# Praise for *Follow Me: The Benefits of Discipleship in the Gospel of John*

"In this thoroughly researched, artfully written book, Mark Zhakevich shows how the rhetoric of the Gospel of John incentivizes its readers to discipleship. The author proffers certain divine benefits to the readers—kinship with God, friendship with Jesus, and more—and bids them come and follow. Zhakevich further shows how this rhetorical strategy fits within the tense social situation in which the author wrote his Gospel."—Matthew V. Novenson, University of Edinburgh

"Zhakevich gives readers of John's Gospel a closer look at discipleship, focusing less on characterization and more on the promises these disciples receive for following Jesus. Instead of shying away from language of reward and benefits, he finds concrete payoffs for the disciples who continue following Jesus, even in difficult circumstances. Zhakevich's work provides another avenue to reflect on the situation of the Johannine community and its unique take on Jesus's gifts for those who remain with him."—Alicia D. Myers, Campbell University Divinity School

"Discipleship is a multifaceted reality in the Fourth Gospel. Mark Zhakevich's study of it highlights the incentives for and benefits of continuous discipleship in the face of possible hostility—discipleship that is comprehensive and costly, but also richly relational and rewarding. Interacting with a wide range of recent scholarship, Zhakevich insightfully reveals interconnections among three major themes and numerous sub-themes that will stimulate all students of this Gospel, including contemporary disciples who might face opposition themselves."—Michael J. Gorman, St. Mary's Seminary & University

"At the heart of John's Gospel is the invitation to 'come and see.' But the call is costly—why would readers persist in abiding along with Peter and the rest of the Twelve? In this insightful study on Johannine discipleship, Mark Zhakevich examines the under-explored nature of the benefits of following Jesus. The costs are high; but so are the rewards."—Andrew J. Byers, author of *Ecclesiology and Theosis in the Gospel of John* and co-chair of the Johannine Literature Seminar for the British New Testament Society

"A well-grounded study of the benefits of Johannine discipleship that will open new lines of inquiry into the purpose, impact, and enduring value of the Fourth Gospel."—Douglas Estes, author of *Question and Rhetoric in the Greek New Testament*

# Follow Me

# Interpreting Johannine Literature

*Series Editor:* Sherri Brown, Creighton University

**Series Advisory Board**
Jaime Clark-Soles, Perkins School of Theology, Southern Methodist University
Alicia D. Myers, Campbell University Divinity School
Lindsey S. Jodrey, Princeton Theological Seminary

The Interpreting Johannine Literature series is born from the desire of a group of Johannine scholars to bring rigorous study and explicit methodology into the teaching of these New Testament texts and their contexts. This series explores critical and perspectival approaches to the Gospel and Epistles of John. Historical—and literary—critical concerns are often augmented by current interpretive questions. Therefore, both a variety of approaches and critical self-awareness characterize titles in the series. Hermeneutical diversity and precision will continue to shed new light on the multifaceted content and discourse of the Johannine Literature.

**Titles in the Series**
*Come and Read: Interpretive Approaches to the Gospel of John*
Alicia D. Myers and Lindsey S. Jodrey, eds.
*What John Knew and What John Wrote: A Study in John and the Synoptics*
Wendy E. S. North
*Follow Me: The Benefits of Discipleship in the Gospel of John*
Mark Zhakevich

# Follow Me

## The Benefits of Discipleship in the Gospel of John

Mark Zhakevich

LEXINGTON BOOKS/FORTRESS ACADEMIC
*Lanham • Boulder • New York • London*

Published by Lexington Books/Fortress Academic
Lexington Books is an imprint of The Rowman & Littlefield Publishing Group, Inc.
4501 Forbes Boulevard, Suite 200, Lanham, Maryland 20706
www.rowman.com

6 Tinworth Street, London SE11 5AL, United Kingdom

Copyright © 2021 by The Rowman & Littlefield Publishing Group, Inc.

*All rights reserved.* No part of this book may be reproduced in any form or by any electronic or mechanical means, including information storage and retrieval systems, without written permission from the publisher, except by a reviewer who may quote passages in a review.

British Library Cataloguing in Publication Information Available

Library of Congress Control Number: 2020944899
ISBN 978-1-9787-1026-9 (cloth)
ISBN 978-1-9787-1028-3 (pbk)
ISBN 978-1-9787-1027-6 (electronic)

# Contents

| | |
|---|---|
| Acknowledgments | ix |
| Abbreviations | xi |
| Introduction | 1 |
| 1 Membership in the Family of God—Divine Initiative and Corollary Benefits | 29 |
| 2 Membership in the Divine Family—Participation in Eternal Life | 51 |
| 3 Abiding with the Father, Son, and Spirit | 85 |
| 4 Royal Friendship with Jesus—The Politics of Friendship in the Ancient World | 111 |
| 5 Royal Friendship with Jesus—The King and His Subjects in the Gospel of John | 129 |
| 6 Answering the Question Why? The Gospel of John in Context | 155 |
| Conclusion | 181 |
| Bibliography | 185 |
| Index | 209 |
| About the Author | 219 |

# Acknowledgments

The following work is a revision of my PhD thesis from the University of Edinburgh. This project could not have been accomplished apart from the input and support from colleagues, friends, and family. I have been fortunate to study with one of the finest New Testament scholars in the world, the late Larry W. Hurtado. I am deeply indebted to Professor Hurtado for his guidance of my thesis and for cultivating within me the skill of critical thinking. He has impressed on me the importance of asking the right questions of the New Testament text and then providing cogent, text-based, and historically plausible interpretations. I am also thankful to Professor Helen Bond for her keen insights as my second adviser. I am grateful to my two examiners, Professors Matthew Novenson and Cornelis Bennema, for their thoughtful input and encouragement to publish my thesis. My brothers, Dr. Iosif Zhakevich and Dr. Philip Zhakevich, and my colleague Dr. Lonnie Bell invested countless hours to assist with revisions. I extend a deep appreciation to Dr. Whitney Gamble for her multiple reviews that improved the quality of this work.

I am thankful to Neil Elliott (and his entire team) for accepting this project for publication and to Sherri Brown for agreeing to include it in the *Interpreting Johannine Literature* series. I am deeply grateful to Professor Brown's insight and counsel that has improved this work.

Most of all, I would like to thank my family: my brothers Iosif and Philip, my sister Anya, and my sister Elizabeth with her husband Alex and their children Andrei, Hannah, Michael, and Mark. They have all been a source of joy and support during this entire process. I especially thank my mother,

Natalya Zhakevich, for her unwavering encouragement during my graduate work. She taught me to aim high, to work hard, and to persevere until the goal is reached. This book is dedicated to her and to her mother, my grandmother Pelogeya Tsvirinko, whose legacy is that she was a follower of Jesus since her childhood in an orphanage until she entered her Father's house in 2015.

# Abbreviations

In addition to the following, all abbreviations in this book are taken from the *SBL Handbook of Style*. 2nd edition. Atlanta, GA: SBL Press, 2014.

| | |
|---|---|
| BTNT | Biblical Theology of the New Testament |
| EGGNT | Exegetical Guide to the Greek New Testament |
| EUS | European University Studies |
| HA | Historische Abteilung |
| HBS | Herders biblische Studien |
| JCHS | Jewish and Christian Heritage Series |
| *Jeev* | Jeevadhara |
| *JTSA* | Journal of Theology for Southern Africa |
| KNT | Kommentar zum Neuen Testament |
| MTS | Münchener theologische Studien |
| NTM | New Testament Monographs |
| PBTM | Paternoster Biblical and Theological Monographs |
| *RevExp* | Review and Expositor |
| RNBC | Readings: A New Biblical Commentary |
| SBEC | Studies in the Bible and Early Christianity |
| *SVTQ* | St. Vladimer's Theological Quarterly |
| *TI* | Testamentum Imperium |
| TSS | Themes in the Social Sciences |
| WBT | Word Biblical Themes |
| ZECNT | Zondervan Exegetical Commentary on the New Testament |

# Introduction

John's Gospel presents a unique call to discipleship. In a way unlike any other Gospel, John invites his readers to follow Jesus because of the glorious rewards extended to faithful followers.[1] In a potential context of severe hostility and persecution, John promises that continuous commitment to Jesus brings three key benefits which outweigh the privileges obtained within the Jewish community. Discipleship with Jesus places Jesus' followers into the divine family, keeps them in an abiding relationship with the Father and the Son through the Spirit, and designates them as royal friends of Jesus.

John intersperses corollary benefits in the surrounding narrative of the three main benefits. These additional benefits are life, love, knowledge of God and of the truth, freedom from sin, walking in the light, salvation, avoidance of judgment, resurrection, protection, performance of great works, affirmation of genuine discipleship, honor, glory, unity, peace, joy, fruit, and answered requests. These gifts come from continuous discipleship, and John offers them as an incentive to remain faithful in light of the cost associated with following Jesus.[2]

## JOHANNINE DISCIPLESHIP DEFINED

Johannine discipleship is devotion to Jesus, characterized by a continuous believing which is derived from rational and relational knowledge of the Father and the Son.[3] This belief is enabled and sustained by the Spirit, who intertwines a disciple in a relationship with the Father and the Son with the resulting expressions of commitment to Jesus such as receiving him, confessing him, continuously believing in him, following him, witnessing to him, loving him, and remaining in him and in his teaching.[4] Johannine expressions of discipleship are listed in table 0.1.

From table 0.1, we observe that for John, discipleship is manifested through belief in Jesus (cognitive) that is accompanied by behavioral change (kinetic).[5]

In classical Greek, "disciple" referred to someone who devoted his mind to something, an apprentice, or an individual in fellowship with another individual. These relationships were characterized by loyalty and inward commitment on the part of the disciple to the master/teacher.[6] The relationship "always implies the existence of a personal attachment which shapes the whole life of the one described as μαθητής."[7] Karl Rengstorf suggests that this attachment is similar to an apprentice who learns from a tradesman:

> The emphasis is not so much on the incompleteness or even deficiency of education as on the fact that the one thus designated is engaged in learning, that his education consists in the appropriation or adoption of specific knowledge or conduct, and that it proceeds deliberately and according to a set plan. There is thus no μαθητής without a διδάσκαλος. The process involves a corresponding personal relation.[8]

The emphasis on learning as part of the teacher-pupil relationship is evident in John's use of the terms "teacher" ('Ραββί, 1:38, 49; 3:2, 26; 4:31; 6:25; 9:2;

Table 0.1  Expressions of Discipleship in John

| | |
|---|---|
| To receive Jesus and his word | 1:11–13; 5:43; 12:48; 13:20; 17:8 |
| To believe in Jesus—as Messiah, as one who is sent by God, as Son of God, as the light, as one with the Father, his works | 1:12; 3:15–21, 36; 4:25–26, 42; 5:34–39; 6:29, 40, 57; 8:23–29; 10:25–26, 31–39; 11:25–27; 12:36, 44, 46; 14:1, 10–12, 31; 16:27, 30; 17:8, 20, 25–26; 20:30–31 |
| To follow Jesus | 1:37–43; 8:12; 10:4–5, 27; 12:26; 13:36–37; 18:15; 21:19–22 |
| To bear fruit | 4:35–38; 12:24–26; 15:1–8, 16 |
| To abide in Jesus | 6:56; 15:1–11 |
| To remain in Jesus' teaching | 8:31; 15:7–11 |
| To hear Jesus' voice | 10:3, 16, 27 |
| To obey Jesus' commands, his sayings, and God's word | 10:16; 12:47–50; 14:15, 21, 23–24; 15:10, 14; 17:6 |
| To hate one's life | 12:25 |
| To serve Jesus | 12:26 |
| To confess Jesus | 12:42 |
| To love other disciples | 13:34–35; 15:12, 17 |
| To wash other disciples' feet | 13:13–17 |
| To know Jesus and the Father | 14:7 |
| To love Jesus and abide in his love | 14:15, 21–24, 28; 15:9–10; 21:15–17 |
| To bear witness to Jesus | 1:7–8, 15, 32, 34; 3:32; 4:39; 12:17; 15:27; 19:35; 21:24 |

11:8; 20:16; διδάσκαλος, 1:38; 3:2; 8:4; 11:28; 13:13–14; 20:16) and "lord" (κύριος, e.g., 6:68; 11:12, 39; 13:13–14, 25; 14:5, 8, 22; 20:13) to refer to Jesus.

Terminology related to the concept of discipleship is sparse in the Hebrew Bible and in the LXX. The noun "disciple" (μαθητής) never appears in the LXX. The verb μανθάνειν appears fifty-six times, but never to describe a teacher-pupil relationship. The Hebrew noun תַּלְמִיד (disciple) appears only in 1 Chronicles 25:8 (LXX: μανθανόντων) in reference to skillful musicians in David's kingdom. The verb לָמַד appears in Isaiah 8:16 in reference to Isaiah's disciples (LXX employs the verb μαθεῖν; also see 50:4, LXX: παιδείας), and in Isaiah 54:13, in reference to sons/daughters being taught by God (LXX: διδακτοὺς θεοῦ). The scarcity of references to discipleship in the Hebrew Bible may be due to the presentation of YHWH in the Jewish Scriptures as the source of teaching and salvation.[9]

## THE PROMINENCE OF DISCIPLESHIP IN JOHN

The theme of discipleship pervades John's Gospel. John demonstrates his emphasis on the concept in three ways: first, in his lexical preference for the term "disciple" (μαθητής) over "apostles" (ἀπόστολοι) and the "twelve" (δώδεκα) as designations for Jesus' followers; second, in his dual use of "believe" (πιστεύω) coupled with the reference to "the disciples" (τῶν μαθητῶν) in the purpose statement; and third, with three illustrations of discipleship in the purpose statement's immediate context (20:30–31).[10]

First, John's emphasis on discipleship is demonstrated by his preference to use the term "disciple" (μαθητής) over the terms "apostles" (ἀπόστολοι) and "twelve" (δώδεκα) as a designation for the followers of Jesus.[11] The noun μαθητής appears seventy-eight times in John, while οἱ ἀπόστολοι appears only in John 13:16, and οἱ δώδεκα appears four times in John (6:67, 70, 71; 20:24). The Johannine referents for μαθητής are the followers of Jesus (seventy-four times), the disciples of John the Baptist (1:35, 37, 3:25), and "the Jews," who claimed to be the disciples of Moses (9:28). The frequency of μαθητής suggests that this is John's featured term for discipleship.

The importance of μαθητής is seen in the term's meaning, which stresses inclusivity. The terms "apostles" and the "twelve" convey exclusivity as they refer to Jesus' inner circle of the twelve followers, whereas the term "disciple" in John indicates inclusivity.[12] This meaning of inclusivity of μαθητής is observable in that μαθητής does not apply exclusively to Jesus' inner circle of disciples (20:19), but also refers to temporary believers in Jesus (6:66).[13] To distinguish between true followers of Jesus (20:19) and temporary sympathizers who defect due to Jesus' difficult teaching (6:60–66), or negative social ramifications (9:22; 12:42), John portrays Jesus as challenging all of his followers to demonstrate allegiance beyond that of outward affiliation (8:31; 15:8) and to commit to continuous discipleship.

Second, the prominence of discipleship is evident in the Gospel's purpose statement through the dual invitation to believe in Jesus alongside the term "the disciples." In 20:30–31 John writes:

> Now Jesus did many other signs in the presence of his *disciples* which have not been written in this book, but these have been written so that you may *believe* that Jesus is the Messiah, the Son of God, and that by *believing* you may have life in his name.[14]

The repeated call to believe in Jesus in the purpose statement indicates that belief is a featured theme. The challenge to continuous belief in Jesus is evident in the repetition of the verb "believe" in 20:31—"that you may *believe* ... and that by *believing* you may have life."[15] There is a textual variant of the verb "believe" in 20:31 that can either be an aorist subjunctive (πιστεύσητε) or present subjunctive (πιστεύητε). This has led to two prominent interpretations of the purpose statement: evangelistic (i.e., begin to believe) or pastoral (i.e., continue to believe). Advocates of the evangelistic view prefer the aorist subjunctive (πιστεύσητε) in 20:31, whereas those who defend the pastoral aim of the Gospel prefer the present subjunctive (πιστεύητε). However, both tenses are well attested in the manuscripts; thus, the decision cannot be made on textual evidence.[16] Moreover, either verb can be shown to support the call to continuous faith in Jesus, since the aspect of the aorist subjunctive does not speak to the kind of action (e.g., punctiliar or progressive) but as to how the action is viewed, that is, from the external viewpoint as simple action. Thus, the aorist tense may reflect John's challenge toward ongoing belief in Jesus just as the present tense.[17] Additionally, the use of the present tense participle "believing" (πιστεύοντες) in 20:31 further suggests ongoing belief. Consequently, these two observations underscore John's emphasis on continuous devotion to Jesus which yields the benefit of life.

Third, the priority of discipleship is further manifested within the context of the purpose statement by means of three illustrations of commitment to Jesus—the Beloved Disciple's, Peter's, and Thomas'. The Beloved Disciple demonstrates his allegiance to Jesus by running fastest to the tomb and by *believing* once he saw the empty tomb (20:1–10).[18] Peter's presence at the tomb also suggests that he is a loyal disciple of Jesus. Despite his triple denial of Jesus (18:15–18, 25–27), and in contrast to his earlier confession (6:68–69) and claim to be committed to Jesus to the point of death (13:37), Peter still arrives at the tomb with the Beloved Disciple. Peter's loyalty to Jesus is also expressed in the pericope immediately after the purpose statement, in which John depicts Peter jumping into the sea to approach Jesus before the other disciples in the boat (21:7–8). The Beloved Disciple and Peter are also presented as following Jesus at the conclusion of the Gospel (21:19–23). The Beloved Disciple's allegiance to Jesus is further expressed in the conclusion of the Gospel in his designation as a witness to Jesus (21:24).

In addition to John's presentation of the Beloved Disciple and Peter as disciples, John also portrays Thomas through his climactic profession, "My Lord and my God" (20:28), as an expression of discipleship. This confession follows Thomas' earlier lapse in allegiance when he declared, "Unless I see the mark of the nails in his hands, and put my finger in the mark of the nails and my hand in his side, I will never believe" (20:25). Jesus returns a week later and responds to Thomas' challenge by offering his hands and his side for Thomas to touch in order to believe. Thomas' response is not to touch Jesus but to affirm Jesus' lordship and divinity (20:28). Jesus responds to Thomas by affirming his belief (20:29), and Thomas is designated as Jesus' disciple (21:1–2). In his response to Thomas, Jesus also elevates the expectation for all future disciples: "Blessed are those who have not seen and yet believe" (20:29). Consequently, the mark of a true disciple in John is not to demand a physical meeting with Jesus but to believe the message about him.

In sum, the prominence of discipleship in John is observable in John's preference of μαθητής, in the dual use of πιστεύω in the purpose statement, and in Peter's, the Beloved Disciple's, and Thomas' examples of belief in the context of the purpose statement and John's designation of them as "disciples" in John 21.

## THE RELATIONSHIP OF DISCIPLESHIP TO ITS BENEFITS

There are four reasons to understand discipleship and its benefits in a close relationship.

First, within the purpose statement, John forges a link between the call to believe in Jesus and the reward for believing by promising life to the believer (20:30–31). This association of belief in Jesus with the promised benefit of life appears shortly after the narrative concerning Jesus' disciples interacting with the risen Jesus (vv. 19–26). Thus, the mention of the disciples, the call to belief, and the promise of life to the believers prompt readers to view the Gospel through the lens of the promise that there are benefits for belief in Jesus.[19]

Second, in addition to the purpose statement, the prologue associates the summons to discipleship with compensatory benefits. Scholars have shown that the prologue sets the focus for the rest of the Gospel, and in the prologue John presents both the call to believe and a reward for such belief.[20] In 1:7,

John the Baptist's testimony contains an implicit call for all to believe in the light. This summons to believe is reinforced in 1:11–13, where the evangelist connects an individual's reception of the *Logos* and belief in the *Logos* with the benefit of becoming a child of God. Moreover, Culpepper has demonstrated that the prologue can be understood as a chiasm with the focal point contained in v. 12b: "He gave them authority to become children of God." The immediate limits of the chiasm are in v. 12a: "those who received him" and in v. 12c: "those who believe in his name." Additionally, the outer limits of the chiasm in v. 11 and in v. 13 focus on the *Logos* and "his own."[21] This chiastic structure in 1:11–13 reveals that the incorporation of the believers into the divine family is the central purpose of the coming of the light and the incarnation of the *Logos* (see also 1:5, 7, 11–14). By including the promise of becoming a child of God in juxtaposition to believing in and receiving Jesus (1:11–13), John indicates that belief in Jesus yields this reward.

John also associates commitment to Jesus with benefits in two additional passages beyond the prologue—10:10 and 12:46. In 10:10, John portrays Jesus as declaring: "I came that they may have life and have it abundantly." This life is promised to the "sheep" that follow Jesus (10:4–5), hear Jesus' voice (10:8–9, 16), and know Jesus (10:14). In 12:46, John writes: "I have come as light into the world, that whoever believes in me may not remain in darkness." Here, John features the promise of not walking in darkness as a reward for belief in Jesus. In both passages, John associates Jesus' coming with benefits to those who believe, which serves to promote belief in Jesus (also see 10:25–26, 37–38; 12:46). These passages indicate that John's call to believe in Jesus should be read alongside these benefits that are promised to believers in Jesus (1:7, 11).

The third reason to view discipleship and benefits in a close relationship is that John intertwines his presentation of discipleship in the context of opposition. Every chapter in John contains elements of antagonism against Jesus or his followers.[22] For example, in 4:1–3, the number of Jesus' disciples had increased, and he left Judea presumably to avoid conflict with the Pharisees, akin to 2:14–19. In 9:28, the reciprocal ridicule between "the Jews" and the blind man concerns the question of whose disciple the blind man was, Jesus' or Moses'?[23] In 12:19, the Pharisees' concern of losing their followers to Jesus is expressed when they say, "You see, there is nothing you can do. Look, the world has gone after him" (for context see 11:53; 12:10–11).[24] In 16:1–2, John depicts Jesus as saying to his disciples, "I have said these things to you to keep you from stumbling." The "things" to which Jesus is referring are mentioned in 14:1–15:27, which are friendship, love, joy, peace, unity, and abiding. These promises, then, serve as benefits that are extended to promote discipleship and dissuade defection, even in the face of violent opposition for following Jesus (16:1–2). The significance of discipleship to the conflict between Jesus and "the Jews" is further demonstrated by the fact that at the trial of Jesus, the High Priest questions Jesus about his *disciples* (18:19) and Peter refuses to acknowledge that he is a follower of Jesus when confronted privately (18:17, 25–27).

The fourth reason to observe a link between commitment to Jesus and rewards is John's promise of life to mitigate against potential abandonment of Jesus. In 6:66–69, John narrates the defection of many followers because of Jesus' difficult teaching on eating his flesh and drinking his blood which is symbolic of abiding in him (6:56).[25] After certain disciples left (6:66), Jesus turns to the twelve and inquires about their loyalty, asking them, "Will you go away also?" (6:67). Peter becomes the spokesperson of "the twelve" when he says, "Lord, to whom will we go? You have the words of eternal life" (6:68). Peter's reply communicates commitment to Jesus that hinges on his belief that Jesus extends eternal life. John constructs this narrative in such a way that his audience may recognize that the antidote to the temptation to defection is the promise of eternal life that is given by Jesus.

In sum, there is a juxtaposition of the call to discipleship with various benefits in the purpose statement, the prologue, passages that describe Jesus' purpose for coming into "the world," and in pericopes that feature opposition to discipleship and defection. Consequently, John's challenge to his audiences to commit to Jesus should be read in light of these benefits that are promised to those who continuously follow Jesus (e.g., 12:25–26).

## THE THREE MAJOR BENEFITS AND THEIR CRITERIA FOR PARTICIPATION

In order to incentivize commitment to continuous discipleship, John deploys certain themes as rewards of discipleship. This book identifies three main benefits of discipleship—membership in the divine family; abiding with the Father and the Son; and royal friendship with Jesus. A benefit is classified as prominent on the basis of its frequency of occurrence in the text, its peculiarity to the Gospel, or its placement in John. The prominence of each benefit is independent of the other, that is, each benefit is uniquely defensible as a key motif in John.

Membership in the divine family is a major benefit because of the prominence of familial terminology and because of the strategic placement of this motif in John. The placement of the family theme further suggests a chiasm in the prologue with the focal point being in 1:12b and thus the family motif forms two *inclusios*: the first *inclusio* in the public ministry of Jesus (1:12–13 with 12:36) and the second *inclusio* of the entire Gospel (1:12–13 with 20:17 and 21:5).

Abiding with the Father and the Son is another prominent benefit because of the frequent occurrence of this theme in John (μένω 40 times; μονή 2 times) and because of the peculiar meaning of abiding in the Gospel.

Royal friendship with Jesus is treated as a major benefit because of the placement and the peculiar presentation of this theme in John. In the Gospel, the noun "friend" (φίλος) appears six times and always in thematic material that is distinctive to the Gospel.[26] Moreover, John devotes an entire paragraph to the theme of friendship with Jesus (15:12–17). By contrast, in the Synoptic Gospels, "friend" appears sixteen times, with only one occurrence functioning as an appellative for the disciples (Luke 12:4).[27] Alternatively in John, placement and peculiarity of the friendship theme establishes it as a prominent motif.

These three main benefits represent literary umbrellas under which corollary benefits fall. These additional, and sometimes overlapping, benefits appear in the near context of one or more of the three key benefits. These additional themes that appear in the orbit of the three main benefits are life, love, knowledge of God and of the truth, freedom from sin, walking in the light, salvation, avoidance of judgment, resurrection, protection, performance of great works, affirmation of genuine discipleship, honor, glory, unity, peace, joy, fruit, and answered requests.

The benefits promised to the believer are qualitatively relational. The opening words of the prologue introduce John's audiences to the *Logos* and their *relationship* to God (1:1–3), thus setting a relational prism for reading the rest of the Gospel. In 1:10–13, the writer deploys relational terminology to distinguish between the antithetical responses to the light: the response of some who received him and that of those who did not. The designation "his own" (τὰ ἴδια, 1:11; see also 10:3, 4, 12; 13:1), in reference to the audience of the light, also evokes a relational framework for the Gospel narrative. The individuals who believe in the light are placed into a familial relationship with God (1:11–13) through the light who is identified as the *Logos* (1:1–5).

Moreover, followers of Jesus experience a relationship not only with the *Logos*, but also with the Father. According to 1:12–13, a believer is in a dyadic relationship with God/Father and with Jesus, a relationship that cannot be dissected into two separate relationships or conflated into a single relationship. And the benefits extended to faithful disciples are obtained through the dual relationship with the Father and the Son. The placement of the relationship motif in the prologue affirms the importance of this motif to the entire Gospel.[28] The rest of the Gospel presents the experience of believers in their relationship to the Son as parallel to their relationship to the Father. For example, to receive Jesus is to receive the Father (13:20); to know the Father is to know Jesus (14:7; 16:3), though they are known distinctly (17:2–3); to be loved by Jesus is to be loved by the Father (14:23;

15:9; 16:27; 17:23); to see Jesus is to see the Father (12:45; 14:9); to hate Jesus is to hate the Father (15:23, 24); and to be with Jesus is to be with the Father (14:2–3).[29]

In sum, three of John's benefits can be set apart from the others by their prominence on account of frequency of occurrence, peculiarity to John, or their placement in the narrative. These three benefits are relational promises that should stimulate the readers' relationship to Jesus.

## THIS STUDY AND ITS PARAMETERS

This book is limited to the Gospel of John and examines it in its final form.[30] This study approaches the Gospel with a close reading of the text, with careful attention given to the literary and narratival features in John.[31] To situate the narrative in a historical context and to expand on the Gospel's concepts that are confined to a specific setting, socio-historical insights are gained from the Greco-Roman and Jewish writings where appropriate.

This study employs "John" as a referent to the writer of the Gospel of John without making a claim about his identity. Helpful surveys have been published that engage the arguments about the authorship of the Gospel of John.[32] The possible historical milieu of the Gospel is presumed to be the conflict between Jewish authorities and Jewish-Christians at the end of the first century CE.[33]

Coupled with the inquiry into the authorship of the Gospel is the question of the identity of the audience.[34] The audience of John is presumed to be the Diaspora-Jews, probably situated in Asia Minor.[35] The references to the followers in Jesus as Jewish believers/Jewish-Christians are not intended as commentary on the provenance of the Gospel. Instead, this ethnic nomenclature is derived from the references to the synagogues (9:22; 12:42; 16:2), the temple (2:13–22), the festivals (2:13; 5:1; 6:4; 7:2; 10:22; 11:55), and other elements of the Jewish identity described in the Gospel (e.g., 1:38, 41). By using these culture-specific references, John seemingly presupposes a Jewish identity of his implied readers.

Although character studies do not feature prominently in this book, where appropriate the characters are employed illustratively to expound on the expressions of discipleship.[36] The term "disciples" is used in the broad sense as a referent to any believer and follower of Jesus who attaches him or herself to Jesus rather than a referent to "the twelve" or to individuals explicitly designated as "disciples" (e.g., 21:1–2).

Finally, the terms "image," "symbol," or "metaphor" are used interchangeably to refer to family, abiding, and friendship as images that John deploys to convey unity in the Jesus-disciple relationship.[37] It is beyond the scope of this book to delve into the philosophical arguments concerning metaphoric language or to build a theory of metaphor.[38]

## JOHANNINE DISCIPLESHIP IN SCHOLARLY CONVERSATION

Scholars of the Gospel of John have generally focused their studies on characterization of the disciples and on discipleship as a theme through the lenses of friendship, family, covenant, life, Christology, agency, mission, and the descent-ascent motif.[39] The theme of the *benefits* of discipleship has not been sufficiently examined. Furthermore, those who have addressed the benefits of discipleship have typically filtered the kaleidoscope of Johannine themes related to discipleship through a single lens (e.g., family, friendship). This book aims to shed light on the neglected category of the Johannine benefits of discipleship. Since many scholars have investigated elements of Johannine discipleship, it is appropriate to examine how the current study complements, or in certain cases diverges from, contemporary scholarship.

The early studies of Johannine discipleship focused on the manifestations of discipleship, often featuring following Jesus as the main expression of commitment to him. Following Jesus is manifested through obedience to his teaching, allegiance to him as a shepherd, and mutual knowledge between Jesus and the disciple.[40] The disciple follows Jesus through suffering and self-denial.[41] Moreover, discipleship was understood to be about attachment to Jesus, which is made visible in the disciples' mutual love and unity.[42]

There was a shift in the 1970s to study discipleship theologically. Ramón Jiménez viewed discipleship through trinitarian theology, while Rudolf Schnackenburg approached it ecclesiologically with a view toward the Johannine community.[43] Marinus de Jonge merged the Johannine community, the centrality of Christology, and the role of the Holy Spirit in discipleship. He identified abiding as the distinguishing mark of the inner circle of the disciples, in contrast with the wider circles of Jesus' followers.[44]

In the 1980s, the primary works on Johannine discipleship focused on the process of becoming a disciple and displaying that commitment.[45] Fernando Segovia argued that discipleship is the execution of Jesus' command to love.[46] He concluded that discipleship is abiding in correct belief and in love, with the latter being the expression and authentication of the former.[47]

D. Francois Tolmie viewed true discipleship in contrast with false discipleship.[48] The three traits of true discipleship are love, knowledge, and obedience, all of which characterize Jesus and thus give Johannine discipleship a Christological base.[49] While Tolmie featured certain expectations of true disciples and mentioned select benefits of discipleship from the Farewell

Discourse "as an encouragement and motivation to the implied reader to be faithful as a disciple," he primarily examined the nature of discipleship rather than the benefits of discipleship.[50]

Andreas Köstenberger evaluated the missions of Jesus and the disciples as a subset of discipleship.[51] He argued that John's focus on Jesus being sent by God, coming into "the world," returning to the Father, and calling people to follow him favors the missionary purpose of the Gospel.[52] Moreover, a new messianic community is formed whose mission is to harvest spiritual fruit within God's eschatological economy of salvation.[53]

Jan van der Watt grouped the diverse themes and imagery in John under the single category of the family construct. He argued it is the most prominent metaphorical network in the Gospel under which all other ideas are subsumed.[54] For example, friendship should not be seen as an independent metaphor but rather "as the enrichment of the existing familial relations."[55] Jan van der Watt's attempt to integrate all of the Johannine imagery, symbols, and teaching related to discipleship within the family network is a massive undertaking that he achieves admirably. Yet, no single image can encompass seamlessly John's depth and breadth of symbolism and metaphorical language.[56] Consequently, it is more appropriate to view John's diverse terminology, symbolism, and themes as belonging to the greater theme of discipleship with many symbolic expressions, one of which is the family metaphor.

In an attempt to understand the dualism in John, James Resseguie examined the Gospel from a narratological point of view.[57] The narrator's perspective is examined through five planes—spatial, temporal, phraseological, psychological, and ideological—to show the narrator's outlook as being "from above."[58] Ultimately, Resseguie shows that the ideological point of view is "from above" in contrast with the material frame of reference that is "from below."[59] The Beloved Disciple is said to represent the ideal perspective in contrast with the other disciples who may at times continue to represent the material point of view.[60] Resseguie only occasionally links the argument to discipleship, and he does not develop the different characteristics of discipleship or the benefits that accompany faithful disciples.[61]

Cornelis Bennema adopted a theological approach to discipleship, specifically through the lens of soteriology.[62] He proposed that the soteriological effect of Wisdom and the Spirit is best understood against the sapiential Jewish background.[63] The Spirit mediates Jesus' presence to his disciples as the second Paraclete, continuing the first Paraclete's work, and functions as the bond of union and the mode of communication between the Father, the Son, and the believer.[64] The individual who enters and continues in such a salvific relationship enjoys benefits derived from continuous discipleship.[65] In light of Bennema's mention of rewards of discipleship, this book complements his portrayal of discipleship by developing the benefits derived from discipleship. Yet, while Bennema limited the conceptual background of his study to sapiential Judaism, this book investigates the Hellenistic background of John's themes related to discipleship.[66]

Rekha Chennattu also approached John theologically by examining discipleship in light of the Old Testament covenant terminology.[67] She argued that in 1:35–51 the disciples are initiated into an Old Testament type of covenant relationship with Jesus. She observed allusions to the Old Testament covenantal relationship in the themes of election, abiding, knowledge of God, witnessing, renaming of individuals, and promises.[68] In her paradigm, John 20–21 contains the "realization of the covenant promises and the actualization of the community of the disciples as God's children."[69] While her proposal of covenant discipleship capitalizes upon the Old Testament imagery in John, the term "covenant" never appears in the Gospel, which is a noteworthy omission considering the Gospel's conceptual and lexical allusions to the Old Testament elsewhere (e.g., σκηνόω in 1:14; Moses in 3:14).[70] Additionally, her thesis primarily hinges on chapters 13–17; however, since discipleship is a central theme in the entire Gospel, her proposal would be more potent if traced throughout the entire Gospel.[71]

David Kaczmarek took the line of inquiry into Johannine discipleship in a slightly different direction when he suggested that the Johannine community strengthened its own membership by adapting and modifying the terminology of the general population to fit the needs of the community. He argued that the terms, "to love (φιλέιν, ἀγαπέιν)," "remain (μένειν)," "friend (φίλος)," and "love (ἀγάπη)," were relexicalized by the Johannine community to define itself as a subset of the general population and as emerging from the Jewish synagogue.[72] Moreover, φιλέω/φίλος is interchangeable with ἀγαπάω/ἀγάπη, functioning according to the classical notion of friendship that connotes unity/equality, inclusivity, and genuine obligation.[73] He then linked the language of love and discipleship with friendship and concluded that "through the character of Jesus, [John] equates discipleship with friendship."[74] The general thesis of relexicalization provides insight into how a community would have established itself through language. However, it seems simplistic to equate discipleship with friendship since discipleship is also juxtaposed with the imagery of family (e.g., 8:31–44) and with abiding (15:6–10), and thus the broader category should be understood as discipleship.[75]

Martin Culy proposed friendship as the main image through which to view discipleship.[76] He examined friendship in the Greco-Roman writings and identified three primary friendship ideals that are also present in John—mutuality, unity, and equality.[77] Since these concepts are present in the relationship between the Father and the Son, John is therefore portraying the relationship between the Father and the Son as friendship. Moreover, since the same three ideals are also true of the friendship between Jesus and the disciples, John must be featuring the Father-Son friendship as paradigmatic for the friendship between Jesus and the disciples.[78] However, Culy's interpretation lacks strong lexical support, since John does not use the term "friend" (φίλος) to describe Jesus' relationship with God but instead uses the verb "love" (φιλέω), which is in fact used interchangeably by John with ἀγαπάω and therefore does not necessarily imply friendship. Yet, in the ancient writings, the three friendship themes of mutuality, unity, and equality are indeed juxtaposed with friendship terminology. While this book presents friendship as a key motif in John, friendship should not be elevated to the status of a "primary vehicle" to characterize relationships in the Gospel.[79]

In the same year as Culy's work, Marianus Hera argued that Johannine discipleship has its basis in Johannine Christology.[80] Whereas the relationship between discipleship and Christology was previously discussed by Marinus de Jonge, Mary Pazdan, and Melanie Baffes, Marianus Hera focuses on John 17 and argued that Christology is a primary motif in the Gospel.[81] Jesus himself is presented as the "prime model of authentic discipleship."[82] John's presentation of Christological discipleship culminates in John 17, a chapter that should be read through the references to "the hour" (ἡ ὥρα), since the passage appears between the coming of ἡ ὥρα (12:23) and the completion of ἡ ὥρα (John 18–20), that is, Jesus' glorification through his suffering, crucifixion, and resurrection.[83]

The following year, Adesola Joan Akala proposed that the Son-Father relationship is central to John's prologue and purpose statement and that the culmination of this relationship is explained in John 17. She posited that the Son-Father relationship is the framework for the rest of the Gospel as Jesus fulfills the mission of God and draws the disciples into this relationship and "ultimately into the transcendent presence of the Father and Son in heaven."[84] As her focus is not on discipleship per se, she only devotes two pages to discipleship in which she affirms that love and unity are fundamental to Johannine discipleship as the disciples continue the mission of Jesus.

Johannine discipleship has also been linked with spirituality. Dorothy Lee approached discipleship as "built on a spirituality that is characterized by believing, learning, abiding, loving, following, and obeying."[85] This type of relationship emanates from Jesus' relationship with God who functions as the model to follow. Michael Gorman similarly viewed Johannine discipleship through the spiritual lens, arguing that abiding and fulfilling the mission of God is the process of imitating Jesus and is the essence of *theosis* in John.[86] Both of these works complement this book in that they focus on the expressions of discipleship while this book advances the rewards of allegiance to Jesus.

Most recently, Sookgoo Shin viewed discipleship as a journey of moral imitation of Jesus.[87] He compared John with Plutarch's *Lives* to show how John uses the ancient literary writing techniques to shape his readers' ethical outlook.[88] He posited that there are two stages of Johannine discipleship. In John 1–12, the evangelist aims to persuade his audiences to adopt Jesus' teachings and worldview which results in faith in him. In John 13–21, the message of discipleship is presented so that the individuals who made a commitment to Jesus can imitate him.[89] Shin then defined moral progress in John as "a total reorientation of worldview and of the understanding of the self which is effected by one's growing knowledge of Jesus's identity and mission, and which further enables one to grow in the likeness of Jesus by embodying the moral traits exemplified by Jesus himself."[90] As his focus was on moral progression of discipleship in four traits—love, mission, unity, otherworldly status—he did not engage the motivations behind that moral change, as such, this book complements his work.

In addition to discipleship, characterization has also been an area of study in Johannine studies. In the 1960s, J. Louis Martyn pioneered the two-level reading of the Gospel of John, arguing that the community behind the creation of the Gospel would have read it not only as a narration of the actual events that occurred at the time of Jesus, but also as a reflection of their own experience.[91] His work prompted the understanding that the characters in John are to be considered as "types of individuals [rather] than as historical persons."[92] In the 1980s, R. Alan Culpepper advanced a flat reading of the Johannine individuals when he posited that "all the characters eventually make their choice."[93] But the flat reading of Johannine characters has been critiqued, since not every character in John demonstrates a clear response to Jesus.[94]

Instead of examining all of the characters' responses to Jesus, in the 1990s David Beck focused on the anonymous individuals in John.[95] He argued that the nameless disciples have active faith that is not based on a sign performed by Jesus *and* these function as his witnesses and paradigms of faith.[96] However, Beck applied his criteria inconsistently, which led him to questionable conclusions about certain individuals.[97] In the early twenty-first century, Nicolas Farelly also selected only a few individuals in his study of characterization. He identified five characters whose faith is observable before and after the resurrection. He concluded that Peter, Judas, Thomas, Beloved Disciple, and Mary Magdalene come to *full* faith and understanding only after the resurrection.[98] While Farelly's study is not about discipleship per se, he nevertheless identified hearing, coming and seeing, following, witnessing, allegiance to Jesus' teaching, and abiding with Jesus as characteristics of discipleship.[99]

## SUMMARY

Modern scholars have investigated the question of *what* discipleship is from historical, theological, and narratological perspectives; however, few have engaged the question of *why* an individual should follow Jesus. This book is the first to draw attention to Johannine themes that are compensatory benefits of continuous discipleship.

## THE OUTLINE OF THIS STUDY

The study commences with membership in the divine family investigated in chapter 1 as the first benefit of discipleship. Chapter 2 focuses on the Johannine concept of "life" (ζωή), which enables the disciple to relate to God and Jesus within the divine family, and to experience corollary benefits that enhance the disciple's participation in the divine family. Chapter 3 examines the benefit of the Father and the Son abiding with the believer through the Spirit in the present (14:15–24) and in the future (14:2–3). Additionally, in 15:1–11, John features "abiding in Jesus" as a condition that a disciple must fulfill, which results in additional benefits that are extended to the believer in Jesus. Chapters 4 and 5 investigate the Johannine depiction of Jesus as a monarch who invites his followers into a royal friendship (15:12–17). Chapter 4 argues that Jesus' statement, "I call you friends" (15:13–15), should be understood against the background of the political and royal friendships of the ancient Near East. Chapter 5 presents the Johannine evidence for royal friendship with Jesus through a study of John's presentation of Jesus as a king and through the exegesis of 15:12–17. Chapter 6 argues that John extends the benefits for faithfully following Jesus in light of the hostility that a believer in Jesus may face as was the probable experience of the Jewish believers in Jesus during the time of Jesus and during the writing of the Gospel. The conclusion synthesizes the argument of this book in light of John's purpose statement.

## NOTES

1. This book employs "John" as a referent to the writer of the Gospel of John without making a claim about his identity.

2. While there have been inquiries into the definition, characterization, and expressions of Johannine discipleship, there has not been a focused study of the benefits conferred on the faithful disciple of Jesus. This project seeks to be a first step toward rectifying this omission in Johannine scholarship.

3. The noun πίστις does not appear in John but the verb πιστεύω is used ninety-eight times, which further lends to the argument that belief is active in John.

4. Bennema's understanding of discipleship containing cognitive and kinetic expressions helped formulate this definition. See Cornelis Bennema, *The Power of Saving Wisdom: An Investigation of Spirit and Wisdom in Relation to the Soteriology of the Fourth Gospel*, WUNT 2.148 (Tübingen: J.C.B. Mohr, 2002), 251. In a recent monograph, Shin defined discipleship as moral progress that is based in a changed worldview through belief in Jesus and results in imitation of his love, mission, unity, and otherworldly identity. His summation of discipleship aligns well with the suggested definition above, which includes cognitive and kinetic expressions of discipleship. Sookgoo Shin, *Ethics in the Gospel of John: Discipleship as Moral Progress*, BIS 168 (Leiden; Boston: Brill, 2019), 48–53, 194–95.

5. Table 0.1 also suggests a more augmented definition of discipleship than Pazdan's, who argued that: (1) the basis of discipleship is belief, (2) the heart of discipleship is knowing, loving, and abiding with Jesus, and (3) the task of discipleship is seeking Jesus and keeping his commands. John also features receiving Jesus, confessing Jesus, and hating one's life as aspects of discipleship. Mary M. Pazdan, "Discipleship as the Appropriation of Eschatological Salvation in the Fourth Gospel" (Ph.D. Diss., University of St. Michael's College, 1982), 309.

6. André Feuillet, *Études johanniques*, Museum Lessianum Section biblique 4 (Paris: Desclée de Brouwer, 1962), 107; *TDNT*, "μαθητής," 4:424.

7. *TDNT*, "μαθητής," 4:441. *Pace,* Lee who affirms that "following" is a personal attachment, nonetheless writes that "discipleship is first and foremost an ecclesial reality in the Gospel." I see the ecclesial reality as the second stage of discipleship after the personal relationship with Jesus has been established. For example, note the call to follow Jesus individually in John 1:43; 8:12; 12:26; 21:19, 22. Dorothy A. Lee, *Hallowed in Truth and Love: Spirituality in the Johannine Literature* (Eugene, OR: Wipf & Stock, 2012), 133, 157.

8. *TDNT*, "μαθητής," 4:416.

9. So Feuillet. However, Hahn suggests that the followers of the prophets prefigured the disciples of Jesus as their relationship seems to mimic that of Jesus and his disciples. Feuillet, *Études*, 100–101; Ferdinand Hahn, August Strobel, and Eduard Schweizer, *Die Anfänge der Kirche im Neuen Testament* (Göttingen; Minneapolis: Vandenhoeck u. Ruprecht; Augsburg Pub. House, 1967), 15–17; *TDNT*, "μαθητής," 4:416–26.

10. I do not elevate the importance of discipleship above Christology. With regard to discipleship, the readers are exhorted to respond to the Christology presented in John by becoming disciples of Jesus. Hera rightly argues that Christology is the basis for discipleship. Hera observes that John depicts Jesus in a way "that leads the audience to a better understanding of their own identity as the disciples and followers of Jesus." Marianus Pale Hera, *Christology and Discipleship in John 17*, WUNT 2.342 (Tübingen: Mohr Siebeck, 2013), citing 36, see also 168.

11. In the Synoptic Gospels, μαθητής appears seventy-two times in Matthew; in Mark forty-six times; in Luke thirty-seven times. John also uses the verb μανθάνω (I

learn) twice (6:45; 7:15). The term οἱ ἀπόστολοι appears nine times in the Synoptic Gospels and οἱ δώδεκα appears twenty-seven times in the Synoptic Gospels.

12. R. Alan Culpepper, *Anatomy of the Fourth Gospel: A Study in Literary Design* (Philadelphia: Fortress, 1983), 115. The inclusive nature of Johannine discipleship was observed by Hera from another perspective when he connected the use of πάντα (all) in 1:3, 7, with 12:32. In 1:3, John writes, "*all* things came into being through him," and in 1:7 we read, "so that *all* may believe through him." In 12:32 John depicts Jesus as promising "to draw all (πάντας) men to himself" by means of the cross. The placement of πάντα with the theme of belief functions as an *inclusio* in the narrative of the public ministry of Jesus (John 1–12) and thereby points to the general call to believe in Jesus. This then buttresses the notion that the Johannine call to discipleship is inclusive. Hera, *Christology*, 49.

13. Köstenberger argues that the meaning of μαθητής widens in the course of John. Andreas J. Köstenberger, *The Missions of Jesus and the Disciples According to the Fourth Gospel: With Implications for the Fourth Gospel's Purpose and the Mission of the Contemporary Church* (Grand Rapids, MI: Eerdmans, 1998), 142–53, 167, 178.

14. All scriptural translations are the author's unless otherwise noted.

15. Farelly, with dependence on Lincoln's lawsuit and witness motif, argues for a pastoral purpose (or perseverance in belief) by noting that John establishes the frame in 1:14, 16, and 21:24 with "we" language, which suggests that the implied author and implied readers share a common faith. That is, as the writer was a witness to Jesus, he now encourages his believing readers to be faithful witnesses for Jesus. Nicolas Farelly, *The Disciples in the Fourth Gospel: A Narrative Analysis of Their Faith and Understanding*, WUNT 2.290 (Tübingen: Mohr Siebeck, 2010), 176–79.

16. For manuscript evidence on the textual variant, see NA28; UBS4; Bruce Manning Metzger, *A Textual Commentary on the Greek New Testament*, 2nd ed. (Stuttgart: Deutsche Bibelgesellschaft/German Bible Society, 1994), 219.

17. For further discussion on the evangelistic, pastoral, or perhaps a dual meaning in the purpose statement, see Constantine R. Campbell, *Advances in the Study of Greek: New Insights for Reading the New Testament* (Grand Rapids, MI: Zondervan, 2015), 106–108, 121; Constantine R. Campbell, *Basics of Verbal Aspect in Biblical Greek* (Grand Rapids, MI: Zondervan, 2008), 91–92. Bennema cautions against putting too much weight on syntax in determining the evangelistic or pastoral aim of the Gospel since John seems to use the present and the aorist to refer to initial and continuous belief. Bennema, *Power*, 108. For additional manuscript evidence of 20:30–31, see Raymond E. Brown, *The Gospel According to John*, 2 vols., AB 29–29A (New York: Doubleday, 1966), 1056. Evangelistic view: John Bowman, "The Fourth Gospel and the Samaritans," *BJRL* 40 (1958): 298–308; D. A. Carson, "The Purpose of the Fourth Gospel: John 20:31 Reconsidered," *JBL* 6 (1987): 639–51; Edwin E. Freed, "Samaritan Influence in the Gospel of John," *CBQ* 30 (1968): 580–87; J. A. T. Robinson, "The Destination and Purpose of St. John's Gospel," *NTS* 6 (1959/60): 117–31; W. C. van Unnik, "The Purpose of St. John's Gospel," *SE* (1959): 382–411. Pastoral: Johannes S. J. Beutler, "Faith and Confession: The Purpose of John," in *Texts about Faith and Confession*, ed. Rudolf Hoppe and Ulrich Berges (Bonn: V & R Unipress; Bonn University Press, 2012), 102; Raymond E. Brown and Francis J. Moloney,

*An Introduction to the Gospel of John*, ABRL (New York: Doubleday, 2003), 152, 182–83; Kenneth L. Carroll, "The Fourth Gospel and the Exclusion of Christians from the Synagogues," *BJRL* 40 no. 1 (1957): 19–32; Farelly, *Disciples*, 85–86, 176–79, 227–28; David Kaczmarek, *An Introduction to Language in the Johannine Community: Love, Friendship, and Discipleship in the Gospel According to John* (Minneapolis, MN: Xlibris, 2008), 36–37; J. Louis Martyn, *History and Theology in the Fourth Gospel*, 3rd ed. (Nashville, TN: Abingdon Press, 2003); Wayne A. Meeks, *The Prophet-King: Moses Traditions and the Johannine Christology*, NovTSup (Leiden: Brill, 1967); Francis J. Moloney, *The Gospel of John: Text and Context* (Leiden: Brill, 2005), 258; Kevin Quast, *Reading the Gospel of John: An Introduction* (New York: Paulist Press, 1991), 7; Fernando F. Segovia, *The Farewell of the Word: The Johannine Call to Abide* (Minneapolis, MN: Fortress, 1991), 301; D. F. Tolmie, *Jesus' Farewell to the Disciples: John 13:1–17:26 in Narratological Perspective*, BIS 12 (Leiden: Brill, 1995), 38–39. Dual purpose: Bennema, *Power*, 108; Saeed Hamid-Khani, *Revelation and Concealment of Christ: A Theological Inquiry into the Elusive Language of the Fourth Gospel*, WUNT 2.120 (Tübingen: Mohr Siebeck, 2000), 208–19; Won-Ha Hwang, Van der Watt, J. G., "The Identity of the Recipients of the Fourth Gospel in the Light of the Purpose of the Gospel," *TS* 63 no. 2 (2007): 683–98; Köstenberger, *Missions*, 200–10; Stephen Motyer, *Your Father the Devil?: A New Approach to John and "the Jews*,*"* PBTM (Carlisle: Paternoster, 1997), 58–61; Walter Rebell, *Gemeinde als Gegenwelt: zur soziologischen und didaktischen Funktion des Johannesevangeliums*, Gemeinde, BBET 20 (Frankfurt: Peter Lang, 1987), 126–29; Derek Tovey, *Narrative Art and Act in the Fourth Gospel*, JSNTSup 151 (Sheffield: Sheffield Academic Press, 1997), 84–92, 97–108; Marianne Meye Thompson, *John: A Commentary*, NTL (Louisville, KY: Westminster John Knox Press, 2015), 430.

18. *Pace*, Moloney who argues that the Beloved Disciple's arrival at the tomb before Peter indicates the Beloved Disciple's greater degree of love and faith for Jesus. However, John presents both disciples misunderstanding the resurrection, returning home, and both disciples are portrayed negatively during the race—the Beloved Disciple does not enter the tomb and Peter runs slower. Thus, Moloney's correlation of the degree of faith with speed in the race is unwarranted. Francis J. Moloney, "John 20: A Journey Completed," *ACR* 59 (1982): 425. Peter, the Beloved Disciple, and Thomas were selected because they reflect development as disciples in John, whereas John does not seem to depict Mary Magdalene in the same light.

19. Similarly, Bennema, *Power*, 109.

20. The following scholars see the rest of the Gospel developing the themes introduced in the prologue. Bennema, *Power*, 110 fn. 29; Raymond E. Brown, "The Prologue of the Gospel of John: John 1:1–18," *RevExp* 62 no. 4 (1965): 429; Sherri Brown, "Believing in the Gospel of John: The Ethical Imperative to Becoming Children of God," in *Johannine Ethics: The Moral World of the Gospel and Epistles of John*, ed. Sherri Brown and Christopher W. Skinner (Minneapolis, MN: Fortress Press, 2017), 3–10; Rudolf Bultmann, *The Gospel of John: A Commentary* (Oxford: B. Blackwell, 1971), 13; Elizabeth Harris, *Prologue and Gospel: The Theology of the Fourth Evangelist*, JSNTSup 107 (Sheffield, England: Sheffield Academic Press, 1994), 189; Stanley E. Porter, *John and His Gospel, and Jesus: In Pursuit*

*of the Johannine Voice* (Grand Rapids, MI: Eerdmans, 2015), 119; Herman N. Ridderbos, "The Structure and Scope of the Prologue to the Gospel of John," in *The Composition of John's Gospel: Selected Studies from 'Novum Testamentum'*, ed. David E. Orton (Leiden: Brill, 1999), 57; John A. T. Robinson, "The Relation of the Prologue to the Gospel of John," *NTS* 9 no. 2 (January 1963): 121, 122, 128; Matthew Vellanickal, *The Divine Sonship of Christians in the Johannine Writings*, Anelecta Biblica 72 (Rome: Biblical Institute Press, 1977), 105; Brooke Foss Westcott, *The Gospel According to St. John* (Grand Rapids, MI: Eerdmans, 1978), 1.

21. The chiasm can be presented as follows:

   A. Word with God (vv. 1–2)
     B. What came to be through the Word: Creation (v. 3)
       C. What we have received from the Word: Life (vv. 4–5)
         D. John sent to testify (vv. 6–8)
           E. Incarnation & Response of the World (vv. 9–10)
             F. The Word and His Own (v. 11)
               G. Those who accepted the Word (v. 12a)
                 H. Became children of God (v. 12b)
               G. Those who believed in the Word (v. 12c)
             F. The Word and His Own (v. 13)
           E. Incarnation & Response of the Community (v. 14)
         D. John's Testimony (v. 15)
       C. What we have received from the Word: Grace (v. 16)
     B. What came to be through the Word: Grace and Truth (v. 17)
   A. Word with God (v. 18)

In support of the chiastic structure of the prologue, see M. E. Boismard, *Le prologue de saint Jean* (Paris: 1953), 106–108; Brown, "Ethics," 11–14; D. A. Carson, *The Gospel According to John* (Grand Rapids, MI: Eerdmans, 1991), 113; R. Alan Culpepper, "The Pivot of John's Prologue," *NTS* 27 no. 1 (1980): 14; André Feuillet, *Le prologue du quatrième évangile* (Paris: Desclée de Brouwer, 1968), 137–77; Andreas J. Köstenberger, *John*, BECNT (Grand Rapids, MI: Baker, 2004), 38; Michael C. McKeever, "Born of God: The 'Virgin Birth' of Believers in the Fourth Gospel," in *But These Are Written: Essays on Johannine Literature in Honor of Professor Benny C. Aker*, ed. Craig S. Keener, Jeremy S. Crenshaw, and Jordan D. May (Eugene, OR: Pickwick Publications, 2014), 121–38; Vellanickal, *Sonship*, 132–36.

22. John 1:11; 2:18–21; 3:11, 36; 4:1–3, 44; 5:16–18; 6:60–66; 7:1, 13, 19–20, 25, 30, 32, 44; 8:20, 37, 40, 59; 9:22, 28, 34; 10:39; 11:8, 46–53, 57; 12:10, 19, 42; 13:2, 21; 14:27, 30; 15:18–27; 16:2, 33; 17:14; chs. 18–19; 19:38; 20:19; 21:18.

23. The use of the title "the Jews" is not intended to be pejorative but is adopted directly from the Gospel to identify the group of individuals who are depicted in certain scenes as antagonistic toward Jesus and/or his followers. For studies on anti-Judaism and John, see R. Bieringer, Didier Pollefeyt, and F. Vandecasteele-Vanneuville, eds., *Anti-Judaism and the Fourth Gospel: Papers of the Leuven Colloquium, 2000*, vol. 1 (Assen, Netherlands: Royal Van Gorcum, 2001).

24. Barrett sees this as a Semitic expression, meaning "everyone." C. K. Barrett, *The Gospel According to St. John*, 2nd ed. (London: SPCK, 1978), 420.

25. Shin rightly sees in the use of abiding in 6:56 an expectation of true disciples to persist "[in]spite of difficult teachings." Moreover, he observes that "discipleship is not a static phenomenon but must involve a growing intimacy and trust between Jesus and his followers." Shin, *Ethics*, 103.

26. The term φίλος refers once to John the Baptist as the friend of the bridegroom (3:29); once to Lazarus (11:11), three times to the disciples (15:12–17), and once to Pilate's friendship to Caesar (19:12).

27. The other uses of φίλος in the Synoptic Gospels refer to neighbors (Luke 11:5–8), associates at meals (Luke 14:10–12), social companions (Luke 15:6–29), business associates (Luke 16:9). The term φίλος is also used with a negative connotation as a designation for Jesus as friend of tax collectors and sinners (Matthew 11:19=Luke 7:34). Elsewhere it is used in reference to a centurion's friends (Luke 17:6), to the friendship of Herod and Pilate (Luke 23:12), and to persecution by friends (Luke 21:16).

28. Aune has observed the importance of opening comments in an ancient letter to the rest of the letter. David Edward Aune, *The New Testament in Its Literary Environment*, LEC 8 (Philadelphia: Westminster Press, 1987), 186, 208. Similarly, Lindsey M. Trozzo, *Exploring Johannine Ethics: A Rhetorical Approach to Moral Efficacy in the Fourth Gospel Narrative*, WUNT2 449 (Tübingen: Mohr Siebeck, 2017), 140.

29. Bultmann identifies a similar duality of a single relationship when he writes, "double knowledge (of God and Christ) is really one single knowledge—for God is only known through the Revealer, and the latter is known only when God is recognized in him." Rudolf Bultmann, *Theology of the New Testament*, 2 vols. (New York: Charles Scribner & Sons, 1951), 2:78. Rainbow also observes duality in the believer's relationship with the Father and the Son. He writes,

> John does not propound two separate objects of religious knowledge. Disciples do not know the Son in addition to the Father, much less instead of the Father. In knowing the Son, it is the essence of the Father that they encounter ... John's christocentric epistemology does not compromise his ontological monotheism, but makes knowledge of the one God accessible by locating the revelation in that agent who is eminently suited to disclose the heart of the personal God.

Paul A. Rainbow, *Johannine Theology: The Gospel, the Epistles and the Apocalypse* (Downers Grove, IL: IVP Academic, 2014), 305.

30. For the development of the text of John, see Brown, *John*, xxxiv–xxxix; Raymond E. Brown, *The Community of the Beloved Disciple* (New York: Paulist Press, 1979); Brown et al., *Introduction*, 74–86.

31. My method closely resembles historical narrative criticism, which has been applied by the following scholars: Cornelis Bennema, *Encountering Jesus: Character Studies in the Gospel of John* (Colorado Springs, CO: Paternoster, 2009), 20–21; M. C. de Boer, "Narrative Criticism, Historical Criticism, and the Gospel of John," *JSNT* 47 (1992): 35–58; Stephen Motyer, "Method in Fourth Gospel Studies: A Way Out of

an Impasse?," *JSNT* 66 (1997): 27–44; Gail R. O'Day, "Toward a Narrative-Critical Study of John," *Int* 49 no. 4 (1995): 341–46. For the benefits of narrative criticism, see James L. Resseguie, *Narrative Criticism of the New Testament: An Introduction* (Grand Rapids, MI: Baker, 2005), 38–40.

32. Barrett, *John*, 100–134; Andreas J. Köstenberger, "Early Doubts of the Apostolic Authorship of the Fourth Gospel in the History of Modern Biblical Criticism," in *Studies on John and Gender: A Decade of Scholarship* (New York: P. Lang, 2001), 17–47. For discussions about the real author, implied author, and narrator, see Culpepper, *Anatomy*, 4–9, 15–49; Tolmie, *Farewell*, 13–21, 33–62; Tovey, *Narrative*, 35, 45–68. For a brief introduction to the Johannine community and the writing of John, see Harold W. Attridge, "Johannine Christianity," in *Essays on John and Hebrews*, ed. Harold W. Attridge (Tübingen: Mohr Siebeck, 2010), 3–19.

33. Chapter 7 investigates the question of the historical setting of John more thoroughly. The common scholarly view of the dating of John is 85–100 CE. See Johannes Behm, Werner Georg Kümmel, and Paul Feine, *Introduction to the New Testament*, trans., Jr. A. J. Mattill, revised ed. (Nashville: Abingdon Press, 1966), 175; Mikael Tellbe, *Christ-Believers in Ephesus: A Textual Analysis of Early Christian Identity Formation in a Local Perspective*, WUNT 242 (Tübingen: Mohr Siebeck, 2009), 35; Paul Trebilco, *The Early Christians in Ephesus from Paul to Ignatius*, WUNT 166 (Tübingen: Mohr Siebeck, 2004), 272. Wallace and Robinson proposed a date before 70 CE; however, most scholars continue to hold the date of 85–100 CE. John A. T. Robinson, *Redating the New Testament* (London: S.C.M. Press, 1976), 307; Daniel B. Wallace, "John 5,2 and the Date of the Fourth Gospel," *Bib* 71 no. 2 (1990): 177–205. Multiple locations have been proposed for the place of writing. Meeks discusses Galilee, Batanaea, and Ephesus as options: Wayne Meeks, "Breaking Away: Three New Testament Pictures of Christianity's Separation from the Jewish Communities," in *'To See Ourselves as Others See Us': Christians, Jews, 'Others' in Late Antiquity*, ed. Jacob Neusner, Ernest S. Frerichs, and Caroline McCracken-Flesher (Chico, CA: Scholars Press Studies in the Humanities, 1985), 93–115. For Ephesus: Tellbe, *Christ-Believers*, 35–39; Trebilco, *Early Christians*, 241–63. For Palestine: Robinson, *Redating*, 296. For Alexandria: William H. Brownlee, "Whence the Gospel According to John?," in *John and Qumran*, ed. Raymond E. Brown and James H. Charlesworth (London: Geoffrey Chapman, 1972), 189–91; William R. Domeris, "Christology and Community: A Study of the Social Matrix of the Fourth Gospel," *JTSA* 64 (1988): 54. For Syria, see Bultmann, *John*, 12. For multiple geographic areas as part of the writing process, see G. R. Beasley-Murray, *John* (Dallas, TX: Word, 1989), lxxix–lxxxi.

34. For summaries of the various views on the background and the audience of John, see Jörg Frey, "The Diaspora-Jewish Background of the Fourth Gospel," *SEÅ* 77 (2012): 169–96; Vhumani Magezi and Peter Manzanga, "A Study to Establish the Most Plausible Background to the Fourth Gospel (John)," *TS* 66 no. 1 (2010): 1–7. Bauckham argues for a general audience, Richard Bauckham, ed. *The Gospels for All Christians: Rethinking the Gospel Audiences* (Grand Rapids, MI: Eerdmans, 1998). For a Hellenistic audience, see Bultmann, *John*. For a Jewish audience, Dodd writes, "In the Fourth Gospel the followers of Christ are threatened with excommunication

from the synagogue—a menace which would have no terrors for any but Jewish Christians. They may have to face martyrdom, but it is clearly at the hands of their fellow-Jews, since the persecutors believe themselves to be rendering service to God." C. H. Dodd, *Historical Tradition in the Fourth Gospel* (Cambridge: University Press, 1963), 412; Hwang, "Identity of the Recipients," 688; Andreas J. Köstenberger, *A Theology of John's Gospel and Letters* (Grand Rapids, MI: Zondervan, 2009), 260; Robinson, *Redating*, 274–75. For Diaspora Jews as the audience, see Frey, "Diaspora," 169–96; Unnik, "The Purpose of St. John's Gospel," 382–411.

35. For Diaspora-Jews: Frey, "Diaspora," 169–96; Culpepper, *Anatomy*, 211–27; Carson, *John*, 91; Frey, "Diaspora," 190–96; Ridderbos, "Prologue," 60; Tellbe, *Christ-Believers*, 58–65. For Ephesus: Brown et al., *Introduction*, 202–206; Mary L. Coloe, *Dwelling in the Household of God: Johannine Ecclesiology and Spirituality* (Collegeville, MN: Liturgical Press, 2007), 5; Frey, "Diaspora," 190; Martin Hengel, *The Johannine Question* (London: SCM, 1989), 124–35; Trebilco, *Early Christians*, 241–63. For Palestine: Robinson, *Redating*, 296 fn. 196. For Syria: Behm et al., *Introduction*, 175; Helmut Koester, *Introduction to the New Testament* (New York: Walter De Gruyter, 1982), 2:178. Conversely, Richard Bauckham and Edward Klink have defended a broad audience for the Gospels based on the understanding that the most probable genre of the Gospels is the Greco-Roman *bios*. I agree with Bauckham and Klink that *bios* is the most fitting genre of John but I do not necessarily see a corollary between genre and the scope of the Gospel's audience. Ashton recently critiqued Bauckham's and Klink's association between genre and audience/setting of John; and Ashton also critiqued Burridge's defense that the Gospels are Greco-Roman *bioi*. Instead, Ashton suggests that the Gospels cannot be called merely *bioi* but should be identified more specifically, keeping in mind the Gospels' theological and pastoral purpose. Ashton elsewhere labels the Gospels as "proclamatory narratives" (27) and defines the Gospel as "a narrative of the public career of Jesus, his passion and death, told in order to affirm or confirm the faith of Christian believers in the Risen Lord" (332). Prior to the dialogue between Bauckham/Klink and Ashton, Aune conveyed a similar position. Aune argued that the Gospels are a subtype of Greco-Roman biography and that the Gospels were "written to persuade their audiences that the crucified and risen Jesus is the Messiah, the Son of God. The Gospels, then, are fundamentally Christian literary propaganda" (59). Aune subscribes to the *bios* genre but maintains the hortatory purpose of each Gospel. Trozzo convincingly argues that John should be understood through the genre of *bios* which includes encomiastic narratives. In the case of John, Jesus is presented as a hero whose union with God forms his ethic that results in Jesus' mission to reach "the world." For the most recent work on Gospel genre, see Craig S. Keener, *Christobiography: Memory, History, and the Reliability of the Gospels* (Grand Rapids, MI: Eerdmans, 2019). For further studies, see John Ashton, *Understanding the Fourth Gospel*, 2nd ed. (Oxford: Oxford University Press, 2007), 332, see also pp. 24–27 for fuller discussion; John Ashton, *The Gospel of John and Christian Origins* (Minneapolis, MN: Fortress, 2014), 23–29; 75–76; Aune, *Literary*, 17–76; Bauckham, ed. *Gospels*; Richard A. Burridge, *What Are the Gospels? A Comparison with Graeco-Roman Biography*, ed. G. N. Stanton, SNTSMS 70 (Cambridge: Cambridge University Press, 1992); Edward W. Klink, *The Audience of the Gospels: The Origin and Function*

*of the Gospels in Early Christianity*, LNTS 353 (London: T & T Clark, 2010); Trozzo, *Ethics*. For a response to Bauckham, see Philip F. Esler, "Community and Gospel in Early Christianity: A Response to Richard Bauckham's Gospels for all Christians," *SJT* 51 no. 2 (1998): 235–48.

36. For character studies in John, see Bennema, *Encountering*; Cornelis Bennema, *A Theory of Character in New Testament Narrative* (Minneapolis, MN: Fortress, 2014); Raymond F. Collins, *These Things Have Been Written: Studies on the Fourth Gospel* 2 (Grand Rapids, MI: Eerdmans, 1990), 1–45, 56–86; Steven A. Hunt, D. F. Tolmie, and Ruben Zimmermann, eds., *Character Studies in the Fourth Gospel*, WUNT 314 (Tübingen: Mohr Siebeck, 2013).

37. For discussion of Johannine symbolism, see Köstenberger, *Theology*, 155–67. For discussion of the symbolism of the Johannine "signs," see Barrett, *John*, 75–78; Köstenberger, *Theology*, 323–35.

38. For a theory of metaphor in John, see J. G. van der Watt, *Family of the King: Dynamics of Metaphor in the Gospel According to John*, BIS 47 (Leiden: Brill, 2000), 1–160.

39. For characterization in John, see Margaret M. Beirne, *Women and Men in the Fourth Gospel: A Genuine Discipleship of Equals*, JSNTSup 242 (London: Sheffield Academic Press, 2003); Bennema, *Encountering*, 11–13, 20; Bennema, *Character*; F. W. Burnett, "Characterization and Reader Construction of Characters in the Gospels," *Semeia* 63 (1993): 3–28; Collins, *These Things*, 1–86; Colleen M. Conway, *Men and Women in the Fourth Gospel: Gender and Johannine Characterization*, SBLDS 167 (Atlanta: SBL Press, 1999); Colleen M. Conway, "Speaking through Ambiguity: Minor Characters in the Fourth Gospel," *BibInt* 10 no. 3 (2002): 324–41; Hunt et al., eds., *Character*; Susan Hylen, *Imperfect Believers: Ambiguous Characters in the Gospel of John* (Louisville, KY: Westminster John Knox Press, 2009). For friendship: Martin M. Culy, *Echoes of Friendship in the Gospel of John* (Sheffield, England: Sheffield Press, 2010); J. Massyngberde Ford, *Redeemer-Friend and Mother: Salvation in Antiquity and in the Gospel of John* (Minneapolis, MN: Fortress, 1997); Sharon H. Ringe, *Wisdom's Friends: Community and Christology in the Fourth Gospel* (Louisville, KY: Westminster John Knox Press, 1999). For family: Van der Watt, *Family*. For covenant themes: Rekha M. Chennattu, *Johannine Discipleship as a Covenant Relationship* (Peabody, MA: Hendrickson, 2006). For life as a lens into John: David Asonye Ihenacho, *The Community of Eternal Life: The Study of the Meaning of Life for the Johannine Community* (Lanham, MD: University Press of America, 2001). Christology: Hera, *Christology*. Agency: Dirk G. van der Merwe, "Towards a Theological Understanding of Johannine Discipleship," *Neot* 31 no. 2 (1997): 339–59. Mission: Michael J. Gorman, *Abide and Go: Missional Theosis in the Gospel of John* (Eugene, OR: Cascade Books, 2018). Köstenberger, *Missions*. For descent-ascent: Van der Merwe, "Johannine Discipleship," 339–59.

40. Eduard Schweizer, *Lordship and Discipleship* (London, England: SCM, 1960), 77–92. Schweizer's emphasis on following Jesus is reaffirmed by Betz (i.e., following is manifested in imitation) and Schultz (i.e., to follow is to be in life community with Jesus). Hans Dieter Betz, "Nachfolge und Nachahmung Jesu Christi im Neuen Testament" (Habilitationsschrift, Mainz, 1967), 36–43; Anselm Schulz, *Nachfolgen*

*und Nachahmen; Studien über das Verhältnis der neutestamentlichen Jüngerschaft zur urchristlichen Vorbildethik*, SANT 6 (München: Kösel-Verlag, 1962), 134–44. Additionally, in 1967 Schweizer published a joint work with Hahn and Strobel as they examined discipleship before Jesus' resurrection, in light of the resurrection-event, and post-resurrection in the Gospels and Pauline literature. While Hahn concludes that in Jesus' pre-Easter ministry, "it is not his person which forms the centre of his own proclamation but rather his mission." Hera more persuasively argued that John's exhortation to discipleship is rooted in the person of Jesus as the Christ. Hahn et al., *Die Anfänge*, citing 22; Hera, *Christology*.

41. Schweizer, *Lordship and Discipleship*, 85.
42. Feuillet, *Études*, 107–12.
43. Ramón Moreno Jiménez, "El Discipulo de Jesucristo segun el evangelio de S. Juan," *Est Bib* 30 (1971): 269–311. For criticism of Jiménez's theological interpretive lens, see Chennattu, *Discipleship*, 3–5; Rudolf Schnackenburg, *The Gospel According to St. John*, trans., David Smith and G. A. Kon, 3 vols. (New York: Crossroad, 1982), 3, 203–17.
44. Marinus de Jonge, *Jesus: Stranger from Heaven and Son of God*, Sources for Biblical Study 11 (Missoula, MT: Scholars Press, 1977), 3, 12–15, esp. 141–68, 193–222.
45. Matthew Vellanickal, "Discipleship According to the Gospel of John," *Jeev* 10 (1980): 131–47.
46. Fernando F. Segovia, *Love Relationships in the Johannine Tradition*, SBLDS 58 (Chico, CA: Scholars Press, 1982), 123–24, 179. Segovia argued that 1 John and the Gospel reflect two different authors who project different meanings to ἀγάπη/ἀγαπάω because their respective works are situated in a different *Sitz im Leben*. He further suggested that due to problems within the community, John 15–17 was inserted into the Gospel in order to affect the ethical tone of the Gospel. Segovia, *Love*, 1–3, 22–24, 117–19, 125, 191, 217.
47. Segovia, *Love*, 117–18, 124.
48. See Tolmie, *Farewell*, 13, 23–28, 64–95, 70–73, 76–77, 191, 228, citing 66. See also A. J. Greimas, "Elements of a Narrative Grammar," *Diacritics* 7 (1977): 23–40.
49. Tolmie, *Farewell*, 70.
50. Tolmie, *Farewell*, 85–95, 185, 190–229, citing 229.
51. Köstenberger, *Missions*, 177. In 1997, Van der Merwe examined the mission of Jesus as a theological setting for discipleship, viewing mission in light of the ancient descent-ascent schema and the agency motif. Van der Merwe, "Johannine Discipleship," 339–59.
52. Köstenberger, *Missions*, 199–210.
53. Köstenberger, *Missions*, 161–85.
54. Van der Watt, *Family*, 161, 397, 400–401.
55. Van der Watt, *Family*, 365 fn. 1053.
56. Culpepper, *Anatomy*, 149–202; Köstenberger, *Theology*, 127–70, 341–54.
57. James L. Resseguie, *The Strange Gospel: Narrative Design and Point of View in John*, BIS 56 (Leiden: Brill, 2001), 1–3, 22.

58. Resseguie, *Strange*, 200–201.
59. Resseguie, *Strange*, 201.
60. Resseguie, *Strange*, 150, 155–63.
61. Resseguie, *Strange*, 65, 96, 107, 149, 150–55, 168, 198.
62. Bennema, *Power*, 35–39.
63. Bennema, *Power*, 1–39, 44–51, 252.
64. Bennema, *Power*, 222.
65. Bennema, *Power*, 131, 136, 154.
66. Bennema, *Power*, 36–37, 42–44.
67. Chennattu, *Discipleship*.
68. Chennattu, *Discipleship*, 41–49.
69. Chennattu, *Discipleship*, 179.
70. Chennattu, *Discipleship*, 210.
71. One additional point of critique is her seemingly unnatural reading of certain texts. For example, she interprets the foot-washing episode as entrance into the covenant relationship with Jesus. She defends her stance by tracing "part" (μέρος, 13:8) to the LXX use of μέρος (חלק) in reference to each tribe's portion in the inheritance of the promised land. Yet the meaning of the foot-washing scene is explained in 13:13–16, which is simply to imitate Jesus in his self-sacrifice. Chennattu, *Discipleship*, 91–99. Similarly, Sandra Schneiders, "Review of *Johannine Discipleship as a Covenant Relationship*," *CBQ* 69 no. 3 (July 2007): 575–76.
72. Kaczmarek, *Language*, 11. For a recent evaluation of antilanguage in John as an expression of antisociety, see David A. Lamb, *Text, Context and the Johannine Community: A Sociolinguistic Analysis of the Johannine Writings*, LNTS 477 (London: Bloomsbury, 2015). Lamb examined the passages that directly address the readers or employ γραφή/ γράφω in order to discern the social context to determine if the author wrote to a specific community. Lamb concluded that there is "little or no *contact* or *affective involvement*" (italics original) that can be observed in John's writings, which would suggest that the author wrote to a "close-knit community." He does allow for some evidence of existence of a "loose network of church groups" in 1–3 John that attached themselves around the text of John. Lamb, *Text*, esp. 145–97, citing 173. Lamb's study provides a unique rebuttal to the Johannine community hypothesis championed by Martyn.
73. Kaczmarek, *Language*, 11, 33, 49.
74. Kaczmarek, *Language*, 47.
75. See chapter 5, below, for a more thorough engagement with Kaczmarek.
76. Culy writes: "The language of friendship pervades the Fourth Gospel from beginning to end and serves as a primary vehicle for characterizing the relationships that are introduced in the Prologue and fleshed out throughout the course of the narrative." Culy, *Echoes*, 178.
77. He also examined the Jewish and early Christian writings but limited the three ideals of friendship to be sourced in the Greco-Roman documents. Culy, *Echoes*, 33, 49, 84, 91, 130, 178–79.
78. Culy, *Echoes*, 32, 87–178.
79. Culy, *Echoes*, 178.

80. Hera, *Christology*, 36, 168.

81. de Jonge, *Stranger*, 3. Mary Pazdan only tangentially noted that Jesus is the model disciple of the Father as illustrated in his fulfillment of a soteriological work on behalf of the disciples. Pazdan, "Discipleship," 337–41. Melanie Baffes similarly affirms a close relationship between Christology and discipleship. She uses this relationship to argue that John 7:37–39 is intentionally ambiguous in order to account for both Jesus and the believer being the sources of living water. Melanie Baffes, "Christology and Discipleship in John 7:37–38," *BTB* 41 no. 3 (2011): 144–50. See also, James D. G. Dunn, "Let John Be John: A Gospel for Its Time," in *Das Evangelium und die Evangelien: Vorträge vom Tübinger Symposium 1982*, ed. Peter Stuhlmacher (Tübingen: Mohr, 1983), 317–18.

82. Hera, *Christology*, 36.

83. Hera, *Christology*, 127, 130, 173.

84. Adesola Joan Akala, *The Son-Father Relationship and Christological Symbolism in the Gospel of John*, LNTS 505 (London: Bloomsbury), citing 188, 209–10, 222–23.

85. Lee, *Hallowed*, 160.

86. Gorman, *Abide and Go*. Gorman does not define *theosis* as ontological but as missiological.

87. Shin, *Ethics*, 48–50. Lindsey Trozzo also investigated the question of ethics in John through rhetorical criticism. She compared John to Plutarch's *Lives* and argued that the encomiastic nature of both works provide imitable ethical lessons for the readers. In John, Jesus' unity with God that extends to believers is the fundamental ethical quality for imitation. Thus, instead of providing certain ethical principles, John invites the readers into Jesus' unity with the Father that affects his mission and directs the readers toward similar behavior in "the world." Trozzo, *Ethics*.

88. Shin, *Ethics*, 26–52.

89. Shin, *Ethics*, 48–53.

90. Shin, *Ethics*, 53.

91. Martyn, *History*. This approach has also been defended by Collins, *These Things*, 49–55.

92. Refer to Collins, *These Things*, 1. See also Edward Lynn Bode, *The First Easter Morning: The Gospel Accounts of the Women's Visit to the Tomb of Jesus*, Analecta Biblica 45 (Rome: Biblical Institute Press, 1970), 75; Craig R. Koester, *Symbolism in the Fourth Gospel: Meaning, Mystery, Community*, 2nd ed. (Minneapolis, MN: Fortress, 2003), 33–77.

93. Culpepper, *Anatomy*, 104; Hylen, *Imperfect*, 1.

94. See Conway, "Speaking," 328; Hylen, *Imperfect*.

95. David R. Beck, *The Discipleship Paradigm: Readers and Anonymous Characters in the Fourth Gospel*, BIS 27 (Leiden: Brill, 1997).

96. Beck, *Discipleship*, 1–2, 137–42.

97. Beck, *Discipleship*, 137. He concludes that the mother of Jesus, the Samaritan woman, the official at Capernaum, the lame man, the blind man, the adulteress, and the Beloved Disciple are paradigms of discipleship. Beck, *Discipleship*, 51–107. At the same time, he rejects John the Baptist, Nicodemus, Peter, Thomas, and others as

model disciples. Beck, *Discipleship*, 133–36, 138–42; Beck, *Discipleship*, 101–107, 140. It is surprising that he concluded that John the Baptist is not a model disciple since John the Baptist bears witness to Jesus (1:6–9, 20–36; 3:27–30; 5:33–36; 10:41). Beck, *Discipleship*, 40–43, 86–91. He also eliminates Nathaniel, Peter, Martha, and Thomas as model disciples, but this seems to be a result of a curious reading of the text since John features their explicit Christological confessions (1:49; 6:68–69; 11:27; 20:28). Beck, *Discipleship*, 139. Additionally, Beck advances a positive interpretation of the lame man (5:1–18), but in doing so, he overlooks John's final comment about the persecution by "the Jews" and the attempted murder of Jesus on account of the lame man's testimony (5:16–18). For additional comments on the lame man, see endnote 75 in chapter 6.

98. Farelly places Mary Magdalene within the broader group of "disciples" and thus he presumes she follows Jesus before and after the resurrection. Farelly, *Disciples*, 4, 10–12, 37, 89–161.

99. Farelly, *Disciples*, 27, 52, 65–66.

*Chapter 1*

# Membership in the Family of God—Divine Initiative and Corollary Benefits

The first key benefit that John confers on a disciple is membership in the divine family. Although the expression "divine family" does not appear in John, the family of God is a prominent motif in the Gospel. Kinship terminology permeates the Gospel, including but not limited to father, son, children, orphans, brothers, his own, and little children.[1] Moreover, God is presented as a Father who procreates, provides, protects, and loves those in relationship with him through his Son. Consequently, it is reasonable to speak of the divine family as consisting of God, his Son, and the believers as children of God. The believers are welcomed into the divine family in order to share the characteristics of the Father. That is, the believers do not become divine but rather resemble the attributes of their divine Father (8:42, 47).[2]

## THE PRIORITY OF THE DIVINE FAMILY

John emphasizes the divine family motif in three ways. First, John frames the entire Gospel with the *inclusio* that features filial terminology—in the prologue (1:11–13) and in the concluding chapters of the Gospel (20:17; 21:5). In the prologue, John presents the *Logos* as coming into "the world," and those who had received the *Logos* were given the authority to join the divine family (1:11–13). In 20:17, Jesus' disciples are designated as Jesus' brothers; and in 21:5, Jesus is portrayed as addressing his disciples as children. Additionally, family imagery forms an *inclusio* in the public ministry of Jesus (John 1–12), as the opening and closing chapters contain promises of amalgamation into the divine family (1:12; 12:36).

Second, the significance of the family theme is evident in the chiastic structure of the prologue with the focal point contained in 1:12b, "he gave them authority to become children of God." A reading of 1:11–13 through the lens of the chiasm suggests that the incorporation of the believers into the divine family is the central purpose of the coming of the light and the incarnation of the *Logos*. Thus, the strategic placement of filial terminology that forms the above *inclusios* in John and the chiasm in the prologue accentuates and distinguishes the family from other images in the Gospel.

Third, John spotlights the divine family through frequent references to the Father-Son relationship between God and Jesus. God is referenced as Father 120 times in the Gospel, more frequently than in the Synoptic Gospels combined (i.e., 58 times). Eighty percent of the references to the Father in John concern Jesus' relationship with the Father, as illustrated by Jesus' appellation of God as "my Father" (25 times).[3] To distinguish Jesus' relationship with the Father, John reserves the term "son" (υἱός) for Jesus, whereas he calls the believers "children" (τέκνα, 1:11–13; 11:52), "little children" (τεκνία, 13:33; παιδία, 21:5), and "brothers" (ἀδελφοί, 20:17).[4] Moreover, the believers are not called children of the *Father* or born of the *Father*, but rather children of God and born of God (1:11–13; 11:52).[5] John is declaring, "There are many 'children' of God, there is only *one* Son."[6]

## THE RELATIONSHIP OF THE DIVINE FAMILY TO DISCIPLESHIP

John deploys the promise of membership in the divine family in conjunction with discipleship terminology to encourage devotion to Jesus. In 1:11–13 and 12:36, John links the language of family to believing in Jesus and to believing in him as the light. Moreover, in 1:11–13, inclusion in God's family is linked with receiving Jesus. That is, from the outset, John's discussion of the believer's integration into the divine family entails the individual receiving Jesus (λαμβάνω) and believing in Jesus (πιστεύω).[7] John features the expressions "his own did not receive him" (οὐ παρέλαβον, 1:11) and "whoever received him" (ὅσοι δὲ ἔλαβον αὐτόν, 1:12) to contrast faith and the lack of faith.[8] Throughout his narrative, John presents belief as assent and allegiance to Jesus.[9] In the first Johannine reference to the divine family in 1:11–13, the present participle τοῖς πιστεύουσιν is used to indicate that continuous believing in Jesus' name is characteristic of a child of God.[10] John's references to "receiving" and "not receiving" Jesus in 1:11–13 encourage his audiences "to read the rest of the narrative with these two opposite responses in mind."[11] As John develops the motif of the divine family, he continues to link it with πιστεύειν (e.g., 3:3–21; 8:20–59) and λαμβάνειν (e.g., 3:11; 17:8). At the close of the Gospel, the kinship terminology is coupled with references to the disciples where Jesus refers to them as brothers (20:17) and children (21:5). It is to the individual who receives Jesus and believes in him that God extends the benefit of membership in the divine family. Consequently, the promise of membership in the divine family can be understood as John's attempt to encourage his audiences toward continuous discipleship.

## MEMBERSHIP IN THE DIVINE FAMILY

Kinship relations dominated social relationships in the ancient Mediterranean milieu and therefore, belonging to the *right* family was chiefly important. The family was the primary social order and was "part and parcel of the everyday life of every person in the ancient Mediterranean world."[12] An individual's identity and success in society depended on belonging to the right family, which led to the prioritization of the group over the individual.[13] This accent on group and on the priority of the family over individualism began at birth. The central event in a person's life was birth, as it determined his or her future societal success.[14] Because of the importance of the family to the ancient audiences, John's promise of the disciple's amalgamation into the divine family would be perceived as a privilege. Moreover, coupling this benefit with the theme of belief in Jesus suggests that John deploys this image to persuade his audiences to commit to Jesus (1:11–13).

John's portrayal of membership in the divine family as a benefit to promote continuous discipleship entails three aspects. First, membership is by divine initiative and thus it is an exclusive privilege of the believer in Jesus. Second, participation in the divine family results in corollary benefits. Third, membership involves attaining eternal life (discussed in the next chapter).

### Birth from Above: Membership Is by Divine Initiative

John's thematization of membership in the divine family begins with God the Father initiating a relationship with the believer in Jesus. John develops God's role as the proactive agent in bringing disciples into his family through the following verbs—become (γίνομαι), beget/born (γεννάω), give (δίδωμι), draw (ἕλκω), and the expression "from God" (ἐκ τοῦ θεοῦ).[15]

*"To Become and Beget"*

John uses two clauses in 1:11–13 to describe God's integration of the believer into the divine family—"to become children of God" (τέκνα θεοῦ γενέσθαι) and "born of God" (ἐκ θεοῦ ἐγεννήθησαν). The verb "become" (γίνομαι) appears eighty-three times in the Gospel, but only the passages in which this verb carries a symbolic meaning related to discipleship are examined here (i.e., 1:12; 8:33; 9:27, 39; 10:16; 12:36).[16] John's second verb to describe the integration of the believer into the divine family is "beget/born" (γεννάω), which appears eighteen times in six separate passages (1:13; 3:3–8; 8:41; 9:2–34; 16:21; 18:37), but the symbolic meaning in reference to following Jesus is only contained in 1:13 and 3:3–8. These passages demonstrate that membership in the divine family is by divine initiative.

## John 1:11–13—Becoming Children of God

The verb "become" (γίνομαι) first appears in 1:12 in reference to the believer becoming a child of God. Here the aorist infinitive form, γενέσθαι, can be understood dynamically/progressively or statically. That is, the advocates of the dynamic/progressive position interpret 1:11–13 as a process of becoming a child of God, whereas proponents of the static interpretation view the references to becoming children of God and being begotten of God (vv. 12, 13) as a simple act which begins at the point of spiritual birth that commences a new relationship of the believer as a child of God. Before defending the static view of vv. 11–13, I first review the scholarly defense of the dynamic/progressive position by highlighting three of their observations.[17]

First, by appending v. 13 to v. 14 instead of keeping vv. 12–13 together, the focus of v. 13 becomes the incarnation of the *Logos*. This is accomplished by bifurcating v. 12 and v. 13 in order to separate the clause "become children of God" (τέκνα θεοῦ γενέσθαι) from "begotten of God" (ἐκ θεοῦ ἐγεννήθησαν), which allows the proponents of this view to read v. 13 in conjunction with v. 14. The emphasis then is that the *Logos* was born of God. Moreover, these scholars advocate for the singular reading of "born" (ἐγεννήθη) over the plural ἐγεννήθησαν in v. 13 and thereby interpret v. 13 and v. 14 as a reference to the begetting of the *Logos*, instead of the begetting of the believers as children of God.[18] However, textual evidence for ἐγεννήθησαν in v. 13 and the teaching of the Johannine corpus undermines the singular reading ἐγεννήθη in v. 13. The earliest manuscripts and the Johannine writings affirm the plural reading ἐγεννήθησαν and thus invalidate the division between v. 12 and v. 13.[19]

The second argument put forward in favor of the dynamic/progressive reading of the aorist infinitive "become" (γενέσθαι) in 1:12 is the use of the same verb elsewhere in the Gospel (i.e., 5:6; 8:58; 9:27).[20] However, a closer inspection of each of these passages indicates that the dynamic interpretation of "become" (γενέσθαι) is not preferable for contextual reasons. In 5:6–9, the lame man becomes immediately healed instead of entering a healing process (note εὐθέως ἐγένετο ὑγιής in 5:9). In 8:58, the reference to Abraham is better understood as his *moment* of birth (πρὶν Ἀβραὰμ γενέσθαι).[21] In

9:27, the blind man's retort to the Jewish authorities—"Do you also want to become (γενέσθαι) his disciples?"—should be understood in light of the response of "the Jews" to the blind man in 9:28, "You are (εἶ) his disciple, we are (ἐσμέν) disciples of Moses." John is depicting "the Jews" as having made a resolute decision against Jesus while confidently affirming their loyalty to Moses. Thus, it is preferable to understand "become" (γενέσθαι) statically rather than dynamically in all three passages. Consequently, the static view of "become" (γενέσθαι) is preferred which understands τέκνα θεοῦ γενέσθαι (v. 12) and ἐκ θεοῦ ἐγεννήθησαν (v. 13) as depicting a simple event of God's begetting of the believer which also makes the believer a child of God.[22]

Third, the dynamic interpretation of "become" (γίνομαι) in 1:12 has also been defended by appealing to its use in v. 14 where the *Logos* becomes flesh (σὰρξ ἐγένετο) and continues to function progressively in the world.[23] Yet a more fitting parallel is the birth analogy in 1:13 and in 3:3–8 through the verb γεννάω.[24] In every instance in the Gospel, γεννάω is in the passive voice, thus stressing the role of the subject rather than that of the object (e.g., 1:13; 3:3–8; 8:41; 9:2, 19, 20, 32, 34; 16:21; 18:37). Moreover, in 3:3–8, the emphasis on the Spirit's proactive work in the new birth is observable in the Spirit blowing where he wishes, suggesting that the Spirit cannot be controlled by the object. This is affirmed in 6:63, "the Spirit is the life-giver, the flesh benefits nothing." John's message in 1:13 is that a believer becomes God's child not because of physiology, or human desire or will, but because the believer is "begotten of God" (ἐκ θεοῦ ἐγεννήθησαν).[25] In the end, the benefit of becoming a member of the divine family is initiated by God.

Instead of viewing the aorist infinitive "become" (γενέσθαι) dynamically/ progressively, γενέσθαι is better understood statically with an ingressive force. This then would indicate a change of condition and entrance into a new perpetual state of being a child of God (1:12).[26] John presents spiritual birth as a simple event after which the child is kept in the relationship with the Father through faith in Jesus. Thus, v. 12 is not describing a "process of becoming a child" that can be likened to a nine-month pregnancy period at the end of which a child is born; instead, the believer's integration into the divine family is a simple act.[27] The change in the tense of the verb, from the aorist "who received" (ἔλαβον, 1:12) to the present participle "those who believe" (τοῖς πιστεύουσιν, 1:12), stresses the need for a continual commitment to Jesus.[28] In the rest of the Gospel, John features both aspects of the relationship between the Father and the children of God, that is, the Father's ongoing commitment to his children (e.g., 6:39–40; 10:28–29; 17:24–26) and the children's continual devotion to the Father (e.g., 8:31–32; 12:35–36; 15:1–17). John features the role of faith that leads toward adoption into God's family, by juxtaposing those who did not receive the *Logos* (v. 11) with those who received him and continuously believe in him (v. 12). But in 1:13, John clarifies that those who believe became children of God because they have been begotten by God.

### John 3:3–8—God Begetting Children

In 3:3–8, "born" (γεννάω) is the preferred Johannine term to describe entrance *into* the kingdom of God by divine initiative. The requirement to see/enter the kingdom of God is birth from above (γεννηθῇ ἄνωθεν, 3:3, 7) or birth through water and the spirit (γεννηθῇ ἐξ ὕδατος καὶ πνεύματος, 3:5, 6, 8).[29] Jesus' response to Nicodemus' misunderstanding indicates that Jesus expected "the teacher" in Israel to understand his reference to the water and spirit, which suggests that an Old Testament background is most appropriate for this passage.[30] The allusion to water and spirit is likely a reference to Ezekiel 36:22–32. The cleansing process in Ezekiel 36:22–32 involves the water, spirit, and a change of heart (vv. 25–27).[31] In John 3:3–8, John features the Spirit as the initiator of the "new birth" process through the consistent use of the passive form of γεννάω. The thematic link between Ezekiel 36:25–27 and John 3:3–8 suggests that the Spirit is the effective cause and sustainer of the new life.[32] While John presents Nicodemus as employing γεννάω in reference to physical birth (3:4), Jesus is portrayed as relying on the Old Testament as he explains to Nicodemus that "being born as a Jew is not sufficient to qualify for entry into the kingdom of God," thus articulating that spiritual birth from above—an act achieved by divine initiative—is necessary for entry into the kingdom of God.[33] The need for spiritual birth arises from the impotency of human flesh (3:6; 6:63). In summary, through the verbs "become" (γίνομαι) and "born" (γεννάω), John stresses God's initiative in inaugurating the believer in Jesus into the divine family because "sonship is based on divine begetting, not on any claim on [the human's] part."[34]

### *"To Give"*

John also uses the verb "give" (δίδωμι) to communicate God's initiative in bringing believers into the divine family.[35] In 6:37, God is the first to act in the process of the disciples coming to Jesus.[36] The Johannine Jesus claims, "Everything that the Father gives me will come to me" (see also 6:39, 44, 65; 17:9, 24). God gives the sheep to Jesus (10:29), Jesus confers eternal life only to those who are given to him by God (17:2), and Jesus manifests God's name (17:6) and prays only for those who have been given to him by God (17:9). Moreover, only those who have been given to Jesus by God will be with Jesus and perceive his glory (17:24). John's use of "give" (δίδωμι) spotlights God's initiative in giving to the Son the believers who thereafter belong to the Father and to the Son (e.g., 17:6, 9–10).

## "To Draw"

John's companion term to refer to the Father's initiative is "draw" (ἕλκω). In the Gospel, this term refers to the Father bringing people to Jesus (6:44) and Jesus drawing people to himself (12:32).[37] The verb ἕλκω also refers to drawing a net filled with fish (21:6, 11) and drawing a sword from its sheath (18:10). Outside of John, ἕλκω appears only four additional times in the New Testament, on three occasions in reference to men being violently dragged (Acts 16:19; 21:30; James 2:6), and once it describes the intensity of inner desires leading an individual to an illicit action (James 1:14). Thus, with the use of ἕλκω John prioritizes the Father's initiative in the process of salvation. John's message to his audiences is that "there is no other way to come to Jesus unless the Father calls you."[38]

## "From/of God"

The expression "from/of God" (θεοῦ, ἐκ θεοῦ, ἐκ τοῦ θεοῦ, 1:13; 7:17; 8:42, 47) also establishes an individual as belonging to the divine family by God's initiative. The accent on the divine origin in the expressions θεοῦ, ἐκ θεοῦ, ἐκ τοῦ θεοῦ can be likened to other phrases that describe Jesus' divine origin. For example, Jesus is said to be from above (ἄνωθεν or ἐκ ἄνω, 3:31; 8:23), from heaven (ἐκ τοῦ οὐρανοῦ, e.g., 3:13, 27, 31; 6:31, 32, 33, 38, 41, 42, 50, 51, 58), and from the Father/God (ἀπὸ θεοῦ, παρὰ πατρός, ἐκ τοῦ θεοῦ, e.g., 1:14; 3:2; 6:46; 7:28–29; 8:40, 42; 13:3; 16:27, 28, 30; 17:8).[39]

John 8:31–59 is the most extensive discussion on the divine family in John, and in 8:31–59 the genitive expression "from/of God" (θεοῦ, ἐκ θεοῦ, ἐκ τοῦ θεοῦ) is used to distinguish between members of God's family and the affiliates of the devil (8:42, 44, 47).[40] In the discussion of the two families in 8:31–59, John juxtaposes Jesus' challenge to remain in his word with true discipleship and with benefits that flow from membership in the divine family. John frames this passage with an invitation to discipleship as he spotlights "the Jews" who believed in Jesus (vv. 30–31). Then John concludes this narrative by showing that presumably these same "Jews" attempted to kill Jesus (v. 59). John depicts Jesus as challenging these supposed believers in Jesus toward discipleship by the use of the third-class conditional sentence, "if you remain in my words" (ἐὰν ὑμεῖς μείνητε ἐν τῷ λόγῳ τῷ ἐμῷ, 8:31).[41] The call to discipleship is also observable in references to believing (8:24, 30, 31, 45, 46), following Jesus (8:12), true discipleship (8:31), abiding in Jesus' teaching (8:31), hearing Jesus' and God's word (8:43, 46), and obeying Jesus' word (8:51–52).[42] The exhortation to believe and become a disciple is juxtaposed with the discussion of family origins.

In order to incentivize his audiences to believe in Jesus, John deploys certain benefits alongside the appeal to follow Jesus.[43] These benefits are discussed next.

## THE COROLLARY BENEFITS OF DIVINE FAMILY MEMBERSHIP

John buttresses the benefit of membership in the divine family with corollary benefits. These are: affirmation of genuine discipleship, knowledge of God and of the truth, freedom from sin, the disciple's unity with the Father and the Son with the other disciples, performance of great works, honor, glory, life, love, walking in the light, salvation, avoidance of judgment/destruction, resurrection, and protection. The following sections trace John's emphasis on each of these additional benefits.

### True Discipleship and Knowledge of the Truth

The first two corollary benefits of membership in the divine family are the ability of the disciples to know the truth and the affirmation of being true disciples (8:31–32). The importance of the concept of truth to Jesus' mission is declared by Jesus to Pilate in 18:37, "For this I was born, and for this I came into "the world," to testify to the truth. Everyone who is of the truth listens to my voice." Truth is sourced in God and is equated to Jesus' words/teaching and God's words (8:26, 28, 31–32, 38; 12:49–50; 14:10; 17:17). Jesus speaks the truth (1:17; 8:32, 40, 44, 45, 46; 16:7; 18:37) and is the embodiment of the truth (14:6).[44] The quality of truth is attributed to the light (1:9), the *Logos* (1:14), God (3:33; 5:32; 7:28; 8:26; 17:3), the Spirit (14:17; 15:26; 16:13), heavenly bread (6:32), Jesus as the true vine (15:1), God's word (17:17, 19), and to Jesus' blood and flesh (6:55). Since God is true, he seeks worshippers whose worship is based in the truth (4:23–24). Those who do what is true come to the light (3:21), and these know the truth because they have been set free by it (8:31–32) and are subsequently designated as true disciples (1:47; 8:31; 19:35). John the Baptist's message (5:33) and the testimony of the Beloved Disciple are designated as true (19:35; 21:24).[45] John uses the adjective "true" (ἀληθῶς) to describe statements made by people (4:18, 37; 8:17), people's knowledge of the truthfulness of Jesus' claims (7:26; 17:8), and affirmation from the lips of Jesus' followers on the identity of Jesus as prophet and savior (4:42; 6:14; 7:40; 10:41).

The relationship the disciples have to the truth as members of the divine family consists in the disciples receiving the ability to know the truth and then remaining in the truth which affirms their status as true disciples (8:31–32). To be a child of God is to accept Jesus'/God's words/truth (vv. 31, 37–38, 40, 47) as having originated from God (vv. 26, 28, 38, 40). To be in the family of God is to believe Jesus'/God's words/truth (vv. 24, 45, 46) by the ability that is initiated by God (v. 47) and confirmed by love for Jesus (v. 42). True disciples are expected to remain in his word (v. 31, μένω), whereas his antagonists do not make a place for his word (v. 37) and are not able to hear it (vv. 43–46) because the words of God are heard by those who are of God (v. 47; see also 1:13). Whereas the devil and the members of his family are characterized by untruth (v. 44), the followers of Jesus are characterized by truth (3:21; 18:37) because they affirm the truthfulness of God (3:33) and Jesus as the agent of God's revelation and the means of salvation (17:8). John challenges his readers to keep (τηρέω) Jesus' word because it affirms their status as his disciples (8:31–32). John presents Jesus as an example of keeping (τηρέω) God's word, which validated his relationship with God (8:55). A willingness to hear, keep, and remain in the words of Jesus confirms the believers in Jesus as true disciples who are in a filial relationship with the Father because they are adhering to the paradigm of obedience to God's word as established by Jesus' obedience to God's word (8:55). John promotes discipleship by noting that only Jesus' disciples are able to hear the truth (8:47) inasmuch as they have been brought into the divine family by God's initiative (ἐκ τοῦ θεοῦ, 8:47); and, in the end, their continuation in Jesus' teaching affirms them as true disciples (8:31b).

## Freedom from Sin

The third benefit of membership in the divine family is freedom from sin. The slavery motif is inserted into the theme of family in 8:31–37.[46] Jesus is portrayed as the agent who frees the believer from slavery to sin (vv. 33, 36). The accusation of enslavement to sin is directed against "the Jews" who had initially believed in Jesus (8:30, 36). The evidence of slavery to sin is the practice of sin (v. 34). Jesus claims to have the exclusive authority to free people from the tyranny of sin (v. 36) and to bring them into a permanent relationship with God as Father in his household (8:35–36) because he is "the Son" (v. 36) who is in a close relationship with the Father (vv. 28–29).[47] Refusal to believe that Jesus is sent by God will lead to the permanent enslavement to sin and ultimate death in sin (v. 24).[48] The negative particle "unless" (ἐὰν μή) in 8:24 restricts the means for deliverance from sin to believing in Jesus as God's agent. In 8:36, the adverb "truly" (ὄντως) emphatically stresses the future reality of the disciples as freed individuals who belong in the divine household (ὄντως ἐλεύθεροι ἔσεσθε).[49]

The opposite of membership in God's household is to be designated a child of the devil.[50] Jesus accuses "the Jews" of being not only slaves of sin (v. 34) but also of being children of the devil (v. 44) because of their actions toward him (vv. 44–47).[51] The notion that the behavior of a child was traced to the father was a staple of the sociology of the ancient family (1 John 3:9–10).[52] During an exchange between "the Jews" and Jesus, "the Jews" link their heritage back to Abraham (v. 33). In response, Jesus compares their behavior to Abraham's as evidence that they do not belong to Abraham (vv. 39–40). Rejection of Jesus (vv. 37, 40, 42) and his message (vv. 37, 43, 45, 46, 47) indicates that a person is under the influence of the devil. In contrast, an individual is "from God" (v. 47) when she is characterized by love for Jesus (v. 42); hearing (vv. 43, 47) and keeping (vv. 51–52) the word of Jesus; honoring Jesus (v. 49); knowing God (vv. 19, 55); and imitating the works of Abraham (vv. 39–40). Consequently, Jesus consigns "the Jews" to the family of the devil (vv. 31–47) because they are seeking to kill him (v. 37) and because they do not accept the truth (vv. 44–47). While John portrays Jesus as accusing "the Jews" of following in the behavioral pattern of the devil, John also presents Jesus as fulfilling the will of God, *his* Father (8:38–47, 55). Jesus illustrates that God is his Father by attributing his own works (5:19; 8:38) and words (8:28; 14:9–10) to the Father's influence, and by claiming obedience to God's word (8:55). The tension over family pedigree escalates (8:41, 44, 48, 52), ultimately climaxing with "the Jews" attempting to kill Jesus (8:59) because he asserted that God was his Father (vv. 54–58).

In sum, in 8:31–59, John features three accompanying benefits to participation in the divine family—the believer understands the truth (vv. 31, 43, 45, 47, 51–52), is affirmed as a true disciple (v. 31), and is freed from slavery to sin (vv. 24, 32–36). John portrays Jesus as extending these promises to "the Jews" (who displayed faith in Jesus) in order to motivate them to commit fully to Jesus (vv. 30–31). The response of "the Jews" in 8:59 demonstrates that they did not accept the challenge to continuous discipleship (vv. 30–31, 45, 47). The placement of these benefits alongside the challenge to discipleship suggests that John is presenting a case to his audience to believe in Jesus on account of the promise of becoming children of God.

### Relational Unity

Membership in the divine family also entails unity among the members as another corollary benefit. The Father-Son relationship functions as the paradigm for the Father-Son-disciples relationship (17:11, 21–23). Since John links the promise of unity/oneness with familial terminology (e.g., 17:21–26), the theme of unity/oneness is appropriately classified as a corollary benefit of membership in the divine family.

The unity/oneness between Jesus and God is foregrounded at the start of the Gospel through the dual use of the pronoun "with" (πρός), which conveys active communion (1:1–2).[53] At the close of the prologue, John introduces the unity of the Father-Son relationship in three ways—by designating the Son as "the only son" (μονογενής, 1:14, 18; 3:16, 18), by denoting the exclusive ability of the Son to see the Father (1:18; 5:37; 6:46; 14:7–11), and by depicting the Son as "in the bosom of the Father" (1:18).[54] John emphatically states that no one has ever seen the Father except the only begotten God, and this assertion, along with the above statements of unity, qualifies Jesus to be the only revealer of the Father (1:18).[55] The Son's revelation of the Father gives those who believe access (14:6) to see the Father as well (12:45; 14:9–11).[56]

John also deploys the expression, "Son (of God)" to portray Jesus in a unique and intimate filial relationship with the Father.[57] The phrase, "Son of God," is "a key christological title in this Gospel, standing for everything unique in Jesus' relationship to God and for the oneness between the Father and the Son."[58] In John, this title spans the entire narrative of the Gospel, from Jesus' initial introduction as the Son of God (1:34) to the same appellation functioning as a cause for his demise (19:7).[59] There are nineteen references in seven distinct passages to Jesus as the Son of the Father.[60] Additionally, there are nine references to Jesus as the Son of God.[61] The expression Son of (God) connotes "the belief that Jesus is in some intrinsic way also divine and of heavenly origin."[62] Throughout the Gospel, the title Son of God takes the readers back to the prologue, where the *Logos*/Jesus was portrayed as the only Son of God who is in an intimate relationship with the Father (1:1, 14, 18).

Additionally, John portrays the unity/oneness of the Father and the Son by featuring the disciple's relationship to both the Father and the Son as being dyadic in nature. This can be seen in the following statements: to know Jesus is to know the Father (8:19; 14:7; 16:3); to believe in Jesus is to believe in the Father (12:44); to receive Jesus is to receive the Father (13:20); to see Jesus is to see the Father (12:45; 14:9); to hate Jesus is to hate the Father (15:23, 24); to be with Jesus is to be with the Father (14:2–3); to be loved by Jesus is to be loved by the Father (14:23; 15:9; 16:27; 17:23); and Jesus and the Father share everything (3:35; 17:7, 10–11). For example, in 17:1–6, the Father and the Son share glory, mission, knowledge, prior co-existence in glory, and they are co-owners of all things (i.e., disciples). The oneness of the Father and the Son is also expressed in the Son deriving his life from the Father (5:26; 6:57), and Jesus acknowledging that his ability to extend life to others is a function of the Father giving Jesus the right to do so (3:35–36; 5:21; 17:2, 7). While the Father and the Son cooperate in conferring life on others, the Father "remains the primary source of life."[63]

The evidence John puts forward to defend Jesus' unity/oneness with the Father is to present Jesus' teaching and works as derived from the Father

(14:10–11).⁶⁴ Jesus promises to integrate the disciples into union with the Father and himself, and the proof of this union would be the works of the disciples (14:12).⁶⁵ That is, just as Jesus' works were accomplished by the Father because Jesus is in the Father, so the disciples' greater works would confirm that they too are in union with the Father.⁶⁶ Jesus assures the performance of these works because he promises to mediate the disciples' requests to the Father so that the Father is glorified through the Son as he answers the disciples' petitions (14:13–14). Consequently, in 14:1, Jesus challenges his disciples to believe in God and in him, and in 14:10–11, he exhorts the disciples to believe that he is in the Father and the Father is in him and that they are united in purpose (10:30).

The Spirit's role in the unity/oneness motif is to dwell with the believer as the Spirit of truth and to reveal the truth to the believer (14:16–17).⁶⁷ John explains the Spirit's involvement in mediating knowledge to the disciple as evident in the genitive "of the truth" (τῆς ἀληθείας, 15:26; 16:13), which describes the cognitive function of the Spirit in communicating truth.⁶⁸ After Jesus' departure, the Spirit will communicate the truth to the believers, leading them into deeper understanding of the truth previously revealed through Jesus (14:26; 16:13), truth that encapsulates the disciples' understanding of their oneness with Jesus and the Father (14:20).⁶⁹ The disciples will experience unity/oneness more fully in "that day," which is the day of the Spirit's arrival (14:20; 16:23, 26).⁷⁰

The Father-Son relational unity/oneness is the paradigm for the unity among the disciples. In 17:11, 21–23, the perfect unity among the disciples is the means by which "the world" will know that Jesus is God's emissary.⁷¹ The basis for the disciples' unity is the unity between the Father and the Son (note the repetition of καθώς in vv. 21, 22).⁷² The paradigmatic function of the oneness of the Father-Son to the oneness of the disciples is further evident through John's application of the same vocabulary to describe the unity/oneness in both relationships (i.e., the cardinal ἕν).⁷³ John also presents the unity of the disciples through the symbols of a sheepfold (10:16) and the vine (15:1–11) and links them to Jesus as the one who is the basis of that unity.⁷⁴ So, John portrays Jesus as promising to integrate the disciples into a relationship with the Father, Son, and Spirit and to create unity between the disciples that resembles the unity of the Father-Son relationship. The unity/oneness of the disciples will be the means of continuing the mission of Jesus (17:20–23).

## Honor and Glory

John's corollary benefits of membership in the divine family also include honor and glory from the Father. In 12:25–26, John portrays Jesus as promising honor to the disciple who continuously serves and follows him. Since

John links the promise of honor to eternal life (v. 25) and to the Father as the one who confers this honor (v. 26), it is appropriate to examine honor as a corollary benefit of membership in the divine family.

Jesus promises honor to the faithful disciples in the context of his own death (12:23–24, 27–34). Jesus responds to the desire of the Greeks to see him by connecting his death to glorification. John then presents Jesus as inviting his audience to be willing to die for him in order to gain eternal life. The condition for the reward of eternal life is to hate one's life to the point of death.[75] Jesus then lays out the expectations one must fulfill to receive honor from the Father that will be granted in the abode where Jesus will be in the future. Honor is extended to the disciples who are characterized by serving and following Jesus.[76] In this way, John depicts Jesus as encouraging his listeners, and by extension, John's audiences, toward faithful service and toward following Jesus by means of the promises of eternal life, residing with Jesus, and honor from the Father. These promises are presented in light of the threat of death, of which Jesus is an example in the immediate context.

The honor that the Father confers on faithful disciples can be understood in light of the ancient "honor and shame" culture that was part and parcel of adoption.[77] The honor associated with membership in the right family is demonstrated by an individual being "raised up from the bottom of society and installed among the nobility."[78] Moreover, "the adoptive son really was to become the son and agent of the adoptive father; he was not a substitute son, nor a second-class son. The adopted son, moreover, assumed the status of the adoptive father and exchanged his own [status]."[79] This privileged status is attributed to the disciples at the outset of the Gospel through filial terminology of "children" (1:11–13) and is carried through until the conclusion of the Gospel where the disciples are called "brothers" (20:17). Jesus' declaration, "I ascend to my Father and your Father, and my God and your God" (20:17) integrates the disciples into a relationship with God the Father that resembles the Father's relationship with Jesus. While some see in this verse an allusion to the Old Testament covenantal formula, "I will be your/their God," it may be better to view this as the ratification of the disciples' membership in the divine family, as this is the first occurrence in the Gospel when Jesus is depicted as calling his followers "brothers."[80] This is the message that Mary Magdalene was commanded by Jesus to communicate to the disciples—that the disciples have been integrated into the divine family (20:17).[81] Whereas previously, the disciples' relationship was primarily with Jesus, by calling the disciples "brothers," John depicts Jesus as placing his disciples into a new and special relationship with his Father (see 14:6).[82] The statement in 20:17 is the result of having a relationship with Jesus and the fulfillment of the promise made in 1:12, "He gave them the right to become children of God," which implies that "[f]rom now on everyone who believes in Jesus can call God,

'My Father.'"[83] Consequently, the Johannine emphasis on the family motif can be understood as a motivation to his audiences to embrace Jesus' call to continuous discipleship because it results in honor and glory that is promised to the believer in Jesus (12:26; 17:22, 24).

## CONCLUSION: THE BENEFITS OF MEMBERSHIP IN THE DIVINE FAMILY

John's first prominent benefit for continuous discipleship is membership in the divine family.[84] Such membership is a privilege for the disciples because it is obtained through the divine initiative. John's use of verbal tenses and his placement of certain benefits in the context of opposition to belief in Jesus suggests that the image of the divine family, along with various corollary benefits, is deployed by John to persuade his audiences to continuous discipleship. In the next chapter we will examine the most prominent Johannine benefit of participation in the divine family—eternal life—along with other corollary benefits that are extended to a child of God in his family.

## NOTES

1. Van der Watt, *Family*, 161, 305, 397.
2. Gorman describes the participation of the believer in the divine family for the purpose of "possessing and exhibiting the divine DNA" as *theosis* (57). Thus, our discussion of membership in the divine family is about sharing the attributes of God that are exhibited in Jesus. Gorman helpfully links the disciple's membership in the divine family with *theosis*, which he defines as "participation and transformation," and this is expressed in the disciple's engagement in the mission of Jesus (17). Gorman, *Abide and Go*, 17, 56–58.
3. D. F. Tolmie, "The Characterization of God in the Fourth Gospel," *JSNT* 69 (1998): 64. The following persons are also called father in John: Jacob (4:12), the forefathers (4:20; 6:31, 49, 58; 7:22), the official in Capernaum (4:52), Joseph (6:42), Abraham (8:39, 53, 56), and the devil (8:38, 41, 44).
4. The appellation, τὰ τέκνα τοῦ θεοῦ, most likely came from the Old Testament concept of "the righteous" being God's children (Genesis 6:2; Psalm 29:1) and Israel being called "God's son" (Exodus 4:22; Deuteronomy 32:6; Jeremiah 31:9, 20; Isaiah 64:8). The righteous are called sons of God in Wisdom 2:13, 16, 18; 5:5. See Craig S. Keener, *The Gospel of John*, 2 vols. (Peabody, MA: Hendrickson, 2003), 400–401; Herman N. Ridderbos, *The Gospel According to John: A Theological Commentary* (Grand Rapids, MI: Eerdmans, 1997), 45; Marianne Meye Thompson, *The God of the Gospel of John* (Grand Rapids, MI: Eerdmans, 2001), 70.
5. Thompson, *God*, 58.

6. Thompson, *God*, 70; Cf., *TDNT*, s.v. "υἱός, υἱοθεσία," 8:366.

7. Receiving Jesus/his words appears in the following passages: 1:11–12; 3:11, 32–33; 5:43; 12:48; 13:20; 17:8. Full treatment of the soteriological concepts are outside the scope of this book. For discussion of the themes involved in the process of becoming and remaining a disciple (e.g., seeing, hearing), see Bennema, *Power*, 110–59.

8. Ernst Haenchen, Robert Walter Funk, and Ulrich Busse, *John: A Commentary on the Gospel of John*, 2 vols. (Philadelphia: Fortress, 1984), 1:118.

9. Barrett, *John*, 164. Of the ninety-eight references to πιστεύω, ninety-three have Jesus as the direct object, in contrast with the seven uses of belief in Jesus in the Synoptic Gospels (Matthew 18:6=Mark 9:42; Matthew 27:42=Mark 15:32; Mark 1:15; Luke 8:12–13; 22:67). For Jesus as the object of faith, see Sigurd Grindheim, "Faith in Jesus: The Historical Jesus and the Object of Faith," *Bib* 97 no. 1 (2016): 79–100.

10. Daniel B. Wallace, *Greek Grammar beyond the Basics: An Exegetical Syntax of the New Testament* (Grand Rapids, MI: Zondervan, 1996), 620–21.

11. Farelly, *Disciples*, 19.

12. Van der Watt, *Family*, 400.

13. Hellerman observes: "For the people in the world of the New Testament, the welfare of the groups to which they belonged took priority over their own individual happiness and relational satisfaction." Joseph H. Hellerman, *The Ancient Church as Family* (Minneapolis, MN: Fortress, 2001), 14–15. For discussion regarding being part of the right family, Bruce J. Malina, *The New Testament World: Insights from Cultural Anthropology*, 3rd ed. (Louisville, KY: Westminster John Knox Press, 2001), 29.

14. J. G. van der Watt, *An Introduction to the Johannine Gospel and Letters* (London; New York: T & T Clark, 2007), 55.

15. The variations ἀπὸ θεοῦ, παρὰ πατρός, ἐκ τοῦ θεοῦ, ἄνωθεν, and ἐκ ἄνω all convey the meaning of being sourced in God.

16. Because the verb γίνομαι in 9:39 appears in passing and its usage does not substantially develop the theme of discipleship, it is not treated here. In 10:16, γίνομαι is appended to ζωή and in 12:36 the verb is attached to light, and both of these passages are examined in chapter 2.

17. For an overview of the debate regarding the dynamic versus static interpretations of "becoming a child of God," see Vellanickal, *Sonship*, 105–12.

18. In support of the singular reading ἐγεννήθη, Vellanickal points to the Latin Codex Veronensis from the fifth century, the Syriac versions Curetonianus (syc) and Sinaiticus (sys) dated by Kurt and Aland to the fourth century, the apocryphal Epistula XI Apostolorum found in Coptic and Ethiopic, which Schneemelcher traces to the Greek original from the second century, and to Tertullian, Irenaeus, and Sulpice Severius. Kurt Aland and Barbara Aland, *The Text of the New Testament: An Introduction to the Critical Editions and to the Theory and Practice of Modern Textual Criticism* (Grand Rapids, MI: Eerdmans, 1987), 190; Wilhelm Schneemelcher and R. McL. Wilson, *New Testament Apocrypha*, Revised ed., 2 vols. (Cambridge; Louisville, KY: J. Clarke & Co.; Westminster/John Knox Press, 1991), 1:251; Vellanickal, *Sonship*, 112–32.

19. There are no Greek mss supporting the textual variant of ἐγεννήθησαν as a singular (ἐγεννήθη) in reference to Jesus. Latin mss chiefly have the singular reading. The patristic witnesses overwhelmingly support the plural reading of ἐγεννήθησαν, which refers to believers. Brown notes that there is a tendency of ancient texts to become more Christological not less as time passes, which would warrant a later change to the singular, instead of the singular being the original reading. Barrett, *John*, 164; Brown, *John*, 11–12; Ford, *Redeemer-Friend*, 120; Murray J. Harris, *John*, ed. Robert W. Yarbrough and Andreas J. Köstenberger, EGGNT (Nashville, TN: B&H Academic, 2015), 32; Maarten J. J. Menken, "'Born of God' or 'Begotten by God'? A Translation Problem in the Johannine Writings," in *Studies in John's Gospel and Epistles: Collected Essays* (Leuven: Peeters, 2015), 14 fn. 4; Bruce Manning Metzger, *A Textual Commentary on the Greek New Testament*, 2nd ed. (Stuttgart: Deutsche Bibelgesellschaft/German Bible Society, 1994), 168–69; Michael Peppard, *The Son of God in the Roman World: Divine Sonship in Its Social and Political Context* (Oxford: Oxford University Press, 2011), 140–45; Van der Watt, *Family*, 179 fn. 88. Brown notes that in all of Johannine literature, the followers of Jesus, instead of Jesus, are described as begotten of God. Brown, *John*, 12. See also John 3:3–8; 1 John 3:9; 4:7; 5:1–4, 18.

20. Vellanickal, *Sonship*, 140–41.

21. Barrett, *John*, 352.

22. For Vellanickal's explanation of the static view, which he rejects, see Vellanickal, *Sonship*, 110.

23. Van der Watt, *Family*, 186. McKeever sees the process of the *Logos* becoming flesh parallel to the divine birth of the believers. McKeever, "Born of God," 121–38.

24. The verb γεννάω can mean "to be born" or "to be begotten" of God. Although most translators prefer the former, the majority of the commentators defend the latter. Barrett, *John*, 206; Beasley-Murray, *John*, 45; Bennema, *Power*, 169 fn. 33; Brown, *John*, 12, 130; Bultmann, *John*, 136 fn. 4; John McHugh, *John 1–4*, ICC (London; New York: T & T Clark, 2009), 46. However, Weissenrieder defends "to be born" because of the embryonic vocabulary in the text of John 3. Annette Weissenrieder, "Spirit and Rebirth in the Gospel of John," *RT* 21 (2014): 77. Moloney prefers "to be born," while Schnackenburg remains agnostic. Francis J. Moloney, *The Gospel of John*, SP 4 (Collegeville, MN: Liturgical Press, 1998), 98; Schnackenburg, *John*, 1:368–69. Menken prefers "to be begotten by God" over "born of God" because it allows for both male and female begetting, while "born" stresses the female role. Menken examined the first century CE Hellenistic texts from a wide geographic area, the passages in the Gospel of John, and the rest of the Johannine literature to conclude that "begotten" is contextually and exegetically preferred for John 1:13. Menken concluded that the translation "begotten" ascribes to God the "metaphorical male sexual role: he is compared to a father who begets children which highlights God as the initiator of the new life of the believer." God as the giver of life is observable in John 5:21, 26. Menken, "Born of God," 13–28, esp. 27–28.

25. Sjef van Tilborg, *Imaginative Love in John*, BIS 2 (Leiden: Brill, 1993), 33–57.

26. *BDAG*, s.v. "γίνομαι"; Herbert Weir Smyth, *Greek Grammar* (Cambridge, MA: Harvard University Press, 1956), §1924.

27. The aorists and the perfect passives of γεννάω in 1:13 and in 3:3–8 emphasize divine initiative.

28. Harris, *John*, 31.

29. Trumbower develops two stages in the new birth—seeing and entering—the former requiring birth from above, whereas the latter results from birth from water and Spirit. However, John employs the verbs "enter" (e.g., 10:9) and "see" (e.g., 1:39, 46; 19:37; 20:8) interchangeably. Additionally, most scholars view seeing and entering as synonymous. Barrett, *John*, 207; Brown, *John*, 130; Bultmann, *John*, 135 fn. 2; Jeffrey A. Trumbower, *Born from Above: The Anthropology of the Gospel of John*, HUT 29 (Tübingen: J.C.B. Mohr, 1992), 74; Vellanickal, *Sonship*, 207. Cf. McHugh, *John 1–4*, 227; Westcott, *John*, 50. The adverb ἄνωθεν appears in 3:3, 7, 31 and 19:11. Since the adverb is a clear reference to heaven in 3:31 and in 19:31, and since 3:11–12 indicates that Jesus is speaking of heavenly things, ἄνωθεν should be understood as birth from above, which is equated to birth from water and Spirit. See Van der Watt, *Family*, 172 fn. 50; Vellanickal, *Sonship*, 172–74; Bultmann, *John*, 136 fn. 4. Cf. Resseguie who sees two meanings of ἄνωθεν, "from above" and "again," as necessary because the "double entendre foregrounds the spiritual act of rebirth against the background of physical birth." Resseguie, *Strange*, 52–53, 122–23.

30. Nicodemus demonstrates his misunderstanding in that he omits Jesus' twice used ἄνωθεν (3:3, 7) when Nicodemus responds to Jesus in v. 4, "how is it possible for a man to be born when he is old?" Menken, "Born of God," 20–21. For Old Testament background, see Barrett, *John*, 208; Bennema, *Power*, 170; Carson, *John*, 195; Keener, *John*, 551–53. For a physiological interpretation of this passage, see Weissenrieder, "Spirit," 58–85, esp. 77–79.

31. Bennema understands water as the "cleansing/purification and the transforming 'indwelling' of God's Spirit which results in a new creation." Bennema, *Power*, 172–73. Cf. Vellanickal who sees water as a reference to baptism. Vellanickal, *Sonship*, 179–91.

32. "The birth of water-and-Spirit is an *initiation metaphor* for entering into salvation, into the kingdom of God, through the cleansing, purifying and renewing work of the Spirit" (italics original). Bennema, *Power*, 180. Köstenberger describes the Spirit as a "stream" who causes and sustains life. Köstenberger, *Theology*, 342. Van der Watt writes, "Life begins and is continued in the presence and working of the Spirit." J. G. Van der Watt, "Everlasting Life in John and the Permanence of Salvation: The Life Metaphor in John's Gospel," *TI* 1 (2005–2007): 12.

33. Bennema, *Power*, 174.

34. Brown, *John*, 11.

35. In 1:12, John deploys δίδωμι to refer to Jesus giving believers the right to be called children of God.

36. Schnackenburg, *John*, 2:46.

37. *BDAG* notes the element of force in the act of dragging/pulling. *BDAG*, s.v. "ἕλκω."

38. Jiménez, "El Discipulo," 291.

39. de Jonge correctly maintains that one should not stress the differences in meaning between prepositions ἀπό (e.g., 3:2; 13:3; 16:30), ἐκ (e.g., 1:13; 7:17), and παρά (e.g., 1:6; 6:46; 8:40; 9:16, 33; 16:27) but instead note the idea these prepositions are conveying—Jesus' origin from God/Father/heaven/above. de Jonge, *Stranger*, 164, fn. 10. Harris notes, "[W]hen God is identified as the source of some benefit, it is often permissible to infer that he is also the agent in its provision . . . when spiritual renewal is depicted as God's work, the apostle John frequently employs the metaphor of rebirth or regeneration . . . [thus] ἐκ θεοῦ may be paraphrased 'as a result of God's initiative and action.'" Murray J. Harris, *Prepositions and Theology in the Greek New Testament* (Grand Rapids, MI: Zondervan, 2011), 105–106.

40. For proposed divisions of this passage, see Barrett, *John*, 333; Carson, *John*, 337; Ridderbos, *John*, 291; Schnackenburg, *John*, 2:187; D. Moody Smith, *John*, ANTC (Nashville, TN: Abingdon Press, 1999), 178. The prominence of the family motif in 8:31–59 is seen in the references to God as Father (vv. 16, 18, 19, 26–27, 28, 38, 40, 41, 42, 47, 49, 54, 55), Abraham as father (vv. 33, 37, 39, 40, 53, 56, 57, 58), the devil as father (vv. 38, 41, 44), children (v. 39), God's household (vv. 35–36), and in the depiction of the two father figures in opposition to one another (vv. 38–44).

41. The aorist subjunctive "remain" (μείνητε) can be viewed as a constative aorist which results in the confirmation of an individual as Jesus' disciple. Harris, *John*, 174.

42. The present tense πιστεύετε in vv. 45–46 stresses continual commitment to Jesus' teaching. The articular present active participle, ὁ ἀκολουθῶν, stresses ongoing commitment. Note the present tense infinitive in v. 43, ἀκούειν τὸν λόγον τὸν ἐμόν, and the use of ἀκούετε in v. 47 in the present tense, stressing continual commitment to hear God's and Jesus' teaching.

43. E.g., the benefits of discipleship in the immediate context are affirmation of being a true disciple (v. 31b), knowledge of the truth (vv. 31–32), freedom from slavery to sin (vv. 24, 36), and protection from death (vv. 51–52). In each of these verses note the use of the third-class conditional clause (ἐάν + subjunctive verb) to persuade the readers to discipleship.

44. Ignace de la Potterie writes that "there is a close relationship between the revealed truth and the actual person of Jesus . . . Jesus is not just a vehicle of revelation like Moses and the other prophets, who remained so to speak, exterior to their message . . . only in Christ has the total and definitive revelation arrived." Ignace de la Potterie, "The Truth in Saint John," in *The Interpretation of John*, ed. John Ashton (Philadelphia: Fortress, 1986), 71. See also Bennema, *Power*, 226 fn. 54; Martin Scott, *Sophia and the Johannine Jesus*, JSNTSup 71 (Sheffield: JSOT, 1992), 126. Adele Reinhartz unconventionally argues that Jesus lied to his brothers (7:8–10), but that is not problematic for Reinhartz as John's main point is not to present Jesus as an ethical model but Christology. Yet her suggestion overlooks John's presentation of Jesus as one who speaks the truth (8:40–46) and as an example to follow (13:15). Adele Reinhartz, "The Lyin' King? Deception and Christology in the Gospel of John," in *Johannine Ethics: The Moral World of the Gospel and Epistles of John*, ed. Sherri Brown and Christopher W. Skinner (Minneapolis, MN: Fortress Press, 2017), 117–33.

45. Conversely, John describes invalid testimony as untrue (5:31; 8:13–14, 16).

46. Vellanickal proposes a chiastic structure of 8:31–36, with the question by "the Jews" to Jesus in v. 33 as the focal point—"how do you say that you will become free?" Vellanickal's chiasm falls short since he does not include v. 37, which continues the themes of σπέρμα Ἀβραάμ and ὁ λόγος ὁ ἐμός. Thus, v. 37 belongs with vv. 31–36. Neyrey more convincingly proposes vv. 31–37 as a chiasm with the outer limits of the chiasm in v. 31b and v. 37c in reference to "my word," and the focal point in v. 35b, "the son continues forever." So, remaining in the word of Jesus is critical to true discipleship and to abiding permanently in the house of the Father. Jerome H. Neyrey, *The Gospel of John in Cultural and Rhetorical Perspective* (Grand Rapids, MI: Eerdmans, 2009), 234–40; Vellanickal, *Sonship*, 286–87.

47. Vellanickal, *Sonship*, 288.

48. Hylen points out that since the conversation between Jesus and "the Jews" occurred during Sukkot (Leviticus 23:39–43), which commemorates freedom from Egyptian slavery, the claim of "the Jews" that they have never been slaves to anyone in 8:32 suggests intentional distancing from ancient slavery but also a misunderstanding of their history and Scripture. Hylen, *Imperfect*, 124.

49. Vellanickal calls this a "permanent standing in the household of [the] Father." Vellanickal, *Sonship*, 292, citing 357.

50. Vellanickal, *Sonship*, 287.

51. Bruce J. Malina and Richard L. Rohrbaugh, *Social-Science Commentary on the Gospel of John* (Minneapolis, MN: Fortress, 1998), 165: "genealogy can be deduced from one's subsequent behavior and character; and behavior and character offer solid indication of one's genealogy."

52. "It was further believed that a person's character and personality were given to him via the seed of his father and was augmented by education and other circumstances. These conditions also determined the expected behavior of that person (8:31–59; 1 John 2:29; 3:9–10)." Van der Watt, *Introduction*, 55.

53. Harris, *John*, 18.

54. Peppard claims that "this verse [1:18] is also not about sonship or begetting, neither of which is present in the text. . . . It is primarily about the combined transcendence and immanence of God in the Incarnate Word/light. The Word is the only God and is thus one with God, as in 1:1, but it also reveals the previously unseen God, as light that shines in darkness (1:5) and Word that becomes flesh (1:14)." However, there is fatherhood and sonship language with every Johannine use of μονογενής in reference to Jesus (e.g., 1:14, 18; 3:16, 18). Moreover, the mention of the Father in 1:18 must imply a son. Additionally, the textual variant "only son" (instead of "only god") suggests at least some of the ancient readers agreed in seeing sonship in the verse. Akala links μονογενής to Genesis 22:2 and Abraham's love for Isaac and Isaac's uniqueness in that he alone carried the covenant promise. From this perspective, Akala understands the function of μονογενής in John 1:14 to reflect the "transcendent, filial relationship between Son and Father" and μονογενής "signifies the Father's self-revelation, glory, and covenantal sacrifice, all manifested in the Son's mission in the world." Akala, *Son-Father*, 140; Peppard, *Son of God*, 144.

55. Note the emphatic οὐδείς and ἐκεῖνος in 1:18. The emphatic pronoun ἐκεῖνος covers all three descriptions of the *Logos*; μονογενής, θεός, and ὁ ὤν. See Harris,

*John*, 39. Bultmann famously said that Jesus came to reveal that he is the revealer. However, John denotes that Jesus also came to reveal his own identity, see 4:25–26; 5:22; 9:35–39; 10:24–25, 36. Note also the ἐγώ εἰμι statements throughout the Gospel. Jesus makes God known (1:18; 5:43; 17:6), reveals his oneness with the Father (8:29; 10:30, 38; 14:10–11, 20; 16:32; 17:11, 21–23), for judgment (9:39), to save "the world" (12:47), to expose sin (15:22), to offer eternal life (10:10; 12:50), to testify to the truth (18:37), to be glorified through the cross (12:27–28), and to free people from darkness (12:46). See Bultmann, *Theology*, 2:66. Peppard, *Son of God*, 143.

56. In 14:6, the predicate statement, Ἐγώ εἰμι ἡ ὁδὸς καὶ ἡ ἀλήθεια καὶ ἡ ζωή, can be understood as "the way" functioning as the primary predicate with "the truth and the life" *explaining* "the way." Segovia writes, "There is no other 'way' to the Father except through Jesus, who is both 'truth' and 'life.'" Brown, *John*, 620–21; Segovia, *Farewell*, 86 fn. 51.

57. Only Jesus is called the Son of God in John.

58. Andrew T. Lincoln, *Truth on Trial: The Lawsuit Motif in the Fourth Gospel* (Peabody, MA: Hendrickson, 2000), 63.

59. For multiple textual variants of Son of God in 1:34, see the Nestle Aland Greek New Testament apparatus, UBS4 apparatus, and Metzger, *Commentary*, 172.

60. John 3:16–18, 34–36; 5:19, 20, 21, 22, 23, 26, 27; 6:40; 8:35–36; 14:13; 17:1.

61. John 1:34, 49; 3:18; 5:25; 10:36; 11:4, 27; 19:7; 20:31. Some mss have Son of God instead of Son of Man in 9:35. See Metzger, *Commentary*, 169–70, 194.

62. Larry W. Hurtado, *Lord Jesus Christ: Devotion to Jesus in Earliest Christianity* (Grand Rapids, MI: Eerdmans, 2003), 362.

63. Van der Watt, *Family*, 206.

64. Shin suggests that the "works" of Jesus are subsumed under the single "work of God" (6:29) to believe in Jesus. Shin, *Ethics*, 106.

65. Tolmie observes that the promise of performing greater works is meant to motivate the implied readers that they need not act like the disciples in John 13–14, but that true discipleship is within their reach if they continue to believe. Tolmie, *Farewell*, 205–206.

66. For example, the Father's sharing of life with the Son demonstrates continuity between the work of the Father and the Son. Barrett, *John*, 260. Gorman concludes that "greater works" refers to the scope of the works. However, Köstenberger more convincingly explains that "greater" does not refer to numerical success or apostolic miraculous acts. Rather, "greater" works are performed by the exalted Jesus through his disciples as they continue his mission post-cross, with the full story of the crucifixion and the resurrection available as part of their message and participation in extending life to others. Köstenberger, *Missions*, 171–75; Gorman, *Abide and Go*, 100.

67. Bauckham observes that the oneness language is binitarian not trinitarian, that is, it includes only the Father and the Son, not the Spirit (10:30; 17:11, 21–23). Richard Bauckham, *Gospel of Glory: Major Themes in Johannine Theology* (Grand Rapids, MI: Baker, 2015), 36. *Pace,* Bauckham, the Spirit is the bond that communicates the relational unity between the Father, the Son, and believers (e.g., 14:15–20).

68. Barrett, *John*, 463.

69. Bennema synthesizes the teaching function of the Spirit as follows: "The Paraclete will lead the disciples into a more perfect knowledge of Jesus' teaching. The Paraclete does not bring independent revelation but interprets Jesus' revelation; he draws out the significance of the historical revelation in Christ." Bennema, *Power*, 228–34, citing 231. Similarly, Barrett, *John*, 467; Beasley-Murray, *John*, 261, 283; Bultmann, *John*, 574–76; de la Potterie, "Truth," 77; Harris, *John*, 278; Andrew T. Lincoln, *The Gospel According to Saint John*, BNTC (Peabody, MA: Hendrickson, 2005), 397; Schnackenburg, *John*, 3:83; Thompson, *John*, 316; Tolmie, *Farewell*, 86 fn. 45. Cf. Painter who argues for new revelation from the Spirit. John Painter, *The Quest for the Messiah*, 2nd ed. (Nashvile, TN: Abingdon, 1993), 431–32.

70. See chapter 3.

71. Note the perfect periphrastic ὦσιν τετελειωμένοι εἰς ἕν in v. 23, which stresses the goal and the result of perfect union. The dual reference to ἀπέστειλας (17:21, 23) links the disciples' unity to mission. Participation in the mission of Jesus is expected of Jesus' followers. John positions the theme of mission with familial terminology (e.g., 4:34–38; 14:12; 15:8, 16, 27; 17:18; 20:21). Part of the mission is to forgive the sins of others, which is a privilege the disciples must fulfill (20:23). Along with being sent into "the world," the disciples are protected from the evil one, who is the ruler of "the world" (12:31; 14:30; 16:33). Jesus prays for protection; thus, we can view it as a benefit joined to engagement in the mission (17:9–19). Because Jesus came to make the Father and his love known (e.g., 17:4–6, 23, 26), Chennattu rightly points out that "the ultimate objective of discipleship is to make God's love known." Chennattu, *Discipleship*, 136. See also Köstenberger, *Missions*; Harris, *John*, 293.

72. The adverb καθώς is both comparative and causative. Brown, *John*, 769.

73. Bauckham traces the Johannine references to the cardinal ἕν back to the Shema, suggesting that John is pointing to the "relational intimacy of Jesus and the Father within the identity of the one God" and uses this as the basis for the developing unity of the disciples into one. Bauckham, *Glory*, 21–41, citing 34.

74. Bennema, *Power*, 136.

75. Note the present tense participle of loving one's life (ὁ φιλῶν), in contrast with the present tense participle of hating one's life (ὁ μισῶν), as an expression of commitment to Jesus.

76. Note the repeated conditional clause ἐάν τις ἐμοὶ διακονῇ with the present tense διακονῇ and the present tense ἀκολουθείτω in v. 26.

77. In reference to family, Hanson observes, "the fundamental and overarching social value has been honor." K. C. Hanson, "All in the Family: Kinship in Agrarian Roman Palestine," in *The Social World of the New Testament: Insights and Models*, ed. Jerome H. Neyrey, Stewart, Eric Clark (Peabody, MA: Hendrickson, 2008), 39.

78. Peppard, *Son of God*, 57. Also see, Van der Watt, *Family*, 175.

79. Christiane Kunst, "Römische Adoption: zur Strategie einer Familienorganisation" (Universität Potsdam, 2005), 294.

80. For Old Testament covenant allusions, see Chennattu, *Discipleship*, 154. For the family of God theme, see de Jonge, *Stranger*, 152.

81. Chennattu proposes that Mary Magdalene's post-resurrection interaction with Jesus that is characterized by joy and yearning qualifies her to be the representative

figure of the new covenant community that is akin to Israel's longing for YHWH. However, there is nothing in 20:11–18 that presents Mary as more than a messenger of Jesus' resurrection. In fact, the disciples are also joyful when they see Jesus (20:20). See endnote 18 in chapter 3 for discussion of Mary the mother of Jesus functioning as the representative of the Johannine community. Chennattu, *Discipleship*, 148.

82. Schnackenburg, *John*, 3:320.

83. Mark Stibbe, "Telling the Father's Story," in *Challenging Perspectives on the Gospel of John*, ed. John Lierman (Tübingen: Mohr Siebeck, 2006), 183.

84. Bauckham cautions that while John features the corporate benefits of following Jesus (e.g., one flock, vine metaphor, unity with other disciples), John also values personal intimacy between Jesus and the individual disciple. This is evident in the example of the individual disciples following Jesus (e.g., Nathaniel, Nicodemus, Peter) and in the sayings that feature the individual responding to Jesus (e.g., πᾶς ὁ πιστεύων, ἐάν τις, ὅς δ' ἄν, οὐδείς). Bauckham, *Glory*, 1–19.

*Chapter 2*

# Membership in the Divine Family—Participation in Eternal Life

The previous chapter introduced membership in the divine family, along with its corollary benefits, as the first of three primary benefits that John offers for continuous discipleship. This chapter focuses on additional benefits in the textual orbit of familial language in John. Participation in the divine family involves God granting life (ζωή) to the believer in Jesus. Whereas birth from above brings an individual into the divine family, ζωή describes the believer's ongoing experience in the divine family.[1] Life refers to the disciple's participation in the life of God and the ability and quality of the disciple's relationship with the Father and the Son within the divine family. This ability and quality are directly proportional to the disciple's knowledge of the Father and the Son, as the disciple is empowered by the Spirit.[2] Moreover, this life is possessed by the disciple in this life and extends into the eschatological future. Thus, ultimately ζωή describes both the quality of life and its duration.[3]

The benefit of life rises above the other corollary benefits derived from participation in the divine family because of frequency and prominence. Consequently, this warrants a more substantial treatment of life in comparison with other benefits derived from membership in the divine family. The prominence of life is evident in its appearance in the prologue (1:4), Peter's confession (6:68), Jesus' declaration that he is life (14:6), Jesus' prayer (17:2–3), and the inclusion of life in the purpose statement (20:30–31). Moreover, only the Johannine Jesus declares, "I have come that they may have life" (10:10). This statement appears in juxtaposition to Jesus' affirmation of having to give up his own life (ψυχή) in order to offer life (ζωή) to his sheep (10:10–18; see also 3:14–15). John presents Jesus as receiving two commandments from his Father—(1) to lay down and take up his own life (ψυχή, 10:18) and (2) to bestow eternal life (ζωὴ αἰώνιος, 12:49–50). John applies distinct terms for physical life (ψυχή) in contrast to spiritual life (ζωή) in order to make certain that Jesus gives up his physical life (ψυχή), not the life (ζωή) that flows from his relationship with God.

Additionally, the strategic placement of life (ζωή) in discourses and pericopes that spotlight discipleship suggests a vital importance of this concept in the Gospel. This, in turn, prompts the question of this book: what are the rewards of discipleship? However, life is not elevated on a par with family, abiding, or friendship because life is integrally embedded into the divine family imagery in the Gospel, so it is more appropriate to understand life as a sub-benefit within the divine family motif.

John distinguishes between life and entering/seeing the kingdom of God. Entering/seeing the kingdom of God refers to the state of an individual who is delivered from sin (8:21, 24, 31–36; 9:41; 16:9), death and judgment (5:21–29; 12:47–50), destruction (3:16; 10:9–10), and the devil (8:44). Life, however, refers to the interaction within the family of God.[4]

While some have asserted that John uses life as a substitute for the Synoptic concept of the kingdom of God, there are good reasons to keep the two concepts separate.[5] First, life is not equated with the kingdom of God because John places both concepts in 3:1–21 as though they are distinct, rather than featuring only one of them. This usage of the two concepts in a single pericope suggests that the two ideas are not identical in meaning.[6] Second, John develops his own version of the kingdom of God especially in his thematization of the kingship of Jesus (e.g., 1:49; 3:3–8; 6:14; 12:13–15; 18:33–37; 19:3, 12, 14–16, 19–21), which suggests that John does not equate life with the Synoptic motif of the kingdom of God. Third, as argued below, it is best to understand life as the disciple's ability and quality of relating with the Father and the Son, which qualifies it as one of the benefits enjoyed *within* the kingdom of God, rather than representing the kingdom of God itself.

Some have argued that John replaces the Synoptic theme of the kingdom of God with life for political and theological reasons.[7] However, John does not refrain from political and theological kingdom imagery (1:49; 6:14; 12:13–15; 18:33–19:21). For example, John presents Jesus both as the Jewish *king* and as the international savior (4:42; 12:21). Moreover, Thomas' confession—"My Lord and my God" (20:28)—can also be seen as politically subversive.[8] Thus, John does utilize both political and theological terminology in reference to Jesus.

Others have suggested that life is the central integrating motif of the Gospel.[9] This proposal rests on the "special places of occurrence" of life, which "flesh out arguments . . . liven up discourses . . . [and] deliver the central message of the passage."[10] This view sees life as a "coping mechanism" in the social context of turmoil. Advocates claim that "most of the sayings associated with Jesus in the Johannine community are all related to the issues of life."[11]

However, the distribution of life in the Gospel undermines the claim that life is the key integrating theme in John because life appears chiefly in chapters 1–12, only three times in the Farewell Discourse, and once in 20:31. The Farewell Discourse contains some of Jesus' most substantial discourses, but contains only three references to life (14:6; 17:2, 3), and in all three instances, life is syntactically placed in proximity to the Father and the Son, consistent with the rest of the Gospel. In fact, in John, life is always interrelated with the family motif.[12] Thus, it seems more appropriate to view life as a benefit that is obtained through membership in the divine family.

The benefit of life and its function within the Johannine imagery of the divine family can be understood in three aspects: linguistic cache, thematic strands, and its related imagery of light, water, and bread.[13] The holistic understanding of these three aspects will support the contention that life in the Gospel supports John's presentation of divine family as a benefit of discipleship.

## THE LINGUISTIC CACHE OF LIFE

John's preferred term for the notion of life is ζωή; it appears fifty-six times in the Gospel.[14] Of the fifty-six occurrences of life, only three references convey physical life and all appear in a single pericope (4:50, 51, 53).[15] John's primary term for physical life is ψυχή, which appears eleven times.[16] John uses ψυχή for physical life and ζωή for the ability and quality of the relationships in the divine family.[17] Consequently, I will use ζωή as the default term for the concept of (eternal) life.

## THE THEMATIC STRANDS OF LIFE

The Johannine presentation of life is clustered around certain themes that enhance the function of ζωή and which are corollary benefits to membership in the divine family. This thematic constellation consists of knowledge; avoidance of judgment, death, and destruction; and resurrection. The imagery of life consists of light, water, and bread. All these concepts are presented by John as benefits of continuously following Jesus.

## Life and Knowledge

John incorporates knowledge of God and Christ into his conception of life. Even though life and knowledge are frequently paired in John, it is difficult to restrict knowledge exclusively to the discussion of life and the divine family because knowledge is also embedded into the imagery of abiding (14:15–24) and friendship (15:12–17).[18] Nevertheless, Paul A. Rainbow is right to suggest that "knowing God and being known by him, then, is the goal and content of life."[19] Therefore, this section focuses on the disciple's knowledge of God and Jesus as a benefit that is derived from possessing life.

John primarily develops the theme of knowledge through the verbs γινώσκω (sixty-three times) and οἶδα (eighty-four times), which are deployed interchangeably in the Gospel.[20] Knowledge in John can be defined as progressive apprehension of revelation that results in a life-giving relationship, which is characterized by affection and cognition.[21] This knowledge pertains to a single relationship that is dyadic in its experience, namely, with the Father and the Son.[22] Thus, one cannot speak of a believer's separate relationship with the Father and a distinct relationship with the Son. Rather, John's presentation of a disciple's knowledge has a dyadic expression as the disciple enjoys life through a relationship with the Father and the Son (8:19). John develops the following aspects about the life-giving knowledge of God: knowledge is an exclusive privilege that is restricted to the disciples, it is progressive in scope, and it yields a relationship with the Father and the Son.

### *Knowledge of God Is an Exclusive Privilege*

Knowing God is an exclusive privilege that is reserved for the disciple in the divine family. John links life to knowledge and discipleship in 17:2–3.[23] Here, John portrays Jesus as summarizing the essence of life in relation to an individual's purpose—to know Jesus and the Father. Rudolf Schnackenburg explains:

> For [humankind] eternal life is thus the goal of his existence and is fulfilled in the "knowledge" of God and Jesus Christ . . . γινώσκειν must on no account be understood in a rational or theoretical sense; as in the Semitic use familiar from the Old Testament, it means an inner apprehension and participation, and ultimately communion.[24]

In 17:2, this knowledge is presented as exclusive since the Son has authority over all flesh, yet the bestowal of life by the Son is restricted to those who have been given to the Son by the Father (6:37, 39, 44, 45, 65; 17:6). Jesus affirmed this to his disciples when he declared to them that he specifically chose them (6:70; 13:18; 15:16, 19). The benefit of the knowledge of God, in effect, is exclusive to the disciples of Jesus.

Table 2.1  Γινώσκω and Οἶδα in John

|  | γινώσκω | οἶδα |
|---|---|---|
| Jesus' common knowledge | 4:1; 5:6; 6:15 | 6:6, 61; 7:15; 8:37; 19:10 |
| Jesus' supernatural knowledge | 1:48; 2:24–25; 5:42; 16:19; 21:17 | 6:64; 13:1, 3, 11; 18:4; 19:28; 21:15, 16, 17 |
| People's common knowledge | 4:53; 7:26, 27, 49, 51; 8:52; 11:57; 12:9; 13:28, 35; 18:15, 16; 19:4, 20 | 2:9; 4:25; 5:13; 6:42; 7:27, 28; 9:12, 20, 21, 25, 29, 31; 11:49; 12:35; 15:15; 18:2, 21; 19:35; 20:2, 13, 14; 21:4, 12, 24 |
| People's understanding of truth | 7:17; 8:28, 32; 10:38; 14:31; 17:23 | 3:2; 4:42; 11:22, 24 |
| People's lack of understanding of truth/ Jesus | 3:10; 8:27, 43, 55; 10:6; 16:3; 17:25 | 1:26, 31, 33; 3:8; 4:10, 22, 32; 7:28; 8:14, 19; 9:24, 25, 29, 30; 15:21 |
| Disciples' knowledge of truth | 6:69; 12:6; 13:7, 12; 14:7, 9, 17, 20; 15:15, 18; 17:3, 7, 8, 25, 26 | 13:17; 14:4; 16:30 |
| Disciples' lack of understanding of truth | 6:69; 12:6; 13:7, 12; 14:7, 9, 17, 20; 15:15, 18; 17:3, 7, 8, 25, 26 | 13:7; 14:5; 16:18; 20:9 |
| Jesus-disciples' intimate knowledge | 10:14, 27 | 10:4, 5; 13:18 |
| Mutual knowledge between the Father and the Son | 10:15; 17:25 | 3:11; 4:22; 5:32; 7:29; 8:14, 55; 11:42; 12:50; 16:30 |

The believer's exclusive privilege to know God is also expressed through the image of "seeing." The concept of "seeing" operates on two levels in the Gospel—literal and spiritual—it is on the latter level that "seeing" connotes the possibility of knowing God (i.e., seeing God).[25] In 14:7–11 Jesus equates knowing the Father with seeing the Father. In this brief dialogue between Jesus, Thomas, and Philip, Jesus challenges his disciples to believe in him three times, and thus forges a link between the benefit of seeing/knowing the Father with believing in Jesus. In 12:44–45, John portrays Jesus inviting people to believe in him, and Jesus appends this invitation to the promise of seeing God: "Whoever believes in me, does not believe in me but in him who sent me. And whoever sees me, sees him who sent me." Here again, belief in Jesus is rewarded with seeing the Father. In 5:37–38, John depicts Jesus declaring that "the Jews" have never seen the form of the Father. Jesus follows this statement by accusing them of not permitting the word of God to abide with them, not believing in Jesus as God's agent, and refusing to come to Jesus to gain life (vv. 38–40). Here John links the inability to see the Father with unbelief and rejection of Jesus (v. 43). The ability to see the Father is explained in 1:18 and 6:46, where John writes that no one has ever seen God but the Son who has "explained" the Father. So, to see the Father is to know the Father through the Son, and seeing the Father is a benefit that is conferred on the believer (12:44–45).

## Knowledge of God Is Progressive

The believer's possession of life entails an increasing knowledge of the Father and the Son, which can be designated as "continuing relating."[26] In 17:3, the purpose clause with the *present* tense verb, "that they may know (ἵνα γινώσκωσιν)," delineates an aim or an end; thus, the aim of eternal life can be understood as a continuous knowledge of God.[27] The progressive nature of this knowledge can be summarized as follows: "Eternal life lies not so much in the possession of a completed knowledge as in the striving after a growing knowledge."[28]

The progressive character of the knowledge of God is also evident in 10:38, where Jesus says, "That they may know you and continue to know that the Father is in me and I am in the Father (ἵνα γνῶτε καὶ γινώσκητε ὅτι ἐν ἐμοὶ ὁ πατὴρ κἀγὼ ἐν τῷ πατρί)." The dual use of "know" (γινώσκω, first in the aorist subjunctive and subsequently in the present subjunctive) stresses the initial and the ongoing commitment that a disciple makes to the recognition of the oneness of Jesus and the Father.[29] The Johannine process of growing in the knowledge of God "is available to the believer through the aid of the Spirit, and this knowledge stimulates and informs further belief, which guarantees access to further knowledge."[30]

The believer's continuous knowledge of the Father and the Son is also affirmed in 17:26, as John transitions from the aorist to the future, "I made known your name (aorist) and will continue to make it known (future)."[31] This seems to be a promise of the coming Paraclete, who will not only remind the disciples of the teachings of Jesus, but will lead the disciples into deeper truth about Jesus (14:26; 15:26; 16:12–15).[32]

## Knowledge of God Is Relational

The believers' knowledge of the Father and the Son integrates them into a relationship with both persons. In 10:1–30, life and knowledge are featured in the figure of the good shepherd. The concept of knowing is weaved through this pericope by means of the verbs γινώσκω (vv. 6, 14, 15, 27, also 10:38 twice) and οἶδα (vv. 4, 5).[33] The good shepherd narrative begins by describing the relationship between the shepherd and the sheep.[34] The sheep hear (vv. 3, 4, 8, 16, 27), follow (vv. 3–5, 27), know (vv. 14–15, 27), and belong to the shepherd's flock (v. 26). In return, the shepherd names (v. 3), leads (vv.

3-4, 16), saves (v. 9), feeds (v. 9), dies for (vv. 11, 15, 18), knows (vv. 14, 27), protects (vv. 28-30), and confers abundant eternal life upon the sheep (vv. 10, 28). John imbeds the theme of relational knowledge into the divine family motif by comparing the mutual knowledge between the shepherd and the sheep (v. 14) with the reciprocal knowledge between the Father and Jesus (v. 15, note the adverb "just" καθώς). The familial language recurs in 10:27-29, where the Father and Jesus protect the sheep that have been given by the Father to Jesus and to whom Jesus grants eternal life; these sheep hear, know, and follow Jesus.

Furthermore, John uses the concept of knowledge to contrast the relationship between the shepherd and his sheep with those who are not the shepherd's sheep. The intimacy of the shepherd-sheep relationship is accentuated with the sheep recognizing the voice of their shepherd (οἴδασιν τὴν φωνὴν αὐτοῦ, v. 4) and not recognizing the voice of a stranger (οὐκ οἴδασιν τῶν ἀλλοτρίων τὴν φωνήν, v. 5). Immediately, the narrator notes in v. 6 that Jesus' listeners did not know (ἔγνωσαν) what he was saying to them. The irony in this passage is that the divine family is characterized by reciprocal knowledge (vv. 4-5, 14-15, 27), whereas those who do not belong to the sheepfold are unable to understand even the simple figure of the shepherd and the sheep (v. 6). The parable about the good shepherd shows that "life exists in intimate knowledge of the members of the family" that is akin to the sheepfold.[35]

In summary, John shows how knowledge, in partnership with life, is a derivative benefit of being a disciple of Jesus and is offered to those who are members of the divine family. John does this by placing knowledge with believing (5:38, 44, 46; 14:7-11), following (10:4-5, 14-15, 27), keeping God's word (5:38; 17:3-8), and receiving Jesus (1:11-18; 5:39-43). John's explanation of knowledge is buttressed by the accompanying benefits of salvation (10:9), protection (10:28-29; 17:11-13), performance of greater works (14:12), and love from God (17:26).

## Life and Eschatology

Life (ζωή) in John describes both the quality and the quantity of the disciple's experience of eternal life. The qualitative benefit that is derived from life is knowing God, which was discussed above. This section focuses on the quantitative benefit of life, that is, life culminates in the eschatological resurrection. In light of the possibility of suffering physical death for following Jesus, John promises eschatological resurrection as a reward of discipleship. Wrapped around the themes of life and eschatology are accompanying ideas of destruction (ἀπόλλυμι), judgment (κρίνω, κρίσις), death (ἀποθνῄσκω, θάνατος), and resurrection (ἀνάστασις). These motifs all appear in narratives that feature life, they frequently appear in proximity to one another, and they are all associated with Johannine eschatology, so they will be investigated below.[36]

Johannine eschatology can be understood as progressively realized.[37] The believers in Jesus receive life upon being integrated into the divine family, which commences a journey of continuously following Jesus until the consummation in the resurrection. This journey is empowered by the Spirit as the disciple increases in the knowledge of God and Jesus (14:26; 16:13–15; 17:2–3), by remaining in Jesus and his word (8:31; 15:1–11; 17:6, 8), until the disciple enters the presence of Jesus and the Father through the resurrection (6:39, 40, 44, 54; 12:26; 14:1–3; 17:24). Death is not a threat in the present time because life (ζωή) is a present possession (5:24; 6:47; 10:28). In addition to the resurrection, the eschatological rewards for continuously following Jesus are an escape from judgment (5:29) and destruction (3:16; 6:39; 10:28), and the conferral of honor (12:26) and glory from the Father (17:22).

## Progressively Realized Eschatology

The key Johannine passage that juxtaposes realized and unrealized eschatology is 5:21–30.[38] The dilemma in this passage concerns the interpretation of v. 25 in contrast to vv. 28–29. Some view 5:25 as referring to *spiritual* resurrection and 5:28–29 to *physical* resurrection.[39] Others understand 5:28–29 as a later redaction to reconcile the Johannine realized eschatology with futuristic eschatology.[40] Some scholars have creatively argued that the discrepancy in 5:21–30 refers to John distinguishing between the individualistic (14:22) and the corporate (5:29) eschatological realization.[41]

The tension between 5:25 and 5:28–29 is eliminated if this passage is understood as teaching progressively realized eschatology.[42] Life is mentioned eight times in 5:19–30 (ζωή, ζῶ, ζωοποιέω); therefore, the Johannine meaning of life can aid the interpreter to arrive at a congruous reading of v. 25 with vv. 28–29. Earlier, life was defined as participation in the life of God and the ability and quality of relating within the divine family. With this definition in mind, the dual aspect of "already" and "not yet" should be taken into consideration in reconciling v. 25 with vv. 28–29. In 5:21, John affirms Jesus' right to extend life to others by utilizing the present tense verbs, "raise" (ἐγείρει) and "give life" (ζωοποιεῖ). In 5:24–25, Jesus extends life in the *present* to the one who hears the words of Jesus and believes in the one who sent Jesus. John uses the present tense of "have" in reference to the believer (v. 24), the Father (v. 26), and the Son possessing life now (v. 26) to emphasize the disciple's present possession of life.[43] That is, the one who continually hears and believes (note the present tense, ὁ…ἀκούων καὶ πιστεύων) shares in the same life that the Father and the Son possess (5:24–26).[44]

The *futuristic* component of life is introduced in 5:29, where Jesus certifies that the life that was previously given to the believer finds its culmination in a future resurrection. This "not yet" element is reaffirmed with the inclusion of the reference to the Son of Man (v. 27), which carries the sense of eschatological judgment.[45] This progressive understanding of life, that it is offered to the believer now but is consummated in the resurrection, is reaffirmed to the crowd in 6:35–59 and to Martha in 11:23–26. Every occurrence of resurrection of individuals in John is in the future tense (5:28–29; 6:39, 40, 44, 54; 11:23, 24) and only in reference to Jesus is it in the aorist (20:9) or present (11:25).[46] Likewise, when the verb "I live" (ζάω) is used with forethought to the resurrection (6:51, 57–58; 11:25–26), the context suggests a future fulfillment of this promise rather than a present reality. Therefore, it is appropriate to understand Jesus' claim, "I am the resurrection and the life" (11:25), in reference to Jesus personifying resurrection and life instead of asserting that resurrection is offered in the present.[47] Consequently, life and resurrection are not equivalent, but the former finds its fullness in the latter.[48]

The distinction between life and the resurrection is seen in 5:29, where both good and evil individuals are resurrected on the last day. Since the evil do not possess life (3:19–21) but are still resurrected (5:29), resurrection and life must not be synonymous. It can be said that participation in the resurrection of the living "seals the verdict"[49] of eternal life that is passed in the present (6:40, 44, 54). This "already-not yet" proposal for 5:25 and 28–29 coheres with other Johannine themes that are portrayed as realized and unrealized throughout the Gospel, for example, judgment: 3:19–21; 12:47–48; life: 6:57–58; 10:10, 28; 14:19; and Jesus' presence with his disciples: 14:1–3, 15–23. Thus, instead of understanding 5:25 and 28–29 as contradictory statements, it is plausible to understand these verses as describing two complementary phases in the Johannine notion of the salvation process.[50]

*Deliverance from Sin, Death, and Destruction*

In addition to resurrection, John promises the believer deliverance from sin, death, and destruction. The themes of death and destruction frequently appear together in juxtaposition to "life" (3:15–18; 5:21–30; 6:39–40; 10:10, 28; 12:25, 47–50), and these concepts convey the idea of being severed from life and the family of God.[51] John uses death (θάνατος) and its derivates in reference to physical death (e.g., 4:49; 11:14) and separation from God (e.g., 8:21–26, 51, 52; 11:26). In his conversation with Martha, Jesus affirms the reality of physical death even in the case of those who possess life; thus the promise made to "the Jews" (5:24; 8:21, 24, 51, 52) should be understood as not merely to live forever physically (e.g., 6:49–51, 58) but rather to avoid a different type of death. In 8:21–26, death is described as being from below, remaining in one's sins, and not being present with Jesus and with the Father. The importance of believing and remaining in Jesus' word to avoid separation from the Father is affirmed in 8:31–36, where Jesus promises freedom from sin (see 8:21, 24; 9:41) and permanent abiding in the house. The importance of Jesus' word to permanent abiding in the Father's house is seen through the *inclusio* of "my word" in 8:31b and 8:37c, with the focus of the chiasm in v. 35b, "the son continues in the house forever."[52] In 17:6, 8, and 13, the reception of Jesus' word indicates ownership by the Father, which leads to being in the presence of the Father (17:24). The other Johannine reference to residing in the house of the Father is 14:1–3, where Jesus promises to return for his own in order to take them to the Father's house (also 12:25–26; 17:24). In 5:24, death is also placed in contradistinction to life, which affirms the meaning of death as permanent separation from the life of God. Thus, Jesus' promise to believers is that they will avoid death, that is, they will never experience separation from the Father because they possess life. This promise is reaffirmed by John's symbolic use of destruction (ἀπόλλυμι), which is always juxtaposed with familial terminology and life (3:16; 6:39; 10:10, 28).[53] And thus like death, destruction similarly conveys the meaning of separation from the life of God within the divine family. In effect, protection from death and destruction is promised when life is conferred in the present, while the threat of death and destruction is not fully extinguished until the believer arrives at the house of the Father (14:1–3). It is at that point when life is ultimately consummated and death and destruction cease to be a threat.

*Deliverance from Judgment*

The final theme in the list of eschatological benefits is deliverance from judgment. Judgment carries a dual meaning—immediate (3:19–21; 5:24) and eschatological (5:27; 12:47–48).[54] Both elements are implied in 3:36, where the wrath of God presently remains (μένει) on the unbeliever who has demonstrated his unbelief through disobedience.[55] This judgment stands in opposition to the promise of present possession of life (ἔχει ζωὴν αἰώνιον, v. 36), which may suggest that God's wrath also reaches into the eschatological future when it will be validated by Jesus (5:27–29; 12:48).[56]

The Johannine notion of judgment can be understood as "separation."[57] In 3:19–21, Jesus as the light enters into the life of the sinner and exposes his deeds. The decision that the sinner makes in favor of darkness and against Jesus separates him from the light. C. H. Dodd aptly described this process:

> [T]he manifestation of the light brings into view the ultimate distinction between truth and falsehood, between good and evil. Hence it is κρίσις, discrimination. Men by their response to the manifestation of the light declare themselves, and so pronounce their own "judgment."[58]

Thus, Jesus is able to claim that he does not judge anyone (3:17; 8:15; 12:47) because the individual has chosen to stand against Jesus and his teaching, and thus the sinner judged/separated himself from Jesus (3:18b–19; 9:39–41).

This same meaning of judgment (i.e., separation) also appears in 8:12–59. In 8:15, Jesus declares, "I judge no one," and this assertion can be reconciled with his saying in 8:26, "I have much . . . to judge," by understanding that 8:12–59 is a forensic narrative in which Jesus acts as a judge over "the Jews" as he separates them into two categories.[59] Jesus exposes their false belief (8:30); he counters their claim that they are Abraham's descendants, and instead reveals their true status as slaves of sin (8:32–40). He contradicts their declaration that they are God's sons and instead demonstrates how their actions prove that they belong to the devil (8:41–47). Consequently, Jesus allows their own words and actions against him to separate/judge them from him (8:15) as he plays the role of a judge (8:26), leading them to the conclusion that they are from below and he is from above (8:23).

In 12:46–50, John also demonstrates how judgment functions both in the present time and in the eschatological future. In 12:47–48, Jesus affirms eschatological judgment that will be mediated by his previously spoken word. Whereas during his earthly career, Jesus' word delivered people out of darkness (3:18–21; 8:12; 12:46), death (8:24, 51), sin (8:32–37), and granted them life (5:38–40); in the eschatological judgment his word will render a verdict on the unbelievers based on what was decided by them during their lifetime (12:48). In other words, the unbelievers' response to Jesus' words (5:31–40, 44–47; 6:63; 8:51–52) will determine their final judgment (12:48–50).[60] Similarly, in 12:31–34, Jesus is depicted as declaring that the judgment by the Son of Man takes place through the cross, an event that transpired during Jesus' incarnation: "Now is the judgment of this world." "The world" that God loves (3:16) rejected the light (1:10–11) by crucifying God's agent of deliverance from judgment. Consequently, God now judges "the world" through the cross, a judgment that is all encompassing, since it extends to "the world" and its ruler (12:31; 16:11).[61] But John promises that the followers of Jesus will evade this future judgment and will be protected from death and destruction because they possess eternal life. Thus, when we collate 3:17–21; 5:21–30; 8:15–16, 26; and 12:46–50, we can conclude that John deploys the notion of judgment (κρίνω/κρίσις) with a present and an eschatological sense, but the meaning remains the same, that is, separation.

*Summary: Johannine Eschatology and Soteriology*

Revisiting the theme of the Johannine presentation of the compensatory benefits of continuous discipleship, two illustrations (negative and positive) demonstrate that the above eschatological benefits are rewards for belief in Jesus. In 5:24–29, Jesus promises eternal life and avoidance of judgment and death to the one who continues to hear and believe (note the present tense participles, ὁ...ἀκούων καὶ πιστεύων, v. 24).[62] In 5:37–43, John depicts "the Jews" as rejecting Jesus' offer to come to him and continually believe (present tense πιστεύετε, v. 38). John denotes their rejection by stating that they do not hear, do not see, do not permit God's word to abide in them, do not believe, and do not receive Jesus, which results in them not having eternal life (5:37–47). While in 5:21–47, "the Jews" reject Jesus' exhortation to believe, in 11:25–27, Martha is portrayed as replying to Jesus, "I have believed that you are the Messiah, the Son of God, who is coming into the world" (v. 27). Martha's declaration is in response to Jesus' promise of a future resurrection (11:25–26) to the person who believes.[63] Thus, in both passages, John features Jesus as encouraging continual belief with the use of the present tense verbs—believe, hear, having God's word abide in a person, and receiving Jesus. Through the use of the present tense verbs, John persuades his readers to continuous allegiance to Jesus, and in return, John portrays Jesus as promising eschatological benefits to those who respond to Jesus' challenge. Martha and "the Jews" function as examples of positive and negative responses to Jesus' challenge that belief is rewarded with eternal life (5:40; 11:25–26).

## The Imagery of Life in John

Three symbols orbit the Johannine presentation of life—light, water, and bread. Since all three images are appended to life in Jesus' declarations of "I am the light/water/bread" (e.g., 4:10, 14; 6:35, 48; 8:12), it is appropriate to conclude that each image presents Jesus as the one who brings life and who is life.[64] The image of light stresses Jesus' deliverance of believers out of darkness and his subsequent guidance of the believers in the path of light. The images of water and bread portray Jesus as the source of life and as the one who continually satisfies.[65]

## Life, Light, and Darkness

In the Gospel, light (φῶς) appears only in John 1–12 and refers chiefly to Jesus.[66] The integration of life and light with the family motif in 1:1–18 and 12:35–36 forms an *inclusio* between the two passages. In 1:1–18, believers become children of God by receiving and believing in the light, and in 12:35–36, believers in the light become sons of the light. The counterpart to light is darkness (σκότος), which is the realm that is opposed to God, characterized by sin, judgment, and confusion (3:19–21; 5:24; 8:12; 12:35).[67] Jesus as the light reveals how an individual can have a relationship with God that would lead to life.[68] Thus, we can define darkness as lacking "a saving knowledge of God" because of the dualism of different realms and the enslavement to sin.[69] So light must be saving knowledge of God that is revealed by Jesus.[70] Within this thematic cluster of light-darkness-life (φῶς-σκότος-ζωή), John features two benefits that a follower of Jesus receives—deliverance from darkness and guidance within the divine family.

The public ministry of Jesus in John 1–12 begins and concludes with a promise of deliverance from darkness. The breadth of this offer is indicated in the prologue where John says, "Life was the light of people" (1:4) and "the true light enlightens every person by his coming into the world" (1:9).[71] "The world" is described as "darkness" (1:5), which, in 3:19–21, 8:12, and 12:35–36, is that from which humanity is delivered by the light. That is, the possibility to have life was extended to all people who would believe in the light (1:7, 11–12) because the light possesses the ability to give life.[72]

At the conclusion of Jesus' public ministry, John presents Jesus articulating that anyone who continually believes (ὁ πιστεύων) in Jesus as the light will not remain in the darkness (ἐν τῇ σκοτίᾳ μὴ μείνῃ, 12:46). The verb "remain" (μένω) appears in the Gospel to describe the intimacy and permanency of the relationship between Jesus and God (e.g., 14:10; 15:10) and the intimacy and permanency of the relationship between the disciples and Jesus, the Spirit, and the Father (e.g., 14:17–23; 15:1–11). By analogy, then, in 12:46, not to remain in darkness (μὴ μείνῃ) is to have the relationship with darkness permanently severed.

In addition to deliverance from darkness, the second benefit of possessing the light of life is the guidance by the light within the divine family. Jesus declares, "I am the light of the world. He who follows me, will not walk in darkness but will have the light of life" (8:12). The expression "the light of life" can carry ethical overtones in relation to how an individual operates within the family of God.[73] Since Jesus personifies light (8:12), this makes Jesus the example of divine life to people.[74] It is also possible to understand the genitive "of life" (τῆς ζωῆς) as an objective genitive, which suggests that light produces life.[75] John presents Jesus as the locus of the light because he acts as the judge who pierces into darkness and separates individuals into those who belong to the light and those who remain in the darkness (1:5; 3:18–21).[76] After deliverance from darkness, an individual is able to *follow* the light. But it is also possible to view Jesus as light in two roles—as the source of light who delivers people from darkness and as the guide who shines for people to walk ethically within God's family.[77] This interpretation reinforces the promise of deliverance from darkness and introduces the ethical component of walking in the light.[78]

John presents the ethical meaning of "the light of life" through the verb "walk" (περιπατέω). In 12:35–36, the present tense command, "walk," results in avoidance of darkness and in knowledge of the way (see also 11:9–10).[79] The concept of "walking" contains an ethical dimension that is expected of the sons of the light as they adopt the quality of the light (e.g., Matthew 5:14–16; Ephesians 5:8–9).[80] Walking in the light produces works (3:21) that indicate the qualitative resemblance to the God of the light (Psalm 18:28; 36:6; 89:15; 1 John 1:5). The way to walk continually in the light is to follow Jesus who is the light (8:12).

Jesus' offer to deliver people from darkness and to lead them ends with his departure. The call to believe in (12:36, 46), walk in (8:12; 12:35), and follow (8:12) the light ceases with Jesus' departure from public ministry, which is why the invitation to walk in the light is only found in John 1–12. Jesus forewarned his disciples and the crowds about his departure which, on the one hand, would bring to an end his offer to serve as the light (7:33; 8:21; 9:4–5; 11:9–10; 12:36), and, on the other, which would commence the judgment of "the world" through Jesus' crucifixion (12:31).[81] The conclusion to John 1–12 is not condemnation but a call to follow the light to become sons of the light (12:36). This is coupled with the command to believe continually in Jesus (note πιστεύετε in 12:36), which is appended to the promise that the believer will be led by the light (12:35–36).

John features the response to the light in between Jesus' final two public exhortations to believe (vv. 35–36 and vv. 44–50). Here, John provides two reasons why the Jewish leaders refused to believe continually in Jesus (note the imperfect ἐπίστευον in 12:37): the fulfillment of Isaiah's prediction of the hardness of their hearts and fear that the Pharisees would expel the believers from the synagogue.[82] In 12:36, the reward for believing in the light is to become *sons* of the light, which further reiterates the promise of membership in the divine family through sonship terminology. In 12:46, belief is rewarded with separation from darkness, avoidance of judgment (vv. 47–48), and eternal life (v. 50). Thus I suggest that in order to promote true discipleship that leads to confession of Jesus as the Messiah, even at the cost of social respectability (12:42–43), John places the inappropriate response from "the Jews" in between two appeals by Jesus to believe in him continuously (note the present tense of πιστεύετε in vv. 36, 44, 46) and to hear, receive, and obey his teaching (vv. 47, 48).

While the light is available only for a limited time, the promise to be led by the light for those who believe in the light extends into the future. This is reinforced by the grammar in 8:12. The association of "light" with "life" suggests continual protection from darkness because life implies eschatological existence (5:29; 10:28).[83] The promise to have the light of life and to avoid darkness is stressed by the emphatic preposition "never" (οὐ μή) with the aorist

## Membership in the Divine Family—Participation in Eternal Life

subjunctive "walk" (περιπατήσῃ) in 8:12, as it is contrasted with the strong adversative "but" (ἀλλά) with the future indicative verb "have" (ἕξει).[84] Rudolf Schnackenburg observes that the future tense of the verb contains the language of immediate promise that never ends.[85] This promise is only conferred on the believer who continually follows Jesus (note the present participle in 8:12, ὁ ἀκολουθῶν) because the benefit to the follower is perpetual existence in the light. Schnackenburg captures the duration of the promise:

> The activity of the *Logos* as "light" begins with creation and extends by means of the Incarnation to the eschatological fulfillment. Indeed, from the very beginning, it is aimed at bringing men home to God's world of light.[86]

John promotes belief in Jesus by juxtaposing the call to follow Jesus with Jesus' declaration to be the light. In 8:12, Jesus declares that he is the light, certain "Jews" initially responded by believing in Jesus (8:30), though subsequently they turn on Jesus and attempt to kill him (8:59). If it is understood that 8:12–59 functions as a single unit spoken by Jesus at Sukkot, then the initial belief and the latter attempt to murder Jesus are responses to all that John portrays Jesus teaching at the festival.[87] During the lighting ceremony that was held at the end of the first day of the feast in the court of the women, commemorating the pillar of fire during the Exodus event (Exodus 13:21), the Johannine Jesus declared that he was the light of "the world" (8:12).[88] The image of light played a significant role in the festival of Sukkot; indeed, as the Mishnah describes, when the candles were lit, "There was not a courtyard in Jerusalem that was not illuminated with the light of the *Beis HaSho'evah*."[89] Jesus' announcement evidently presented Jesus as the fulfillment of the Old Testament symbolism of the light and "the light emanating from the temple, for all the world, is Jesus himself."[90] It is to this declaration that "the Jews" initially respond with belief (8:30–31), but ultimately with aggression (8:59).

The second occurrence of Jesus declaring to be the light is in 9:5, where John weaves in the story of the blind man to illustrate Jesus' pronouncement (9:1–41). John features the story of the blind man to teach that everyone is born blind (9:2–3) and needs to be delivered from darkness into light through an encounter with Jesus (9:5–7). Refusal to come to Jesus as the light (8:12; 9:5) and acknowledge blindness prolongs the blindness and guilt (9:39–41).[91] Those who believe in Jesus as the light are promised to have their deeds exposed (3:19–21), to escape darkness and walk in perpetual light (3:19; 8:12; 12:35–36, 46), and to see the one who was previously unseen (1:18; 12:45; 14:7, 9).[92]

While "the Jews" illustrate a negative response to Jesus' declaration (8:59; 9:40–41), the blind man exemplifies the positive response which is affirmed through his confession (9:17), willingness to be ridiculed for Jesus (9:28), and reverence toward Jesus (9:35–38).[93] The blind man confesses Jesus as a prophet (9:17) and as a messenger from God (vv. 31–33). Additionally, the double use of "lord" (κύριος) in 9:36–38 may demonstrate development in the blind man's understanding of Jesus' identity—from politely addressing Jesus as "sir" to acknowledging him as "Lord."[94] Moreover, the association of worship with "lord" in v. 38 enriches both terms, possibly suggesting worship that is not mere homage to a human, but is, rather, similar to the Old Testament worship that reflects an individual's response to the revelation of God (e.g., Genesis 17:3; Exodus 34:6–8).[95] The juxtaposition of "worship" (προσκυνέω) with "lord" (κύριος) can be understood in the strongest sense of the word, that is, that "the accompanying act makes his confession equivalent to the later one by Thomas—my Lord and my God (20:28)."[96]

The previous Johannine reference to worship appeared in John 4, in the narrative of the Samaritan woman. In that pericope, worship was described in respect to a proper sphere (4:21) and according to the right knowledge (4:23). John's description of Jesus' response to the Samaritan woman is similar to Jesus' response to the blind man's inquiries about Jesus' identity. To the Samaritan woman Jesus replies, "I am he, the one who is speaking to you" (Ἐγώ εἰμι, ὁ λαλῶν σοι, 4:26). To the blind man, Jesus responds: "It is he who is speaking with you" (ὁ λαλῶν μετὰ σοῦ ἐκεῖνός ἐστιν, 9:37).[97] Moreover, in both instances there is a benefit that is extended to the individual. In the case of the Samaritan woman, she is offered eternal life (4:10, 14), while sight is offered to the blind man (9:36, 39–41). In the blind man's question to Jesus (9:36), we can observe John's appeal to his readers to answer the same question with which the Pharisees and the blind man were faced—who is Jesus? (9:29–30, 33, 36; see also 8:25). The unbelief of the Pharisees/"the Jews" consigns them to ongoing blindness and judgment. John encourages a response comparable to that of the blind man inasmuch as he presents the benefits of deliverance from darkness and of the subsequent leading by the light that prevents stumbling (11:9–10).

## Life and Water

To enhance the value of life for his readers, John deploys the image of water in juxtaposition with life in two passages: 4:10–15 and 7:38–39.[98] In 4:10, Jesus offers living water (ὕδωρ ζῶν) to the Samaritan woman who eventually receives Jesus' message (vv. 29, 39–42). The antecedent of the water must be determined in this passage. Jesus could not be the water of life since he offers it.[99] Additionally, the chiasm in v. 10 equates the gift of God with the water of life. John writes, "Jesus answered her, if you knew the gift of God, and who it is that is saying to you, 'Give me a drink,' you would have asked him, and he would have given you living water." Since Jesus is the focus of the chiasm as the giver of the water of life, he cannot be the referent for the "living water."[100] The combination of the discussion concerning water in these two passages indicates that the water of life refers to Jesus' revelation, which conveys salvific content that leads to eternal life and the Spirit who collaborates with Jesus to confer eternal life (see also 6:63).[101]

The benefit of "living water" in both passages concerns quenching one's thirst (4:15; 7:37). In the dialogue with the Samaritan woman, John moves from physical thirst (vv. 7, 15) to spiritual thirst that can be satiated by Jesus.[102] The present tense participle "living" (ζῶν) that modifies "water" (ὕδωρ, vv. 10, 11) highlights the continual spiritual fulfillment that is gained from the "living water" and the inclusion of "eternal life" (v. 14) affirms the permanency of the satisfaction in the present and into the eschatological period. Additionally, the fulfillment that a believer receives from Jesus' gift is stressed in the contrast between the need for continual drinking of physical water (πᾶς ὁ πίνων, note the present participle) with the gratification gained from a single drink of living water, "whoever should drink . . . will never thirst" (ὃς δ' ἂν πίῃ...οὐ μὴ διψήσει εἰς τὸν αἰῶνα).[103] That is, God's gift of living water as conferred by Jesus through his teaching (6:63b) and the Spirit's application of that teaching (6:63a) permanently satisfies spiritual thirst.[104]

Initially, Jesus' offer of the living water is misunderstood by the Samaritan woman.[105] She responds to Jesus' remarks about the living water by expressing a desire to quench her thirst permanently and to stop coming to the well altogether to draw water for herself (v. 15). However, after Jesus demonstrates that he has supernatural knowledge of her life, after he explains to her the meaning of true worship, and after he announces to her that he is the Messiah, she understands the meaning of the water to which Jesus was referring.[106] That she finally understands Jesus' words is made evident in her abandonment of the water jar (v. 28), her confession of Jesus' messiahship (vv. 29, 42), and her participation in Jesus' mission as a witness (vv. 28–30, 38b–42).[107] She becomes a positive example of what Jesus challenges his disciples to do (vv. 31–38), that is, to engage in his mission, and in this way she models "faithful discipleship."[108]

The story of the Samaritan woman contains the promise of the benefit of life in exchange for belief in Jesus as the Messiah and commitment to discipleship. Moreover, in order to witness to her villagers (μαρτυρούσης, v. 39) the Samaritan woman overcame two aspects of adversity: the stigma of confessing her unhappy marital history (v. 39) and the stigma for talking to a Jewish man.[109] Thus, it appears that John inserts the story of the Samaritan woman into the narrative not only to present Jesus as the international savior

(v. 42), but also to demonstrate that the benefit of eternal life may motivate an individual to follow Jesus even in the face of the possibility of adverse social consequences that the Samaritan woman could have endured for speaking with a Jewish man.[110]

John 7:37–39 is the second passage that refers to the water of life. Here, it is mediated through the work of the Spirit. Sukkot is the setting for Jesus' declaration, "If anyone thirsts, let him come to me and drink. He who believes in me, as the Scripture has said, rivers of living water will flow from his inner part" (7:37–38).[111] Many have argued for the Christological interpretation of this passage that Jesus is depicted as the new temple from whom the waters will flow. Thus, the Old Testament eschatological promises are fulfilled in Jesus (Ezekiel 47:1–12).[112] Others see the believer as the source of the living water, since Jesus has granted life to the individual who now becomes that source of living water.[113]

Arguably, John permits both options: to view Jesus as the source of water and to see the believer as the source of water. On the one hand, Jesus is consistently portrayed in the Gospel as the source of eternal life (10:10, 28); on the other hand, the Spirit (15:26; 16:7; 20:22) joins the process of conferring life upon the believer (6:63).[114] The believer is said to possess eternal life (11:25) and the Spirit (14:16–17) permanently.[115] Thus, John presents Jesus as the source/spring (=κοιλία) from whom the Spirit (=rivers of living water or the stream) will flow to the believer, who, in turn, will become a "derivative source" of the Spirit for other people.[116]

In this context, Jesus' invitation to continuous commitment to him is conveyed through the present tense participles, "the one who believes" (ὁ πιστεύων, v. 38) and "those who believe" (οἱ πιστεύσαντες, v. 39), which result in the benefits of possessing the Spirit and having one's thirst assuaged. These benefits are extended by Jesus to individuals who are paralyzed by fear of "the Jews," such that the crowd would not even mention Jesus' name (7:13). In the end, the benefits of the relief of thirst, eternal life, and possession of the Spirit should encourage the readers of the Gospel to come, drink, and believe (7:37–39) in Jesus even if one is dominated by fear because of potential arrest (7:30, 45) or death (7:1, 20, 25).[117]

## Life and Bread

The third image that is appended to "life" is bread. In the narrative on the bread of life (6:22–71), John depicts Jesus as the bread of life in whom one can find permanent satiation. The imagery of the bread of life follows the narrative of Jesus' sign of the feeding of the 5,000 (6:1–14, 25–34).[118] The crowd responds to the miracle of the bread by seeking Jesus for perpetual free bread (vv. 22–26). However, John portrays Jesus as redirecting the discussion from physical bread to himself, the bread from heaven, who provides true satisfaction by granting eternal life (vv. 27–33).[119]

Here, Jesus invites his listeners to come and feast on him as the eternally satisfying manna.[120] In light of the conclusion to the narrative featuring two responses to Jesus' teaching, either defection or devotion (vv. 66–68), attention needs to be drawn to the benefits of continuous discipleship and how these benefits prompt devotion to Jesus.[121] In other words, John depicts Jesus as promising satisfaction from eating the true bread (vv. 35, 55–56), eternal life (vv. 27, 33, 35, 40, 47, 50–51, 53, 54, 57, 58, 63, 68), and resurrection (vv. 39, 40, 44, 54), and this serves to persuade John's audiences to continuous discipleship, in contrast with the defectors (6:60–67). John also emphasizes discipleship in this context through the repeated use of the verb "believe" (πιστεύω, vv. 29, 30, 35, 36, 40, 47, 64, 69) and the accompanying imagery of coming (vv. 35, 37, 44, 45, 65), seeing (vv. 30, 36, 40, 62), eating (vv. 50, 51, 53–58), drinking (vv. 53–56), and walking with Jesus (v. 66).[122]

Similar to the discourse with the Samaritan woman where Jesus is portrayed as contrasting the physical water with living water, in 6:22–71, Jesus demonstrates the eternal gratification a believer experiences from consuming the bread of life. The difficulty in earning bread and the negativity toward hunger in the ancient society gives the metaphor of the bread of life more potency.[123] Jesus contrasts perishable nourishment with eternal satisfaction from the bread of life. The former is gained through physical labor (v. 27) whereas the latter through belief in Jesus (v. 29); and the former results in death (v. 49) while the latter in resurrection (v. 54). The adjective "true" (v. 32) contrasts the Old Testament provision of manna with Jesus being the *true* bread who sustains life.[124] The crux of the discussion is satiation of hunger, and Jesus is depicted as the bread that continually satisfies.[125] Life, in other words, is found only in "feeding" on Jesus.[126] The metaphorical interpretation of eating and drinking is evident in 6:55–56, where the verb "remain" (μένω) is used to explain the eating of the flesh and drinking of the blood of Jesus as confirmation of possessing a relationship with Jesus through his death (v. 51).[127] Subsequently, in v. 57, Jesus identifies the origin of his life and his ability to grant life to others as being in the living Father. The present participle "living" (ὁ ζῶν) modifying "Father" (πατήρ) signifies the perpetual existence of God and, by derivation (5:26), the perpetual existence of Jesus who is the *Logos* (1:1–4). With the reference to the living Father providing for and sustaining the life of Jesus (5:26)—who, in turn, confers life upon those who continually abide in him, delivers them from death (v. 50), and promises future resurrection (v. 54)—John brings us into the metaphor of the divine family.[128] This work of conferring life is possible only with the cooperating work of the words of Jesus and the Spirit, because flesh is impotent in spiritual matters (3:6; 6:63).[129] Thus, the portrayal of Jesus as the bread of life appears in the Gospel as a benefit within the context that bears overtones of the divine family.[130]

Moreover, the narrative in John 6 provides an antidote to defection. For John's intended audience, the conclusion of the narrative in vv. 60–71 creates a fork in the road with two contrasting disciples as potential models to imitate—Judas who represents defectors and Peter who represents the followers of Jesus. As a response to the desertion of some of his disciples, Jesus asked the twelve, "Do you also wish to go away?" Peter's response is: "Lord, to whom will we go? You have the words of eternal life. We have believed and we have come to know that you are the Holy One of God," and this response communicates the message that to follow Jesus is to receive eternal life.[131] This response, then, functions in this narrative to motivate commitment to Jesus because of the benefit of eternal life. Peter's reply reaches back to the beginning of the discourse, where Jesus claimed to be sent by God (v. 29) and sealed by God (v. 27). Jesus' origin from God was the repeated claim of which he hoped to persuade his listeners (vv. 33, 38, 39, 41, 42, 44, 46, 50, 51, 57, 58), and this is precisely what Peter affirms with certainty: "You are the holy one of God" (v. 69). Peter's confession mirrors the confessions of Martha (11:27) and Thomas (20:28), both of whom are depicted as faithful followers of Jesus.[132] John's readers can reach forward in the Gospel and recognize that Peter's discipleship will be flawed (18:15–18, 25–27).[133] Nonetheless, John's readers would also see that Peter reaffirms his commitment to his Lord and so Peter "never stops his journey with Jesus" (21:15–22).[134] In the bread of life narrative, John portrays Jesus as offering eternal life, satisfaction in him, and the promise of a future resurrection as benefits of continuous discipleship, so that his audiences would emulate Peter, not Judas or other defectors, in their response to Jesus' call to follow him by consuming him as the bread of life.

**Summary: The Imagery of Life**

To enhance the value of life for his audiences as a reward of discipleship, John features life alongside the images of light, water, and bread. Each of these symbols appear in Jesus' "I am" declarations in association with life which suggests that each image portrays Jesus as the one who brings life and who is life (e.g., 4:10, 14; 6:35, 48; 8:12). The image of light spotlights Jesus' role as the one who delivers his followers out of darkness (1:9; 12:46) and guides them in the path of light (8:12; 12:35–36). The images of water and bread feature Jesus as the source of life and as the one who continually satisfies (4:15; 6:35, 55–56; 7:37). In deploying light, water, and bread as rewards of following Jesus, John pairs each image with a call to discipleship through one or a combination of the following verbs: believing (1:4–13; 6:29, 30, 35, 36, 40, 47, 64, 69; 12:36, 46), following (8:12), coming (3:21; 6:35, 37, 44,

45, 65), seeing (6:30, 36, 40, 62), eating (6:50, 51, 53–58), drinking (4:10–15; 6:53–56; 7:37–39), and walking with Jesus (6:66; 12:35).

## CONCLUSION: THE BENEFITS OF MEMBERSHIP IN THE DIVINE FAMILY

This chapter presented eternal life as the featured benefit that is derived from membership in the divine family. Eternal life can be defined as the ability and quality of relating within the divine family. This life is eternal in that it culminates in a future resurrection and permanent presence with God. John's description of how a disciple procures life involves the activity and the teaching of the Father, the Son, and the Spirit. In John, the living God (5:21; 6:57) begets members into the divine family (1:13), as he awards life to the disciples of Jesus (5:21). The Son's life is dependent on the Father (6:57) but is also said to be rooted in himself (1:4; 5:26, 40; 6:33, 57, 63; 14:19) as he grants life to whomever he will (5:21; 17:2) in cooperation with the Spirit (6:63). The words of Jesus are the means through which life is bestowed to the disciples (5:39–40; 6:63b, 68; 12:50). The Spirit participates in the conferral of life upon the believers by impressing the words of Jesus upon his followers (3:5–8; 16:13–15). Jesus' association with his Father provides him with the ability to contain life in himself (5:26; 6:57) and to grant this life to those who believe in him (1:4; 3:15–16; 5:21, 40; 6:27, 33, 40, 54, 68; 10:10, 28; 11:25; 14:6; 17:2, 3; 20:31). The Son grants life to his followers in the present time (3:16; 5:40; 6:47, 53, 54) and in the eschatological future (6:50–51, 58), culminating in the resurrection (5:29; 6:39, 40, 44, 54; 11:25–26). Life results in abundant living (10:10) that is secured by Jesus (10:28–30) and is dependent on Jesus (6:57; 14:19). Life is found in close association with the light (1:4; 8:12), water (4:10–14), bread (6:35, 48, 58), words of Jesus (6:63, 68; 12:48), word/commandment of God (5:37–40; 12:48–50), judgment (3:16, 36; 5:21–29; 12:48), and the Holy Spirit (4:14; 6:63; 7:38). John extends the above benefits, which are derived from eternal life as part of participation within the divine family to the committed disciple (6:60–71; 8:31).

## NOTES

1. As Van der Watt notes, "Birth is the introduction to life and life is the consequence of birth. . . . Life and birth are both spiritual, the one leads to the other." Van der Watt, *Family*, 177.

2. Van der Watt has a similar definition of ζωή in John. Van der Watt, "Everlasting Life," 9; Van der Watt, *Family*, 178.

3. Dodd observes, "[The] Hebrew conception of life is always one of action, movement and enjoyment," thus *quality* is a fitting term to describe these aspects of ζωή. C. H. Dodd, *The Interpretation of the Fourth Gospel* (Cambridge: University Press, 1953), 150.

4. Similarly, Bennema, *Power*, 154 fn. 164, 174, 180.

5. For the substitution of the kingdom of God motif with ζωή, see Brown, *John*, 159; Bultmann, *John*, 152 fn. 2; André Feuillet, *Johannine Studies* (Staten Island, NY: Alba House, 1964), 175–89; J. Alexander Findlay, *The Way, the Truth and the Life* (London: Hodder and Stoughton, 1940), 225; Jörg Frey, "From the 'Kingdom of God' to 'Eternal Life': The Transformation of Theological Language in the Fourth Gospel," in *John, Jesus, and History, Volume 3: Glimpses of Jesus through the Johannine Jesus*, ed. Paul N. Anderson, Felix Just, and Tom Thatcher (Atlanta, GA: SBL Press, 2016), 439–58, citing 452; Archibald M. Hunter, *The Work and Words of Jesus*, Rev. ed. (London: SCM, 1950), 77; Archibald M. Hunter, *According to John: The New Look at the Fourth Gospel* (Philadelphia, PA: Westminster Press, 1968), 107; J. Richard Middleton, *A New Heaven and a New Earth: Reclaiming Biblical Eschatology* (Grand Rapids, MI: Baker, 2014), 246; Rainbow, *Theology*, 277–78; Shin, *Ethics*, 64; Vellanickal, *Sonship*, 209, 213, 225. Van der Watt similarly views life and kingdom as close but not identical soteriological concepts. Van der Watt, *Family*, 377, 381.

6. U. E. Simon, "Eternal Life in the Fourth Gospel," in *Studies in the Fourth Gospel*, ed. F. L. Cross (London: A. R. Mowbray & Co., 1957), 98.

7. Köstenberger, *Theology*, 285–86.

8. For a discussion of the use of the title *dominus et deus* in reference to Domitian, see Suetonius, *Dom.* 13.1–2; Martial, *Epigrams*, 5.8.1; 7.34.8; 8.2.6. Warren Carter, *John and Empire: Initial Explorations* (New York: T & T Clark, 2008), 71–72, 195–97; Chennattu, *Discipleship*, 165–66; Adolf Deissmann, *Light from the Ancient East: The New Testament Illustrated by Recently Discovered Texts of the Graeco-Roman World*, 4th ed. (London: Hodder and Stoughton, 1927), 362.

9. Ihenacho writes: "[L]ife is at the center of the Johannine language, symbolism, and spirituality, and that it is the common meaning of the Johannine community and its chief integrative concept." Ihenacho, *Community*, xx. Similarly, Quast and Mussner see eternal life as John's main concept for salvation. Gorman has recently argued that all of the themes in John relate to eternal life which led him to conclude that the Gospel has a missional purpose of life, light, and love. While I agree that there is *a* missional purpose in John, on account of the predominant appearances of life in John 1–12, and since there are other themes that overshadow life (e.g., belief, discipleship), it seems best to view life as a motivating factor for belief in Jesus which aligns well with 20:30–31. Gorman, *Abide and Go*, 44–70. See also Franz Mussner, *Zōē; Die Anschauung vom "Leben" im vierten Evangelium*, Münchener theologische Studien, 1. Historische Abteilung, 5 (München: Karl Zink Verlag, 1952), 186–87; Quast, *Reading*, 25.

10. Ihenacho, *Community*, xix, 44.

11. Ihenacho, *Community*, 208.

12. Every use of ζωή and αἰώνιος ζωή in John is in association with familial terminology in the near context or as in the case of 1:4, in the broader context of 1:1–14.

13. For the conceptual background of life, see Ashton, *Understanding*, 399–405; Floyd F. Filson, "The Gospel of Life: A Study of the Gospel of John," in *Current Issues in New Testament Interpretation in Honor of O. A. Piper*, ed. W. Klassen and G. F. Snyder (New York, NY: Harper, 1962), 115–18; Ihenacho, *Community*, 235–89; Abiola Mbamalu, "'Life' in the Fourth Gospel and Its Resonances with Genesis 1–3," *In die Skriflig* 38 no. 1 (2014): 1–5; George W. E. Nickelsburg, *Resurrection, Immortality, and Eternal Life in Intertestamental Judaism and Early Christianity*, Expanded ed., HTS 56 (Cambridge, MA: Harvard University Press, 2006). Bennema argues that sapiential Jewish writings form the background to John. Mussner argues that ζωή in John is the continuation of the Old Testament, Pauline, and Synoptic teaching on life. Feuillet views ζωή through the lens of oriental religions. Dodd sees Hellenistic mysticism in John's use of life. Appasamy contextualized ζωή in Indian religious thought, comparing it to the spiritual life of the *bhaktas*. Bultmann viewed the entire Gospel as situated in Gnosticism. A. J. Appasamy, *The Johannine Doctrine of Life: A Study of Christian and Indian Thought* (London: Society for Promoting Christian Knowledge, 1934), 6, 12, 44; Bennema, *Power*, 42–99; Bultmann, *Theology*, 2:10; *TDNT*, s.v. "ζάω," 2:832–75; Dodd, *Interpretation*, 201; Feuillet, *Études*, 175–80; Mussner, *Zōē*, 186.

14. The fifty-six uses are distributed as follows: seventeen times as αἰώνιος ζωή or ζωὴ αἰώνιος; nineteen times as ζωή; seventeen times as ζάω; and three uses of the verb ζῳοποιέω. Van der Watt has shown that John's use of αἰώνιος ζωή or the absolute ζωή carries the same meaning. J. G. van der Watt, "The Use of αἰώνιος in the Concept ζωὴ αἰώνιος in John's Gospel," *NT* 31 no. 3 (1989): 217–28. Most scholars view ζωή and ζωὴ αἰώνιος interchangeably. See Bultmann, *Theology*, 2:19; Dodd, *Interpretation*, 144. Knight observes that ten of seventeen references of ζωὴ αἰώνιος and twenty-four of thirty-six uses of ζωή are contained in John 5–12, which describe the hostility of "the Jews" and the crowds toward Jesus. This leads Knight to conclude that "by using language that points beyond persecution and natural life in this manner, the implied author allows the readers to view the temporal effects of hostility and persecution against the backdrop of the eternal promises spoken from Jesus' own lips. The implied author thus encourages the implied readers to remain faithful in their commitment to Jesus." William E. Knight, "Defining Discipleship in the Fourth Gospel: A Narrative Analysis of the Motif for the Implied Reader" (Ph.D. Dissertation, New Orleans Baptist Theological Seminary, 2001), 169.

15. The use of ζῇ in 4:50–53 can be understood in reference to the official's son's life as a Hebraism with the simple meaning of revived back to physical life (see Numbers 21:8 LXX where ζήσεται is used for restoration to physical life). So Barrett, *John*, 248. Cf. Ihenacho, *Community*, 185 fn. 11, 209.

16. John 10:11, 15, 17, 24; 12:25 (2x), 27; 13:37, 38; 15:13; 18:18.

17. The juxtaposition of ψυχή with ζωή in 12:25 spotlights the permanency of ζωή in that the former ends while the latter is modified by αἰώνιον to describe its duration. Schnackenburg, *John*, 354.

18. The proximity between life and knowledge is noted by Westcott who writes, "knowledge which is life." Westcott, *John*, 239. Kee notes that the theme of knowledge is more prominent in John than in the other Gospels as evidenced by the

more frequent occurrence of γινώσκω, οἶδα, and γνωρίζω. H. C. Kee, "Knowing the Truth: Epistemology and Community in the Fourth Gospel," in *Neotestamentica et Philonica: Studies in Honor of Peder Borgen*, ed. D. E. Aune, T. Seland, and J. H. Ulrichsen (Leiden: Brill, 2002), 254.

19. Rainbow, *Theology*, 308.

20. Table 2.1 indicates the interchangeable use of γινώσκω and οἶδα in John. For additional support, see Cornelis Bennema, "Christ, the Spirit and the Knowledge of God: A Study in Johannine Epistemology," in *The Bible and Epistemology: Biblical Soundings on the Knowledge of God*, ed. M. Healy and R. Parry (Milton Keynes, U.: Paternoster, 2007), 115 fn. 28; *TDNT*, s.v. "γινώσκω," 1:689; Rainbow, *Theology*, 301 fn. 69; *NIDNTT*, s.v. "Knowledge," 390–409. Cf. Ignace de la Potterie, "Οἶδα et γινώσκω: Les deux modes de la connaissance dans le quatrième évangile," *Biblica* 40 no. 3 (1959): 709–25; Vellanickal, *Sonship*, 245.

21. Bennema shaped the above definition by observing that Johannine knowledge is "cognitive perception of the truth on the basis of sensory perception . . . [in other words] . . . the saving content of what has been cognitively retrieved from what has been heard and seen." Bennema, *Power*, 127–28.

22. "The knowledge which is life, the knowledge which from the fact that it is vital is always advancing, is two-fold; a knowledge of God and his sole, supreme Majesty, and a knowledge of the revelation which He has made in its final consummation in the mission of Christ." Westcott, *John*, 239.

23. Scholars deem this passage as containing the definition of eternal life. Barrett, *John*, 503; Lincoln, *John*, 435; George Barker Stevens, *The Johannine Theology: A Study of the Doctrinal Contents of the Gospels and Epistles of the Apostle John* (New York: C. Scribner's Sons, 1894), 314; Thompson, *John*, 350; Van der Watt, "Everlasting Life," 5; Westcott, *John*, 239. Cf. Schnackenburg, *John*, 360.

24. Schnackenburg, *John*, 360.

25. Bennema, *Power*, 124.

26. Van der Watt, *Family*, 216. The progressive sense of knowing God is supported by the present subjunctive, γινώσκωσιν, in 17:3.

27. Westcott, *John*, 239. The other proposed functions of "ἵνα γινώσκωσιν" are telic: Stevens, *Theology*, 314–15. Semitic: Keener, *John*, 1055. Purpose clause: Westcott, *John*, 239.

28. Westcott, *John*, 239.

29. Bennema, *Power*, 128.

30. Bennema, "Johannine Epistemology," 127.

31. The dual use of γνωρίζω (aorist followed by the future tense) stresses continuity between the past and future ministry. Harris, *John*, 293; Lincoln, *John*, 440; Schnackenburg, *John*, 3:196; Smyth, *Grammar*, §1910b.

32. Harris notes, "In 14:26, the two verbs should be seen as aoristic futures suggesting 'successive occurrences.'" Harris, *John*, 263; Westcott, *John*, 248.

33. The other prominent concepts are hearing: ἀκούω, vv. 3, 8, 16, 27, and verbs of motion: i.e., ἐξάγω, vv. 3, 16; ἀκολουθέω, vv. 4, 5, 27; ἐκβάλλω, v. 4; πορεύομαι, v. 4; φεύγω, v. 5; εἰσέρχομαι, v. 9 (2x); ἐξέρχομαι, v. 9.

34. The sheep can refer to the Jewish people and Gentiles (10:16). So, Carson, *John*, 390; Köstenberger, *Missions*, 163; Cf. Martyn and Brown, who see "other sheep" as other Christians who are either scattered or from other communities. Raymond E. Brown, "'Other Sheep not of this Fold': The Johannine Perspective on Christian Diversity in the Late First Century," *JBL* 97 (1978): 20; J. Louis Martyn, *The Gospel of John in Christian History: Essays for Interpreters* (New York: Paulist Press, 1978), 115–21.

35. Quoting Van der Watt, "Everlasting Life," 12.

36. Life is paired with destruction (3:16; 6:39; 10:28), judgment (5:21–30; 8:12–16; 12:46–50), death and resurrection (5:21–30; 6:39–40, 44, 54, 58; 10:28; 11:23–26). For Johannine eschatology, see Barrett, *John*, 67–70; Beasley-Murray, *John*, cxxvii–cxlii; Rainbow, *Theology*, 280–85; Schnackenburg, *John*, 2:426–37.

37. Defended by Beasley-Murray, *John*, 77; R. Alan Culpepper, "Realized Eschatology in the Experience of the Johannine Community," in *The Resurrection of Jesus in the Gospel of John*, ed. Craig R. Koester and R. Bieringer (Tübingen: Mohr Siebeck, 2008), 253–76; J. C. Davis, "The Johannine Concept of Eternal Life as a Present Possession," *RQ* 27 (1984): 164–65; Köstenberger, *Theology*, 346; Mbamalu, "Life," 1–5; Rainbow, *Theology*, 280–85; Simon, "Eternal Life," 102; Stevens, *Johannine Theology*, 328–54; Thompson, *John*, 87–91, 129–31; Van der Watt, *Family*, 436. For proponents of realized eschatology, see Josef Blank, *Krisis: Untersuchungen zur johanneischen Christologie und Eschatologie* (Lambertus-Verlag: Freiburg im Breisgau, 1964), 344; Brown, *John*, cxv–cxxi, esp. cxx; Bultmann, *Theology*, 3–92; Bultmann, *John*, 431; Jaime Clark-Soles, "'I Will Raise [Whom?] Up on the Last Day': Anthropology as a Feature of Johannine Eschatology," in *New Currents through John: A Global Perspective*, ed. Francisco Lozada and Tom Thatcher (Atlanta: SBL Press, 2006), 29–53; Dodd, *Interpretation*, 7, 395; Robert Kysar, *Voyages with John: Charting the Fourth Gospel* (Waco, TX: Baylor University Press, 2005), 19–25; Quast, *Reading*, 3; John A. T. Robinson, *Jesus and His Coming: The Emergence of a Doctrine* (London: SCM, 1957), 160–85.

38. For a survey of scholarly reconciliation of 5:25 with 5:28–29, see J. G. van der Watt, "A New Look at John 5:25–9 in the Light of the Use of the Term 'Eternal Life' in the Gospel According to John," *Neot* 19 (1985): 74–76; Rainbow, *Theology*, 278–85.

39. Barrett, *John*, 262–63; Beasley-Murray, *John*, 76–77; G. R. Beasley-Murray, *Gospel of Life: Theology in the Fourth Gospel* (Peabody, MA: Hendrickson, 1991), 11–12; Harris, *John*, 114–15; Moloney, *John*, 179–84; Westcott, *John*, 87.

40. Bultmann, *John*, 258–61; Schnackenburg, *John*, 2:116. Similarly, *EDNT*, s.v. "ζῶ, ζωή, ἧς, ἡ," 2:108.

41. For corporate versus individualistic interpretation, see C. F. D. Moule, "A Neglected Factor in the Interpretation of Johannine Eschatology," in *Studies in John: Presented to Professor Dr. J. N. Sevenster on the Occasion of His Seventieth Birthday* (Leiden: Brill, 1970), 155–60. Boismard argues that 5:25 is a later addition inserted to accommodate the evolving Christian theology toward realized eschatology. M. E. Boismard, "L'évolution du thème eschatologique dans les traditions johaniques," *RB* 68 (1961): 507–24. Brown suggests that multiple Johannine eschatological traditions

converge in 5:25–30. Brown, *John*, 219–21. Kysar supposes that 5:21–30 is contradictory because it describes the Johannine community parting ways with the Jewish theology of futuristic eschatology, whereas Christian theology evolved toward realized eschatology. Kysar, *Voyages*, 25, 48. Van der Watt argued that 5:25 refers to the death of individuals who lived and died before interacting with Jesus, whereas 5:28–29 describes a future resurrection. Van der Watt, "New Look at 5:25–9," 71–86. However, his view is not supported by context and is unjustified in light of John's assertion that all people interact with the light (1:3–4, 9–10).

42. Also known as "already-not yet." This term is adopted from Bennema, *Power*, 121 fn. 63; I. Howard Marshall, *New Testament Theology: Many Witnesses, One Gospel* (Downers Grove, IL: InterVarsity, 2004), 524.

43. John repeatedly states that a proper response to the word of Jesus/God indicates that one belongs to Jesus/God. See 3:34; 6:63; 8:43, 47; 10:3, 16, 27; 12:47–50; 17:6–14. Note the verb μεταβέβηκεν in the perfect tense in 5:24 indicating the ongoing effect of having life, μεταβέβηκεν ἐκ τοῦ θανάτου εἰς τὴν ζωήν.

44. In 5:24 and 5:39–40, Jesus equates the efficacy of his words with the Scriptures in their life-giving potency. In 5:24, the single article controlling the two present tense participles, ὁ τὸν λόγον μου ἀκούων καὶ πιστεύων…ἔχει ζωὴν αἰώνιον, stresses the close relationship between continuous hearing and believing of Jesus' words with eternal life. Smyth notes that a single article with two nouns connected with a καί indicates a single notion. Smyth, *Grammar*, §1143; Wallace, *Grammar*, 270–90.

45. For "Son of Man" in John, see Richard Bauckham, "Messianism According to the Gospel of John," in *Challenging Perspectives on the Gospel of John*, ed. John Lierman (Tübingen: Mohr Siebeck, 2006), 34–68; André Feuillet, "Le triomphe du fils de l'homme," in *La venue du messie: messianisme et eschatologie* (Desclée de Brouwer, 1962), 149–71; Larry W. Hurtado and Paul Owen, *'Who Is This Son of Man?': The Latest Scholarship on a Puzzling Expression of the Historical Jesus*, LNTS 390 (London; New York: T & T Clark, 2011); Benjamin E. Reynolds, *The Apocalyptic Son of Man in the Gospel of John*, WUNT 249 (Tübingen: Mohr Siebeck, 2008); Schnackenburg, *John*, 2:114.

46. *Pace*, Van der Watt who critiques eschatological resurrection and maintains that "in the person of Jesus it seems evident that the resurrection is already there." Van der Watt, *Family*, 214 fn. 235.

47. So Peder Borgen, *Bread from Heaven: An Exegetical Study of the Concept of Manna in the Gospel of John and the Writings of Philo*, NovTSup 10 (Leiden: E. J. Brill, 1965), 168 fn. 2; Filson, "Gospel of Life," 113. Cf., Dodd, *Interpretation*, 148.

48. Thompson, *John*, 130.

49. Thompson, *John*, 130.

50. Similarly, Coloe, *Dwelling*, 100.

51. Van der Watt, *Family*, 212.

52. Neyrey, *John in Cultural*, 234–35. Also see endnote 46 in chapter 1.

53. John's other uses of ἀπόλλυμι refer to food that perishes (6:12, 27), destruction of a nation (11:50), loss of physical life (12:25), and loss of relationships (17:12; 18:9).

54. Cf. Bultmann who rejected a cosmic eschatological judgment and the *parousia* because Jesus' arrival was the *krisis* of "the world" (12:31). However, there seems

to be an indication of an eschatological reunion between Jesus and his disciples in 12:26; 14:2–3, 28. Bultmann, *Theology*, 2:33–40, 56–58; Bultmann, *John*, 167.

55. Brown links God's wrath with God's reaction to Israel's disobedience in the context of Old Testament covenantal language. Thus, the individual who does not believe in Jesus does not receive the gift of life but instead incurs God's judgment. Sherri Brown, "John the Baptist: Witness and Embodiment of the Prologue in the Gospel of John," in *Characters and Characterization in the Gospel of John* (London: Bloomsbury T & T Clark, 2013), 163.

56. Similarly, Clark-Soles, "I Will Raise," 46.

57. Judgment with the meaning of separation also appears in Matthew 13:36–43, 47–50; 22:11–14; 25:1–13, 31–46; Ephesians 5:8–14.

58. Dodd, *Interpretation*, 210.

59. So Neyrey, *John in Cultural*, 227–51.

60. Dodd explains, "[I]nevitably, those who do not respond to His words, but prefer darkness to light, condemn themselves. Hence the word of judgment on the 'Last Day' is no other than the revelation of life and light which Christ gave in his incarnation." Dodd, *Interpretation*, 211.

61. Barrett, *John*, 426–27; Beasley-Murray, *John*, 213; Thompson, *John*, 270–72.

62. Wallace observes that ὁ πιστεύων is a gnomic substantival participle but the progressive sense can be obtained from the meaning of πιστεύω in soteriological contexts. Wallace, *Grammar*, 620–21.

63. Beck rejects Martha as a paradigmatic disciple. However, Martha's confession reiterates the Gospel's purpose statement and incorporates the dominant theme of agency/sending; thus she can be viewed as positive model of discipleship. Beck, *Discipleship*, 100.

64. Bultmann, *Theology*, 2:59.

65. Van der Watt, *Family*, 231–32.

66. The light-darkness dualism is predominantly Johannine, sparsely appearing in other New Testament writings (e.g., Luke 11:35; 2 Corinthians 6:14; Ephesians 5:8–14; 1 Thessalonians 5:4–5; 1 Peter 2:9). Brown, *John*, 515. Light is a reference to Jesus in 1:4, 5, 7, 8, 9; 3:19–21; 8:12; 9:5; 12:35–36, 46. The exceptions are John the Baptist (1:7–8; 5:35) and a symbolic use of the light (9:4–5; 11:9–10).

67. For background to the light-darkness motif, see Ashton, *Understanding*, 389–95; Bultmann, *John*, 7–9, 342 fn. 5; Schnackenburg, *John*, 1:247–49.

68. Bennema writes, "As the light, Jesus brings illuminating revelation that gives life." Bennema, "Johannine Epistemology," 129.

69. Bennema, "Johannine Epistemology," 111–13, citing 124.

70. Bultmann, *John*, 43; Bultmann, "ζάω," 2:871.

71. For exegesis of this verse, see Harris, *John*, 29.

72. Harris notes that since ἡ ζωή and τὸ φῶς are both articular and are joined by ἦν, it is a reciprocating proposition. Harris, *John*, 23.

73. Van der Watt, *Family*, 236.

74. Van der Watt, *Family*, 238–39, 250–56.

75. So Brown, *John*, 344; Bultmann, *John*, 342 fn. 5; Carson, *John*, 338; Harris, *John*, 168; Thompson, *John*, 183; Herman C. Waetjen, *The Gospel of the Beloved Disciple* (London: T & T Clark, 2005), 236. Westcott, however, points to the other two sayings, "water of life" and "bread of life," to argue that all three should be understood with the dual meaning of springing from life and issuing life. Westcott, *John*, 129.

76. So Culpepper, *Anatomy*, 191.

77. Van der Watt seemingly arrives at the same conclusion when he says that these two positions are two sides of the same coin. Van der Watt, *Family*, 249–50, 259.

78. Shin similarly sees ethical overtones in the coupling of "walking" with "darkness" on account of the Jewish understanding of περιπατέω being used to refer to conducting one's life in a certain way. Shin, *Ethics*, 103.

79. Moloney, *John*, 355.

80. Barrett, *John*, 429.

81. Jesus had previously hidden himself to avoid arrest (4:3; 10:39–40) and death (7:1; 8:59; 10:53–54), but in 12:36, he disappears and focuses on his disciples until he reappears in the Garden of Gethsemane to initiate the judgment of "the world" and its ruler (12:31). Dodd, *Interpretation*, 211.

82. The imperfect ἐπίστευον may be durative, which could be used by John to suggest obstinacy to continuous belief in Jesus. In light of the triple use of the present tense in vv. 36, 44, 46, it is plausible to understand the imperfect as John's attempt to expose "the Jews'" refusal to fully commit to Jesus (v. 42). See Friedrich Blass, Albert Debrunner, and Robert Walter Funk, *A Greek Grammar of the New Testament and Other Early Christian Literature* (Chicago: University of Chicago, 1961), §327; Harris, *John*, 237; Schnackenburg, *John*, 3:413.

83. Bultmann, *John*, 42 and Schnackenburg, *John*, 1:244 who also point to the Old Testament for light as part of eschatological salvation in Amos 5:18, 20; Micah 7:8; Habakkuk 3:4; Isaiah 2:5; 9:1; 51:5 (LXX Isaiah 58:8, 10; 60:1–3, 19–20; 61:1); Baruch 5:9.

84. Thompson similarly observes the emphatic promise. Thompson, *John*, 183 fn. 164.

85. See also 4:14; 6:35; 11:25; 12:25. Schnackenburg, *John*, 2:191. It is possible to take the genitive τῆς ζωῆς in 8:12 as a reference to eschatology, since ζωή carries a futuristic component, thus the meaning would refer to arriving at the life/kingdom of light. Beasley-Murray, *John*, 128; Schnackenburg, *John*, 2:191. In addition to the present benefits of walking in the light (e.g., not stumbling), there is an eschatological deliverance from God's final judgment that is promised (e.g., 5:29; 12:48).

86. Schnackenburg, *John*, 1:244.

87. In defense of 8:12–59 as a single unit with sub-units from the events at Sukkot, see Barrett, *John*, 333; Carson, *John*, 337; Ridderbos, *John*, 291; Schnackenburg, *John*, 2:187; Smith, *John*, 178.

88. The ceremony occurred on the first day of Sukkot, whereas Jesus' declaration, "I am the light of the world," is placed after the last day of the feast (7:37).

Thus, Poirier connects 8:12 to the Feast of Dedication in 10:22. See John C. Poirier, "Hanukkah in the Narrative Chronology of the Fourth Gospel," *NTS* 54 (2008): 465–78; Thompson, *John*, 183 fn. 167. Dodd, defends the unity of John 7–8 by appealing to κρυπτῷ in 7:4 and 8:59 which unifies the narrative. Dodd, *Interpretation*, 348, 356.

89. *m. Sukkah IV* 5:2–3. As cited in Yisroel Gornish, *The Mishnah Volume 3: Rosh Hashanah, Yoma, Succah*, ed. Nosson Scherman and Meir Zlotowitz, 4 vols. (Brooklyn, NY: Mesorah Publications, Ltd, 1980). See also, *ABD*, s.v. "Mishnah," 4:871–73. For a study on the background to the light imagery (i.e., primitive Christian, Jewish, or Hellenistic), refer to Barrett, *John*, 335–38; Keener, *John*, 381–87. For Wisdom background to the light imagery, see Schnackenburg, *John*, 1:241–42; Scott, *Sophia*, 119–21; Michael E. Willett, *Wisdom Christology in the Fourth Gospel* (San Francisco, CA: Mellen Research University Press, 1992), 88–95. For a summary of the light-darkness motif in the Old Testament, see Elizabeth Achtemeier, "Jesus Christ, the Light of the Word: The Biblical Understanding of Light and Darkness," *Int* 17 (1963): 439–49.

90. Thompson, *John*, 183. Thompson notes that Jesus enacts the role of the Servant of Isaiah as the light to the nations (Isaiah 42:6; 49:6).

91. Culpepper writes, "They have chosen to live in darkness because they love it (cf. 3:19) . . . they recognize their blindness, and their sin "remains." Culpepper, *Anatomy*, 192. For a psychological interpretation of blindness, see Resseguie, *Strange*, 144.

92. It is noteworthy that the first time the promise to see God is given in John is in the context of believing in Jesus as the light in order to be freed from darkness (12:45) whereas up to that point, only Jesus was privileged to see the Father (1:18; 6:46; 8:38). Following Jesus as the light opens the eyes of the believer to the unseen God in the face of Jesus (12:45; 14:7–11).

93. Shin sees the blind man's bravery to be ridiculed and expelled from the synagogue as proof of his progress in discipleship, which involves moral progress as evident in the blind man's "complete reorientation of one's whole being including values and behavior." Shin, *Ethics*, 120.

94. Köstenberger, *John*, 294. Similarly, Brown, *John*, 375; Carson, *John*, 376–77; Hunt et al., eds., *Character*, 436; Lincoln, *John*, 286–87; Shin, *Ethics*, 118.

95. Barrett, *John*, 365; Beasley-Murray, *John*, 159–60; Brown, *John*, 376; Bultmann, *John*, 339, fn. 3; Köstenberger, *John*, 295; Schnackenburg, *John*, 2.254. The term προσκυνέω is used in John 4:20–24 and 12:20 to refer to the worship of God.

96. Lincoln, *John*, 287.

97. Moloney observed this parallelism. Francis J. Moloney, *Signs and Shadows: Reading John 5–12* (Minneapolis, MN: Fortress, 1996), 128, fn. 44.

98. Barrett notes the value of water due to its scarcity to the ancient desert dweller. Barrett, *John*, 233. Water is also mentioned in 3:5 and 6:35 and the immediate context of each passage contains a reference to life (i.e., 3:16; 6:40). Both of these passages are discussed elsewhere in this book. For additional discussion, see Dale C. Allison, "The Living Water (John 4:10–14; 6:35c, 7:37–39)," *SVTQ* 30 (1986): 143–57.

99. Brown, *John*, 178.

100. Bennema writes that the gift of God is parallel to the gift of living water, which implies that Jesus is the giver at the center of the chiasm. Bennema, *Power*, 182 fn. 81.

101. See Bennema, *Power*, 187. Other suggestions for "water of life" are life/eschatological salvation, cleansing/purification, the spirit, divine Wisdom/teaching, revelation, Jesus, or Jesus' teaching. For different views, see Bennema, *Power*, 183–87. Allison adds God and Torah as options with supporting Jewish texts. Allison, "Living Water," 144–45. Van der Watt, *Family*, 228–35. Bennema, *Power*, 186–87, 195. See also Willett, *Wisdom*, 94; Bennema, *Power*, 185; Bultmann, *John*, 181. For the water metaphor in Jewish literature, see Barrett, *John*, 233–34. Culpepper, *Anatomy*, 194. Brown, *John*, 178–79. Zahn suggests it is Jesus or the Spirit. Theodor Zahn, *Das Evangelium des Johannes*, Kommentar zum Neuen Testament (Leipzig: Diechert, 1921), 237–38; F. J. McCool, "Living Water in John," in *The Bible in Current Catholic Thought: In Honor of M. Gruenthaner*, ed. J. L. McKenzie (New York: Herder & Herder, 1962), 226–33.

102. Brown argues that in John, "Jesus' power over water identifies him with God" and affirms his messianic mission. In the conversation with the Samaritan woman, Brown suggests that Jesus identifies himself with the "I am" of God (v. 26). Sherri Brown, "Water Imagery and the Power and Presence of God in the Gospel of John," 72 no. 3 (2015): 290, 294.

103. Barrett, *John*, 234.

104. Bennema, *Power*, 182 fn. 81; Van der Watt, *Family*, 231–32.

105. For misunderstanding in John, see D. A. Carson, "Understanding Misunderstandings in the Fourth Gospel," *TynBul* 33 (1982): 59–91. Farelly notes that misunderstanding is a reminder that discipleship is a process of growth as the disciples develop as witnesses for Jesus. Farelly, *Disciples*, 179–84, 227.

106. So Bennema, *Power*, 188; Bultmann, *John*, 192; Schnackenburg, *John*, 1:442. Contra Barrett, *John*, 239, 291–92, 342. For discussion on Jesus' use of ἐγώ εἰμι see Brown, *John*, 537; Schnackenburg, *John*, 2:79–89; Thompson, *John*, 156–60. The ἐγώ εἰμι formula is probably derived from the LXX statements of divine announcements in Isaiah 41:1; 43:10, 25; 45:18–19; 46:4; 51:12; 52:6. So Brown, *John*, 533–38; Culy, *Echoes*, 113–17; Lincoln, *John*, 178; Thompson, *John*, 160. Note the linguistic similarity between Isaiah 52:6 (LXX) and John 4:27:
Isaiah 52:6—ὅτι ἐγώ εἰμι αὐτὸς ὁ λαλῶν
John 4:26—ἐγώ εἰμι, ὁ λαλῶν σοι

107. Many scholars see her leaving behind the jar as evidence of satiation with the living water. Beck, *Discipleship*, 75; Bennema, *Power*, 189–90; Carson, *John*, 227; Mary L. Coloe, "The Woman of Samaria: Her Characterization, Narrative, and Theological Significance," in *Characters and Characterization in the Gospel of John*, ed. Christopher W. Skinner (London: Bloomsbury T & T Clark, 2013), 192; Keener, *John*, 621. Others understand this gesture as indicative of her eagerness to inform the villagers of Jesus' presence and identity, which is supported by the urgency in her tone as indicated by the grammar in v. 29, δεῦτε ἴδετε ἄνθρωπον. Haenchen et al., *John*, 1:224; Lincoln, *John*, 179. Or perhaps she intended to return

to Jesus, Beasley-Murray, *John*, 63; J. H. Bernard and A. H. McNeile, *A Critical and Exegetical Commentary on the Gospel According to St. John*, 2 vols., ICC (New York: Charles Scribner & Sons, 1929), 152; Lincoln, *John*, 179. Resseguie suggests that the Samaritan woman understands that the "living water" requires a new jar, herself. Resseguie, *Strange*, 79–80. Bennema supposes that the villagers' confession includes hers. See Bennema, *Power*, 190–91, esp. fn. 123. Her statement to the villagers in the interrogative, μήτι οὗτός ἐστιν ὁ Χριστός, can be viewed positively, for example: "That must be the Messiah at last, perhaps this is the Messiah." Blass et al., *Greek Grammar*, §427.2. See also Beirne, *Women and Men*, 90–91. Cf., Robert Gordon Maccini, *Her Testimony Is True: Women as Witnesses According to John*, JSNTSup 125 (Sheffield: Sheffield Academic Press, 1996), 121. O'Grady and Reinhartz call the Samaritan woman a missionary. Chennattu and Raymond Brown attribute to her an apostolic function as a witness in John. Brown, *Community*, 188; Rekha M. Chennattu, "Les femmes dans la mission de l'église: interprétation de Jean 4," *BLE* 108 no. 3 (2007): 382, 384, 392; John F. O'Grady, *According to John: The Witness of the Beloved Disciple* (New York: Paulist Press, 1999), 25; Adele Reinhartz, "Women in the Johannine Community: An Exercise in Historical Imagination," in *A Feminist Companion to John*, ed. Amy-Jill Levine and Marianne Blickenstaff (London: Sheffield Academic Press, 2003), 21.

108. Beirne, *Women and Men*, 92; Bennema, *Power*, 190–91; Bennema, *Encountering*, 91; Chennattu, "Les femmes," 385; Hylen, *Imperfect*, citing 55. Chennattu recognizes her discipleship efforts when she affirms her as an apostolic witness to the citizens of Sychar. Chennattu, "Les femmes," 392. Note the allusion to 1:39, 46 in the Samaritan woman's invitation to "come and see" (v. 29). So, Maccini, *Her Testimony*, 129–31. Shin insightfully notes that in the story of the Samaritan woman, John aims to moralize his readers by teaching them that following Jesus "requires one to move beyond conventional social and religious borders," which moves the disciples to reconsider the scope of Jesus' mission which extends to the Samaritans. Moreover, part of discipleship is to engage in the mission of Jesus whether in Judaea as illustrated through the pericope about Nicodemus or in Samaria. Shin, *Ethics*, 94–99.

109. For the social stigma related to her marital life, see Barrett, *John*, 235; Bennema, *Power*, 182; Harris, *John*, 92; Thompson, *John*, 102–103. In 4:27, the disciples' amazement that Jesus was speaking to a Samaritan woman is highlighted with the emphatic placement of the imperfect ἐθαύμαζον before ὅτι μετὰ γυναικὸς ἐλάλει. Likewise, the Samaritan woman herself was astounded that Jesus as a Jew would speak to her (v. 9). See Barrett, *John*, 232–33; Keener, *John*, 585. On the impropriety of a private conversation between a man and a woman, see Mishnah: *Pirke Aboth* 1.5; *Qidd* 4.12; Babylonian Talmud: *Ber* 43b; *Erub* 53b; *Kidd* 70a, b; 81a. *ABD*, s.v. "Mishnah," 4:871–73; *ABD*, s.v. "Talmud," 6:310–15.

110. *Pace,* Bultmann who asserts that John views the function of the Samaritan woman "only to bring the Samaritans to Jesus." Bultmann, *John*, 193. For Jewish-Samaritan tension, see Keener, *John*, 587–601.

111. For a description of the water libation ceremony at Sukkot, see *m. Sukkah* 4.1, 9–10. The major commentaries take Sukkot as the setting. See Keener, *John*, 703.

112. Barrett, *John*, 328; Beasley-Murray, *John*, 115–17; Brown, *John*, 320–24; Bultmann, *John*, 304–305; Richard B. Hays, *Echoes of Scripture in the Gospels* (Waco: Baylor University Press, 2016), 314–16; Kee, "Knowing," 260; Keener, *John*, 728–30; Joel Marcus, "Rivers of Living Water from Jesus' Belly John 7:38," *JBL* 117 (1998): 328–30; Moloney, *John*, 252–53; Wai-Yee Ng, *Water Symbolism in John: An Eschatological Interpretation* (New York: Peter Lang, 2001), 75–81; Jeffrey L. Rubenstein, *The History of Sukkot in the Second Temple and Rabbinic Periods*, BJS 302 (Atlanta: Scholars Press, 1995), 90; Van der Watt, *Family*, 234.

113. Baffes, "Christology," 144–50; Barrett, *John*, 328; Bennema, *Power*, 193–95; Thompson, *John*, 175–76; Van der Watt, *Family*, 234.

114. The cause for this disagreement lies in three areas. First, the antecedent of αὐτοῦ in v. 38 is left unspecified, that is, as to whether it is ὁ πιστεύων or ἐμέ. Second, it is unclear if the citation in v. 38, ποταμοὶ ἐκ τῆς κοιλίας αὐτοῦ ῥεύσουσιν ὕδατος ζῶντος, is part of Jesus' words in v. 37 or the narrator's commentary. Third, the citation in v. 38 does not correspond to any particular Old Testament text. Thus, to explain the Old Testament allusion, scholars have relied on texts that portray water flowing either from the eschatological Jerusalem (Ezekiel 47:1–12; Zechariah 12:10; 13:1; 14:8; Joel 3:18) or from the rock in the wilderness that quenched Israel's thirst (Exodus 17:6; Numbers 20:8–11; Psalm 78:16, 20; 105:41; Isaiah 48:21; Nehemiah 9:15, 20; 1 Corinthians 10:4). Moreover, there is no clear Old Testament text that contains the statement "rivers of living water"; nor is there a text that portrays water flowing from an individual. Thus, grammar and the Old Testament texts do not settle the matter with any certainty. See Brown, *John*, 321; Ng, *Water Symbolism*, 79–80. The summary of these three questions of the text is adopted from Thompson, *John*, 175. For a discussion of the grammatical disagreements in the text, see Bennema, *Power*, 192–95; Brown, *John*, 320–24; Ng, *Water Symbolism*, 75–81. The following texts are candidates for the river of water flowing from an individual: Proverbs 13:14, 25; Sirach 24:30–31; 39:6.

115. Bennema rightly discusses the predicament concerning the Spirit's work before and after Jesus' crucifixion in light of 7:39. His conclusion is that the Spirit was not yet active in the same extent/way that he would be after Jesus' crucifixion, but was active in a salvific manner prior to the cross (e.g., 3:5–6; 6:63). *Pace*, Wes Howard-Brook, *Becoming Children of God: John's Gospel and Radical Discipleship* (Maryknoll, NY: Orbis Books, 1994), 325; Schnackenburg, *John*, 2:157.

116. Bennema, *Power*, 195. See also Culpepper, *Anatomy*, 194.

117. Although the descriptions of hostility refer to Jesus, the comment in 7:13 would be gratuitous unless the crowd believed there was danger involved in following Jesus. The threat was real not only to Jesus but also for anyone who publicly associated with him (9:22; 12:42; 20:19).

118. See Borgen's seminal study, *Bread from Heaven*, where he examines John 6 in light of Philo and Jewish midrashim, especially Merkabah mysticism, haggadic and halakhic traditions that may have shaped Johannine thought. Borgen argues for the giving of the law at Sinai as a model for the bread from heaven discourse in John. Borgen, *Bread*, 147–92. Painter in Culpepper's work provides a source-critical and narrative-critical study of John 6 in light of the Synoptic accounts. John Painter,

"Jesus and the Quest for Eternal Life," in *Critical Readings of John 6*, ed. R. Alan Culpepper (Leiden: Brill, 1997), 61–94. Ford observes feminine aspects of God's redemption and nourishment of his people through the image of Wisdom's feast in John 6. Ford argues that John 6:56 refers to lactation, a scene in which God/Christ feeds "his children from his breasts." Ford relies on the Hellenistic texts concerning Wisdom as the nurturing mother and on the cult of Isis for her interpretation of John 6. Ford, *Redeemer-Friend*, 124–35, citing 133. For eucharistic implications, see Maarten J. J. Menken, "John 6:51c–58: Eucharist or Christology," in *Critical Readings of John 6*, ed. R. Alan Culpepper (Leiden: Brill, 1997), 183 fn. 3; P. J. Temple, "The Eucharist in St. John 6," *CBQ* 9 (1947): 442–52; Moloney, *John*, 207, 223–24. McGrath critiques the eucharistic interpretation, arguing that the focus of John 6 is that Jesus is the bread of life not the Christian Eucharist. James F. McGrath, *John's Apologetic Christology: Legitimation and Development in Johannine Christology*, SNTSMS 111 (Cambridge: Cambridge University Press, 2001), 172–82. For a critique of the eucharistic view but with allowance for an allusion to the early church practice of the sacrament, see Paul N. Anderson, *The Christology of the Fourth Gospel: Its Unity and Disunity in the Light of John 6*, WUNT 2.78 (Tübingen: Mohr, 1996), 110–36, 254; Barrett, *John*, 284, 297; Beasley-Murray, *John*, 95; Culpepper, *Anatomy*, 197; James D. G. Dunn, "John VI—A Eucharistic Discourse?," *NTS* 17 (1971): 328–38; Feuillet, *Études*, 47–129; Painter, "Eternal Life," 88; Dorothy A. Lee, *The Symbolic Narratives of the Fourth Gospel: The Interplay of Form and Meaning*, JSNTSup 95 (Sheffield: JSOT Press, 1994), 152; Menken, "John 6:51c–58," 183–204; Thompson, *John*, 149. Cf., Bauckham and Bennema who reject eucharistic overtones, Bauckham, *Glory*, 18; Bennema, *Power*, 200 fn. 171.

119. Contra Miroslav Volf, Trozzo perceptively notes that the feeding of the 5,000 is not about Jesus' compassion but about his divine identity and his unity with God. According to Trozzo, this unity with God forms the foundation of Johannine ethics. Trozzo, *Ethics*, 88–96; Miroslav Volf, "Johannine Dualism and Contemporary Pluralism," in *The Gospel of John and Christian Theology*, ed. Richard Bauckham and Carl Mosser (Grand Rapids, MI: Eerdmans, 2008), 41.

120. Bennema understands the bread of life as Jesus' personification of Wisdom incarnate who came down from heaven to offer eternal life. Bennema, *Power*, 196–208. Similarly, Feuillet, *Études*, 72–99.

121. Painter suggests that the association of Judas with the twelve (v. 71) casts a shadow on the loyalty of the twelve (vv. 67, 70) and Peter's confession (vv. 68–69). However, John is not contrasting Judas with the twelve or with Peter. He contrasts the disciples who walked away with the faithful twelve through the imagery of walking with Jesus (vv. 66–68) and believing in Jesus (vv. 64, 69). Moreover, Judas was previously included with the faithless defectors (v. 64), thus the contrast is best seen as the defectors and Judas versus Peter with the remaining ten disciples. Painter, "Eternal Life," 90–91. Note the present tense of πιστεύω which stresses Jesus' call to ongoing discipleship in 6:29, 35, 36, 40, 47, 64 and ὁ τρώγων 6:57.

122. The verbs φαγεῖν (vv. 23, 26, 39, 49, 50, 51, 52, 53, 58) and τρώγω (vv. 54, 56, 57, 58) are used interchangeably. Menken, "John 6:51c–58," 196. Painter similarly sees the theme of discipleship in these images. Painter, "Eternal Life," 88, 93.

123. Van der Watt, *Family*, 217–20.

124. Feuillet, *Études*, 48.

125. Van der Watt, *Family*, 222–23.

126. Lee, *Symbolic*, 127.

127. Bennema, *Power*, 200–202; Menken, "John 6:51c–58," 194.

128. Harris sees διά in κἀγὼ ζῶ διὰ τὸν πατέρα as affirming the cause/source of Jesus' life being the Father. Harris, *John*, 142. Also, Barrett, *John*, 300; Beasley-Murray, *John*, 95; Brown, *John*, 283. Cf. Westcott who takes the Father as the object of Jesus' life. Westcott, *John*, 108.

129. There are two primary interpretations of σάρξ in 6:63, anthropological or Christological. For Christological, see Bennema, *Power*, 202–4; Schnackenburg, *John*, 2:71–72. For anthropological, see Beasley-Murray, *John*, 96; Brown, *John*, 299–300; Harris, *John*, 146; Moloney, *John*, 231; Udo Schnelle, *Das Evangelium nach Johannes* (Leipzig: Evangelische Verlagsanstalt, 1998), 139; Thompson, *John*, 162; Westcott, *John*, 109. For the ambiguous view of σάρξ, see Barrett, *John*, 304; Bultmann, *John*, 446.

130. Feuillet, *Études*, 58.

131. The perfect verbs πεπιστεύκαμεν and ἐγνώκαμεν signify existence of knowledge and faith that preceded the current scene and are confidently affirmed in the present. Farelly notes that the perfect tense stresses the stative sense of the disciples' belief and knowledge in the present, in contrast with the defectors who abandon Jesus on account of "ongoing lack of understanding Jesus' teaching." Barrett, *John*, 306; Blass et al., *Greek Grammar*, §342; Farelly, *Disciples*, 47–48.

132. Bennema, *Encountering*, 145–50, 164–70.

133. Resseguie suggests that John presents two Peters: the eager and self-willed (13:36–37; 18:15–18, 25–27) versus the new Peter who follows the will of another, loves the shepherd, and cares for the sheep (21:15–19). However, Resseguie's paradigm of two Peters is problematic, since in the final mention of Peter in 21:20–22, he is portrayed as wavering as he looks back at the Beloved Disciple. Also, by relegating Peter's positive traits to 21:15–19, Resseguie devalues Peter's confession in 6:68–69. Resseguie, *Strange*, 150–55.

134. Chennattu, *Discipleship*, 100.

*Chapter 3*

# Abiding with the Father, Son, and Spirit

In addition to membership in the divine family, John deploys abiding with the Father and the Son through the Spirit as the second key benefit that is conferred on the believer as a means of incentivizing continuous discipleship. The rationale for identifying the theme of abiding as a key benefit of discipleship is the prominent and peculiar meaning of abiding in John. The prominence of the theme of abiding is expressed in the frequent terminology of "abide/abode" (μένω, 40x; μονή, 2x). The motif of abiding is peculiar to John in that it carries a symbolic meaning in reference to the mutual abiding between the Father and the believer, the Son/Jesus and the believer, and the Spirit and the believer.

There are three aspects to abiding in the Gospel. First, according to 14:2–3, abiding is a promise that is experienced by the disciple in the eschatological future. Second, in 14:15–24, John promises that the Father and the Son will abide in the believer through the Spirit in the present time. Third, in 15:1–11, John portrays abiding as a condition that the believer in Jesus must fulfill if she is to experience corollary benefits—fruit, the presence of the Paraclete, peace, joy, answered requests, love, confirmation of being a genuine disciple of Jesus, avoidance of judgment, and the ability to perform great works. Consequently, the Johannine theme of abiding is a present and a future benefit that is a reward for continuous discipleship, and, at the same time, it is also a condition for the disciple of Jesus, which, if fulfilled, yields additional benefits.

Prior to examining the theme of abiding in John, it is necessary to show the Johannine dependence on the Old Testament imagery of God abiding with humans.

# GOD DWELLS WITH HIS PEOPLE

## God's Presence and the Tabernacle

The Johannine allusions to Moses and to the Pentateuch have been observed by many commentators who have demonstrated that it is instructive to read the Gospel in light of the Old Testament.[1] In the Exodus narrative, Moses mediated God's presence (Exodus 13:19–22; 33:7–11; 34:30–35; Numbers 14:14; Deuteronomy 1:30–33); in John, Jesus came as the one who reveals God and provides access to God (John 1:18; 14:6–10).[2] John first establishes the relationship between God and the *Logos* by noting that the *Logos* was with God (1:1). Subsequently, the *Logos* became flesh and dwelt with people (1:14). John employs the verb "dwell" (ἐσκήνωσεν) to describe the dwelling of the incarnate *Logos* with humanity.[3] John links the Gospel to the wilderness narrative with the verb "dwell" (ἐσκήνωσεν, 1:14), which is a cognate of the noun "tabernacle" (σκηνή) that describes God's presence with his people in the tabernacle (e.g., Exodus 25:9; 29:42–46; 40:29–38). Thus, similar to the Old Testament wilderness narrative that identifies the tabernacle as the dwelling place of God with his people, John depicts the incarnation of the *Logos* as God "tabernacling" with people in the person of Jesus.[4]

## Jesus Is the Mediator of the Presence of God

In addition to John's allusion to the presence of God in the Exodus narrative through the imagery of the tabernacle, the mention of glory in John 1:14 further substantiates that Jesus mediates the presence of God in John. God's presence with Israel was not merely symbolized in the pillar of cloud and a pillar of fire (Exodus 13:21–22), the ark (Exodus 25:22), the tent of meeting and the tabernacle (Exodus 33:8–11; 40:34–38), and the temple (2 Chronicles 7:1–3), but God's presence with Israel is also designated as glory (Exodus 29:43–46).[5] In the narrative concerning the inauguration of the Solomonic temple, the Chronicler describes the filling of the temple with God's presence when he writes:

> Now when Solomon had finished praying, fire came down from heaven and consumed the burnt offering and the sacrifices, and the glory of the Lord filled the house. The priests could not enter into the house of the Lord because the glory of the Lord filled the Lord's house. (2 Chronicles 7:1–2)[6]

The presence of God's glory through the pillar and through the fire in the tabernacle and in the temple suggests "these locations as the chosen dwelling places for God."[7]

The relationship between God's presence, glory, and the temple is also affirmed negatively in Ezekiel 10:18–19. There, the prophet describes the departure of the glory of God as symbolic of the withdrawal of his presence from the temple and subsequently from Jerusalem, signifying the removal of God's presence from Israel (Ezekiel 11:23). The prophet reintroduces the discussion concerning the presence of God with a prediction about the return of God's glory (Ezekiel 43:4–7). This prediction is embedded into Ezekiel's eschatological narrative in which he describes the rebuilding of the temple (Ezekiel 40–48).[8] The prophet predicts the dwelling of God with his people through the presence of the Spirit (Ezekiel 36:26–28). Ezekiel's depiction is akin to John's portrayal of the coming of the Spirit: "He abides with you and will be in you" (John 14:17). But the Spirit is merely perpetuating what Jesus represented, which was a continuation of the Old Testament imagery of God's presence with his people. In the Old Testament, the temple functioned as the locus of God's presence and glory and was the venue for the worship of God. In John, Jesus is depicted as sharing and expressing the glory of God (1:14) and the presence of God (14:6–10). Upon Jesus' departure, his presence is continued through the Spirit (14:18–23).

In sum, John's reference to God "tabernacling with humans" (1:14) calls to mind the Old Testament passages describing God's presence with his people. Whereas in the Torah and the prophetic literature God's symbolic presence was temporarily expressed through the pillars of cloud and fire, the ark of the covenant, the tent of meeting, the tabernacle, the temple, and the glory motif, in the Gospel of John, Jesus personifies God's presence (1:14; 14:6–10).[9]

## ABIDING IN THE GOSPEL OF JOHN

John develops the theme of abiding through the verb abide (μένω, 40x) and through the noun "abiding place" (μονή, 2x). The term abide is used in reference to remaining in a location (1:38, 39; 2:12; 4:40; 7:9; 8:35; 10:40; 11:6, 54; 14:25; 19:31), to being alive (12:24, 34; 21:22, 23), and with a symbolic meaning.[10] In the symbolic category, abide refers to the abiding relationship of the Father with the Son (14:10), the abiding of Jesus in the Father's love (15:10), the obligation of believers to abide with(in) Jesus/Jesus' love (6:56; 15:4–10), and the believers' dwelling with God (14:2, 23).[11] It is within this category of symbolic meaning that abiding intersects with the theme of discipleship in 14:2–3, 15–24, and 15:1–11. More specifically, in these three passages, the theme of abiding is presented as a compensatory benefit that is extended to the disciples in light of hostility that they may suffer for their allegiance to Jesus (e.g., 15:18–27; 16:1–2). This benefit is experienced by the disciples both in the present time (14:15–24) and in the eschatological future (14:2–3), as the disciples are challenged to abide in Jesus (15:1–11).[12]

## The Promise of Abiding in the Future

In 14:2–3, John utilizes the noun "abiding places" (μοναί) as a reference to the eschatological fulfillment of Jesus' promise to his disciples of a permanent dwelling place with God. John writes:

> In my Father's house there are many dwelling places (μοναὶ πολλαί). If it were not so, would I have told you that I go to prepare a place for you? And if I go and prepare a place for you, I will come again and will take you to myself, so that where I am, there you may be also.

There are four leading proposals to understanding the use of "abiding places" (μοναί) in 14:2. First, this noun may be referring to the physical rooms in the Jerusalem temple.[13] However, if this is the case then Thomas' question in 14:5 is irrelevant, since he would have known the location of the Jerusalem temple. Second, this passage may be referring to Jesus making an individual feel at home with the Father.[14] Yet this interpretation overlooks the fact that the promise of 14:2 is fulfilled after Jesus' departure, not during the time of Jesus' presence with the disciples on earth (14:3–6, 28; 17:24). Additionally, this view discounts the eschatological meaning of "abiding places" (μοναί) in Second Temple Jewish literature.[15]

The third view is that the noun "abiding places" (μοναί) in 14:2–3 refers to God dwelling relationally with his people in the Christian community.[16] Proponents of this view point to three observations of the text. First, John redefines the temple from the physical structure in Jerusalem to Jesus' body and then to the Johannine community.[17] Second, the phrase "the house of the father" (οἶκον τοῦ πατρός, 2:16) should be distinguished from "the house of my father" (τῇ οἰκίᾳ τοῦ πατρός μου, 14:2) with the former referring to a building, and the latter to a household and to the relationships in God's family because Jesus established the divine family in John 19:26.[18] Third, Mary Coloe, an advocate of this view, observes that:

> The subject of the verb dwell throughout chapter 14 is not the believer, but God. The action, therefore, is not the believers coming to dwell in God's heavenly abode, but the Father, the Paraclete, and Jesus coming to dwell with the believers. It is a "descending" movement from the divine realm to the human, not an "ascending" movement from the human to the divine.[19]

The cumulative effect of these observations has led certain scholars to suggest that in 14:2–3, "many abiding places" (μοναὶ πολλαί) is not a designation for heaven but to relationships within God's family that make up the household of God (8:35).[20] These arguments are discussed below in conjunction with a more satisfying alternative.

A fourth interpretation of 14:2–3 is that John is referring to the eschatological reunion of believers with Jesus in heaven.[21] Within this view, there are two aspects to the meaning of "abode" (μονή) in John 14:2 and 23. In 14:2 "abiding places" refers to a *future* dwelling of the believer with the Father and Jesus in a different locale. In 14:23, John uses "abiding place" to designate the relationship between Jesus and the Father with the believer in the *present*.[22] There are four reasons in defense of this view.

First, the subject of the verb abide (μένω) in John 14 is God/Spirit/Jesus (vv. 10, 17, 25) and that God/Jesus is the subject in the saying, "we will come to him and make an abiding place with him" (πρὸς αὐτὸν ἐλευσόμεθα καὶ μονὴν παρ' αὐτῷ ποιησόμεθα, v. 23). Proponents of the third interpretation stated above affirm this observation; however, they overlook the general tenor of 14:1–6 in that the believers are taken by Jesus to a place that he has prepared for them in his Father's presence.[23] The key question in 14:1–6 is Jesus' departure and how the disciples can follow him. Jesus' words of comfort in vv. 1–6 is that he is going to the Father in order to prepare a place for them *after* his departure and that he will return for them so they could be with him.[24] John emphasizes the language of travel in vv. 1–6 with the following sayings: go, place, I will come again, where I am going, where I am, where I go, I am going to the Father (πορεύομαι, τόπον, πάλιν ἔρχομαι, ὅπου εἰμὶ ἐγώ, ὅπου [ἐγὼ] ὑπάγω, τὴν ὁδόν, ἔρχεται πρὸς τὸν πατέρα, see also v. 12). So, to interpret "many abiding places" (μοναὶ πολλαί) as anything other than dwelling places in God's presence is to miss the flow of thought—that Jesus is going to the Father and he will return for his disciples.[25]

The second reason why John 14:2 is referring to heaven as the locale of the Father's house with many rooms is because of Jesus' reply to Thomas' question in 14:5. Thomas is depicted as saying to Jesus: "We do not know where you are going, how will we know the way?" Jesus does not respond with directions to the physical temple, but rather speaks of himself as the path to the Father. Although the only two other New Testament references to "my Father's house" refer to the Jerusalem temple (Luke 2:49; John 2:16), in John 14:2, if the phrase "my Father's house" also refers to the Jerusalem temple then Thomas' question is nonsensical because Thomas would know the way to the temple. However, since Jesus was speaking of leaving this world and going to the Father, it is reasonable to view heaven as the locale of the Father's house.[26]

Third, contrary to the argument that John redefines the temple from a physical structure to Jesus' body to the community of believers, John's terminology for the "temple" argues against the association of the temple imagery with the community of believers. Mary Coloe understands the term "house" (οἰκία) in 14:2 as "the household of God," which is the community of believers indwelt by the Spirit with many interpersonal relationships (μοναί).[27] She points to 1 Corinthians 3:16–17; 6:19; 2 Corinthians 6:16; and Ephesians 2:21 to support the claim that the temple has been redefined in John as the people of God.[28] However, in all of these passages, the noun "temple" (ναός)—rather than "household" (οἰκία) or the cognate "house" (οἶκος)—is used to explain the Christian community as God's temple. To refer to the *temple* as a building, the New Testament writers use three terms—ἱερόν, οἶκος, and ναός.[29] To refer to Jesus' body as the temple only ναός is used.[30] And the New Testament writers use only ναός to describe the community of believers as the temple of God that is indwelt by the Spirit (1 Corinthians 3:16–17; 6:19; 2 Corinthians 6:16; Ephesians 2:21). Yet John does not use ναός in 14:2; rather he uses οἰκία. Indeed, some New Testament writers use οἶκος, though not οἰκία (1 Timothy 3:15; Hebrews 3:6; 10:21; 1 Peter 2:5; 4:17) to refer to the church as the household of God; but in none of these passages are the notions of indwelling by God/Jesus/Spirit associated with the household of God as the divine family. In considering John's terminology, three words frame the discussion about the temple—ἱερόν, ναός, and οἶκος. The term ἱερόν always refers to the physical temple in John (e.g., 2:14–15; 5:14; 7:14). The noun ναός is used exclusively for Jesus' body (2:19–21). The term οἶκος refers to the physical temple (2:16, 17) and to a house (7:53; 11:20). Additionally, the noun οἰκία refers to the house as a dwelling place (11:31; 12:3), to the members of a household (4:53), and to a household (8:35); but οἰκία does not refer to a temple.[31] In sum, John distinguishes between the temple of God (ἱερόν and οἶκος), Jesus' body (ναός), and a household (οἰκία). Based on the above passages, we can conclude that οἰκία in John 14:2 cannot refer to the "indwelling of the Father, Jesus and the Paraclete with the believer" because New Testament writers use ναός instead of οἶκος/οἰκία to refer to the church as the temple of God that is indwelt by the Spirit.[32] Moreover, as shown above, the New Testament writers do not use οἰκία but only οἶκος to refer to the church as the household of God, but devoid of the notion of the indwelling by God/Jesus/Spirit. Consequently, the term οἰκία in John 14:2 refers to the heavenly abode with God rather than to the Jerusalem temple or to the community of believers indwelt by the Spirit.

The fourth reason to understand 14:2 as referring to a heavenly locale is that the saying "my father's house" and the term "abiding place" (μονή) appear in the Second Temple Jewish literature in reference to the heavenly dwelling place with God. "Father's house" in Philo refers to heaven as a paternal house to which a sojourner returns after this life.[33] In 1 Maccabees 7:38, "abiding place" (μονή) refers to a locale in God's presence.[34] In this passage, the Jewish people pray to God that he would kill their enemies and "not give them an abiding place" (μὴ δῷς αὐτοῖς μονήν). The prayer calls for vengeance, death, remembrance of their mockery, and a plea not to permit them to have a place of abiding. This is a request for permanent cessation of life due to (1) the increasing severity of these petitions and (2) an appeal for God to remember the offenses against the Jewish people and to respond with judgment. This prayer parallels John 3:36, where John uses the verb μένω to describe the presence of God's wrath on the individual who does not believe in the Son and thereby forfeits the gift of eternal life.[35]

First Enoch similarly provides evidence that heaven was the referent for "dwelling places." The contribution from 1 Enoch to the study of John 14:2–3 is conceptual rather than lexical, as the only surviving copies of the passage which refer to "dwelling places" are in Ethiopic rather than Greek.[36] However, there is evidence that the New Testament writers were aware of this composite work (several parts of which were written between the fourth century BCE and the first century CE) because allusions to 1 Enoch appear in the New Testament writings (e.g., 2 Peter 2:4; Jude 1:14–15) and in other early Christian writings.[37] It is possible that the ideas contained in 1 Enoch that refer to the heavenly dwelling places were known to the author of the Gospel of John. First Enoch 39:4–8 reads:

> (4) There I saw other *dwelling places* of the holy ones, and their resting places too. (5) So there my eyes saw their *dwelling places* with the holy angels, and their resting places with the holy ones and they interceded and petitioned and prayed on behalf of the children of the people, and righteousness flowed before them like water, and mercy like dew upon the earth, and thus it is in their midst forever and ever. (6) And in those days my eyes saw the Elect One of righteousness and of faith, and righteousness shall prevail in his days, and the righteous and elect ones shall be without number before him forever and ever. (7) And I saw a *dwelling place* underneath the wings of the Lord of the Spirits; and all the righteous and the elect before him shall be as intense as the light of fire. Their mouth shall be full of blessing; and their lips will praise the name of the Lord of the Spirits, and righteousness before him will have no end; and uprightness before him will not cease. (8) There (underneath his wings) I wanted to *dwell*; and my soul desired that *dwelling place*. Already my portion is there; for thus has it been reserved for me before the Lord of the Spirits (italics mine).[38]

Heaven seems to be the setting of the fourfold use of "dwelling places," and the singular use of "dwell," which further supports the Jewish expectation of dwelling in heaven with God. The above passage appears in the section from 1 Enoch called Similitudes (37–71), in which the author develops the themes of "the coming judgment of the righteous and the wicked; the Messiah, the Son of Man, the Righteous One, and the Elect One; the exposition of additional heavenly secrets; the measuring of Paradise; the resurrection of the righteous; and the punishment of the fallen angels."[39] Thus, the overlap of these themes with John's Gospel warrants the inclusion of 1 Enoch 38:4–8 in support of a celestial and eschatological understanding of John 14:2–3.

The writer of 2 Enoch also discusses heavenly dwelling places. The only surviving manuscripts of 2 Enoch are in Slavonic, and there is no consensus among scholars on its dating, opinions ranging from the first century BCE to the tenth century CE.[40] However, because of the apocalyptic nature of this pseudepigraphal document and the parallel themes of dwelling places as heavenly residences in 1 Enoch 38:4–8 with 2 Enoch 61:2–3 and with John 14:2–3, it is possible that 2 Enoch may serve as a further witness to the use of the equivalent terminology as mentioned also in John.[41] The first half of 2 Enoch (chs. 1–68) primarily consists of eschatological material that "describes how Enoch was taken up to the Lord through the seven heavens and then returned to report to his family what he had learned."[42] It is in this eschatological section of 2 Enoch that the writer mentions houses in the future age. Second Enoch 61:2–3 states:

> That which a person makes request from the LORD for his own soul, in the same manner let him behave toward every living soul, because in the great age many shelters have been prepared for people, very good houses, bad houses without number. Happy is he who enters into the blessed dwellings; and indeed in the bad ones there is no conversion.[43]

As a result of the references to the heavenly place as an abode in God's presence in Philo, 1 Maccabees, 1 Enoch, and 2 Enoch, the term "abiding places" (μοναὶ) in John 14:2 likely refers to dwelling places in heaven that are prepared for the disciples.[44] Jesus' words to his troubled disciples were meant to convey a promise to "prepare for them the universal and permanent possibility of an abiding communion with his Father" in the same locale as Jesus.[45] In light of the repeated present tense command in John 14:1 "to believe," the promise of abiding in vv. 2–3 can be read as a compensatory benefit that is conferred on faithful disciples because it declares to the believers that their relationship with Jesus continues into the eternal future where they will dwell with Jesus and with the Father permanently.[46]

## The Promise of Abiding in the Present

In addition to experiencing the abiding presence of the Father and the Son through the Spirit in the eschatological future, disciples experience that abiding presence is experienced in the present. This means that the term "abiding place" (μονήν, 14:2, 23) bears two different but corresponding referents in

John—in 14:2–3 it refers to the future dwelling with God, and in 14:23 it refers to the abiding relationship between God, Jesus, and the believer by means of the Spirit in a time that precedes the *eschaton*.[47]

John addresses the timing of this promise in 14:18, where he portrays Jesus as promising: "I will not leave you as orphans, I will come to you," and in 14:20, "In that day you will know that I am in my Father and you in me, and I in you." Scholars have explained the timing of this promise in three primary ways. First, some view the saying "in that day" as Jesus' post-resurrection appearance to his disciples; however, this view undermines Jesus' promise not to leave his disciples as orphans in 14:18, which would necessarily occur after his ascension.[48] The second interpretation is that it refers to the *parousia* as supposed by the early church fathers.[49] However, as with the first proposal, the disciples would be orphans in the time between Jesus' ascension and before his *parousia*. Moreover, in 14:19 John states that "the world" will not see Jesus while the disciples will, which contradicts the appearance of Jesus at *parousia* when everyone is expected to see him (e.g., Revelation 1:7).[50]

The third option is to understand the phrase "in that day" as Jesus' coming through the Spirit/Paraclete.[51] The promise of Jesus to return (14:18) was initially fulfilled in Jesus' appearances to his disciples after the resurrection and subsequently through the presence of the Paraclete.[52] In this sense, the Paraclete continues the work of Jesus, the first Paraclete. This interpretation coheres with the references to "in that day" in 16:23 and 16:26, since in both verses the disciples are encouraged to bring their requests directly to God in the name of Jesus, which implies that Jesus is not present with them when they bring their requests to God, since they would otherwise bring their requests directly to Jesus. This understanding leaves open the possibility of a future *parousia* as argued above from 14:2–3, because none of the mentions of "in that day" (14:20; 16:23, 26) prohibit another return of Jesus after the arrival of the Paraclete. Consequently, the three uses of "in that day" can refer to the coming of the Paraclete after Jesus' resurrection, which leaves open the possibility of understanding 14:2–3 as the promise of abiding with Jesus in the future.[53]

Abiding can be designated as triadic abiding in John for Jesus (14:2–3, 20, 23; 15:4; 17:21), the Spirit (14:16–17), and the Father (14:2–3, 23; 17:21) are all presented as abiding with the believer. Concerning Jesus' abiding with the believer, he initially returns to the disciples after the resurrection and subsequently in the form of the Paraclete (14:18–20). The correspondence between the ministries of Jesus and the Paraclete (e.g., knowledge, teaching, guiding, announcing, witnessing), and the description of each (e.g., both come, are sent, are given, hated by "the world") suggests that "since the Paraclete can come only when Jesus departs, the Paraclete is the presence of Jesus when Jesus is absent" (12:26; 14:2–3; 17:24).[54] The promise in 14:16 is that the Paraclete will be with the disciples forever. And according to 14:23, the Father and Jesus are said to abide with the believer. The relational aspect of abiding between the believer, the Father, and the Son is to be experienced through the agency of the Spirit.[55] John previously discussed the theme of God and Jesus dwelling with the believer (1:14; 6:56), but in 14:17–23, the notion of God dwelling with the disciples is amplified in a triadic direction with the Father and the Son dwelling with the believer through the Spirit.

John frames triadic abiding in 14:15–24 to be a relational experience for the disciple by presenting it in the context of love for Jesus and obedience to Jesus' commandments. John establishes this framework through the fourfold pairing of the verbs "love" and "keep" (vv. 15, 21, 23, 24). Each appearance of this pair of verbs communicates the same message—love for Jesus is expressed in the keeping of his commands (vv. 15, 21) and his words (vv. 23, 24). And as Jey J. Kanagaraj notes: "John speaks of love and obedience as one single component in his theology of mutual indwelling (cf. 14.23) and they are presented as the highest mark of Christian life (13.35; 15.12–17)."[56] The zenith manifestation of the link between love and abiding appears in 14:21–23, where Jesus promises to manifest himself to the individual who keeps his commands and who loves him. This special self-manifestation is further defined in v. 23 through Jesus' promise to make an abode jointly with the Father in that individual's life. There is a plausible connection with covenantal overtones between Jesus manifesting himself to his followers as he manifests the glory of God (1:14–17; 14:23) and Moses seeing God's glory (Exodus 33:13, 18).[57] The disciple's participation in this revelation and the abiding of the Father and the Son through the Spirit with the disciple is contingent upon the disciple's demonstration of love through obedience to Jesus' commands (14:23a, 24a).

The pairing of love and abiding appears also in 15:9–10. John writes, "Just as the Father loved me, I also loved you; abide in my love. If you keep my commandments, you will abide in my love, just as I have kept my Father's commandments and abide in his love." The paradigm for fulfilling this command is Jesus' obedience to the Father, which proves that Jesus remains in the Father's love and knows the Father (8:55). In 17:26, John indicates that the Father's love for the Son will be replicated in the Father's love for the disciples, which will result in Jesus' presence with the disciples. The promise of abiding then is inseparable from the requirement of love that the disciples are to manifest to one another (13:34) and toward Jesus (14:15).

In addition to the love between Jesus and the Father functioning paradigmatically for the disciples, John portrays the mutual abiding between the Son and the Father as a model for the abiding between the disciples and the Son and the Father. In 14:10, John identifies Jesus' works as evidence of the Father abiding with the Son. Then in v. 12, Jesus promises his disciples that they will do greater works than he performed. Subsequently, in 14:20 Jesus affirms, "I am in my Father, and you are in me and I am also in you." The reciprocal abiding between Jesus and the Father empowered Jesus to do his works, and the disciples' abiding with Jesus will empower them to perform even greater works (14:12). Thus, these greater works performed by the disciples will confirm that the disciples are experiencing a similar abiding with the Father that was experienced by Jesus with the Father.

John presents abiding as a benefit that is enjoyed by a continuous follower of Jesus both in the present (14:15–24) and in the future (14:2–3).[58] In the present, the Spirit mediates the abiding of the Son and the Father to the disciple. The mutual abiding between the Father and the Son is paradigmatic for the abiding that is promised to the disciple for continuously believing in Jesus (14:1). As Jesus' abiding in the Father was confirmed by his obedience to the Father, so would a disciple's abiding with the Son be confirmed by the disciple's obedience to the Son's teaching. And the longevity of this abiding relationship is addressed by Jesus in his prayer: "Father, I desire that they also, whom You have given Me, be with Me where I am." (17:24).

## The Challenge to and the Benefits of Abiding in Jesus

In 15:1–11, John develops the disciples' abiding in Jesus as a condition that the disciples must fulfill to demonstrate their commitment to Jesus and to experience additional benefits in the context of fruit-bearing (15:2, 4, 5, 8, 16).[59] The disciples will also experience corollary benefits if they fulfill the condition of abiding in Jesus. These benefits are analyzed below.

### The Challenge to Abide in Jesus

In 15:1–11, John reveals five aspects of bearing fruit that relate to abiding and to discipleship. John presents fruit as a benefit (15:5, 8, 16) and as a condition (15:2).

First, the nature of fruit must be defined. What precisely is fruit and how does it manifest itself? In the context of chapter 15, John suggests that fruit manifests itself in relation to Jesus in a variety of ways—love, obedience, participation in mission, and witnessing (e.g., 4:36; 12:24). While some interpreters see love as the main referent for fruit, there is no explicit statement in 15:1–17 that demands that love be equated with fruit.[60] To be sure, one expression of "fruit" is love, and Jesus expects his disciples to follow his model (15:13; 12:24–26)—he becomes the standard against which the disciples are to measure their love.[61] Love is a prominent theme in 15:9–17 in relation to fruit, but the other two occurrences of "fruit" in John appear in the context of mission (4:36; 12:24); therefore, the Johannine notion of fruit can be understood as a general expression of commitment to Jesus with diverse manifestations—love, obedience, participation in mission, and witnessing.[62] It can be summarized that "bearing fruit is simply living the life of a Christian disciple."[63]

The second aspect of fruit-bearing is that it is accomplished by abiding in Jesus. The disciple is not commanded to bear fruit but to remain in Jesus, which will result in fruit (v. 4).[64] John stresses the abiding relationship with Jesus through the following sayings: abide in me (μείνατε ἐν ἐμοί, v. 4); unless it abides in the vine (ἐὰν μὴ μένῃ ἐν τῇ ἀμπέλῳ, v. 4); unless you abide in me (ἐὰν μὴ ἐν ἐμοὶ μένητε, v. 4); the one who abides in me (ὁ μένων ἐν ἐμοί, v. 5); unless one abides in me (ἐὰν μή τις μένῃ ἐν ἐμοί, v. 6); abide in me (μένῃ ἐν ἐμοί, v. 6); if you abide in me (ἐὰν μείνητε ἐν ἐμοί, v. 7); my words abide in you (τὰ ῥήματά μου ἐν ὑμῖν μείνῃ, v. 7); and abide in my love (μείνατε ἐν τῇ ἀγάπῃ τῇ ἐμῇ, v. 9; μενεῖτε ἐν τῇ ἀγάπῃ μου, v. 10). The interplay between the aorist and the present tenses is noteworthy. John begins with the aorist imperative, "remain in me" (μείνατε ἐν ἐμοί, v. 4), to stress the urgency of the disciple's need to remain in Jesus in order to bear fruit, since the branch that does not bear fruit is removed (vv. 2, 6).[65] Then John proceeds from the aorist to the present subjunctive, "remain" (μένητε, vv. 4b, 6), and to the present participle, "the one who remains" (ὁ μένων, v. 5), and thereby stresses the continuous nature of fruit-bearing that characterizes every genuine disciple (v. 8). The repetition of the conditional conjunction with a negative particle, "unless" (ἐὰν μή, vv. 4, 6), further stresses the need for continual abiding of a disciple in Jesus, inasmuch as this determines whether one will produce fruit or fail to produce fruit, and, in effect, whether one will enjoy the benefits of following Jesus or suffer the consequences for ceasing to follow Jesus.[66] John returns to the aorist tense in v. 7 (μείνητε...μείνῃ), and shifts from the third person "anyone" (τις, v. 6) to the second person (ἐὰν μείνητε, v. 7), to reiterate the personal nature of abiding in Jesus, and the urgency of such a relationship in light of the consequences for someone who fails to abide in Jesus. The dependence on Jesus for fruit-bearing is stressed in the repetition of the negative particle (οὐ δύνασθε ποιεῖν οὐδέν, v. 5), which is John's emphatic declaration that a disciple can do "nothing at all" apart from abiding in Jesus.[67]

Third, John associates fruit-bearing with keeping Jesus' words and obeying his commandments, which continues the disciple's abiding in Jesus. The importance of Jesus' words to the relationship with Jesus has been noted before (5:38; 8:31, 37, 51), including in this passage where Jesus' word is the agent of the disciples' cleansing (15:3). In 15:7–8, John reiterates the significance of Jesus' words to abiding with him, which results in answered requests, bearing much fruit, and in affirmation of genuine discipleship. Then, in vv. 9–10, John introduces love and the keeping of Jesus' commands as a necessary trait to abiding in Jesus. John's promise is that the keeping of the commandments will lead to abiding in Jesus' love (future tense, μενεῖτε ἐν τῇ ἀγάπῃ μου, v. 10). John then portrays Jesus as an example of abiding in God's love as expressed in obedience to the Father's commandments (v. 10; 8:55).

Fourth, fruit-bearing glorifies the Father. The importance of the fruit-bearing of the disciples to the Father is evident in the Father's personal involvement in the process. To enhance the productivity of the branches, the vinedresser/Father prunes the productive branches (v. 2) and removes the dead branches (vv. 2, 6).[68] The goal is that the branches "remain attached to the vine, vigorous, healthy, drawing life, and producing fruit."[69] It is noteworthy that it is the Father who is glorified rather than Jesus, even though Jesus is the means through which the fruit is produced. The disciples are engaged in "the work of the Son and remain united to him, [and so] there is only one mission shared by the Son and his disciples. In this one mission the Father is glorified."[70] Thus John features God's involvement in the disciples' continuous fruit-bearing (vv. 2, 8, note the present tense of φέρω), which glorifies the Father (v. 8).

Fifth, lack of fruit-bearing leads to judgment and destruction. John introduces the image of judgment in 15:2 by denoting the fruitless branches that are removed and then, in v. 6, by comparing these branches to the disciples who do not abide in Jesus and are, therefore, cast off, wither, are gathered, are thrown into the fire and burned.[71] In contrast to the fruitless branches, the fruitful branches glorify the Father with much fruit, which is a demonstration of authentic abiding in Jesus and in his love (15:8). To these disciples, John portrays Jesus as declaring that their fruit evidences their abiding in him (v. 5) and in the end, their commitment to abide in Jesus secures them in Jesus' abiding presence (v. 6).

## *The Benefits of Abiding in Jesus*

John enhances his presentation of the need for disciples to abide in Jesus by offering corollary benefits alongside fruit-bearing: (1) the presence of the Paraclete, (2) peace, (3) joy, (4) answered requests, (5) love from Jesus, (6) confirmation of being a disciple of Jesus, (7) escape from judgment, and (8) performance of great works. The last two benefits—escape from judgment and performance of greater works—were examined in chapter 2, consequently they will not be discussed below.

The first two benefits—the presence of the Paraclete/Holy Spirit and peace—appear together and therefore will be treated jointly. John presents the Spirit as granting life (3:5–8; 6:63). Subsequently, the Spirit is promised to the believer in the discussion of the water of life (7:39) and again in the context of abiding (14:16–17, 26; 15:26; 16:7, 13). The Spirit is designated as the "Spirit of truth" (14:17; 15:26; 16:13) and the "Holy Spirit" (14:26).

The general meaning of Paraclete (παράκλητος) carries a legal connotation of an attorney or an advocate (e.g., 1 John 2:1).[72] However, in John, the allusion to Jesus as the former Paraclete and the presentation of the Spirit as the agent who discloses truth implies that "he does not function so much to advocate the disciples' cause before God as to mediate the presence of Jesus to his disciples."[73] Concerning the disciples, the Spirit's role is (1) to be with them forever (14:16–17), (2) to teach them (14:26; 16:14), (3) to remind them about Jesus and his words (14:26), (4) to testify concerning Jesus (15:26), (5) to guide the disciples into the truth (16:13), (6) to glorify Jesus before the disciples (16:14), and (7) to facilitate peace (14:26–27; 16:33; 20:19–23, 26).[74]

John always features the promise of peace in conjunction with the presence of the Spirit/Paraclete. In 14:26, Jesus promises that the Father will send the Holy Spirit in Jesus' name. Then in v. 27, Jesus is portrayed as declaring, "Peace I leave with you," which is immediately followed by the exhortation to his disciples not to let their hearts be troubled or fearful. The Spirit is the mediator of peace, which should quell all anxiety. In 16:33, peace is promised after the prediction of the Paraclete's coming to encourage the disciples not to be disturbed by the tribulation in "the world" because Jesus has overcome "the world" (16:23–27). This passage illustrates John's presentation of certain benefits as a reward for continuous belief in Jesus against the potential opposition from "the world" (16:30–33). The final mention of peace is in 20:19–23, where it is once more juxtaposed with the presence of the Spirit. In this post-resurrection episode, John portrays Jesus as giving the Spirit to the disciples as Jesus charges them to continue his mission, which includes forgiving sins.[75] Here again, peace is in the context of turmoil, for the disciples had locked the doors "for fear of 'the Jews'" (20:19). The benefit of the Spirit given as part of the abiding relationship, on the one hand, yields peace, and on the other, as discussed above, the Spirit is the agent who maintains the abiding relationship in the present era between the Father, the Son, and the disciples.

The third and fourth benefits—joy and answered requests—are portrayed jointly in 14:13–14; 15:7–11; and in 16:20–24. In 15:11, John depicts Jesus as declaring that the reason for his exhortation to abide in him is so that the disciples experience complete joy (3:29; 16:20–24; 17:13). The present subjunctive of the verb of being (εἰμί in the clause ἡ χαρὰ ἡ ἐμὴ ἐν ὑμῖν ᾖ, 15:11) stresses the continual experience of the disciples' joy, which parallels Jesus' experience of joy and joy that will be made full.[76] According to the context, joy is obtained by remaining in Jesus (15:4), producing fruit (15:5, 8), remaining in his love through the keeping of his commands (15:9–10), and experiencing answered requests (15:7). The notion of answered requests, which serves as a motivation for joy, is also mentioned alongside complete joy in 16:20–24. In both passages (15:7; 16:24), the verb "ask" appears in the imperative mood to exhort the disciples to be bold in their requests in order to experience joy through answered requests (15:11; 16:22–24). John also links answered requests with the Father being glorified by the Son as he answers the disciples' requests (14:13–14). In 17:13, Jesus promises complete joy to his disciples even after he is gone, which has eschatological implications because this joy will not be taken from them (16:22).[77] In 17:13, the promise of complete joy is bracketed with the promise of God's protection (17:11, 15), and so this joy is brought to completion with God's personal care of the disciples.

The fifth benefit associated with abiding is love from the Father and Jesus (14:21–24; 15:9–10). John stresses the wholeness of the Father's love for the Son and Jesus' love for the disciples through the constative aorist of "love" (15:9–10).[78] Jesus' love for the disciples finds its origin in the Father's love for the Son (note καθώς...κἀγώ in 15:9) and it reflects the same intensity and the same constancy (3:35; 5:20; 10:17; 14:21–23; 15:9; 17:23, 26).[79] The importance of love to the relationship between Jesus and his followers is observable by the *inclusio* in the discussion of this love in the Farewell Discourse (13:1; 17:26).[80] This love is contingent upon the disciples' love, obedience, and belief in the Son (8:42, 45–46; 14:21–24; 15:10; 16:27). The urgency of the exhortation for the disciples to remain in Jesus' love is expressed in the aorist imperative "to remain" (μείνατε, 15:9); and the condition for remaining in Jesus' love (μείνατε ἐν τῇ ἀγάπῃ τῇ ἐμῇ) is keeping the commandments (14:21; 15:10) in the same manner that Jesus kept his Father's commandments (8:55; 15:10). One of Jesus' commandments is for his disciples to love each other (13:34; 15:12, 17).[81] The result of experiencing God's love is the presence of the Spirit (14:17, 26; 15:26), the Father, and the Son (14:20, 23). This benefit of love, however, is reserved for those who continue in their love for Jesus (14:15, 21–24; 15:10).

The sixth benefit of abiding is the confirmation of genuine discipleship by means of the disciple's fruit-bearing. In 15:8, John writes, "By this my Father is glorified that you bear much fruit (note the present tense of φέρητε) and become my disciples." This verse is the climax of vv. 1–7, since the epexegetical "that" (ἵνα) in v. 8 links the production of fruit with the glory of the Father and with the authenticity of discipleship.[82] John makes "bearing much fruit" emphatic by placing "fruit" and "much" before the verb "bear" (ἵνα καρπὸν πολὺν φέρητε). The closeness between fruit-bearing and discipleship is seen in John's affirmation of the former being the outward sign of the latter.[83] That is to say, "in bearing fruit they show that they are disciples."[84] The promise of demonstrating the genuineness of discipleship echoes the message of 8:31, which affirms a true disciple as someone who remains in Jesus' teaching.

Furthermore, the exhortation for the disciples to love each other can be linked with genuine discipleship (13:34–35; 15:12, 17) as the command to love each other in 13:34–35 appears in the narrative of Judas' betrayal of Jesus and Peter's desire to be in union with Jesus (13:8–38). So, Judas and Peter portray false and true discipleship, respectively. The next appearance of the command to love each other (15:12, 17) is also linked with true discipleship, since the command is in the context of abiding in Jesus and fruit-bearing, which demonstrates true discipleship (15:7–8). Since fruit confirms the Son's love for the Father and the Son's abiding in the Father's love, fruit becomes the confirmation of the disciple's genuine abiding in Jesus.

## Abiding and Discipleship

By way of reminder, the argument of this volume is that John encourages his audiences to continuous discipleship by presenting the theme of abiding as one of the three key benefits of belief in Jesus. The following section focuses on four indicators of John's juxtaposition of the call to discipleship with the benefit of abiding.

First, the promise of abiding with Jesus in the future appears alongside comments regarding Jesus' imminent departure (14:1–3) and remarks regarding defection from following Jesus (16:1–2). In 14:1, the pathos of the passage is the disciples' anxiety concerning Jesus' departure to the Father as observable in John's depiction of Jesus' words of comfort, "Let not your hearts be troubled." John presents Jesus as exhorting the disciples to ongoing belief in him through the dual usage of the verb "believe" in the present tense (πιστεύετε), suggesting continuous commitment to Jesus (see also 14:11–13).[85] At the same time, Jesus' encouragement of his disciples must be seen in light of Jesus' warning against the potential abandonment by his followers (16:1–2). John elsewhere notes the desertion of many other disciples (6:66) and Judas' betrayal (6:70; 13:2, 17–19, 21–31; 18:2–6).[86] The placement of the narrative concerning Judas' betrayal (13:2, 21–30) in the near context of the repeated exhortation for the disciples to believe and abide in Jesus (14:1, 11–12, 15–24; 15:1–11; 16:30–31) accents the importance of believing and abiding to avoid defection. Jesus admonishes that even in the face of potential hostility (14:27; 15:18–27; 16:1–2, 33), the disciples ought to remain loyal to him, inasmuch as in the end Jesus will ultimately see victory over any opposition, and by abiding in Jesus the disciples will experience corollary benefits.

Second, John's repeated use of the verb "believe" in the present tense signals his promotion of continuous belief in Jesus. John deploys "believe" in the present tense as an imperative (14:1, 11), indicative (14:10), participle (14:12), and he also depicts the disciples' affirmation of their belief in Jesus in the present tense (16:30), which, taken altogether, stress the continuous nature of belief that is expected of the disciples who would experience the benefits of abiding in Jesus.[87] John encourages belief beyond the present time by depicting Jesus' teaching as motivation toward the disciples' belief after he is gone (14:29).

Third, the conditional statements throughout the Farewell Discourse (e.g., 15:4, 6, 7, 10) also stress the exhortation to continuous discipleship. These statements feature the conditions of remaining in Jesus (15:4, 6, 7) and in his word (15:10) in the protasis, and the promises of bearing fruit (15:4), protection from judgment (15:6), answered requests (15:7), and love from Jesus (15:10) in the apodosis. These promises further serve to encourage the disciple to abide in Jesus/Jesus' teaching and thereby exhibit true discipleship (e.g., 8:31).

The fourth indicator of John's exhortation toward continuous discipleship is John's depiction of the disciples' response to Jesus' promise of abiding. In the Farewell Discourse, John denotes the disciples' responses to Jesus only infrequently, and in those instances their response is in the form of a question (13:6–9, 24–25, 36–38; 14:5, 8, 22; 16:17–18), with the exception of 16:29–30. In 16:29–30, John features the disciples' unified response to Jesus—"We believe that you came from God," a confession that characterizes Jesus' committed disciples throughout the Gospel (e.g., 6:69; 11:27; 17:8, 25; 20:28). Thus, although John does not immediately narrate the disciples' response after each benefit is presented, John's portrayal of their final words in 16:29–30 indicates a positive belief response to Jesus' teaching presented in the Last Discourse.

## CONCLUSION: ABIDING WITH THE FATHER, SON, AND SPIRIT

This chapter developed the argument that Johannine abiding is a benefit that has both a present and a future dimension. "Abiding" in John refers to the permanency of the "immanence" of the relationship between the disciple and God and Jesus.[88] The present and future abiding presence of God with his people was observed in Jewish writings which affirm the "realized-unrealized" understanding of abiding place(s) (μοναί, μονήν) in John 14:2–3 and 14:23. The promise of God's abiding presence reaches its zenith in eschatology, when Jesus will provide an abiding place for his faithful disciples (14:2–3). Thus, John's presentation of abiding takes on a progressive sense, a journey of the disciple toward the Father's house.[89] Meanwhile, in the present dimension of abiding with the Father and the Son through the Spirit, the disciple is exhorted to abide in Jesus by loving him through obedience to his commands and bearing fruit. Faithful disciples will abide in Jesus and thereby enjoy additional benefits, namely, fruit, the Paraclete, peace, joy, answered requests, love, confirmation of true discipleship, avoidance of judgment, and the ability to perform great works. John offers the promise of abiding with its associated benefits to his intended audiences to encourage them to maintain their commitment to Jesus.

## NOTES

1. See Mary L. Coloe, *God Dwells with Us: Temple Symbolism in the Fourth Gospel* (Collegeville, MN: Liturgical Press, 2001), 123–24; T. F. Glasson, *Moses in the Fourth Gospel*, SBT 40 (Naperville, IL: A.R. Allenson, 1963); Stan Harstine, *Moses as a Character in the Fourth Gospel: A Study of Ancient Reading Techniques*, JSNTSup 229 (London: Sheffield Academic Press, 2002); McGrath, *Apologetic Christology*, 149–95; Meeks, *Prophet-King*; Claus Westermann, *The Gospel of John in the Light of the Old Testament* (Peabody, MA: Hendrickson, 1998), 76–77.

2. Marshall contends that Jesus is to be understood primarily not as a revealer or mythological divine figure but as a "counterpart to Moses (Jn 1:17) who establishes the new community." Boismard calls Jesus the "new Moses" due to the parallelism of fear and preparation of a place between Deuteronomy 1:29–33 and John 14:1–3. Ashton also argues that Jesus replaces Moses. Ashton, *Origins*; Boismard, "L'évolution," 520–21; Marshall, *Theology*, 512–13.

3. The Hebrew noun מִשְׁכָּן behind ἐσκήνωσεν, appears 139x in the Hebrew Bible and in 136 occurrences (exceptions are Numbers 16:24, 27; Isaiah 22:16) refers to the abode of YHWH (σκηνή in the LXX). McHugh explains that John is intentional in employing the cognate ἐσκήνωσεν in 1:14 because it alludes back to Exodus 25:9 where σκηνή is used for the first time to refer to God's place of abode with his people. McHugh, *John 1–4*, 55–56.

4. Coloe also translates ἐσκήνωσεν the "tabernacling presence of God's glory." Coloe, *God Dwells*, 11. For parallelism between John 1:14–18 and Exodus 33–34, see Craig S. Keener, "'We Beheld His Glory!' (John 1:14)," in *John, Jesus, and History, Volume 2: Aspects of Historicity in the Fourth Gospel*, ed. Paul N. Anderson, Felix Just, and Tom Thatcher (Atlanta: SBL Press, 2009), 24.

5. The tannaitic (70–250 CE) and amoraic (250–550 CE) midrashim develop the concept of the cloud representing divine protection and intimacy. Rubenstein, *Sukkot*, 301; *NIDB*, s.v. "Midrash."

6. See also Exodus 24:16–17; 40:34–35; Leviticus 9:23–24; 1 Kings 8:10–11; 1 Chronicles 21:26. Josephus notes that when the temple was dedicated, the aroma of the sacrifices was carried away into the distance and this was perceived as God's presence and dwelling with his people (*Ant.* 8.102).

7. Mary B. Spaulding, *Commemorative Identities: Jewish Social Memory and the Johannine Feast of Booths*, LNTS (London: T & T Clark, 2009), 139.

8. Coloe, *God Dwells*, 47.

9. Akala argues that John draws the readers into a Son-Father relationship through symbolic imagery. Thus, all the imagery in the prologue (i.e., tabernacle, the temple) culminates in Jesus as he represents God's glory and faithfulness as part of his mission to make God known. Akala, *Son-Father*, 137–39.

10. Symbolically, μένω refers to the Spirit abiding on Jesus (1:32–33) and with(in) the disciples (14:17), the presence of God's wrath (3:36), the word of God/Jesus inhabiting an individual (5:38; 8:31), the spiritual food that results in eternal life (6:27), sin that remains (9:41), abiding in darkness (12:46), and the permanency of the disciples' fruit (15:16). Lee suggests that the literal uses of μένω carry metaphorical overtones as John is not merely presenting Jesus as staying with his followers but establishing an abiding relationship with them (e.g., 1:38–39; 4:40). Lee, *Hallowed*, 143–45.

11. For studies on abiding in John, see Pascal-Marie Jerumanis, *Réaliser la communion avec Dieu: croire, vivre et demeurer dans l'évangile selon S. Jean*, Études bibliques 32 (Paris: J. Gabalda, 1996), 412–17; Klaus Scholtissek, *In ihm sein und bleiben: die Sprache der Immanenz in den johanneischen Schriften*, Herders biblische Studien Bd 21 (Freiburg; New York: Herder, 2000), 155–56.

12. Lee similarly sees both dimensions in Johannine abiding. Dorothy A. Lee, "Abiding in the Fourth Gospel: A Case-study in Feminist Biblical Theology," *Pacifica* 10 (1997): 128. In addition to the verb μένω, John uses the prepositions ἐν and μετά, the verb εἰμί, and the cardinal ἕν to describe the union of the Son with the believer (14:20; 15:4–5), the union of the Spirit with the believer (14:16), and the intimate relationship of the Father and the Son that is the basis for the intimate relationship between the Father and the Son with the believer (8:29; 10:30, 38; 14:10–11; 16:32; 17:11, 21–23, 26).

13. Keener, *John*, 936.

14. Haenchen et al., *John*, 2:124–28.

15. Further discussion below.

16. Coloe, *God Dwells*, 157–78; Coloe, *Dwelling*, 145–66; Barrett, *John*, 457. Chennattu, *Discipleship*, 103–104; Dodd, *Interpretation*, 395; C. F. D. Moule, "The Meaning of 'Life' in the Gospels and Epistles of St. John: A Study in the Story of Lazarus, John 11:1–44," *Theology* 78 (March 1975): 124; Van der Watt, *Family*, 344–50.

17. Coloe, *God Dwells*, 160–78; Coloe, *Dwelling*, 109–12.

18. Coloe, *God Dwells*, 160–67; Coloe, *Dwelling*, 108–109. Oliver and Van Aarde suggest that God's household is his kingdom with his people. However, this view is not defensible contextually from John 14. Moreover, none of the twenty-three references to kingship in John is juxtaposed with a reference to household or fatherly terminology. W. H. Oliver and A. G. van Aarde, "The Community of Faith as a Dwelling-Place of the Father: βασιλεία τοῦ θεοῦ As Household of God in the Johannine Farewell Discourse(s)," *Neot* 25 no. 2 (1991): 395. Farrelly argues that Mary and the Beloved Disciple represent Christian communities in John 19:26–27. Trozzo affirms the formation of a new spiritual family in this text. Shin sees the church prefigured in the union of Mary and the Beloved Disciple. However, Bennema more convincingly defends the literal meaning of the Beloved Disciple providing care for Mary. Bennema, *Encountering*, 74–75; Farelly, *Disciples*, 135–38; Shin, *Ethics*, 188–89; Trozzo, *Ethics*, 118–19.

19. Coloe, *God Dwells*, citing 163; Coloe, *Dwelling*, 110, 146–48.

20. Coloe maintains a parousian return even though she understands the μοναὶ πολλαί as relationships in the family of God. Coloe, *God Dwells*, 162–63, 174, 177;

Coloe, *Dwelling*, 110–12; 146–48. Van der Watt also sees 14:2–3 as teaching, "close relations within the house or family in which the believers will find themselves. They will really *come home*" (italics original). Van der Watt, *Family*, 347.

21. Moloney, *John*, 394; BDAG, s.v "μονή." Simon views it through a Gnostic eschatological lens. Simon, "Eternal Life," 108.

22. So Lincoln, *John*, 389–90, 395–96. In 14:2–3, Lincoln sees a traditional eschatology of a parousian return; while in 14:23 he sees God and Jesus coming to dwell with believers.

23. Coloe, *God Dwells*, 160–67.

24. For other mentions of going to the Father, see John 12:26; 13:36; 14:6; 16:5, 10, 28; 17:11, 13, 24. Harris, *John*, 255.

25. Similarly, Edward W. Klink, *John*, ed. Clinton E. Arnold, ZECNT (Grand Rapids, MI: Zondervan, 2016), 615, and Schnackenburg, *John*, 2:361; 3:59–62.

26. James McCaffrey, *The House with Many Rooms: The Temple Theme of Jn. 14, 2–3*, Analecta biblica 114 (Roma: Editrice Pontificio Istituto Biblico, 1988), 30–31.

27. Coloe, *God Dwells*, 160–67.

28. Coloe, *God Dwells*, 169–71.

29. E.g., ναός—Matthew 27:51=Mark 15:38=Luke 23:45; οἶκος—Matthew 12:4; ἱερόν—Matthew 4:5.

30. John 2:19–21=Matthew 26:61=27:40=Mark 14:58=15:29.

31. In the rest of the New Testament, οἰκία refers to the members of a household in Matthew 12:25=Mark 3:25–27; Mark 6:4; Acts 17:5; 1 Corinthians 16:15; Philippians 4:22; and to an earthly and heavenly body in 2 Corinthians 5:1; while over 80 uses refer to a physical house. For discussion of οἰκία, see Coloe, *God Dwells*, 161; Robert Gundry, "In My Father's House Are Many *Monai* (John 14:2)," *ZNW* 58 (1967): 71.

32. Coloe, *God Dwells*, 163; Coloe, *Dwelling*, 110.

33. Philo writes: "For so shalt thou be able also to return to thy father's house (εἰς τὸν πατρῷον οἶκον), and be quit of that long endless distress which besets thee in a foreign land." *Somn.* 1.256 (Colson and Whitaker, LCL).

34. First Maccabees 7:38 is the only usage of μονή in the LXX. It reads, "Take vengeance on this man and on his army and let them fall by the sword, remember their blasphemies and do not give them an abiding place" (μὴ δῷς αὐτοῖς μονήν).

35. The concept of a long-term dwelling place is also seen in Josephus's use of μονήν in his description of Jonathan's restoration of his residence in Jerusalem. Josephus writes: "So Jonathan took up his residence (τὴν μονὴν ἐποιεῖτο) in Jerusalem, making various repairs in the city and arranging everything according to his own liking. Thus, he ordered the walls of the city also to be built of square stones in order that they might be more secure against the enemy." Josephus, *Ant.* 13.41 (Thackeray and Marcus, LCL).

36. James H. Charlesworth, ed. *The Old Testament Pseudepigrapha*, 1st ed., 2 vols. (New York: Doubleday, 1983), 6.

37. *NIDB*, s.v. "Enoch, First Book of," 258; *ABD*, s.v. "Enoch, First Book of," 2:508–16. For critical comments on 1 Enoch, see Craig A. Evans, *Ancient Texts for New Testament Studies: A Guide to the Background Literature* (Peabody, MA: Hendrickson, 2005), 29–30. For references to 1 Enoch in early Christian writings,

see Nestle Aland Greek New Testament and Charlesworth, ed. *OT Pseudepigrapha*, 8, 10.

38. Translation from Charlesworth, ed. *OT Pseudepigrapha*, 1:30–31. Charles translates this phrase as "the mansions of the holy and the resting-places of the righteous." The remaining citations of "dwelling place" agree with references in Isaac's account. R. H. Charles and August Dillmann, *The Book of Enoch* (Oxford: Clarendon Press, 1893), 5, 115–17.

39. Charlesworth, ed. *OT Pseudepigrapha*, 5.

40. *ABD*, s.v. "Enoch, Second Book of," 2:520–21; Charlesworth, ed. *OT Pseudepigrapha*, 1:91–221; Evans, *Ancient Texts for New Testament*, 30; *NIDB*, s.v. "Enoch, Second Book of," 261.

41. Keener notes that 2 Enoch may be a commentary on 1 Enoch. Keener, *John*, 935.

42. Charlesworth, ed. *OT Pseudepigrapha*, 1:91.

43. Similarly, 2 Enoch 65:10 refers to future eternal dwelling places as reward for the righteous. The passages reads: "But they will have a great light, a great indestructible light, and paradise, great and incorruptible. For everything corruptible will pass away, and the incorruptible will come into being, and will be the shelter of the eternal residences." Translation from Charlesworth, ed. *OT Pseudepigrapha*, 1:192.

44. So Beasley-Murray, *John*, 249–51; Klink, *John*, 614–15, 659; Lincoln, *John*, 389–90, 395–96; Moloney, *John*, 394; Segovia, *Farewell*, 82 fn. 45; Thompson, *John*, 307–308; Westcott, *John*, 200. Cf. Barrett, who rejects any eschatological significance in 14:2–3, and 23. Barrett, *John*, 456–57, 466.

45. Quoting Moloney, *John*, 394.

46. Similarly, Tolmie, *Farewell*, 203–204.

47. *Pace*, Moloney, who sees the future tenses in 14:23 as promising a future eschatological abiding relationship with the Father, Son, and the believer. Beasley-Murray, *John*, 259–60; Moloney, *John*, 404–405.

48. Barrett, *John*, 464; Beasley-Murray, *John*, 258–59; Farelly, *Disciples*, 72; Lincoln, *John*, 395; Schnackenburg, *John*, 2:430; 3:76–77, 159.

49. Brown, *John*, 645–46. Chennattu critiques the eschatological understanding of 14:23 in favor of the Paraclete mediating God's and Jesus' presence because the eschatological view does not seriously consider the subject of ποιησόμεθα as being the Father and Jesus rather than the disciples who will make a μονήν. However, as the timing is not addressed explicitly in the text, her objection does not seem viable. Chennattu, *Discipleship*, 105–106.

50. Bennema, *Power*, 222–23 fn. 45.

51. Bennema, *Power*, 222–23; Brown, *John*, 645–46; Chennattu, *Discipleship*, 105–106; Haenchen et al., *John*, 2:126–28; Keener, *John*, 2:974; Segovia, *Love*, 154; Tolmie, *Farewell*, 206–10. Bultmann merges the *parousia*, Easter, and the coming of the Paraclete into a single event described in vv. 18–20, but this view does not comport with the promise of the disciples seeing Jesus again. Bultmann, *Theology*, 2:57. Chennattu rightly sees God's dwelling with his people as one of the key principles of the covenant motif that John picks up from the Old Testament. Chennattu, *Discipleship*, 43–44, 61, 83–84, 103–104.

52. Brown, *John*, 645–46. Similarly, Coloe, *God Dwells*, 174–76; Harris, *John*, 261–62, 281; Thompson, *John*, 314–16, esp. fn. 82.

53. Tolmie also allows for both options. Tolmie, *Farewell*, 203–204, 209.

54. Raymond E. Brown, "The Paraclete in the Fourth Gospel," *NTS* 13 (1967): 126–28, citing 128.

55. "The Paraclete will mediate, as the mode of communication, Jesus' presence and life to the believer so that they will 'see', i.e., perceive, Jesus and participate in his life (14.18–19). Thus, we suggest that the indwelling of the believer by the Father and Son (14.23) is (experienced by) the indwelling of the believer by the Paraclete (14.17)." Bennema, *Power*, 222–23. Similarly, Lincoln, *John*, 396.

56. Jey J. Kanagaraj, *'Mysticism' in the Gospel of John: An Inquiry into Its Background*, JSNTSup 158 (Sheffield: Sheffield Academic Press, 1998), 268.

57. Chennattu, *Discipleship*, 107–108.

58. In her extensive discussion of Johannine abiding, Pazdan does not delve into the question of the eschatological fulfillment of this promise. She focuses on the present aspects of abiding as part of the disciple's relationship with Jesus which entails "knowing, loving, seeking, and finding [Jesus]." Pazdan, "Discipleship," citing 308–309, 315, see also 210–36, 315–16.

59. As agreed upon by the majority of commentators, 15:1–17 is a unit that is distinct within the Farewell Discourse because of the repetition of the themes of fruit, love, commandment, and answered requests. John 15:1–17 is further divided into vv. 1–11 (abiding) and vv. 12–17 (friendship). See Barrett, *John*, 470–83; Beasley-Murray, *John*, 223; Brown, *John*, 658–702; Bultmann, *John*, 529–47; Coloe, *Dwelling*, 151; Harris, *John*, 266–75; Lincoln, *John*, 401–14; Thompson, *John*, 322–30. For the relationship between abiding and vine imagery, see J. Becker, *Das Evangelium des Johannes*, 2 vols., ÖTK 4/1–2 (Gütersloh: Gerd Mohn; Würzburg: Echter: 1979–81), 2:482; Bennema, *Power*, 140; Coloe, *Dwelling*, 157; Francis J. Moloney, *Glory not Dishonor: Reading John 13–21* (Minneapolis, MN: Augsburg Fortress, 1998), 56–57; Leon Morris, *The Gospel According to John*, Rev. ed., NICNT (Grand Rapids, MI: Eerdmans, 1995), 592–600. The standard works on John 15 are C. P. Bammel, "Farewell Discourse in Patristic Exegesis," *Neot* 25 no. 2 (1991): 193–207; Rainer Borig, *Der wahre Weinstock: Untersuchungen zu Jo 15, 1–10*, SANT 16 (München: Kösel, 1967); William R. Domeris, "The Farewell Discourse: An Anthropological Perspective," *Neot* 25 no. 2 (1991): 233–50; J. A. Du Rand, "Perspectives on Johannine Discipleship According to the Farewell Discourses," *Neot* 25 no. 2 (1991): 311–25; P. J. Hartin, "Remain in Me (John 15:5): The Foundation of the Ethical and its Consequences in the Farewell Discourses," *Neot* 25 no. 2 (1991): 341–56; Jürgen Heise, *Bleiben: Menein in den johanneischen Schriften* (Tübingen: J. C. B. Mohr (Paul Siebeck), 1967), 80–92; George Johnston, "The Allegory of the Vine: An Exposition of John 15:1–17," *CJT* 3/4 (1957/58): 150–58; Fernando F. Segovia, "The Theology and Provenance of John 15:1–17," *JBL* 101 no. 1 (1982): 115–28; Fernando F. Segovia, "John 15:18–16:4a: A First Addition to the Original Farewell Discourse?," *CBQ* 45 (1983): 210–30; Segovia, *Farewell*; J. C. De Smidt, "A Perspective on John 15:1–8," *Neot* 25 no. 2 (1991): 251–72. For ecclesiological motifs from John 15, see Köstenberger, *Missions*,

164, 169; Schnackenburg, *John*, 3:211–12. For eschatological themes, see Ford, *Redeemer-Friend*, 161. For Christological themes, see Anne Jaubert, "L'image de la vigne (Jean 15)," in *Oikonomia: Heilsgeschichte als Thema der Theologie*, ed. Felix Christ (Hamburg–Bergstedt: Herbert Reich Evang. Verlag GmbH, 1967), 97; Andrew Streett, *The Vine and the Son of Man* (Minneapolis, MN: Fortress, 2014), 219. Chennattu suggests the Old Testament covenant background with Jesus and the disciples being depicted by John as the true Israel and the new vineyard for YHWH. Chennattu, *Discipleship*, 114. For redaction criticism of 15:1–17, see Brown, *John*, 666–67; Schnackenburg, *John*, 3:89–93; Segovia, *Love*, 81–101; Segovia, *Farewell*. For a source-critical study, see Borig, *Der wahre Weinstock*, 19–194. Bultmann suggests Gnostic and Mandean sources. Bultmann, *John*, 530, fns. 3, 4, 5. The following passages have been suggested as background texts to John 15:1–17: Isaiah 5:1–7; 27:2–6; Jeremiah 2:21; 6:9; 8:13; 12:10; Ezekiel 15:1–8; 17:1–10; 19:10–14; Hosea 10:1; Psalm 80; Sirach 24:17–21; 2 Esdras 5:23; 2 Baruch 36–40. Barrett, *John*, 472; Beasley-Murray, *John*, 272; Brown, *John*, 669–70; Carson, *John*, 513; Keener, *John*, 988–93; Köstenberger, *John*, 449–50, fn. 6; Lincoln, *John*, 402; Moloney, *John*, 419; Morris, *John*, 593; Stanislaw Pisarek, "Christ the Son and the Father-Farmer in the Image of the Vine (Jn 15.1–11, 12–17)," in *Testimony and Interpretation: Early Christology in Its Judeo-Hellenistic Milieu: Studies in Honor of Petr Pokorný*, ed. Jiri Mrazek and Jan Roskovec (London; New York: T & T Clark, 2004), 243; Schnackenburg, *John*, 3:104–106; Thompson, *John*, 322–24; Van der Watt, *Family*, 51, fn. 123; Ben Witherington, *John's Wisdom: A Commentary on the Fourth Gospel* (Louisville, KY: Westminster John Knox Press, 1995), 255.

60. For love as the primary fruit, see Brown, *John*, 676; Coloe, *Dwelling*, 162.

61. Segovia lists five love relationships in vv. 9–17: (1) the Father's love for Jesus, (2) Jesus' love for the disciples, (3) Jesus' love for the Father, (4) the disciples' love for Jesus, and (5) the disciples' love for one another. Jesus' love for the disciples becomes the ground for the disciples' love for each other. Segovia, *Love*, 189–92.

62. Schnackenburg similarly notes that "the fruit" should not be restricted to love, but that it should be understood broadly to include "all the fruits of a Christian life lived in close union with Christ and especially of a 'fruitful' community life which bears witness to itself in faith and love." Schnackenburg, *John*, 3:100.

63. Barrett, *John*, 474. Similarly, Kanagaraj who writes: "φέρειν καρπόν... [denotes] all forms of Christian life lived in close communion with Christ." Kanagaraj, *Mysticism*, 268.

64. Thompson, *John*, 325.

65. Harris notes the urgency to remain in Jesus. Harris, *John*, 267.

66. Schnackenburg observes that these linguistic variations are typical in John and accent the same principle of abiding. Schnackenburg, *John*, 3:100.

67. Quoting Harris, *John*, 267.

68. Harris, *John*, 266. Notice the paronomasia between removing (αἴρει) and pruning (καθαίρει). Barrett, *John*, 473; Beasley-Murray, *John*, 268 note (a); Harris, *John*, 266.

69. Thompson, *John*, 324.

70. Brown, *John*, 662.

71. Lee explains that "without adherence to the vine, without pruning and sculpting by the vinedresser, the branches wither and die; they die of isolation and neglect and their only use is as firewood." Lee, "Abiding," 129.

72. *TDNT*, s.v. "παράκλητος," 5:800–14; Smith, *John*, 274; Mark W. G. Stibbe, *John* (Sheffield: JSOT Press, 1993), 152.

73. Quoting Smith, *John*, 274. See also, *TDNT*, s.v. "παράκλητος," 5:800, fn. 1, 813.

74. Beasley-Murray sees no significance in the use of two prepositions in 14:17 in reference to the Spirit being *with* (παρά) and *in* (ἐν) the disciples. Schnackenburg views the two prepositions as a single figure of speech pointing to the "the Spirit's inner presence in individual believers." Beasley-Murray, *John*, 257–58; Schnackenburg, *John*, 3:76.

75. Jesus' greeting of peace to Thomas in 20:26 can perhaps be understood as Jesus' inclusion of Thomas into the same promise of peace and the giving of the Spirit that was extended to the other disciples in vv. 19–23.

76. Harris, *John*, 269.

77. Bultmann, *John*, 505–507, 541. Similarly Schnackenburg, *John*, 3:104.

78. Barrett, *John*, 475.

79. Harris, *John*, 269.

80. Attridge compares the theme of love in John 13–17 to Plato's *Symposium* and Plutarch's *Amatorius*. While there are significant differences between John and the latter two works which focus on erotic love, Attridge suggests there are similarities of characterization, irony, and revelatory quality of each literary piece. For more of the analysis, see Harold W. Attridge, "Plato, Plutarch, and John: Three Symposia about Love," in *Beyond the Gnostic Gospels: Studies Building on the Work of Elaine Pagels*, ed. Elaine H. Pagels, Eduard Iricinschi, Lance Jenott, et al. (Tübingen: Mohr Siebeck, 2013), 367–78.

81. Trozzo persuasively argues that the love command is not to be exclusively exercised within the Johannine community, but is to be extended to the outsiders because God's love for "the world" sent Jesus into "the world," thus the disciples are to "build mutual love for the purpose of an inclusive mission that seeks to meet the world's spiritual and physical needs." Trozzo, *Ethics*, 154–56, 165–76, citing 176. Okure similarly concludes, "Though historically Jesus exercised his mission in Palestine, the scope of this mission is the whole world . . . and its destined audience, 'all flesh.' . . . As Jesus' immediate audience…were challenged to respond to him, so are all peoples of the world challenged to make the same faith response to the same mission of Jesus . . . whether personally proclaimed by him or reported later by his disciples." Teresa Okure, *The Johannine Approach to Mission: A Contextual Study of John 4:1–42*, WUNT 2.31 (Tübingen: J.C.B. Mohr, 1988), 198.

82. Segovia, *Love*, 107.

83. Similarly, Barrett, *John*, 475.

84. Brown, *John*, 662–63.

85. Segovia observes that in 14:1–2, the call to courage and the call to believe are interrelated. The disciples will find comfort if they continue to believe. Segovia, *Farewell*, 81–83. Similarly, Farelly, *Disciples*, 69.

86. Resseguie suggests that the spatial distance between Jesus and his followers as they cease to follow him reflects an inner spiritual distancing from Jesus that reveals apostasy. Resseguie, *Strange*, 95–96. Tolmie sees the reference to "night" as Judas leaves (13:30) with symbolic overtones, indicating that Judas "has become part of the forces of darkness." Tolmie, *Farewell*, 193, citing 200. Similarly, Resseguie, *Strange*, 61.

87. In 14:1, the form of both verbs can be the imperative (Barrett, *John*, 456; Beasley-Murray, *John*, 243 note e; Carson, *John*, 488; Klink, *John*, 613–14; Thompson, *John*, 306) or indicative (Brown, *John*, 618). Contextually, it is appropriate to view both uses of πιστεύετε imperatively since the imperative μὴ ταρασσέσθω precedes πιστεύετε. Nevertheless, the meaning of the verse is not drastically altered with either view—in both cases a call to continuous discipleship is implied.

88. Kanagaraj, *Mysticism*, 264.

89. Kanagaraj, *Mysticism*, 266. Lee similarly links abiding with the homecoming imagery of the disciple into the Father's presence. She points out that Jesus makes his home with people in a human body so that people can find a home with the Father through him. She writes, "he represents, therefore, both God's abiding with believers and believers' abiding with God. Without him, according to John, no such abiding, no sense of home, can exist." Lee, *Hallowed*, citing 149.

*Chapter 4*

# Royal Friendship with Jesus—The Politics of Friendship in the Ancient World

The Johannine call to discipleship promises membership in the divine family and abiding with the Father and the Son through the Spirit as encouragements to persevere in commitment to Jesus. A third major benefit to continuous discipleship is the promise of royal friendship with Jesus. In John 15:15, Jesus says to his disciples, "No longer do I call you slaves. . . . I have called you friends." With this declaration, Jesus invites his disciples into a royal friendship. This friendship results in benefits which are linked to the new status of the disciples. In the Johannine context, the term "friends" (φίλοι) in 15:12–17 can be understood with a royal-political meaning. Consequently, the relationship between Jesus and the disciples can be designated "royal friendship." This chapter will lay the groundwork by showing that classical Greek, Roman, and Hellenistic writings provide a literary context in which the term "friend" (φίλος) bears political overtones, thus supporting royal friendship as a suitable interpretation of 15:12–17.

Prior to investigating friendship as a theme in the ancient Mediterranean political context, I note three reasons why "royal friendship" is a major benefit in John. First, the infrequent designation of Jesus' disciples as his friends in the New Testament in contrast with John devoting an entire paragraph to the same motif spotlights the prominence of friendship in John.[1] Moreover, 15:12–17 is the only passage in the Gospel in which John portrays Jesus as calling his disciples "friends," thus making this passage peculiar *within* John. Second, the strategic placement of 15:12–17 within the Farewell Discourse is observable in the transitional clauses in v. 11, "these things I have said" (ταῦτα λελάληκα) and in v. 17, "these things I command" (ταῦτα ἐντέλλομαι). Third, the command to "love one another" in vv. 12 and 17 functions as an *inclusio* and thereby sets this paragraph apart from the rest of the narrative. Therefore, the peculiarity of friendship to the Gospel and its placement in the

Farewell Discourse warrant a closer evaluation of the meaning of friendship in John, which I argue has royal overtones.

## FRIENDSHIP IN THE ANCIENT MEDITERRANEAN CONTEXT

Multiple proposals have been offered to explain the theme of friendship in John 15:12–17. The prominent interpretations are discussed below, along with their weaknesses, to show that the royal-friendship interpretation advanced here is the most consistent explanation of the passage in its historical and literary context. Johannine friendship has been variously explained as friendship with God, a Greek-fictive relationship, friendship within a household, Father-Son friendship, friendship between and agent and a patron, as *amicitia/clientele*, and as Hellenistic political friendship.

### Friendship with God

Some have observed parallel ideas between John and Jewish sapiential writings, which present Wisdom seeking out her friends, enlightening them, leading them to God, and making her seekers friends with God.[2] The argument is based on parallels between Wisdom in Jewish writings and Jesus being Wisdom incarnate in John who similarly makes the disciples "friends of God."[3] Jesus expresses friendship through his care for the sick and the dying (e.g., Lazarus), through his death for his sheep, and through his meals.[4] In this view, Jesus' example of love and the disciples' continuation of the same quality of love (e.g., 15:12, 17; 21:15–18) form the foundation of Christology and ecclesiology, which result in the "community defined by the gift and demand of friendship with God, Christ, and one another."[5] To be sure, there are parallel themes between Johannine friendship and Jewish sapiential writings, which qualify the Wisdom motif as a candidate for the background of Johannine friendship.[6] However, there are two reasons why friendship with God is not the most fitting model for understanding John 15:12–17.[7] First, the text of John focuses on friendship between *Jesus* and the disciples not between *God* and the disciples. In John, Jesus is continually presented as God's agent (e.g., 3:2, 16–17; 5:36–37; 10:36; 17:8–9) and in 15:16, Jesus continues to function as a mediator between the two parties, particularly in prayer (see also 17:8–9, 20). Jesus' role in praying on behalf of his disciples (15:16) is comparable to Moses, as God's friend, who had direct access to petition God on behalf of Israel (Exodus 33:11, 18; 33:19–34:8).[8] That is, both Moses and Jesus function as mediators between God and humans through prayer, and thus it would be more appropriate to draw a parallel between Moses and Jesus as God's friends. John's declaration, however, is not that Jesus is God's friend, but that the disciples are Jesus' friends.[9]

Second, friendship with God is not a pervasive concept in the Old Testament and Jewish literature.[10] Only Abraham, Levi, and "the righteous" are called friends of God.[11] In the Jewish writings, of Moses it says that God spoke to him face to face as to a friend.[12] While examples of friendship with God do exist in ancient Jewish literature, these examples are too few to serve as a background for John 15:12–17.

## Greek Fictive-Kinship Friendship

Greek fictive-kinship has been suggested as a prism for understanding 15:12–17.[13] In such a relationship, both parties seek the well-being of one another.[14] Scholars point to the themes of sacrificial love and concern for the welfare of the other person in the immediate context of 15:12–17 as evidence of fictive kinship friendship.[15] Their defense rests on Aristotle who discusses friendship in more detail than any other classical writer.[16]

Aristotle understands friendship as a partnership in which friends share life's joys and sorrows, for a true friend is an extension of self.[17] Jürgen Moltmann summarizes the Aristotelian notion of commitment in friendship as follows:

> Friendship is no passing feeling of affection. It combines affection with faithfulness. You can rely upon a friend. A friend remains a friend even in misfortune . . . [faithfulness] has to do not with acting and possessing but with the individual person and with being.[18]

Moreover, for Aristotle, friends should be willing to sacrifice for each other. He writes, "a friend is one who exerts himself to do for the sake of another what he thinks is advantageous to him."[19] Furthermore, "the virtuous man's conduct is often guided by the interests of his friends and of his country, and that he will if necessary lay down his life in their behalf."[20] Seneca similarly affirmed that friendship entailed mutual concern between friends when he wrote:

> I am not your friend unless whatever is at issue concerning you is my concern also. . . . There is no such thing as good or bad fortune for the individual; we live in common. And no one can live happily who . . . transforms everything into a question of his own utility; you must live for your neighbor, if you would live for yourself.[21]

The writings of Aristotle and Seneca indicate that concern for a friend even to the point of death was prevalent in the thinking of ancient writers.[22] Johannine friendship reflects a similar notion of faithfulness, sacrifice, and commitment. John writes, "No one has greater love than this, that someone should lay down his life for his friends" (15:13).

In addition to sacrificial partnership, the notion of the friend as an extension of self is present in John in the themes of sharing of all things and the disciples' participation in Jesus' mission. In 15:15, John depicts Jesus as telling his disciples, "I have called you friends, because the things which I heard from my Father, I made known to you." This aligns with the Aristotelian notion of holding all things in common. Subsequently Jesus declares, "I appointed you to go and bear fruit and your fruit should last, so that if you ask anything from the Father in my name, he will give it to you" (v. 16), a statement that reflects the intimacy between Jesus and the disciples and is akin to the Aristotelian rubric of a friend being an extension of self.

Coupled with the principles of sharing joys and sorrows in friendship is the duty of demonstrating frankness of speech toward a friend. Honesty in conversation was prized as a means of distinguishing a true friend from a false one. First, Hellenistic philosophical schools incorporated teaching on open and frank conversations (παρρησία) in the context of instruction on friendship. Second, during tense political times, παρρησία was seen as possible only among friends.[23] Cicero illustrates this principle in his letter to his friend Atticus:

> I must tell you that what I most badly need at the present time is a confidant—someone with whom I could share all that gives me any anxiety, a wise, affectionate friend to whom I could talk without pretense or evasion or concealment.[24]

Similarly, Plutarch called frankness of speech the "language of friendship," while Seneca wrote, "Speak as boldly with him as with yourself . . . why need I keep back any words in the presence of my friend? Why should I not regard myself as alone when in his company?"[25] Philo also understood frankness (παρρησία) as an essential element in friendship, making the two concepts nearly inseparable when he wrote, "And frankness of speech is akin to friendship. For to whom should a man speak with frankness but to his friend?"[26]

In John, frankness is mentioned nine times but with relevance to our discussion only in two verses (16:25, 29). The remaining passages refer to Jesus' boldness in ministry (7:26; 10:24; 11:14; 18:20) or his lack of boldness (7:4; 11:54), and the crowd's lack of boldness in confessing Jesus as the Christ for the fear of "the Jews" (7:13). The two verses which depict Jesus' frankness in his relationship with his disciples appear in John 16. In 16:25, Jesus promises to speak frankly with his disciples rather than in metaphors, while in 16:29, frankness is attributed to the disciples who affirm Jesus' candid speech. John depicts Jesus' frankness as grounded in the love relationship between the disciples and the Father (16:23, 27).[27]

John also associates open speech with friendship in 15:12–17, even though the term frankness (παρρησία) is not used. In 15:15, John credits Jesus' full revelation of the Father to the disciples as evidence of their transition from slavery to friendship. Thus, the distinguishing mark of their friendship is the "fullness of revelation."[28] This openness in conversation stresses "absolute relational transparency."[29] The ancient Mediterranean custom was for the master to keep his slaves uninformed, whereas the friends of the master were his equals and thus had the right to engage in free conversation.[30] In John, this practice was a privilege that was enjoyed only by Jesus' disciples to the exclusion of others from this special revelation (17:6–9, 26). In the end, the entire Farewell Discourse may be considered to be an example of this open speech between friends, for, as Udo Schnelle opines, "among true friends, it is possible to speak the truth in all candor and thus cultivate friendship, so that the Farewell Discourses themselves function as a kind of friendship maintenance."[31]

John does not simply follow the typical Greco-Roman inclusion of frankness in friendship; rather, he surpasses it. On the one hand, John reverses the Aristotelian logic of entering into friendship in that Jesus reveals himself to the disciples *in order* to make them his friends rather than *because* they had become his friends. John T. Fitzgerald explains:

> In the standard Greco-Roman understanding of friendship, revelation presupposes friendship . . . one might have expected the Johannine Jesus to have said to his disciples, ". . . inasmuch as we are now friends, I shall disclose to you everything that I have heard from the Father." But Jesus in the Fourth Gospel does not do that. . . . Instead, he reverses the standard logic: "I have called you friends because I have made known to you everything that I have heard from my Father" (15:15). Revelation here creates friendship rather than presupposes it. . . . By treating his followers as friends, Jesus makes them precisely that.[32]

So Johannine friendship exceeds the Aristotelian concept of friendship. On the other hand, John also indicates that the disciples became Jesus' friends because they received Jesus' words. John 17:8 states: "For I have given them the words which you gave me, and they have received them." Fernando Segovia suggests that the disciples became friends because they accepted the "whole of Jesus' teaching and revelation as entrusted to him by the Father. In other words, the given status of the disciples in the chain of love, as those loved by Jesus, is due to their own reception and acceptance of Jesus' teaching and revelation."[33] Thus, while Jesus' frankness of speech makes the disciples friends, the disciples' reception of Jesus' frank speech about the Father demonstrates that they belong to Jesus and to the Father (17:6–8).

While certain features of fictive-kinship friendship are present in 15:12–17, there are compelling reasons to choose against it as a lens for Jesus' friendship with his followers. First, fictive-kinship friendship was typically exercised by social peers, but in 15:12–17, there are indications of social disparity between Jesus and his disciples as "friends" as apparent in the language of servants, master, friends, command, obedience, choosing, appointment, and sending, all of which suggest a divergence from the fictive-kinship friendship paradigm.[34] Second, 15:12–17 arguably contains elements of fictive-kinship friendship; however, as will be shown in the next chapter, these elements of relational intimacy that describe Jesus' friendship with his disciples surpass the Greek fictive-kinship model.

### Friendship in the Family Household

Jesus' friendship with his disciples has also been compared to friendship between family members. That is, Jesus "creates an *oikos* [household] of mutual friends who have found each other on the basis of mutual freedom and of kinship relationships."[35] Jesus is part of the household of the Father, and he functions as the mediator who enlarges the Father's household by adding friends into it for the purpose of "the enrichment of the existing familial relations."[36] So friendship in John describes "the intimate relation between Jesus and his own . . . [It] is not ordinary friendship, but friendship with the unique Son. . . . this contributes to the global familial network."[37] Sjef van Tilborg explains:

> A man's friends are part of his *oikos*. They determine the social position of the *oikos* and are determined by it. The greater and more important the *oikos* is, the more numerous and important are the friends; but also, the more important it is to be a friend of the *kyrios* of such an *oikos*. Jn 15,12–17 presupposes imaginarily a powerful *oikos* with a father-*kyrios* who heads a household in which the son plays an important role as mediator between selected friends and the absolute sovereignty of the Father.[38]

Admittedly, the family motif is dominant in the Gospel and John mentions the Father twice in 15:15–16. However, friendship within a household paradigm does not align with John 15:13–15 for three reasons.

First, whereas the above interpretation suggests that the friends in the household are friends of the Father figure, in John, the disciples are made Jesus' friends and are *never* called God's friends. Second, the household explanation assumes the Father of the household is the lord (κύριος) of the house, but in 15:12–17 *Jesus* is called "the lord" (κύριος) not the Father.[39] Thus the household model requires Jesus to be the master of the household with friends, not the Father, and yet in the Gospel of John, Jesus is never presented as having a household, only the Father has a household (8:35; 14:2–3). Consequently, viewing Johannine friendship in 15:12–17 through the lens of the family/household imagery is not consistent with the passage.

Third, the hierarchical statements in 15:14 and 16 (i.e., "do what I command you . . . I chose you and appointed you") necessitate an explanation as to their place within the family dynamic. One can appeal to the lord-slave model and suggest that "friendships could also exist between unequals."[40] However, this explanation still demands that the Father is the lord since he is the head of the household and slaves would be designated as friends in relation to him. However, as stated above, in John 15, Jesus is the lord not the Father who establishes a friendship with his disciples and himself. Thus, a more nuanced understanding of Johannine friendship is warranted that accounts for the relational disparity in v. 14 and v. 16, a disparity that is not considered by the family household model.[41] Admittedly, proponents of this view allow for regal overtones in the friendship relationship, but they ascribe the royal character to God as the Father-king.[42] However, John does not portray God as the Father-king in 15:12–17, yet John repeatedly depicts Jesus as a royal figure.[43]

In sum, while household terminology is present in the context of 15:12–17, the main point of the passage is not that Jesus brings the disciples into the divine family, but that he integrates them into friendship with himself as a benefit of continuous discipleship (e.g., 15:8). Therefore, to view friendship within the family motif minimizes the distinctiveness of the friendship image in John and does not fully integrate the hierarchical and friendship terminology in 15:12–17.

## Father-Son Friendship in John

Some scholars have classified the relationship between Jesus and God as a friendship on account of ancient Greco-Roman ideals of mutuality, unity, and equality.[44] Proponents suppose that since John applies these three traits to the relationship between Jesus and God, John is presenting Jesus as God's friend.[45] By extension, since 15:13–16 contains elements of mutuality, unity, and equality, friendship between Jesus and his disciples mirrors the God-Jesus friendship.[46]

There are two weaknesses in the above interpretation of 15:12–17. First, it lacks lexical support, since John does not use the term friend (φίλος) to describe Jesus' relationship with God or vice versa. Admittedly, the arguments rest on the conceptual background that may suggest an ideal friendship between God and Jesus, but in the passages that are used to support the principles of ideal friendship (i.e., unity, mutuality, and equality), John stresses Jesus' sonship, not friendship with the Father.[47] Thus, the notion of friendship between God and Jesus is overstated.[48]

Second, the assertion that friendship language pervades John overlooks the scarce use of friend in the Gospel (φίλος appears six times, 3:29; 11:1–16; 15:13–16; 20:2).[49] Even if we grant that John develops ideal friendship imagery through the concepts of unity, equality, and mutuality, the image of family is evoked more naturally than friendship due to explicit references to sonship and fatherhood throughout the Gospel. Additionally, the elevation of friendship language results in forcing friendship imagery into certain passages that do not have friendship in the immediate context. For example, 19:12–15 has been interpreted as "the Jews" rejecting "friendship with God" because they choose Caesar. But John never discussed friendship between people and God, only between Jesus and people; thus, it would be more appropriate to suggest that "the Jews" are rejecting friendship with Jesus in favor of Caesar.[50] Similarly, it has been suggested that through the use of frankness (παρρησία) Jesus extended friendship to "the world." But this ignores the natural reading of 18:20–21, which seems to be a reference to Jesus' public teaching in the synagogues and in the temple, which is substantiated by Jesus directing the high priest to ask his listeners about the content of his teaching.[51] Thus, the God-Jesus relationship is not the most fitting paradigm for the Jesus-disciples friendship in 15:12–17.

## Friendship and Commissioning

The language of mission in 15:16 may point to Jesus' commissioning of his disciples as the motivation behind the rhetoric of slavery and friendship.[52] The slave's effectiveness as an agent was dependent on the authority granted to him by the superior to make decisions, a privilege a slave did not have. First, a slave does what is commanded without personal knowledge of the details. Second, a slave does not have the ability to express reciprocal love to his master.[53] Thus, in order to allow the commissioned agent to fulfill his function, intimacy with additional rights and privileges was provided.

It is undeniable that John stresses agency in the Gospel (e.g., 4:38; 13:20; 14:12; 17:18; 20:21) including in 15:16 where John has Jesus saying: "I appointed you to bear fruit." However, 15:16 is the only reference to the motif of agency in the entire pericope of 15:12–17; therefore, to prioritize agency over the other themes is unwarranted. John presents the relationship between Jesus and the disciples as follows: he chose them (6:70; 13:18; 15:16); he was their teacher (1:38, 49; 4:31; 9:2; 11:8; 13:13); the disciples addressed him as lord (13:13–14); there was hierarchy in their relationship

(13:16–17; 15:20); and he called them little children (13:33), which is not merely a term of endearment but simultaneously a term of relational hierarchy. Although there is no explicit reference to Jesus calling his disciples "slaves" or treating them as such, there is hierarchy in their relationship. This hierarchy is reinforced by Jesus' command for the disciples to love one another (15:12, 17) and to bear fruit (15:16). Consequently, we can conclude that "their obedience to his ἐντέλλεσθαι (v. 14) brings out very sharply the fact that this is not at all a friendship between equals. He remains the κύριος."[54] Thus the hierarchical language in 15:12–17 does not merely convey the agency motif, but rather the language of subordination and affection is more appropriately understood as royal friendship and commissioning is a subset of this category.

## Roman *Clientela* and *Amicitia* as Friendship

Roman writings confirm the practice of royal friendship in the ancient Near East, which lend support to the understanding that John 15:12–17 is featuring royal friendship.[55] Both *amicitia* and *clientela* refer to friendship between a superior and an inferior (Cicero, *Amic.* 71–73; Suetonius, *Aug.* 66.4).[56] *Clientela* refers to a relationship between a superior and an inferior in which a superior offered protection in exchange for services or political support from the inferior.[57] There was an element of expected reciprocity in these relationships such as exchange of goods (e.g., food, homes, cities, building projects, hospitality, gifts, and family alliances) for political loyalty, honor, and military support.[58] The ancient practice of political friendships rested on the "assumption that favors will be returned: a man who helps his friend usually does so with the expectation that some return for his favor will be made."[59] This expectation was present in imperial friendships in which client kings were called *amicitiae* (Suetonius, *Aug.* 66.4).[60] Roman emperors had *amicitiae* in their court, allowing them to influence the government.[61] Pliny further illustrates the benefits derived from friendship with the emperor, such as appointment to a priestly office (*Ep.* 10.13) or a praetorship (*Ep.* 10.12). Philo mentions that a "friend of Caesar" would be protected from public insult, both verbal and physical (*Flacc.* 6.40). A man who was a "friend of Caesar," this was a "publicly known and significant fact about him."[62] The prominence of ancient friendship between a ruler and his select group of subjects is observable in the "coins of Herod Agrippa I [which] frequently read 'Philokaisar,' a designation that Philo also gives him (*Flacc.* 6.40)."[63] Additionally, "royal friendship" is also apparent in John 19:12. In this passage, Pilate is faced with a choice either to prefer friendship with Caesar and consign Jesus to the cross or to release Jesus and thereby jeopardize his friendship with Caesar.[64] From this we can deduce that the title "friend of the king"/"friend of Caesar" was used throughout the Roman provinces, which adds credence to the possibility of interpreting 15:12–17 as royal friendship.[65]

## Hellenistic Political Friendship

The Maccabean literature provides additional examples of royal friendships in the ancient world. The relationships between the Ptolemaic, Seleucid, and Jewish rulers as depicted in the Maccabean literature provide a lens for understanding John 15:13–16 as royal friendship between Jesus and his disciples.[66] The writers of 1–4 Maccabees employ "friend" (φίλος, 56 times) and "friendship (φιλία, 20 times) to describe political relationships with mutual benefits to the patron and the client.[67] In contrast to the other writings in the LXX, 1–4 Maccabees have a high concentration of the terms friendship (φιλία) and friend (φίλος); therefore, the following analysis of these terms is limited to the occurrences in the Maccabean writings.[68]

The usage of friend(s) (φίλος/φίλοι) in the Maccabean literature demonstrates that the superior ruler chose his friends and decided to whom he would grant public honors and gifts along with the title "friend of the king."[69] In exchange, the superior expected the loyalty of the inferior. In 1–4 Maccabees, friend(s) (φίλος/φίλοι) refer to rulers of different nations who are friends (1 Maccabees 2:15–22), military personnel in the same unit (2:39; 3:38; 7:8–25; 9:26–28, 39), national alliances (8:17–32; 12:1–12), and inherited political friendships (14:18–22, 38–40; 15:15–22). During the Maccabean rebellion, the officers of Antiochus Epiphanes IV promised to Mattathias and his sons the title "friend of the king," as well as silver, gold, and other gifts in exchange for loyalty to Antiochus (2:15–22). Antiochus IV considered friendship a matter of loyalty either to God or to him, but not both, and in return Antiochus IV promised wealth, title, and political influence (2 Maccabees 7:24; 4 Maccabees 8:5; 12:4–5).

Another instance of royal friendship is apparent in the relationship between Alexander, the son of Antiochus IV, and Jonathan, the son of Mattathias. These two men shared a political friendship in which Alexander appointed Jonathan as the high priest, granted to him the title "friend of the king," gave him a purple robe and a gold crown (1 Maccabees 10:18–20), appointed him as the general and governor of the province (1 Maccabees 10:65), and enrolled him into the first class of the order of friends (1 Maccabees 10:65).[70] In response, Alexander expected military partnership and loyalty from Jonathan (1 Maccabees 10:16, 20, 26).

Friends of the king were appointed as viceroys (1 Maccabees 3:32), vice-regents (1 Maccabees 6:10–14; 2 Maccabees 11:1), chief ministers (2 Maccabees 3:7), and regents (2 Maccabees 4:31); they also received the gifts of a crown, the king's robe, and the king's signet ring (1 Maccabees

6:14–17). When friendship alliances were made at the national level, the benefits included national peace, extradition, and military aid (1 Maccabees 8:17–32; 12:1–12).[71] The friends of the king were elite politicians who exercised significant influence in the affairs of the state, functioned as guardians of the king's son (1 Maccabees 6:14–17), and assisted the king in matters of war and persecution of religious sects (3 Maccabees 7:3–5). The above illustrations from the Maccabean literature indicate that royal friendships existed at the individual and national level, and that royal friendships were characterized by reciprocal obligations and benefits. The benefits included influencing foreign and domestic policies, tangible wealth, upward social mobility, and even the opportunity to influence pedagogically the king's children (1 Maccabees 6:14–17).

The Johannine depiction of friendship incorporates the notion of benefits. For example, John depicts Jesus as integrating his disciples into his circle of the royal friends (15:12–17), which is coupled with promises of dwelling in his Father's residence (14:2–3), additional knowledge (15:15), and answered requests (15:16). Being part of this friendship, the disciples would, in turn, bear fruit (15:16) and keep Jesus' commandments (15:10, 12, 14, 17). Some of the earliest uses of royal friendship language trace back to the successors of Alexander, and John's usage of friendship language in 15:12–17 is akin to the political titles that were applied to the friends of Egyptian kings.[72] Because Hellenistic documents and John 15:12–17 share common features in their portrayal of friendship, these documents are helpful lenses through which to view Johannine friendship as royal friendship.

## CONCLUSION: ROYAL FRIENDSHIP IN THE ANCIENT WORLD

This chapter examined multiple ancient paradigms used by Johannine scholars to investigate Jesus' friendship with his disciples. The royal political friendship paradigm aligns most seamlessly with the language of John 15:12–17 as a possibility for the ancient literary context of this passage. Consequently, the next chapter will argue that Jesus' friendship with his disciples is akin to a political friendship between a royal figure and his subjects.

## NOTES

1. Luke 12:4 is the only other reference to Jesus calling his disciples friends in the New Testament.

2. Scott, *Sophia*, 155–57. In addition to the Jewish sources, there are mentions of friendship with a god in Greek and Roman writings. In these texts, writers invoke friendship with a god to guarantee military victory (Aeschylus, *Sept.* 174), to obtain favor from a god (Iamblichus, *Vit. Pyth.* 10.5), or to share in the divine character (Iamblichus, *Vit. Pyth.* 33.240). Moreover, certain people are free because of friendship with a god (*Disc.* 2.17.29–30; 3.24.60; 4.3.9) and there can be no friend dearer than a god (*Disc.* 2.16.44–45). However, these Greek and Roman sources lack parallel themes with John 15.

3. For parallels between wisdom and Jesus, see Ringe, *Wisdom's Friends*, 46–63. For friendship with God, see Ringe, *Wisdom's Friends*, 1, 3, 62, 67, 72, 83, 93.

4. Ringe, *Wisdom's Friends*, 76–77.

5. Quoting Ringe, *Wisdom's Friends*, 3. For ecclesiology, see Ringe, *Wisdom's Friends*, 81–83. Lee similarly sees Jesus making the disciples friends of God and with each other. Lee, *Hallowed*, 151–52. For soteriological overtones in Johannine friendship through the Paraclete as "the bond of friendship" between Jesus and the disciples, see Bennema, *Power*, 9, 21–22, 62, 114, 117–18, 223–25, 243, 247.

6. Bennema, *Power*, 224–25; Ringe, *Wisdom's Friends*, 69–72, 77–82.

7. Chennattu compares the friendship between Jesus and his disciples to the Old Testament covenant relationship between YHWH and Israel. However, Israel is not designated as YHWH's friend in the Old Testament. Chennattu, *Discipleship*, 117.

8. Keener sees a parallel between Moses in Exodus 33:11 and the disciples since God revealed his glory to Moses and to the disciples through Jesus, the "embodiment of torah in flesh (2 Corinthians 3)." Keener, *John*, 410, 1013.

9. *Pace*, Ringe, *Wisdom's Friends*, 67; Van der Watt, *Family*, 365.

10. For treatment of friendship in the Old Testament and other Jewish literature, see Ringe, *Wisdom's Friends*, 71–74.

11. For Abraham: 2 Chronicles 20:7; Isaiah 41:8; *Jub.* 19:9; *Apoc. Ab.* 10:6; *T. Ab.* 15:12–14; James 2:23. Philo also refers to Abraham as God's friend in *Sacr.* 77; *Abr.* 50, 89, 273; *Sobr.* 55–56. For Levi: *Jub.* 30:18–20. For "the righteous": *Wisdom* 7:14, 27; 8:18.

12. Moses: Exodus 33:11; Numbers 12:8; Deuteronomy 34:10; *Wisdom* 7:27. Philo also refers to Moses as a friend of God in *Mos.* 1.156; *Sacr.* 130; *Ebr.* 94; *Migr.* 45; *Her.* 21; *Somn.* I.193–94, 231–32. In *Wisdom* 7.27–28, the person who seeks Wisdom and acts wisely is called a "friend of God" and is loved by God. Brown focuses on the phrase "loved by God," and appends it to Isaiah 41:8, which states that Abraham is "loved by God." Brown concludes that in John 15 we should see the disciples as beloved of Jesus rather than as his "friends." Brown, *John*, 664. For similarities between Philo *Ebr.* 55–56 and John 15:12–17, see Bernard et al., *John*, 487–88.

13. Bruce J. Malina and Richard L. Rohrbaugh, *Social-Science Commentary on the Gospel of John* (Minneapolis, MN: Fortress, 1998), 235.

14. Malina et al., *Commentary*, 236.

15. Malina et al., *Commentary*, 236. Similarly, Shin concluded against the possibility of a political/royal friendship because the relationship between Jesus and his disciples is one of personal intimacy and mutual trust. But neither of these

characteristics precludes the possibility of royal friendship, as affection was a part of this friendship. Shin, *Ethics*, 187.

16. For studies on classical friendship, see Culy, *Echoes*; John T. Fitzgerald, *Friendship, Flattery, and Frankness of Speech: Studies on Friendship in the New Testament World*, NovTSup 82 (Leiden: Brill, 1996); John T. Fitzgerald, *Greco-Roman Perspectives on Friendship*, RBS 34 (Atlanta: Scholars Press, 1997); David Konstan, *Friendship in the Classical World* (Cambridge: Cambridge University Press, 1997); Johns Varghese, *The Imagery of Love in the Gospel of John* (Rome, Italy: Gregorian & Biblical Press, 2009), 207–77.

17. *Eth. nic.* 8.9.2; 9.4.1; 9.9.1. For more examples, see *Nicomachean Ethics* books eight and nine; *Eudemian Ethics* book seven; and *Politics, Rhetoric*, and *Magna Moralia*. For critical comments on these works, refer to Fitzgerald, *Perspectives on Friendship*, 35, fn.1.

18. Jürgen Moltmann, "Open Friendship: Aristotelian and Christian Concepts of Friendship," in *The Changing Face of Friendship*, ed. Leroy S. Rouner (Notre Dame, IN: University of Notre Dame, 1994), 30–31.

19. Aristotle, *Rhetoric* 1.5.16 (John Henry Freese, LCL).

20. Aristotle, *Eth. nic.* 9.8.9 (Rackham, LCL).

21. Seneca, *Ep.* 48.2 (Gummere, LCL).

22. Diogenes Laertius, *Lives* 10.120; Epictetus, *Disc.* 2.7.3; Lucían, *Tox.* 37; Plato, *Apol.* 28d; *Symp.* 179b; Seneca, *Ep.* 9.10–11.

23. These two points were adopted from Konstan, *Friendship*, 15, 103–105.

24. Cited in Konstan, *Friendship*, 15; Cicero, *Att.* 1.18 (Bailey, LCL).

25. Plutarch, *Flatterer* 5; Seneca, *Ep.* 3.3 (Gummere, LCL).

26. Philo, *Her.* 21 (Colson and Whitaker, LCL).

27. Van der Watt points to παρρησία (16:27) as the expression of God's love for the disciples as evidence for friendship in a household setting. Van der Watt, *Family*, 366.

28. Segovia, *Farewell*, 158–59.

29. Culy, *Echoes*, 154.

30. See Gail. R O'Day, "Jesus as Friend in the Gospel of John," *Int* (April 2004): 157; Rainbow, *Theology*, 285–86. Both O'Day and Rainbow see only fictive-kinship friendship in 15:12–17 without royal overtones. See O'Day, "Jesus as Friend," 144–57.

31. Udo Schnelle, *Theology of the New Testament* (Grand Rapids, MI: Baker, 2009), 739.

32. John T. Fitzgerald, "Christian Friendship: John, Paul, and the Philippians," *Int* (July 2007): 285.

33. Segovia, *Farewell*, 159.

34. For parity in ancient friendship, see Malina et al., *Commentary*, 119, 236.

35. Van Tilborg, *Imaginative*, 116.

36. Van der Watt, *Family*, 365 fn. 1053.

37. Van der Watt, *Family*, 367. For additional discussion on the intersection of friendship with the family motif, see Van Tilborg, *Imaginative*, 154; Van der Watt, *Family*, 362 fn. 1031.

38. Van Tilborg, *Imaginative*, 149. Coloe also understands 15:13–16 as teaching about friendship within the household and she cites Van Tilborg for support. Coloe, *Dwelling*, 162–64.

39. Out of 52 uses of κύριος in John, only three uses (1:23; 12:38 (2x)) refer to God from Isaiah's prophecies, the remaining forty-nine uses refer to Jesus.

40. Quoting Van der Watt, *Family*, 365. For the lord-slave paradigm, see Van der Watt, *Family*, 364–65, 367–69.

41. Van Tilborg points to the feet washing scene and the subsequent command to love in 13:4–38 as illustrative of the household in which Jesus is the hospitable friend who sacrifices for his friends. The overlapping themes of love and laying down one's life in 15:12–17 with 13:4–38 confirm the link between these two passages. Van Tilborg, *Imaginative*, 158–60.

42. Van Tilborg also suggests a regal character to the friendship relationship but he views God as the Father-king. See Van Tilborg, *Imaginative*, 163. Van der Watt similarly affirms God as Father-king. See Van der Watt, *Family*, 378–81, fn. 1123.

43. There is only one text that refers to the "kingdom of God" (3:3–5), and it is discussed in the next chapter.

44. Culy adopts these three ideals from the Greco-Roman writings. Culy, *Echoes*, 33–91, 130, 178–79, especially 49, 84.

45. Culy, *Echoes*, 87–129.

46. Culy, *Echoes*, 152, 165. This argument is linked to the household motif in John 8:34–36 with God, Jesus, slaves, and sons as characters that can parallel the slavery and friendship language in 15:13–16. This language of friendship in John highlights intimacy within a family and "clarif[ies] what a familial relationship should look like." Culy, *Echoes*, 88–95, citing 89. Bennema makes the same connection between 8:34–36 and 15:13–16, observing that Jesus' friends are the children of God. Bennema, *Power*, 224–25.

47. For friendship motifs of mutuality, unity, and equality, see Culy, *Echoes*, 118–24. E.g., John 5:19–29; 10:30; 17:1–26. There is not a single passage that contains the themes of unity, mutuality, and equality between God and Jesus that designates Jesus as God's friend or vice versa. Instead, Jesus is portrayed as calling God his Father 25 times, and of the 120 times that God is called "Father" in John, 80 percent refer to God being the Father of Jesus. *Pace*, Culy, *Echoes*, 118–29.

48. Lamb similarly critiques Culy for "giving undue prominence" to the motif of friendship between Jesus and the Father. David Lamb, "Review of *Echoes of Friendship in the Gospel of John* by Martin Culy," *BTB* 42 no. 1 (2012): 51–52.

49. Culy asserts that "the language of friendship pervades the Gospel from beginning to end and serves as a primary vehicle for characterizing the relationships that are introduced in the Prologue." Culy, *Echoes*, 178–80. I suggest that friendship is one of the three key benefits in John with a peculiar meaning of "royal friendship."

50. Culy, *Echoes*, 169.

51. Culy, *Echoes*, 168–69. Elsewhere Culy suggests that "the pervasive friendship language in the Fourth Gospel may have led to subtle echoes of friendship motif when this term [παρρησία] was used." Culy, *Echoes*, 107 fn. 73.

52. Susan M. Elliott, "John 15:15—Not Slaves but Friends: Slavery and Friendship Imagery and the Clarification of the Disciples' Relationship to Jesus in the Johannine Farewell Discourse," in *Proceedings of the Eastern Great Lakes and Midwest Society of Biblical Literature* (Toronto, 1993), 31–46.
53. Elliott, "John 15:15," 31–46.
54. *TDNT*, s.v. "φιλέω," 9:165.
55. For studies on Roman friendship, see David Braund, *Rome and the Friendly King: The Character of the Client Kingship* (London; New York: Croom Helm; St. Martin's Press, 1984); P. A. Brunt, *The Fall of the Roman Republic and Related Essays* (Oxford: Clarendon Press, 1988); S. N. Eisenstadt and L. Roniger, *Patrons, Clients and Friends: Interpersonal Relations and the Structure of Trust in Society*, Themes in the Social Sciences (Cambridge: Cambridge University Press, 1984); Barbara K. Gold, *Literary Patronage in Greece and Rome* (Chapel Hill, NC: University of North Carolina, 1987); Horst Hutter, *Politics as Friendship: The Origins of Classical Notions of Politics in the Theory and Practice of Friendship* (Waterloo, ON: Wilfrid Laurier University Press, 1978); Konstan, *Friendship*; Fergus Millar, *The Emperor in the Roman World: 31 BC–AD 337* (London: Duckworth, 1977), 110–22; Richard P. Saller, "Patronage and Friendship in Early Imperial Rome: Drawing the Distinction," in *Patronage in Ancient Society*, ed. Andrew Wallace-Hadrill (London; New York: Routledge, 1989), 49–87; E. Wolf, "Kinship, Friendship, and Patron-Client Relations," in *The Social Anthropology of Complex Societies*, ed. Michael Banton (London: Tavistock Publications, 1966), 1–22.
56. Ernst Badian, "Amicitia," in *Brill's New Pauly*, ed. Hubert Cancik, Helmuth Schneider, Manfred Landfester, et al. (Leiden: Brill, 2005). For a bibliography of ancient writers addressing friendship, see Fitzgerald, *Perspectives on Friendship*, 7–11.
57. Konstan, *Friendship*, 136. Additionally, Judge observes that the status of friendship when conferred by the superior on the inferior "implied full conformity with the wishes of the initiator—as Jesus stated when he formulated the terms upon which the disciples would be counted as his friends ('if you do what I command you', John 15:14)." David M. Scholer, ed. *Social Distinctives of the Christians in the First Century: Pivotal Essays by E. A. Judge* (Peabody, MA: Hendrickson, 2008), 167.
58. Peter Garnsey and Richard P. Saller, *The Roman Empire: Economy, Society, and Culture* (Berkeley, CA: University of California Press, 1987), 154; John E. Stambaugh and David L. Balch, *The New Testament in Its Social Environment*, LEC 2 (Philadelphia: Westminster Press, 1986), 63–64. Josephus recounts an incident between Antipater and Jewish residents of Onias who initially resisted Antipater's army, until Antipater showed them a letter from the high priest Hyrcanus who urged these residents to stand down and promised friendship with Julius Caesar in return for military support. *Antiq.* 14.131.
59. Lionel Ignacius Cusack Pearson, *Popular Ethics in Ancient Greece* (Stanford, CA: Stanford University Press, 1962), 136.
60. Suetonius writes that Augustus expected his friends to leave something for him in their wills. Suetonius, *Aug.* 66.4.
61. There is an account of Domitian having righteous friends in his court while Trajan had evil friends in his court. *Scriptores Historiae Augustae, Severus Alexander*

LXV. See also Badian, "Amicitia." At the same time, the emperor could terminate his friendship at any moment as the relationship depended on the whims of the emperor. See Millar, *Emperor*, 111–12. An emperor's displeasure with a friend could result in death (Plutarch, *Mor.* XI). Millar, *Emperor*, 113.

62. Millar, *Emperor*, 116.

63. Helen K. Bond, *Pontius Pilate in History and Interpretation*, SNTSMS 100 (Cambridge: Cambridge University Press, 1998), 190; Brown, *John*, 879.

64. John 19:12 is examined below.

65. Dominique Cuss, *Imperial Cult and Honorary Terms in the New Testament*, Paradosis, Contributions to the History of Early Christian Literature and Theology 23 (Fribourg: University Press, 1974), 169.

66. For a thorough treatment of friends in the Maccabean period, see E. J. Bickerman, *Institutions des Séleucides*, Haut-commissariat de la république française en Syrie et au Liban service des antiquités bibliothèque archéologique et historique XXVI (Paris: P. Geuthner, 1938), 40–50; Ceslas Spicq, *Notes de lexicographie néo-testamentaire*, I, II, + Supplément vols., Orbis biblicus et orientalis 22/1–3 (Fribourg, Suisse; Göttingen: Éditions universitaires; Vandenhoeck & Ruprecht, 1978–1982), 3:940–43; G. Herman, "The 'Friends' of the Early Hellenistic Rulers: Servants or Officials?," *Talanta* 12–13 (1980–1981): 103–49.

67. There is an exception in 4 Maccabees 2:10–13 where φιλία/φίλος refers to relationships between parents and children, a spousal relationship, and affection between friends.

68. The LXX employs φίλος 186 times and φιλία 36 times. The Hebrew equivalent for friend (also translated as "neighbor") is רֵעַ, appearing 193 times in the Hebrew Bible.

69. There are additional passages in the LXX which designate individuals as friends of the king. A review of these additional passages confirms the observations made of friends of the king in the Maccabean literature. That is, φίλος refers to men who functioned as the king's counselors (2 Samuel 15:32–37; 16:15–17:23; 1 Chronicles 27:33; 1 Esdras 8:11, 13, 26; Esther 3:1; 6:9; Daniel 5:23; 6:14; Bel and the Dragon 6:2), to friendship with international rulers (Esther 1:3, 13; 2:18), to public officials (Esther 8:12e LXX), and to friends of King Hezekiah (Proverbs 25:1). In sum, the other LXX passages which refer to friends of the king do not negate the benefits and responsibilities that are associated with friends of the king as depicted in 1–4 Maccabees.

70. Goldstein notes that "friends of the king had the privileges of members of the royal court. They were entitled to wear purple broad-brimmed Macedonian hats and purple robes." Jonathan A. Goldstein, *I Maccabees*, AB 41 (New York: Doubleday, 1976), 232. The same confirmation was made by King Ptolemy on Jonathan when Jonathan brought him silver, gold, clothing, and other gifts as narrated in 1 Maccabees 11:26–33, 57.

71. Goldstein explains two types of Roman treaties: (1) friendship and (2) alliances. In defending these categories, he relies on Silvio Accame, *Il dominio romano in Grecia dalla guerra acaica ad Augusto*, Studi pubblicati dal R. Istituto italiano per la storia antica fasc 4 (Roma: Roma. A. Signorelli, 1946), 48, 54–55; Alfred Heuss,

*Die völkerrechtlichen Grundlagen der römischen Aussenpolitik in republikanischer Zeit*, Klio Beiheft XXXI (Leipzig: Dieterich, 1933), 54, fn. 1; Eugen Täubler, *Imperium romanum* (Leipzig and Berlin: Teubner, 1913), 47, 420–22. For further analysis on the Roman treaties, see Goldstein, *I Maccabees*, 360–65.

72. Deissmann understands the root of the title "friends of Caesar" that appears in John 19:12 as being Ptolemaic. He sees it as being parallel to *amicus Caesaris*. Adolf Deissmann, *Bible Studies: Contributions Chiefly from Papyri and Inscriptions to the History of the Language, the Literature, and the Religion of Hellenistic Judaism and Primitive Christianity* (Edinburgh: T & T Clark, 1901), 168, fn.1. In his 1901 study, Deissmann concluded that φίλος in John 15:15 had the simple meaning of friend. However, in his fourth edition of *Light from the Ancient East* (1922), he rescinded his conclusion and saw John's reference in line with ancient Egyptian usage of royal friendship. Deissmann, *Bible Studies*, 168–69; Deissmann, *Light*, 378, fn. 2.

*Chapter 5*

# Royal Friendship with Jesus—The King and His Subjects in the Gospel of John

This chapter continues the argument from the previous chapter that Jesus' friendship with his disciples should be understood as royal friendship by building upon the established Greco-Roman context for understanding the term "friend" (φίλος) in John 15:13–15 through a royal-political background. In the current chapter, two additional reasons are offered in defense of the royal friendship interpretation. First, there are five Johannine passages that are evaluated (1:49; 3:3–5; 6:14–15; 12:13–15; 18:33–19:21) in order to demonstrate that John presents Jesus as a royal figure. Second, the exegetical study of 15:12–17 demonstrates that John features Jesus as establishing royal friendship with his disciples. This chapter concludes with a focus on the responsibilities and benefits surrounding royal friendship with Jesus. John features royal friendship with Jesus along with its corollary benefits—love, knowledge of the Father, fruit, joy, and answered requests—in order to encourage his audiences to continuous discipleship, even in the face of opposition.

## FRIENDSHIP IN THE NEW TESTAMENT

Prior to examining 15:12–17 grammatically and contextually, it is appropriate to review John's use of friendship language in contrast with the rest of the New Testament to demonstrate John's emphasis on friendship. The noun "friendship" (φιλία) is mentioned once in the New Testament (James 4:4), while "friend" (φίλος) appears twenty-nine times with a wide range of meanings. Φίλος refers to public associates (Luke 14:10), private friends (Luke 14:12; 15:29; Acts 10:24; 19:31; 27:3), neighbors (Luke 11:5, 6, 8; 15:6, 9), military personnel (Luke 7:6), Jesus as a "friend of tax collectors and sinners"

(Matthew 11:19; Luke 7:34), unfaithful friends (Luke 21:16), Christian relationships (3 John 15), and to friends that last beyond this life (Luke 16:9). Additionally, φίλος refers to the friendship between Herod and Pilate (Luke 23:12) and friendship with God (James 2:23). In addition to the nouns φιλία/φίλος, the verb for "love" (φιλέω) is used twenty-five times by New Testament writers with a similar broad range of meanings. Φιλέω refers to the desire for public honor and respect (Matthew 6:5; 23:6; Luke 20:46), familial relationships (Matthew 10:37), Judas' kiss of betrayal (Matthew 26:48=Mark 14:44=Luke 22:47), love for Jesus (1 Corinthians 16:22), believers' love for each other (Titus 3:15), Jesus' love for the church (Revelation 3:19), and the habitual practice of lying (Revelation 22:15).

Luke 12:4 is the only New Testament verse where Jesus calls his disciples friends outside of John 15:12–17. In Luke 12:4–12, Jesus is presented as teaching his disciples not to fear physical death because God cares for them. The passage states that God knows the number of hairs on their head (v. 7) and has greater concern for them than for the sparrows (vv. 6–7). Because the larger context of these two passages makes reference to opposition to Jesus' followers (John 15:18–25; Luke 12:4, 11) and the assistance of the Spirit (John 15:26–27; Luke 12:12), it is possible to understand the term "friends" (φίλοι) as bearing a similar meaning in these two passages.[1] However, John develops the concept of friendship around the themes of hierarchy, obedience, slavery, and mission, all of which are absent from Luke 12:4–12. Thus, John's usage of "my friends" in 15:12–17 is more nuanced, demands closer attention, and aligns more with the meaning of a political friendship than its use in Luke 12:4.

## FRIENDSHIP IN THE GOSPEL OF JOHN

John employs friend (φίλος) six times in four passages (3:29; 11:11; 15:12–17 (3x); 19:12). In 3:29, John the Baptist is a friend of Jesus or his best man (3:29). This friendship is characterized by disparity between John the Baptist and Jesus. For example, John the Baptist is portrayed as confessing, "He must increase, but I must decrease" (3:30); Jesus attracts more disciples than John the Baptist (3:26; 4:1–3); and John the Baptist affirms that he is not the Messiah (3:28; see also 1:20–28, 29–36). In addition to inequality, this first use of "friend" in the Gospel also entails trust, since the best man provides oversight of the wedding.[2] The next use of φίλος is in reference to Lazarus, whom Jesus calls "our friend" (11:11), and who is someone whom Jesus loved (11:3, 36). Jesus' love for Lazarus is characterized by self-sacrifice, since Jesus is willing to put himself in the way of danger for the benefit of his friend (11:8). In 19:12, friend (φίλος) carries political overtones and sheds light on the use of φίλοι in 15:12–17, which is the only other passage with three uses of φίλος.

The verb "love" (φιλέω) appears thirteen times in John and consistently carries the meaning of affection (5:20; 11:3, 36; 12:25; 15:19; 16:27 (2x); 20:2; 21:15, 16, 17 (3x)). The term φιλέω refers to the Father's affection for the Son (5:20); the Father's affection for Jesus' followers and their love for Jesus (16:27 (2x)); Jesus' love for Lazarus (11:3, 36); the love of Jesus' followers for him to such a degree that it appears as self-hatred (12:25); "the world's" love for those who belong to it (15:19); the Beloved Disciple (20:2, note the interchangeable use of ἀγαπάω with φιλέω—13:23; 20:26; 21:7, 20–24); and the affection between Jesus and Peter (21:15, 16, 17 (3x)).[3]

The above survey indicates that there is a close relationship between John's vocabulary for love and friendship (e.g., ἀγαπάω, φιλέω, φίλος). It has been suggested that these terms have gone through a relexicalization process in the Johannine community, and that love and friendship have become linked to authentic discipleship such that discipleship should be equated with friendship and love.[4] This argument is based on the interchangeable meaning of φιλέω and ἀγαπάω in John and on the three characteristics of the love-friendship-discipleship language—(1) unifying power, abiding, unity/equality, (2) comfort, change of relationship, inclusivity, and (3) service and obligation.[5] To be sure, there is a close relationship between the language of love, friendship, and discipleship in John; however, it is too simplistic to equate these concepts for four reasons. First, the verbs φιλέω and ἀγαπάω do not always refer to discipleship (e.g., 3:19; 15:19). Second, John presents discipleship through a series of additional concepts—following, believing, remaining in Jesus' teaching, bearing fruit—all of which portray discipleship as extending beyond friendship. Third, the characteristic of equality that described ancient friendship does not align with the hierarchical description of friendship in 15:14–16. Fourth, friendship is not the only image associated with discipleship; the imagery of family is also juxtaposed with discipleship (8:30–44). Consequently, instead of limiting the latitude of John's presentation of discipleship to friendship, it is more appropriate to view discipleship as an overall category of commitment to Jesus with diverse expressions of that commitment (e.g., 8:31; 12:24–26, 42; 13:34–35; 14:15; 15:14, 16, 27) and with different benefits that are derived from the discipleship relationship, one of which is friendship (15:12–17). We now turn to John's depiction of Jesus as a royal figure, which validates the argument that Jesus' friendship with his disciples is to be designated as royal friendship.

## JESUS AS A ROYAL FIGURE IN THE GOSPEL OF JOHN

John presents Jesus as a royal figure from the beginning of the Gospel. Andrew C. Brunson argues that "Jesus begins his ministry as king, enters Jerusalem as king, and is crucified as king."[6] The noun "king" (βασιλεύς) appears sixteen times in John, fifteen times referring to Jesus and once to Caesar (19:15).[7] Even in 19:15 where "the Jews" declare "we have no king but Caesar," the title of "king" is implicitly attributed to Jesus, since the declaration of "the Jews" that Caesar is their king is made in contradistinction to Jesus as the king. John intertwines the presentation of Jesus as a king from chapter 1, in which Nathaniel affirms Jesus to be the "king of Israel" (1:49), to the passion narrative at the end of the Gospel where the sign is posted above Jesus' head on the cross, reading, "The King of 'the Jews'" (19:19–21). Moreover, additional kingdom terminology is associated with Jesus throughout the Gospel, thus further presenting him in a royal light (see table 5.1).

This section examines John's presentation of the royal motif in 1:49; 3:3–5; 6:14–15; 12:13–15; and 18:33–19:21 in order to demonstrate that Jesus' regal status in John buttresses the royal friendship between Jesus and his disciples in 15:12–17.

### John 1:49—Jesus as the King of Israel

John commences his theme of Jesus' kingship in 1:49. During a conversation between Nathaniel and Jesus, Nathaniel affirms Jesus as the "king of Israel."[8] Some view Nathaniel's affirmation of Jesus' kingship as evidence that Nathaniel believes in Jesus as the Messiah.[9] Nathaniel's confession may be rooted in Psalm 2, where the messenger of God is called "his anointed" (τοῦ χριστοῦ αὐτοῦ, v. 2), the king (βασιλεύς, v. 6), and son (υἱός μου εἶ σύ, v. 7).[10] The titles Son of God and the "king of Israel" (John 1:49) appear alongside other designations for Jesus: the Lamb of God (vv. 29, 36), rabbi (v. 38), Messiah (vv. 41, 49), "him about whom Moses in the law and also the prophets wrote" (v. 45), and Son of Man (v. 51). These sayings contribute to the messianic tone of the entire passage as John builds toward Nathaniel's

Table 5.1 Royal Terminology in John

| | |
|---|---|
| The kingdom of God (βασιλείαν τοῦ θεοῦ) | 3:3, 5 |
| My kingdom (ἡ βασιλεία ἡ ἐμή) | 18:36 (3x) |
| King (βασιλεύς) | 6:15; 18:37 (2x); 19:15 |
| The king (ὁ βασιλεύς) | 12:15; 19:12, 14, 15 |
| The "king of Israel" (βασιλεὺς τοῦ Ἰσραήλ) | 1:49; 12:13 |
| The "king of 'the Jews'" (ὁ βασιλεὺς τῶν Ἰουδαίων) | 18:33, 39; 19:3, 19, 21 (2x) |

confession in v. 49, "Rabbi, you are the Son of God! You are the king of Israel!" Because John 1:49 echoes the themes of Psalm 2, it is reasonable to suggest that John immediately launches into a royal messianic Christology to establish Jesus' identity as Messiah-king.[11]

## John 3:3–5—Jesus and the Kingdom of God

The Johannine royal motif continues in the conversation between Jesus and Nicodemus. The use of the possessive genitive (τὴν βασιλείαν τοῦ θεοῦ, 3:3, 5) depicts Jesus' understanding of the kingdom as belonging to God. However, there is a shift in the literary presentation of the kingdom in John from God's kingdom in 3:3–5 to Jesus' kingdom in 18:36.[12] The thematic parallels between 3:3–13 and 18:36–37 suggest that the kingdoms of God and Christ are identical.[13] Specifically, both passages mention: the two worlds (i.e., earthly and heavenly, 3:12; 18:36), Jesus' arrival into "the world" as a foreigner (i.e., Son of Man, 3:13) and as a foreign king (18:36–37), the sending motif (3:2; 18:37), and the term "from above" (ἄνωθεν, 3:3, 19:11).[14] Not only do these references indicate that Jesus' kingdom does not originate in this "world," they even equate the kingdoms of God and Christ.[15] Thus, the emphasis on the kingdom in 3:3–13 and 18:36–37, coupled with the repeated references to the spiritual realm (3:2, 4, 7, 12, 27, 31), indicates that God's kingdom can be understood as Jesus' kingdom.[16]

## John 6:14–15—Jesus and the Failed Coronation

In 6:15, Jesus is portrayed refusing the forceful attempt of the crowd to make him king.[17] This incident can be ascribed to popular messianic expectations coupled with the apparent correspondence between Jesus' ministry and Moses' ministry.[18] Moreover, the crowd's witness of and amazement by Jesus' miracles also arguably prompted the crowd to move to install Jesus as the king. However, while the crowd saw Jesus as a king whose kingdom belonged to this "world," Jesus refused to concede to this act of coercion.[19]

Jesus' refusal to accept the attempt at his coronation is, in the view of John, to be explained theologically—the time of Jesus' kingship had not yet come. To be sure, one might surmise that Jesus' swift escape from the attempted coronation to an isolated area (6:15) might be credited to his desire to avoid capture by Antipas, who would have viewed Jesus as a threat if the attempt to make Jesus king succeeded.[20] However, it seems more natural to understand Jesus' evasion of the crowd as an attempt to avoid being made king prematurely. That is, in the view of John, Jesus' coronation is a matter of timing.[21] John demonstrates that Jesus acts according to his own timeline. Indeed, in 12:23, John does depict Jesus as finally admitting that his hour of glorification had come. In other words, just as Jesus rejects his mother's pressure to be glorified (2:4), and just as he rejects his brothers' insistence that he "show himself to the world" (7:1–6), so in 6:14–15 Jesus refuses to be glorified through a premature coronation by the crowd. In the end, John's portrayal of Jesus' reaction demonstrates that the crowd had a misconception both of the nature and timing of Jesus' kingship.

### John 12:13–15—Jesus and His Royal Entry

In this passage, John depicts Jesus as being greeted by the crowd as the prophesied "king of Israel." The scene is reminiscent of the aforementioned coronation attempt in 6:1–15. John 12:13–15 parallels the triumphant entry narrated in the Synoptic Gospels (Matthew 21:1–11; Mark 11:1–11; Luke 19:29–38), with Matthew being the only one who does not include royal allusions. However, all four Evangelists place Psalm 118:26 on the lips of the crowd—"Blessed is he who comes in the name of the Lord."[22] The entire scene suggests a triumphal military or a royal entrance.[23] While the Synoptic Evangelists discuss the finding of the donkey prior to the entrance into Jerusalem, John places the same detail in the narrative *after* the crowd's triumphant shouts, which allows John to depict Jesus as a humble king in contrast with the nationalistic fervor of the large crowd.[24] John's divergence from the Synoptic Gospels stresses Jesus' rejection of the crowd's triumphant shouts in order to accent the uniqueness of his kingship—it does not belong to this "world" (18:36). The broader context of 12:13–15 reveals the chief priests' and Pharisees' concern that Jesus will be welcomed as a political ruler (12:19) and that he will undermine their rule (11:47–50), a fear that was warranted in light of the large crowd's welcoming of Jesus as king with the shouts of "hosanna."

### John 18:33–19:21—Jesus and Kingship Not of This World

In the Johannine passion narrative, there are ten references to Jesus as king (18:33, 37 (2x), 39; 19:3, 12, 14, 15, 19, 21) and three references to his kingdom (all in 18:36). This makes kingship the dominant Christological theme in this section.[25] The motif of Jesus' kingship takes a different tone in John 18, where a distinctive royal title is attributed to Jesus—"king of 'the Jews'" (ὁ βασιλεὺς τῶν Ἰουδαίων)—in contrast to the previously noted title, "king of Israel" (ὁ βασιλεὺς τοῦ Ἰσραήλ).[26] John deploys the two titles in contradistinction to each other, the former being a title of derision and the latter being a title of euphoric excitement. This distinction comes from the observation that these two titles are used by different groups of people. Both Nathaniel and the crowd at the triumphal entry use the title "king of Israel," and in this way they allude to the Old Testament prophecies of a coming Davidic king (Isaiah 9:7; Jeremiah 23:5; Ezekiel 37:21–25; Zechariah 9:9), whereas Pilate, the soldiers, and the antagonistic Jewish leaders use the latter title with derision.[27] The soldiers address Jesus as the "king of 'the Jews'" as they physically and verbally abuse him (19:3). Pilate addresses Jesus as the "king of 'the Jews'" (18:33, 39) and writes it on the plaque placed above Jesus' head on the cross (19:19). In response, the chief priests appeal to Pilate to change the title on the plaque from the "king of 'the Jews'" to "This man *said* I am the king of 'the Jews'" (19:21). This attempt to edit the plaque signals the leaders' rejection of Jesus as their king.

The royal motif in the passion narrative reaches its climax in 19:14–15, where the Jewish leaders view Jesus as a messianic pretender who is a political rival to Caesar (19:15).[28] In 19:14, Pilate exclaims to "the Jews," "Here is your king," and the chief priests respond with, "Take him away! Take him away! Crucify him!" (19:15). The response of the Jewish leaders to Pilate's question "Shall I crucify your king?" (19:15) delineates the choice they have made in regard to Jesus' claims of messianic kingship. That is, in stating "We have no king but Caesar" (19:15), the Jewish leaders chose the Roman emperor over Jesus. In this second mention of Caesar/the emperor, Van Tilborg claims the change in person in v. 15 indicates that the Jewish leaders "no longer profess that God is the only king of Israel. Raymond Brown furthers that in this way the dilemma 'Jesus or the emperor' is not only Pilate's dilemma; it is just as much the dilemma for the leaders of Israel."[29] The Jewish response to Pilate suggests that "the real trial is over for in the presence of Jesus 'the Jews' have judged themselves; they have spoken their own sentence."[30] In sum, while the Jewish leaders reject Jesus as the Messiah, John's portrayal of the trial of Jesus overflows with royal themes and irony: while Jesus received the punishment of a criminal, the charge against him was for claims of royalty.

The Jewish leaders' explicit rejection of Jesus as king in 19:15 is related to the theme of friendship in light of the dialogue between the Jewish leaders and Pilate in 19:12. In an attempt to pressure Pilate to execute Jesus, "the Jews" proclaim to Pilate: "If you release this man, you are no friend of Caesar. Everyone who claims to be a king sets himself against Caesar" (19:12).[31] In this statement, "the competing powers of Rome and Israel confront each other."[32] The narrative contains various responses to Jesus and in this case, "like Judas, Pilate must make a decision about friendship."[33] The mention of "friend of Caesar" (φίλος τοῦ Καίσαρος) would remind the readers of John's last mention of friendship in 15:12–17.[34] Just as Judas and Pilate must make a decision about friendship (18:1–5; 19:12), the Jewish leaders are also forced to choose with whom to align politically and in whose royal circle of friends to remain. John seeks to show that the Jewish leaders prefer the earthly and Roman royal friendship instead of royal friendship with God's agent.

Furthermore, the expression "friend of Caesar" (φίλος τοῦ Καίσαρος) in 19:12 functions as a technical title that refers to a political relationship.[35] This title was conferred on individuals with whom the emperor enjoyed a close friendship and who were therefore pronounced to be his friends as a reward for their loyalty.[36] In the early period of the Roman Empire, "friends of Augustus" were a "well-known society."[37] Moreover, "friendship with Caesar could be warm or purely formal; it provided the emperor with loyal support and his friends with prestige and the ability to secure benefits for themselves and others."[38]

The technical use of the title "friend of Caesar" can be traced back to the Roman imperial practice.[39] Lucius Aelius Sejanus was Pilate's patron who brokered the process of the emperor Tiberius conferring upon Pilate the title "friend of Caesar" (Tacitus, *Ann.* 6.7). Sejanus was subsequently suspected of plots against the imperial family and as a result he was arrested, tried by the senate, and executed in 31 CE.[40] In fact, Sejanus' treason against the imperial family was so offensive that even his youngest children were killed; and Sejanus' clients were deposed (Tacitus, *Ann.* 6.19).[41] Pilate, however, survived for another five years, which speaks to Pilate's stable rule over Judea, until he was finally deposed in 36 CE.[42] In view of the turn of events involving Sejanus, it is reasonable to suggest that Pilate was especially mindful of his political friendship with Tiberius because of Sejanus, albeit as a means of self-preservation.[43] These events can account for Pilate's capitulation to the pressure from the Jewish leaders as an attempt to keep peace in Judea and not jeopardize his career as a Roman governor. In light of Pilate's friendship with Tiberius through Sejanus, John's mention of a "friend of Caesar" in 19:12 not only illustrates the Roman practice of royal friendships, but it also implies that Jesus can be understood as a royal patron who is viewed to be in opposition to Caesar.[44] Indeed, even if the Jewish leaders regard Jesus as an impostor, "the Jews" apply the title "king" to Jesus in their response to Pilate: "Everyone who makes himself king, sets himself against Caesar" (19:12). It is against this background that "the Jews" challenge Pilate concerning his loyalty and friendship with Caesar, as if Pilate must choose friendship with Caesar or Jesus.[45]

## Summary: The Kingship of Jesus in John

John carefully weaves the details concerning Jesus' royal identity from the start of his Gospel to the Passion narrative. John opens and closes the book of Signs (chs. 1–12) with a reference to the kingship of Jesus (1:49; 12:13–15), once again returning to it in the passion narrative (chs. 18–19). Throughout the Gospel, Jesus was recognized as a king by different individuals. Jesus' committed followers saw him as a king (1:49), Jesus' half-hearted followers saw him as a king (6:14–15), and the crowd at the triumphal entry into Jerusalem greeted Jesus as the "king of Israel" (12:15). The enemies of Jesus also understood his claim to kingship but chose to reject it and instead pledged their allegiance to Caesar (19:12, 15, 17–22). Pilate was the final character in John who engaged Jesus concerning his claim to royalty (18:36–37), which ultimately resulted in mockery and derision of Jesus as a king.[46] Since the royal motif is part of the fabric of the entire Gospel, it is plausible to understand Jesus' words, "I call you friends," as coming from a royal figure speaking to his followers and conferring on them the benefit of being friends of a king in response to their devotion to him through abiding, fruit-bearing, love, obedience, and witnessing (15:1–17, 27). The promise of friendship is offered in exchange for continual obedience to Jesus' commands (15:14) and in juxtaposition with a warning about hatred from "the world" that may cause the disciples to defect (16:1–4).[47]

In addition to the evidence discussed in the previous chapter about the Hellenistic writings that support the royal-political view and the survey above of John's portrayal of Jesus as a royal figure, the exegesis of 15:12–17 yields four additional arguments in support of the royal friendship paradigm. These four reasons will be discussed after cursory comments about the structure of 15:1–17.

## ROYAL FRIENDSHIP AND DISCIPLESHIP IN JOHN 15:12–17

In the Farewell Discourse, John injects a brief discussion about the disciples' relationship to Jesus as his friends.[48] In 15:13–16 John writes:

> No one has greater love than this, that someone should lay down his life for his friends. You are my friends if you do what I command you. I no longer call you servants because the servant does not know what the master is doing; but I have called you friends, because the things which I heard from my Father, I made known to you.[49]

The scholarly dialogue concerning Johannine friendship pivots on the statement, "I no longer call you servants . . . but I have called you friends" (15:15). The implication of this phrase is that there was a previous incident when Jesus called his disciples servants; however, no such incident appears in the Gospel. This could be an example of an analepsis in the text, in which John's readers are being informed of an event that has not yet occurred in the temporal progression of the narrative. One option is that it is a completing analepsis, in that the readers are pointed to an event that has occurred, but of which they have not been informed yet.[50] Conversely, it could be a repeating analepsis, which alludes back to a previous event for the purpose of clarification, emphasis, or recollection for the readers. It is possible to understand the foot-washing scene as the prior event in which Jesus demonstrates an act of friendship to his disciples rather than superiority over them.[51] Alternatively, by viewing the adverb "no longer" (οὐκέτι) in v. 15 logically, it is possible to understand the statement "I no longer call you servants . . . but I have called you friends" as a redefinition of Jesus' relationship with his disciples.[52] That is, they are no longer servants, but they are now his close friends.

Prior to offering an exegesis of 15:12–17, we need to understand why 15:12–17 should be treated distinctly from 15:1–11. There are two reasons to divide 15:1–17 into two parts—vv. 1–11 and vv. 12–17.[53] First, the clause "these things I have said" (ταῦτα λελάληκα, v. 11; also in 14:26; 15:25; 16:1, 4, 6, 25, 33) signals a transition from the theme of the vine and the branches (15:1–11) to friendship (15:12–17).[54] This is further supported by the parallel clause "these things I command" (ταῦτα ἐντέλλομαι, v. 17) which indicates a transition from v. 17 to v. 18.[55] Second, 15:12–17 can be seen as a separate unit because these verses are framed by an *inclusio* "to love one another" (vv. 12, 17).[56] The mention of love in vv. 9–10 does link vv. 1–11 with vv. 12–17; however, the focus in vv. 9–10 is to love Jesus, whereas in vv. 12–17 the command is to love each other.[57]

Seeing that 15:12–17 can be understood in distinction from vv. 1–11, there are four reasons why the preferred interpretation of 15:12–17 is royal friendship between Jesus and his disciples. First, the verb τίθημι appears in 15:13 and in the good shepherd narrative (10:11, 15, 17, 18), which establishes a lexical link between the two passages and confirms that Jesus is the Shepherd-King in John. Second, the language of social disparity in 15:12–17 indicates royal overtones. Third, election terminology in 15:12–17 is in accord with the ancient royal-political imagery of a king choosing his inner circle of friends. The fourth reason to interpret 15:12–17 as royal friendship are the benefits promised to the friend of Jesus in return for their loyalty to him. These four arguments are expounded below.

### Royal Friendship and the Shepherd-King Motif

The first reason to interpret John 15:12–17 as royal friendship is the lexical link of this passage with 10:1–18 which features Jesus as the shepherd-king. The use of the verb "lay down" (τίθημι) in 15:13 parallels the use of the same verb in the pericope concerning Jesus as the good shepherd (10:11, 15, 17, 18). The association of these two passages is strengthened by John's use of the verb "lay down" (τίθημι) in reference to Jesus' death only in 10:11–18 and 15:13. In 10:1–18, John likens Jesus to the shepherd-king who cares for his people as a shepherd cares for his sheep.[58] The reference to the good shepherd evokes Old Testament texts where rulers were depicted as shepherds of their people. For example, David (Psalm 78:70–72), the Messiah (Ezekiel 34:23; 37:24; Micah 5:2 with Matthew 2:6; Psalm 2:9), and Joshua (Numbers 27:15–18).[59] Even God is presented in the Old Testament as shepherding his people.[60] Similarly, the Roman emperor Tiberius is reported as describing his servants from Egypt as his sheep (Cassius Dio, *Roman History* 57.10.5). In another instance, Suetonius presents Tiberius as advising the prefect of Egypt on being a good shepherd of his people (Suetonius, *Tib.* 32.2).[61] The depiction of emperors and kings as "shepherds" and especially the depiction of Jesus as the good shepherd who lays down his life for his followers helps to recognize the royal overtones in the language of 15:13–16.[62] When this is coupled with John's portrayal of Jesus as king in the passion narrative, we can understand the Johannine Jesus as a "friendly monarch" and as the suffering friend-king who dies for his friends.[63]

## Royal Friendship and Social Disparity

The second reason to view 15:12–17 as royal friendship is on account of the language of disparity between Jesus and his disciples. Ancient friendship typically involved social peers and "in no ancient definition of friendship does one find that a friend is one who does what he is commanded. A lack of status equality must be present in order for one 'friend' to command another."[64] Moreover, regarding hierarchical relationships, Zeba Crook suggests, "Friendship language was often used to place a veneer over relationships of dependence precisely because of the status consciousness of these cultures. To be a dependent was common, yet shameful."[65] In 15:12–17, John depicts Jesus as superior to his disciples, for Jesus reserves the right to command them even after calling them friends (vv. 14, 16, 17; see also 13:14–18, 34; 14:15, 21–24; 15:10, 12).[66] In 15:14, social disparity is evident by means of the conditional particle with the present tense command "if you do the things I command you" (ἐὰν ποιῆτε ἃ ἐγὼ ἐντέλλομαι ὑμῖν), which indicates that friendship with Jesus is contingent upon continuous obedience to his commands.[67] In fact, obedience to Jesus' commands is the first expectation of friendship with Jesus (vv. 10, 12, 14, 17).[68] The command that immediately follows the discussion of hierarchy and one that frames the entire pericope is the charge for the disciples to love each other (vv. 12, 17).[69] In v. 14 John employs the personal pronoun "you" (ὑμεῖς) in the emphatic position at the front and at the end of the verse to spotlight the disciples as those who must fulfill the command to love. While Jesus' command for the disciples to love one another demonstrates his superior status over them, the fact that Jesus himself demonstrates this love (v. 13) implies that Jesus is not just their superior, but also their friend. The disciples' continual obedience to Jesus' command to love will keep them in friendship with Jesus.[70]

Some have suggested that the disciples' transition from the designation of slaves to friends means they are no longer "δοῦλοι depending upon the wishes and the whims of a master, but φίλοι, intimate and equal associates with Jesus."[71] However, this perspective overlooks how the friendship between Jesus and the disciples is to be reconciled with the statements about Jesus' right to demand obedience and Jesus' right to send his disciples on a mission.[72] In fact, in the succeeding pericope (15:18–27), John portrays Jesus as the master and his disciples as the servants—"Remember the word that I said to you, a slave is not greater than his master. If they persecuted me, they will also persecute you; if they kept my word, they will keep yours also" (15:20; 17:14). If Jesus intended to eradicate any notion of hierarchy, why does John portray Jesus as addressing his disciples as slaves in v. 20, after he already declared in v. 15, "I no longer call you slaves"? John seems to present Jesus as retaining the hierarchical distinction akin to a royal figure within his circle of advisers through the terminology of "master" and "slaves." Ferdinand Hahn explains this hierarchical difference and the expectation to serve as follows:

> The fact that a disciple is not above his master means that his authority is mediated and that he is always bound to the person of Jesus. On the other hand, he can become like his master, and this means that he may represent his Lord in the fullest sense. Discipleship is thus characterized by this peculiar subordination of the disciple to his master and yet at the same time by being his equal in the service to which he is called.[73]

This same distinction between Jesus as Lord and the disciples as slaves was previously introduced at the foot-washing scene, with a charge to the disciples to imitate their Lord. After washing his disciples' feet (13:1–11), Jesus says, "A slave is not greater than his master, neither is the one sent greater than the one who sent him" (13:16).[74] There was an expectation of the inferior's dependence on the superior, and thus conditions for friendship "would not have seemed odd to anyone in antiquity, because that is what friendship meant. It was a close bond of intimacy which depended upon conformity to the wishes of the more powerful."[75] Jesus' wishes are explained in 13:14–15: "So if therefore, I, your Lord and teacher, washed your feet, you also ought to wash one another's feet. For I gave you an example, just as I have done for you, you should do also."[76] Likewise, in 15:12–13 John writes, "This is my commandment that you love one another just as I have loved you." Jesus' love extends beyond washing his disciples' feet; it climaxes with him sacrificing his life on their behalf (10:11, 15, 17; 15:13), and they are expected to lay down their lives also (12:24–25).[77]

Jesus' expectation of his disciples to imitate him is also seen in the play on the meaning of the verb τίθημι in "lay down his life" (θῇ) in 15:13 and in "appointed" (ἔθηκα) in 15:16. That is, the commissioning of the disciples involves the anticipation of the disciples' self-sacrifice for the work of Jesus (e.g., 12:25–26; 15:18–20; 16:2; 21:18–19).[78] Peter understood Jesus' expectation of love unto death because John depicts Peter using the verb τίθημι (13:37) to express his devotion to Jesus unto death, a devotion that Jesus questions since he declares that Peter will deny him (v. 38).[79] Although Peter failed under pressure during Jesus' trial, he would receive another opportunity to prove his love to and to give his life for Jesus (21:18–19).

In sum, in 15:12–17, friendship is a relationship between a superior and an inferior. The disparity in the relationship is evident through the repeated command to love other disciples (vv. 12, 17; 13:34) and a reminder that this kind of sacrificial love should characterize the community of those who claim the title friend-disciple of Jesus.[80] Craig Koester argues that the expectation of self-sacrificial love substantiates the hierarchical nature of the friendship:

> [Disciples] adopted a Christological understanding of friendship through which Jesus' commands to love one another could be brought to expression. Friendship with Jesus was not egalitarian—he retained a singular position—yet it brought Jesus' followers into a relationship of reciprocal love, creating a community in which people who addressed each other as 'friends' could realize the ideal mutual self-sacrifice (15:12–14).[81]

Consequently, "Friendship with Jesus is not a status automatically conferred but a response to the revelation of God in Jesus by living out his commandment to love."[82]

## Royal Friendship and Election Imagery

The third reason to understand 15:12–17 through the lens of royal friendship is because the language of election portrays Jesus as a royal figure who has the prerogative to choose his friends. John previously remarked on Jesus' choosing of his disciples in 13:18: "I know whom I have chosen." In 15:19, Jesus distinguishes his disciples from "the world" because he chose them out of "the world," which alludes to the reference of those who belong to Jesus and who are "his own" (13:1). In 15:16, Jesus also affirms his election of his disciples when he states: "You did not choose me, but I chose you" (οὐχ ὑμεῖς με ἐξελέξασθε, ἀλλ' ἐγὼ ἐξελεξάμην ὑμᾶς). The emphasis in 15:16 on Jesus' absolute right to choose his disciples is evident (1) in the emphatic position of οὐχ ὑμεῖς with the contrastive ἀλλά, (2) in the emphatic personal pronoun ἐγώ that is followed by the verb ἐξελεξάμην, and (3) in the repetition of the personal pronoun (ὑμεῖς and ὑμᾶς), which focuses on the disciples and thereby stresses Jesus' authority to choose whomever he wills.[83]

One option is to interpret the election terminology through the Old Testament covenant motif (e.g., Deuteronomy 7:6–11).[84] There are certainly parallel themes between God's election of Israel in the Old Testament and John 15:16, namely, God's love, promises, and humankind's commitment to God through obedience. However, the absence of covenant terminology (i.e., διαθήκη, בְּרִית) weakens this proposal. Instead, Jesus' choice to elect certain individuals to be his friends is reminiscent of a monarch's right to establish his circle of friends.[85] Election alongside friendship should be interpreted as expressing a special relationship between Jesus and his followers within the paradigm of discipleship.[86] The special relationship is evident not only in the benefits the disciples receive (e.g., joy, love, frankness of speech, 15:11, 15, 16), but also in the fact that it (special relationship) also demands obedience to the king's commission to participate in his mission.[87] Jesus' expectation of his disciples is evident in 15:16 in the purpose clause that contains three elements that are to be fulfilled on a continuous basis (note the present tense of each verb)—so that you would go (ὑπάγητε), so that you would bear fruit (καρπὸν φέρητε), and so that your fruit would remain (ὁ καρπὸς ὑμῶν μένῃ).[88]

The charge to bear fruit is naturally intertwined with the theme of discipleship.[89] John indicates that friendship cannot be separated from fulfilling Jesus' mission to bear fruit, which is accomplished by abiding in the vine and in the reciprocal love between the disciples, a love that is rooted in Jesus' love for his disciples (15:1–9).[90] The result of obeying Jesus' command manifests itself in answered requests (15:7), which links friendship to discipleship, because the same promise of answered requests is seen in 14:12–14, where it is linked to belief and to bearing fruit in 15:7–8 where fruit-bearing confirms one's status as a disciple of Jesus (16:23–24).[91]

## Royal Friendship and Its Benefits

The fourth reason in defense of royal friendship is the fact that benefits are promised to the disciples in return for fulfilling Jesus' obligations. The broader context indicates that the disciples experience abiding fruit that glorifies the Father and confirms them as authentic disciples (15:8); sacrificial love from their royal patron (15:9, 12); complete joy (15:11); knowledge of the Father (15:15); access to the Father (15:7, 16); answered requests from the Father (15:7, 16); and the new title of "friends" (15:14–15). While some have argued against the idea of royal friendship in 15:12–17 because Jesus is not in a position to provide benefits, and the disciples do not experience any material benefits from their friendship with Jesus (e.g., influence, financial gain, protection from enemies); this view overlooks Jesus' declaration in 18:36, "My kingdom is not from this world."[92] The benefits conferred on Jesus' friends are not restricted to physical benefits since Jesus' kingdom is not from this "world." Thus, to expect immediate tangible benefits from the new royal friendship with Jesus is to miss the greater relational and eternal promises featured in the Gospel (5:24, 29; 10:10, 28; 20:31). The conferral of additional benefits to the disciples in the context of friendship is akin to the ancient monarch's treatment of his friends, as he offered various gifts in exchange for loyalty (see chapter 4 for examples), which further affirms royal friendship as the most fitting understanding of 15:12–17.

## SUMMARY: JESUS, DISCIPLES, AND ROYAL FRIENDSHIP

The above section demonstrated that the exegesis of 15:12–17 supports the royal friendship paradigm. First, 15:12–17 is set apart as a separate unit within the Farewell Discourse through (1) the use of ταῦτα λελάληκα (v. 11) and the parallel clause ταῦτα ἐντέλλομαι (v. 17), and (2) through the repeated command "to love one another" (vv. 12, 17). Second, the royal friendship motif is buttressed through the verb τίθημι that links 15:12–17 with 10:1–18 and suggests that John features Jesus as the shepherd-king. Third, Jesus' commands to his disciples signal relational subordination which would be typical of royal friendship. Fourth, the imagery of election and commissioning similarly confirms Jesus as a monarch with the prerogative to select his friends. Fifth, the obligations stipulated and the benefits promised in the context of 15:12–17 establish royal friendship as the most compelling interpretation of this passage.

## ROYAL FRIENDSHIP IN RELATION TO DISCIPLESHIP

The link between friendship and the overall argument of this book—John promotes continuous discipleship—is discernible in four aspects.[93] First, friendship is associated with serving as witnesses for Jesus; thus, as John the Baptist functioned as a witness and a friend to Jesus (3:26–29), so the disciples are expected to fill a similar role and this expectation appears in the immediate context of the friendship narrative (15:13–16, 27). Second, love is inherent to friendship and discipleship, thus a link is formed between the two themes (13:34–35; 14:15; 15:13–14). Third, both discipleship and friendship are characterized by obedience, knowledge, and intimacy (8:31–32; 15:9, 13–16; 16:25–29; 17:6–26). Fourth, fruit-bearing through participation in Jesus' mission (15:8, 16; 17:18; 20:21), answered requests (15:7, 16; 16:23–24), and election (6:70; 13:18; 15:16, 19) are themes that John associates with friendship and discipleship.[94]

The argument of this book is that John deploys friendship as a compensatory benefit in order to prompt continuous discipleship with Jesus. This is seen in John's exhortation to continuous belief in the near context of 15:12–17 (e.g., 14:1–3, 11–12). Additionally, the warning concerning hatred from "the world" in 15:18–27 appears in the context of the promise of royal friendship, thus friendship should be understood as an incentive to remain faithful during opposition from "the world." In encouraging his disciples to endure opposition from "the world," Jesus reminds them that he endured it before them (15:18, 20, 25), that opposition confirms the disciples' separation from "the world" by his election (15:19), and that enduring opposition signifies that they know the Father (15:21–24). Moreover, in 16:33, Jesus commands his disciples to be of good cheer because he overcame "the world" that opposes them. Additionally, in order to keep the disciples from defecting during difficult times, Jesus warns them of potential persecution in the form of expulsion from the synagogues and death (16:1–2). In light of the looming threat of "the world's" hatred, murder, and expulsion from the synagogues, John portrays Jesus as promising to change the status of his loyal followers to royal friends. This benefit is conferred on those who manifest allegiance to him amidst opposition from "the world" and thus functions as a motivator for continuous discipleship.

## CONCLUSION: ROYAL FRIENDSHIP BETWEEN THE KING AND HIS COURT

This chapter continued the discussion commenced in chapter 4 that in 15:12–17, John portrays Jesus as a royal figure who transforms his relationship with his disciples from being servants to friends. Jesus is depicted as a royal patron who invites his disciples into his inner circle of friends, which forges a hierarchical relationship that promises privileges to the disciples in return for their loyalty to Jesus.[95] Following a linguistic study of friendship terminology (φίλος/φιλέω), we saw that (1) John's presentation of Jesus as a monarch in 1:48–49; 3:3–5; 6:14–15; 12:13–15; 18:33–19:21 and (2) the exegesis of 15:12–17 support royal friendship as the interpretation of 15:12–17. These two reasons should be added to the evidence presented in chapter 4 that the references to the political friendships in the classical Greek, Roman, and Hellenistic sources provide a conceptual context for John 15:12–17. Thus, these three arguments demonstrate that John presents Jesus as the "king of Israel" who refuses public coronation (6:14–15) until the hour of his glorification (12:23). It is in the conversation with Pilate that Jesus affirms that his kingdom is not of this earth (18:36–37). This confession is further substantiated by the Johannine narration of Jesus' self-assertion of being the good shepherd, a metaphor that evokes imagery of monarch-shepherds in the Old Testament, in Roman texts, and in Egyptian texts. John deploys this concept of royal friendship as a compensatory benefit of continuous discipleship in light of the cost of following Jesus.[96]

## NOTES

1. Garland suggests that in Luke 12:4, Jesus' disciples are viewed similar to "loyalists in the emperor's favored circle." Marshall, however, sees this designation as merely describing "the close relationship between Jesus and those who do his will and are entrusted with his secrets." David E. Garland, *Luke*, ZECNT (Grand Rapids, MI: Zondervan, 2011), 504; I. Howard Marshall, *The Gospel of Luke*, NIGTC (Grand Rapids, MI: Eerdmans, 1978), 513.

2. Keener, *John*, 579–80.

3. For discussion on the alternation of φιλέω and ἀγαπάω in 21:15–17, see Ann Graham Brock, "The Significance of Φιλέω and Φίλος in the Tradition of Jesus Sayings and in the Early Christian Communities," *HTR* 90 no. 4 (October 1997): 393–409; Sherri Brown, "What's in an Ending? John 21 and the Performative Force of an Epilogue," *Perspectives in Religious Studies* 42 no. 1 (2015): 29–42; Ilaria Ramelli, "'Simon Son of Jonah, Do You Love Me?' Some Reflections on John 21:15," *NovT* 50 (2008): 332–50; David Shepherd, "'Do You Love Me?' A Narrative-Critical Reappraisal of ἀγαπάω and φιλέω in John 21:15–17," *JBL* 129 no. 4 (2010): 777–92.

4. Kaczmarek, *Language*, 21–23, 40–55.

5. Kaczmarek, *Language*, 21, 33–39, 68–69. Kaczmarek's observation that the meaning of φιλέω and ἀγαπάω is interchangeable is correct (see 5:20 with 3:35; 11:3 with v. 5; 13:23 with 20:2; 14:21 with 16:27). Similarly, Bennema, *Power*, 224 fn. 51; Brown, *John*, 497–99; Bultmann, *John*, 711 fn. 5; Kaczmarek, *Language*, 21, 24–39; Ringe, *Wisdom's Friends*, 65; Segovia, *Love*, 134; Willett, *Wisdom*, 75–76. However, Brock's argument that φιλέω and ἀγαπάω represent different Christian communities who preferred these terms, i.e., the Petrine community preferred φιλέω, while Johannine preferred ἀγαπάω remains unconvincing. Brock argues that the Johannine community employed a Petrine term (i.e., φιλέω) to demonstrate unity with Peter's followers. Kaczmarek relies on Brock and espouses a similar position, that is, the redactor added John 21 to establish the equality of the John's and Peter's witness. However, in 21:15–18, the focus is Peter's relationship to Jesus, not to John. Moreover, Jesus' inquiry focuses on Peter's restoration and assignment to shepherd the flock, rather than the superiority or inferiority of his testimony to Jesus in

comparison to the Beloved Disciple's testimony. Brock, "Significance of Φιλέω and Φίλος," 393–409; Kaczmarek, *Language*, 62–73.

6. Andrew C. Brunson, *Psalm 118 in the Gospel of John: An Intertextual Study on the New Exodus Pattern in the Theology of John*, WUNT 2.158 (Tübingen: Mohr Siebeck, 2003), 224 fn. 32.

7. The Johannine presentation of Jesus as king is consistent with the other three Gospel writers. See Matthew 2:2; 27:11, 37, 42; Mark 15:2–12, 18, 26; Luke 19:38; 23:2, 37.

8. Keener suggests that "king" in John usually refers to the Davidic ruler. Keener, *John*, 670. Anderson similarly sees the Davidic ruler behind this title. Anderson, *Christology*, 229. Meeks argues for Moses as the prophet-king in the background of Johannine royal language. Meeks, *Prophet-King*. Brunson argues that Psalm 118 is the background of the Johannine royal language, especially in John 12:13–15, where the entrance of Jesus as king into Jerusalem can be understood as the coming of YHWH. Brunson, *Psalm 118*, 227–39. Cf. Hurtado, who engages Wright on a similar proposal. Hurtado concludes that in the New Testament, there is a "remarkable christological appropriation of the theme of YHWH's return. Despite Wright's urgings, however, it is not clear that the theme of YHWH's return was appropriated initially to interpret Jesus's ministry, death, and resurrection. Instead, the identifiable New Testament instances of the appropriation of the theme present Jesus's *parousia* as effectively being YHWH's eschatological return/manifestation." Larry W. Hurtado, "Participationism and Messiah Christology in Paul: YHWH's Return to Zion. A New Catalyst for Earliest High Christology?" in *God and the Faithfulness of Paul: A Critical Examination of the Pauline Theology of N.T. Wright*, ed. Christoph Heilig, J. Thomas Hewitt, and Michael F. Bird (Tübingen: Mohr Siebeck, 2016), 417–38, citing 434.

9. Brown, *John*, 87.

10. For the messianic theme in John 1:45–49, see Bauckham, "Messianism," 57–59.

11. Additional Old Testament messianic references that John could have relied upon to fill in his royal messianic theology are Isaiah 9:7; Jeremiah 23:5; Ezekiel 37:24–25; Zechariah 9:9. See Nestle Aland Greek New Testament.

12. Köstenberger, *Theology*, 448.

13. Hengel notes that the conversations about the kingdom occur at the beginning and at the end of John, both occurred between Jesus and a person in authority, both individuals address Jesus, and both individuals reject Jesus. Martin Hengel, *Studies in Early Christology* (Edinburgh: T & T Clark, 1995), 350–55.

14. For further study on the descend-ascend motif in John, see the seminal study by Wayne A. Meeks, "The Man from Heaven in Johannine Sectarianism," *JBL* 91 no. 1 (1972): 44–72. The motif of "sending" in John (4:34; 5:23–24, 30, 37; 6:38, 39, 44; 7:16, 18, 28, 33; 8:16, 18, 26, 29; 9:4; 12:44, 45, 49; 13:20; 14:24; 15:21; 16:5; 20:21) further substantiates John's depiction of Jesus' claims that he is from another world.

15. Brown, *John*, 869; Bultmann, *John*, 654, 135 fn. 4; David K. Rensberger, "The Politics of John: The Trial of Jesus in the Fourth Gospel," *JBL* 103 no. 3 (1984): 408.

16. Frey, "Kingdom of God," 455; Keener, *John*, 1112; Moloney, *John*, 93, 494. See also Schnackenburg, *John*, 3:249. Van der Watt explains that Jesus and God "work together not in opposition to each other" in the kingdom. He continues, "God and his anointed king ruled Israel. Their eschatological expectations culminated in the hope of the restoration of this Kingdom, which will be ruled by the messiah." Van der Watt, *Family*, 379.

17. The term ἁρπάζω appears four times in John (6:15; 10:12, 28, 29) and always has the meaning of violent snatching or seizing of an object. *BDAG* defines it as forceful snatching, theft, and dragging away of something. *TDNT* defines it as a firm, quick, violent capture of an object. *BDAG*, s.v. "ἁρπάζω"; *TDNT*, s.v. "ἁρπάζω," 1:472–74.

18. Carson, *John*, 162, 272; Keener, *John*, 670.

19. Bultmann, *John*, 214.

20. Note that in Matthew 14:13, Jesus withdrew from the region in which Herod executed John (see also Mark 6:14–44; Luke 9:7–17). Antipas presided over the trial of Jesus (Luke 23:8–12). *NIDB*, s.v. "Herod, Family"; Keener, *John*, 670.

21. Meeks, *Prophet-King*, 89.

22. The cry of "Hosanna" was a shout of praise adopted from the festival of the Tabernacles and from Psalm 118:26. During the feast of the Tabernacles, Psalm 113–118 was sung every morning by the temple choir. When the verse containing the "Hosanna" cry was reached (118:26), each male in the temple shook willow and myrtle branches tied with palm branches and called them "hosannas." Thus, when Jesus entered Jerusalem, it was completely appropriate for the crowds to welcome him with these branches and with the Hosanna greeting. Beasley-Murray, *John*, 210.

23. See 1 Maccabees 13:51; 2 Maccabees 10:7; 14:4. Keener, *John*, 869; Meeks, *Prophet-King*, 86; Schnackenburg, *John*, 2:374.

24. Brown, *John*, 463; Stibbe, *John*, 133–34.

25. The only other title employed in this section for Jesus is Son of God (19:7). Reimund Bieringer, "My Kingship is Not of This World," in *The Myriad Christ: Plurality and the Quest for Unity in Contemporary Christology*, ed. Terrence Merrigan and Jacques Haers (Leuven: University Press; Uitgeverij Peeters, 2000), 160.

26. In John, the term "Israel" has a positive connotation, which is not always the case with "the Jews." This distinction can be extended to the titles "king of Israel" and "king of 'the Jews.'" So Meeks, *Prophet-King*, 82–83; Sjef van Tilborg, *Reading John in Ephesus*, NovTSup 83 (Leiden: Brill, 1996), 26. Bauckham dissents and suggests that "king of Israel" is a Jewish title, while "king of 'the Jews'" is a Gentile title, and both carry messianic overtones. Richard Bauckham, *The Testimony of the Beloved Disciple: Narrative, History, and Theology in the Gospel of John* (Grand Rapids, MI: Baker, 2007), 230–31; Bauckham, "Messianism," 59–60. Dunn indicates that "Israel" is a self-designating title, whereas "Jews" is employed by an outsider like Pilate. James D. G. Dunn, *Jesus Remembered* (Grand Rapids, MI: Eerdmans, 2003), 263. North suggests that "the Jews" is not a remarkable title in John and is not to be viewed in terms of "us" versus "them" designation by John because: (1) John's infusion of Israel/Israelite with religious meaning is not unique to him, thus the use of the term is not a particular feature of his circumstances;

(2) John deploys Israel/Israelite so infrequently that it cannot function as a robust alternative to "the Jews"; (3) Jewish writers seem to use both "Jew" and "Israelite" in self-reference and in communication with one another. Thus, she concludes that "the Jews" is not remarkable and merely functions as a referent to Diaspora-Jews. Wendy E. S. North, *A Journey Round John: Tradition, Interpretation, and Context in the Fourth Gospel*, ed. Chris Keith, LNTS 534 (London: Bloomsbury, 2015), 165–67.

27. Rensberger calls Pilate's use of this title "ironic" and sardonic with the intent of embittering "the Jews." Brown observes that Pilate's use of the title "king of the Jews" betrays his mockery, since he had just determined Jesus was not a pretender to the throne. Sherri Brown, "What Is Truth? Jesus, Pilate, and the Staging of the Dialogue of the Cross in John 18:28–19:16a," *CBQ* 77, no. 1 (2015): 77–78; Rensberger, "Politics," 402–403.

28. Brown, *John*, 872.

29. Van Tilborg, *Reading*, 173. Meeks similarly affirms that the rejection of Jesus by "the Jews" is equivalent to their rejection of God as their king. Brown understands that the chief priests are spokesmen for "the Jews," and therefore sees no significance in the change in person. Raymond E. Brown, *The Death of the Messiah: From Gethsemane to the Grave a Commentary on the Passion Narratives in the Four Gospels*, 2 vols., ABRL (New York: Doubleday, 1994), 849; Meeks, *Prophet-King*, 81.

30. Brown, *John*, 894. See also Lance Byron Richey, *Roman Imperial Ideology and the Gospel of John*, CBQMS 43 (Washington, DC: Catholic Biblical Association of America, 2007), 176, fn. 75.

31. Brown observes the dramatic irony of Pilate forcing "the Jews" to choose between Barabbas and Jesus, but here "the Jews" turn the tables on Pilate and raise the stakes for Pilate and challenge him to choose between Jesus and Caesar. Brown, "What Is Truth?," 82.

32. Ford, *Redeemer-Friend*, 185.

33. Ford, *Redeemer-Friend*, 186.

34. The title "friend of Caesar" has no parallel in the New Testament. Richey, *Roman*, 168.

35. There is no consensus among scholars whether φίλος τοῦ Καίσαρος is a technical title or if it only describes Pilate's loyalties to Tiberius. The following scholars associate the political relationship between Sejanus and Pilate as friends of Tiberius and interpret the title "friend of Caesar" as a technical political title, akin to *amicus Caesaris*: Von Ernst Bammel, "φίλος τοῦ Καίσαρος," *TLZ* 77 no. 4 (1952): 205–10; Brown, *John*, 879–80; Brown, *Death*, 693–98; 843–44; Cuss, *Imperial Cult*, 48; Schnackenburg, *John*, 3:262–63; Van Tilborg, *Reading*, 172; *EDNT*, s.v. "Καῖσαρ," 2:235–36. Cf., Jean-Pierre Lémanon, *Pilate et la gouvernement de la Judée: textes et monuments* (Paris: Gabalda, 1981), 275; Morris, *John*, 706; Van der Watt, *Family*, 362 fn. 1032. Carson calls it a semi-technical honorific. Carson, *John*, 607. Lincoln remains agnostic. Lincoln, *Truth*, 133; Lincoln, *John*, 468–69. See Michael Theophilos' recent article defending the technical title from additional Roman primary sources and Numismatic evidence: Michael P. Theophilos, "John 15.14 and the

ΦΙΛ-Lexeme in Light of Numismatic Evidence: Friendship or Obedience?," *NTS* 64 (2018): 33–43.

36. Cuss, *Imperial Cult*, 49.
37. Brown, *John*, 879.
38. Koester, *Symbolism*, 241.
39. Bammel also links φίλος τοῦ Καίσαρος to the Ptolemaic and Seleucid political practice of friendship with the king. Bammel, "φίλος τοῦ Καίσαρος," 205–10.
40. Bammel, "φίλος τοῦ Καίσαρος," 205–10; Brown, *John*, 893–94.
41. *OCD*, s.v. "Aelius Seianus, Lucius (Sejanus)," 19.
42. Brown, *Death*, 693–95.
43. Van Tilborg, *Reading*, 172. For Pilate's conflict with the Jews, see Josephus, *J.W.*, 2.169–74.
44. *BDAG*, s.v. "Καῖσαρ"; Deissmann, *Light*, 377–78. Meeks similarly observes: "[O]ne of the characteristics of the Johannine treatment of the trial and the events that lead up to it is that the *political* implications are emphasized. In 11.48 a specifically political motivation is injected into the plotting of the Jewish authorities. John alone mentions the presence of Roman soldiers (ἡ…σπεῖρα καὶ ὁ χιλίαρχος) [19:12] at the arrest of Jesus. In the trial itself, the political-realistic element is introduced by the Jews at 19.12: If you release this man you are not Caesar's friend; anyone who makes himself a king opposes Caesar's. The climactic rejection of Jesus by the Jews is the statement 'We have no king but Caesar' in which the 'religious' and 'political' questions are shown to be inextricably merged." Meeks, *Prophet-King*, 64.
45. Keener explains Pilate's initial reticence to condemn Jesus by suggesting that Pilate viewed Jesus as a sage, comparable to the Cynics, who was not a political threat to the state because Jesus' kingship was "a hypothetical kingship focused only on 'truth.'" Nevertheless, Keener admits that Pilate condemned Jesus because it was "politically imprudent to release a defendant charged with treason." Craig S. Keener, "'What is Truth?': Pilate's Perspective on Jesus in John 18:33–38," in *John, Jesus, and History, Volume 3: Glimpses of Jesus through the Johannine Jesus*, ed. Paul N. Anderson, Felix Just, and Tom Thatcher (Atlanta, GA: SBL Press, 2016), 77–94, citing 93.
46. Ford observes that the entire passion narrative is an allusion to the consecration of a monarch. She points to: "(1) The anointing by Mary (John 12:1–8), (2) the entry into Jerusalem (John 12:12–19), (3) the crowning and homage of a king (John 19:1–3), (4) the proclamation (John 19:4–5), (5) the acclamation (John 19:6–7), (6) the enthronement on the *bema*, judgment seat (John 19:13–6), (7) the naming (John 19:19–22), (8) the regal burial with abundance of spices (John 19:38–42)." Ford, *Redeemer-Friend*, 176.
47. In 15:14, note the present tense verbs, ἐὰν ποιῆτε ἃ ἐγὼ ἐντέλλομαι ὑμῖν.
48. The Farewell Discourse has been interpreted as Jesus' final speech, comparable to the typical Greek or Roman death scene. See Lincoln, *John*, 384; Segovia, *Farewell*, 5; Stibbe, *John*, 152–53. For the structure of the Farewell Discourse, refer to Brown, *John*, 586–96; Bultmann, *John*, 457–631; Segovia, "John 15:18–16:4a: A First Addition to the Original Farewell Discourse?," 210–30; Segovia, *Farewell*, 20–58.

49. For discussions concerning the authenticity of Jesus declaration in 15:12–17, see J. G. van der Watt, "Some Reflections on the Historicity of the Words 'Laying Down Your Life for Your Friends' in John 15:13," in *John, Jesus, and History, Volume 3: Glimpses of Jesus through the Johannine Jesus*, ed. Paul N. Anderson, Felix Just, and Tom Thatcher (Atlanta, GA: SBL Press, 2016), 481–91.

50. Culpepper, *Anatomy*, 59.

51. Culy, *Echoes*, 158–60. Moloney, Ford, and Schneiders similarly link friendship to foot-washing. Ford, *Redeemer-Friend*, 136–46; Moloney, *Glory*, 64; Francis J. Moloney, *Love in the Gospel of John: An Exegetical, Theological, and Literary Study* (Grand Rapids, MI: Baker, 2013), 117; Sandra Schneiders, "The Foot Washing (John 13:1–20): An Experiment in Hermeneutics," *CBQ* 43 (1981): 76–92.

52. Schnackenburg, *John*, 110–11.

53. Although Segovia writes that the discourse of 15:1–17 "can be regarded as a coherent artistic whole that is carefully developed from the beginning to the end," he still divides the passage into vv. 1–8 and vv. 9–17 because of the theme of abiding in the vine (vv. 1–8) and abiding in love (vv. 9–17). Segovia, *Farewell*, 125–31, citing 163. Elsewhere, Segovia suggests that vv. 1–8 is about belief and vv. 9–17 features love. Segovia, *Love*, 117–20, 189. Brown and Keener divide the text into vv. 1–7 and vv. 8–17. Brown, *John*, 665–68; Keener, *John*, 988–1016. Bernard divides the passage into vv. 1–8, 9–11, and 12–17. Bernard et al., *John*, 2:477–85. Bultmann sees parallelism in these two sections—"remain in me" (vv. 1–8) and "remain in love" (vv. 9–17). Bultmann, *John*, 529, 537, 546. Schnackenburg sees vv. 1–25 as a unit. Schnackenburg, *John*, 3:91–92. The two-fold division espoused here is affirmed by Barnabas Lindars, *The Gospel of John*, NCB (London: Oliphants, 1972), 488–93; John Marsh, *The Gospel of St. John* (Harmondsworth: Penguin, 1968), 518, 523; Schnackenburg, *John*, 3:92–93, 95–96.

54. For the change of topic in 15:12, see Barrett, *John*, 467; Beasley-Murray, *John*, 261, 269; Brown, *John*, 650; Köstenberger, *John*, 441; Moloney, *Glory*, 56; Ridderbos, *John*, 519; Schnackenburg, *John*, 3:82.

55. Segovia similarly sees a break after 15:17. Segovia, *Farewell*, 125–31.

56. Moloney, *Love*, 119.

57. Segovia, *Farewell*, 125, 130, 162. There are other common themes between vv. 1–11 and vv. 12–17, such as the preeminence of the Father (vv. 1, 9, 15, 16), fruit (vv. 2, 4, 5, 8, 16), commandment/word (vv. 3, 7, 10, 12, 14, 17), abiding (vv. 4, 5, 6, 7, 16), love (vv. 9, 10, 12, 13, 17), and answered requests (vv. 7, 16). However, the summary statement in v. 11 along with the inclusio of love in vv. 12–17 suggests a literary distinction between vv. 1–11 and vv. 12–17.

58. Ford writes, "'Shepherd' is a synonym for 'ruler' and thus the discourse could be called 'the ideal sovereign.'" Ford, *Redeemer-Friend*, 180–81. See also Meeks, *Prophet-King*, 307–12.

59. Negative examples come from Jeremiah 23:1–4; Isaiah 56:9–12; Ezekiel 34; Zechariah 11.

60. Psalm 80:1; 23:1; Isaiah 40:11.

61. Ford notes, "With the advent of Hellenization, the concept of 'friendship' changed. There was an emphasis not so much on the 'friendship' of the body of citizens but on the *philoi* of the monarch." Ford, *Redeemer-Friend*, 87.

62. Meeks affirms the parallelism between Jesus as king and the good shepherd, arguing that the emphasis on his death demonstrates the inauguration of his kingship. Meeks, *Prophet-King*, 68, 80–81. *Pace,* Culy who does not see royal imagery in 15:12–17. See Culy, *Echoes*, 165 fn. 146, 169.

63. For Jesus as friendly monarch and suffering king, see Ford, *Redeemer-Friend*, 168–93, citing 180.

64. For equality in friendship, see Malina et al., *Commentary*, 119, 236; Zeba A. Crook, "Fictive-Friendship and the Fourth Gospel," *TS* 67 no. 3 (2011): 1–7, quoting 6.

65. Crook, "Fictive-Friendship," 7.

66. Puthenkandathil notes the aspect of subordination in Johannine friendship when he defines it as "master-disciple relationship." Eldho Puthenkandathil, *Philos: A Designation for the Jesus-Disciple Relationship—An Exegetico-Theological Investigation of the Term in the Fourth Gospel*, European University Studies 23.475 (Frankfurt am Main: P. Lang, 1993), 6, 243.

67. *Pace,* Brodie who suggests that John's teaching on friendship removes all authoritarianism and command language in favor of genuine mutuality. Thomas L. Brodie, *The Gospel According to John: A Literary and Theological Commentary* (New York: Oxford University Press, 1993), 483–84.

68. So Segovia, *Farewell*, 158. Tolmie also stresses the intimacy of friendship to the discipleship relationship by noting that the disciples do not merely obey Jesus because he commands them but as his friends, they want to obey him. Surprisingly, Tolmie does not discuss the hierarchical structure in v. 14 and v. 16. Tolmie, *Farewell*, 213.

69. The importance of love to the Farewell Discourse and to 15:12–17 is affirmed through the repeated references to love in the Farewell Discourse (31 times–ἀγαπάω/ἀγάπη; 3 times–φιλέω), four of which appear in 15:12–17. Additionally, the inclusio of love that frames the friendship motif between v. 12 and v. 17 stresses the link between love and friendship. The definite article and the emphatic personal pronoun ἐμή in 15:12 (αὕτη ἐστὶν ἡ ἐντολὴ ἡ ἐμή, ἵνα ἀγαπᾶτε ἀλλήλους) identifies the love command to be preeminent. The emphasis on love continues in v. 14 through the reference back to the command in v. 12 and through the personal pronoun ἐγώ preceding the verb ἐντέλλομαι.

70. Segovia acknowledges that "the status of φίλοι is said to be preserved only by carrying out Jesus' commands," but Segovia does not entertain the possibility of royal friendship being the basis for Jesus' demand for obedience. Segovia, *Love*, 114–16, citing 279 fn. 197. See also, Segovia, *Farewell*, 158.

71. Moloney, *Love*, 119.

72. Moloney, *Love*, 118.

73. Hahn et al., *Die Anfänge*, 30.

74. Summers provides an interesting insight about the relationship between a disciple and his rabbi when he says, "The understanding of μαθητής, disciple, was changing to encompass not only a learner but one who adhered to a great master . . . there is no reference in the literature to a rabbi calling his disciples 'friends' . . . ; therefore, this is an unusual passage." This further accents the humility displayed by Jesus toward his disciples through washing their feet. Steve Summers, *Friendship:*

*Exploring Its Implications for the Church in Postmodernity*, T & T Clark Theology 7 (London; New York: T & T Clark, 2009), 25, fn. 44.

75. Scholer, ed. *Social Distinctives*, 105–106.

76. Shin correctly observes two meanings in the foot-washing episode—the theological basis for the cross due to the mention of "the hour" (13:1) and the ethical imitation of humility for the disciples and readers to follow (13:15). Additionally, he rightly points out that ὑπόδειγμα is only used of Jesus in John, thus signifying that while many characters are presented as examples of discipleship, Jesus is the example *par excellence*. Moreover, the adverb καθώς appears thirty-one times in John and in the Farewell Discourse καθώς is coupled with four themes—love, unity, mission, ἐκ-status—that feature Jesus as an example for his disciples to follow. Gorman helpfully notes that if the foot-washing scene is to be understood through the cross and if the cross is a missional act of God's love (3:16), then the invitation for the disciples to participate in the foot washing is an invitation into the divine mission and to participate is to "take on the divine DNA." Gorman, *Abide and Go*, 90–96; Shin, *Ethics*, 132–42. While Lee understands foot washing as mainly Jesus' act of friendship with symbolism of ritual cleansing, she also sees foot washing metaphorically for Jesus' humility and death. Lee, *Hallowed*, 152.

77. Tolmie notes that foot washing was typically performed by slaves. Tolmie, *Farewell*, 194. Moloney observes that the climax of Jesus' love is his death. Moloney, *Love*, 117–18.

78. The Book of Signs and the Book of Glory both contain a call to follow Jesus, and it may cost the disciples their lives (12:24–25; 21:19). Shin, *Ethics*, 191.

79. "Love is *the* hallmark of friendship and finds its ultimate expression in the laying down of one's ψυχή for one's friends" (italics original). Bennema, *Power*, 224.

80. For comparison of the love commandment in 13:34 with 15:12, 17, see Segovia, *Love*, 122–24.

81. Koester, *Symbolism*, 241.

82. Willett, *Wisdom*, 109.

83. There are a total of six uses of the second personal pronoun ὑμεῖς in v. 16, stressing the division between Jesus' function in election and his *right* to commission his disciples. See, Klink, *John*, 658.

84. So Chennattu, *Discipleship*, 59–61, 116–18.

85. See examples from the analysis of the Maccabean Literature in chapter 4. *Pace*, Brodie who contends that "Jesus does not address them [disciples] as an exclusive club. Rather they are . . . [to bring] their friendship with Jesus to others." However, the privilege of being a friend of a king and being commissioned by the king are not mutually exclusive, since a disciple can enjoy a unique relationship with king Jesus and fulfill the mission of inviting others into such a relationship (15:16). Brodie, *John*, 484.

86. So Schnackenburg, *John*, 3:111.

87. Haenchen et al., *John*, 2:132.

88. Segovia, *Farewell*, 160.

89. Bennema, *Power*, 245–46, fn. 137.

90. Gorman has recently linked the themes of mission, abiding, eternal life, and imitation of God. He argues that *"mission is a primary mode of theosis"* for it brings the disciple into God's mission through participation in the vine which results in fruit. Thus, the disciple engages in Jesus' mission in extending God's love to "the world." Gorman convincingly shows that the verb "do/make" sets up a parallel between Jesus' work and the disciples' ministry in John 13–17, as the disciples continue Jesus' work of fulfilling the mission of God. Beyond that, Gorman rightly points out the importance of fruit-bearing to discipleship when he suggests that "it is actually in bearing fruit that the disciples become disciples." Gorman, *Abide and Go*, citing 104, 130–31.

91. Note the result clause, ἵνα ὅ τι ἂν αἰτήσητε τὸν πατέρα ἐν τῷ ὀνόματί μου δῷ ὑμῖν. Segovia, *Farewell*, 161.

92. *Pace*, Summers who declares that Jesus is in no position to confer rewards. Summers, *Friendship*, 18.

93. The first three points are adopted from Bennema, *Power*, 223–25.

94. Because the corollary benefits of royal friendship overlap with the corollary benefits of abiding and membership in the divine family, they are treated in chapters 1–3.

95. Keener agrees that the best understanding is a type of friendship with a king. Keener, *John*, 1007.

96. In his exegesis of 15:1–17, Segovia similarly sees the real and immediate possibility of the disciples faltering "in terms of belief, praxis, or both" and the disciples "being under the pressure from the world" as the prompt for this passage. Segovia, *Farewell*, 166–67, 209.

*Chapter 6*

# Answering the Question Why? The Gospel of John in Context

The present study has argued that certain Johannine themes associated with discipleship can be packaged under three primary rewards for continuous devotion to Jesus—membership in the divine family, the abiding of the Father and the Son with believers through the Spirit, and royal friendship with Jesus. This chapter argues that John promises these benefits to the faithful followers of Jesus in light of the potential cost of discipleship. John situates his Gospel in the setting of hostility from "the Jews" and from "the world" toward believers in Jesus. John depicts this hostility through the expulsion passages (9:22; 12:42; 16:2) and in the references to the fear of "the Jews" (7:13; 9:22; 12:42; 19:38; 20:19).[1] In addition to the conflict between "the Jews" and Jesus and his followers, John presents "the world" in opposition to Jesus and his followers (e.g., 7:7; 15:18–19; 17:14). This chapter suggests that antagonism to Jesus' disciples from "the Jews"/"the world" functions as the canvas on which John spotlights the benefits of commitment to Jesus in order to incentivize continuous discipleship.

## THE HISTORICAL SETTING OF THE GOSPEL OF JOHN

Three dominant approaches have been suggested for the reconstruction of the historical setting of the writing of the Gospel of John. A more thorough review of each proposed solution will aid us in establishing the most plausible *Sitz im Leben* of the Gospel of John.

### The Destruction of the Temple and the Johannine Community

The trauma associated with the destruction of the Jewish temple in 70 CE is one of the possible incentives for the writing of John for three reasons.[2]

First, following the scholarly consensus that John was written in the late first century CE, the destruction was an indisputable event that occurred in a historical datum that was recent from the Johannine perspective.[3] Therefore, the destruction of the temple must have "had at least some bearing on the way this Gospel was written."[4] Second, the destruction of the temple shaped the Jewish residents in Palestine and in the Diaspora and thus must have influenced the author of the Gospel.[5] Third, John presents the temple as a provisional manifestation of God's presence, and the destruction of the temple provides the opportunity for the Messiah "to inaugurate a more permanent form of God's presence with his people."[6] This proposal brings prominence to the temple in John by linking the temple motif with the destruction of the temple and the Christological purpose of the Gospel, especially since both passages refer to Jesus' resurrection (see 2:19–22; 20:1–31).[7]

The destruction of the temple was almost certainly a factor for the composition of the Gospel of John (e.g., 2:19–22), but this theory only partially explains the Gospel's background. It neglects passages that do not relate to the temple (e.g., 2:1–11; 5:1–47; 6:1–71; 12:12–50; chs. 18–19), which is perhaps the reason that this view has not obtained much traction in scholarship.[8]

## The Johannine Community at the End of the First Century

Fifty years ago, J. Louis Martyn's two-level reading of John reshaped the landscape of Johannine studies.[9] He suggested that the story of the blind man in John 9 was a window into the experience of the Johannine community at the end of the first century CE.[10] He could then interpret this pericope as a reflection of the trauma of the Jewish believers in Jesus due to the conflict with "the Jews" which resulted in the expulsion of believers from the synagogues (ἀποσυνάγωγος), which was rooted in the curse against the heretics, designated as the *Birkat ha-Minim*.[11] Martyn further argued that the Johannine "expulsion passages" do not reflect the events of the historical Jesus, but rather the experience of the Johannine community at the end of the first century CE.[12] Although the majority of Johannine scholars continue to support a variation of this hypothesis, there are two concerns evaluated below that expose weaknesses in the two-level reading approach.[13]

### *The Birkat ha-Minim and the Gospel of John*

The link between the *Birkat ha-Minim* and the Gospel of John is highly speculative and continues to be debated in scholarship.[14] In his recent defense of the connection between the *Birkat ha-Minim* and the Gospel of John, Marius Heemstra appealed to the *fiscus Judaicus*, a tax introduced by Vespasian in 70 CE for the temple of *Jupiter Capitolinus* as a replacement for the Jewish temple tax.[15] Since certain Jews began to evade this tax, Domitian and Nerva amplified their collection efforts by means of directing these Jews to the synagogue to pay the tax, imprisonment, and the confiscation of property.[16] In response, Jewish synagogue leaders implemented the *Birkat ha-Minim* in order to unify faithful Jews and expel the heretics who only joined to avoid the tax. In this way, a link is forged between the *Birkat ha-Minim* and *fiscus Judaicus*.

Moreover, Marius Heemstra joins *fiscus Judaicus* with ἀποσυνάγωγος (9:22; 12:42; 16:2) by understanding the latter through the Old Testament passages that banned certain individuals from the congregation of Israel. That is, "if Jewish Christians were considered to be heretical in saying that 'the Torah is not from Heaven,' then they were expelled from 'all Israel.'"[17] Thus, the Johannine ἀποσυνάγωγος "should perhaps not so much stress the point of putting Jewish Christians out of the synagogue, but rather creating a formal (legal) distance between them and the Jewish community."[18] Consequently, after the year 96 CE, Jewish believers in Jesus could no longer claim the label "Jew" due to the legal action of ἀποσυνάγωγος.[19] Heemstra applies this approach to the use of ἀποσυνάγωγος in John 16:2 to suggest that the term referred to two events—first, a legal separation of the Jewish believers in Jesus from the Jewish community, which led to the second, the Romans began to view Jewish believers in Jesus as atheists who deserved death. Thus according to Heemstra, John 16:2b refers to the Romans, not to "the Jews."[20] By linking ἀποσυνάγωγος to *fiscus Judaicus* and to the *Birkat ha-Minim*, 96 CE is offered as the date for the "parting of the ways" between "the Jews" and the believers in Jesus which would suggest 100 CE as the date for the writing of John.[21]

There are four weaknesses to this proposal. First, the assertion that the Jewish Christians denied the heavenly origin of the Torah merely because they claimed that the Messiah was from heaven is *non sequitur* for two reasons.[22] First, the two views—the "Torah from Heaven" versus the "Messiah from Heaven"—are not mutually exclusive concepts. Second, there are no "instances of Jewish Christian documents which deny the divine origin of the Torah."[23] Thus, the lack of historical evidence to validate the legitimacy of this alleged Christian theological error weakens the assertion that ἀποσυνάγωγος was in response to this *alleged* Christian practice.

Second, the re-interpretation of ἀποσυνάγωγος to mean that the Jewish Christians were excluded from the Jewish community rather than merely from the synagogue is not incontrovertible. Lawrence Schiffman critiques this suggestion:

> It cannot be overemphasized that while the benediction against the *minim* sought to exclude Jewish Christians from active participation in the synagogue service,

it in no way implied expulsion from the Jewish people. In fact, heresy, no matter how great, was never seen as cutting the heretic's tie to Judaism (italics original).[24]

Thus, it is not sustainable to assert that *fiscus Judaicus* compelled "the Jews" to set boundaries for inclusion and exclusion of certain members within the Jewish community through the *Birkat ha-Minim*.

Third, on account of other New Testament evidence, ἀποσυνάγωγος and the "parting of ways" must have taken place earlier than the enactment of *fiscus Judaicus* (70 CE) and the *Birkat ha-Minim* ca. 100 CE.[25] In the words of Martin Hengel, it seems more reasonable to view the "parting of ways" between "the Jews" and Jewish Christians as "a lengthy and painful process which began even before Paul with the martyrdom of Stephen."[26] Thus, 96 CE as the proposed date of the separation between "the Jews" and the Jewish Christians overlooks other New Testament evidence that points to an early starting point for this conflict and ultimate divergence of paths.

Fourth, it is more convincing to understand "the Jews" as the persecutors of Jewish Christians rather than the Romans in John 16:2. There is a lack of evidence that the Romans viewed their execution of Christians as an act of service to their gods.[27] However, reading 16:2 as a reference to Jewish antagonism toward Christians is far more congruous with Paul's aggression toward believers in Jesus, as he dragged them out of the synagogues and condemned them to death on account of his zeal for God (e.g., Acts 8:1–3; 9:1–2; 22:3–4; Galatians 1:13–14).[28] Moreover, "the Jews" as the antagonists is more plausible than the Romans because elsewhere in John "the Jews" put Jesus' sympathizers out of synagogues (9:22, 34; 12:42).

In addition to the above weakness, Jonathan Bernier, who argues that the *Birkat ha-Minim* and ἀποσυνάγωγος ought not to be associated together, offers two compelling points of critique. First, the *Birkat ha-Minim* edict does not mention expulsions and the Johannine expulsion passages do not mention the edict; therefore, no explicit correlation can be identified between the two.[29] Second, the historicity of the practice of ἀποσυνάγωγος can be defended with the verb συντίθημι in John 9:22 in light of the two other occurrences of this verb in the New Testament (Luke 22:5; Acts 23:20), the use of συντίθημι in Luke 22:5 and Acts 23:20 imply an informal decision rather than a formal decree in John 9:22.[30] Additionally, in John 12:42 it is the Pharisees who are behind the application of the ἀποσυνάγωγος not the rulers, which implies that this was not a formal decree.[31] Thus, we can surmise that the expulsions of Jesus' followers were accomplished informally and occurred during the time of Jesus rather than having any connection with the *Birkat ha-Minim* in the late first century CE.[32]

The informal nature of this decree would have been executed through mob or police violence (e.g., John 7:32; 9:34; Luke 4:29–30).[33] Jonathan Bernier's conclusion that ἀποσυνάγωγος in John was not an official decree compelled him to postulate a new suggestion for the rationale and the process behind the practice of ἀποσυνάγωγος. He argued that the fascination with Jesus as the possible Messiah prompted the Jewish leaders to curb support for Jesus through the expulsion of Christians from the synagogue, which at times resulted in physical violence.[34] Jesus' popularity challenged the religious status quo in Jerusalem, since people were attracted to Jesus (John 11:48; 12:11, 19). Popular support of Jesus threatened the influence of the Jewish authorities, and thus they responded by attempting to terminate the Jesus movement (11:48–50). When that failed, the Jewish leaders orchestrated the death of Jesus and continued similar hostility against Jesus' followers (Acts 8:1–3; 9:1–2).[35] John's account of the hostility toward Jesus and his followers coincides with the evidence from the Synoptic Gospels and Acts that similarly recount instances of Jesus' sympathizers being forced out of the synagogues (e.g., Matthew 5:11; 10:17; 23:34; Mark 13:9; Luke 12:11; 21:12; Acts 6:9; 8:1–3; 9:2; 13:45–50; 17:1–5; 22:19; 26:9–11).

## The Two-Level Reading of the Gospel of John

The argument favoring the *Birkat ha-Minim* as a historical background for John is coupled with the two-level reading of the Gospel. The story of the blind man in John 9 is read on two levels—as a story of Jesus and as the story of the Johannine community. Even though many scholars view John 9 through this lens, some scholars criticize this approach for not being transferable to other passages in John.[36] For example, as Jesus' followers, Martha and Mary would need to represent Johannine Christians who were expelled from the Jewish community, but in 11:19 they are still surrounded by Jewish mourners.[37] Additionally, certain individuals openly believed in Jesus and yet they suffered no repercussions from "the Jews" (e.g., 11:1–42; 12:11).[38] Thus, while these passages should confirm the two-level reading of John, instead they undermine this theory.[39] Moreover, the two-level approach to John seems to be circular for it reads the text as a reflection of the Johannine community and then proceeds to use that history to account for the details in the Gospel.[40] In contrast to the two-level reading of the Gospel, John wrote a historical account of the time of Jesus.[41] Indeed, Adele Reinhartz argues that John's references to fulfilled prophecy (e.g., 12:12–16; 18:32; 19:24, 32–37) and John's claims of writing a truthful account of his observations (19:35; 21:24–25) indicate that "the earliest readers may have viewed the Gospel primarily as historical and cosmological tales rather than an ecclesiological tale, the story of their community, as such."[42]

Additionally, certain Johannine passages present the author as an eyewitness who conveyed a truthful account of the events he narrated (e.g., 1:14; 2:18–22; 19:35; 21:24–25), as he relied on his memory with the aid of the Paraclete (14:26) in his aim to prompt belief through the Gospel (19:35; 20:30–31). This is evident in John's knowledge of the life of Jesus, and so he wrote the Gospel with the intent to include factuality, while being free of the suspicion to commit fraud.[43] Therefore, the passages featuring expulsion from the synagogue are historically plausible to have occurred in the time of Jesus, and perhaps extended into the time of the readers of the Gospel of John (16:2).[44]

## Jesus and Moses in the Gospel of John

A recent defense of the conflict between the synagogue and the Jewish Christians suggests that "around the end of the first century CE, the opposition between Moses and Jesus was at the heart of the conflict between these two groups."[45] A review of select passages that seemingly set Jesus in opposition to Moses (e.g., 1:14–17; 1:19–2:11; 4:1–42; 3:14; 5:31–47; 6:30–33; 7:15–24; 9:27–28) led John Ashton to conclude that "the Gospel represents a deliberate decision to supplant Moses and to replace him with Jesus, thereby substituting one revelation, and indeed one religion, for another."[46] That is, "[by the] ousting of Moses from his central place as God's representative in his dealings with his people, the fourth evangelist (along with those on whose behalf he spoke and wrote) was effectively establishing a new religion."[47]

Proponents of the hypothesis that Jesus ousts Moses point to four "family quarrels"—ancestry, sacred space, festivals/feasts, and the law—that allegedly function as assaults on the Jewish religion in the Gospel.[48] The attack on ancestry is evident by Jesus being depicted as greater than Jacob (1:51; 4:12) and Abraham (8:53). Next, Jesus supersedes the temple (2:19) and declares Jerusalem to be less central to Jewish worship (4:21, 23), which abolishes the sacred space of Judaism. The festivals/feasts are completed in Jesus since Jesus is presented as embodying Sukkot (7:37), as applying the consecration of Hanukkah to himself (10:36), and as being the true paschal lamb of Passover (19:36). Finally, Jesus declares to be the focus of the Law (5:39) and the Writings (5:46) and is presented as a mediator of revelation that is superior to Moses, on account of which the primacy of Moses is undermined (1:17).[49] Consequently, these four "family quarrels" convey the replacement of Moses with Jesus, which function as the basis for the Jewish antagonism toward the Johannine community.[50]

John 9:27–28 is viewed as a key passage that demonstrates Jesus' usurpation of Moses.[51] However, it seems that it is "the Jews" who see Jesus in opposition to Moses, not the author of the Gospel. In contrast, John views

Jesus as the successor to Moses, that is, as one who maintains and perpetuates Moses' role, not as one who usurps and abolishes his role. The Jewish perception of Jesus' usurpation is seen in the narrative by John's presentation of the pronounced Jewish allegiance to Moses over Jesus. First, the Jewish leaders assert, "we are disciples of Moses" (note the emphatic position of ἡμεῖς, 9:28). Second, the parallel placement of the pronouns σύ and ἡμεῖς in v. 28 (i.e., σὺ μαθητὴς εἶ ἐκείνου with ἡμεῖς δὲ τοῦ Μωϋσέως ἐσμὲν μαθηταί) heightens the contrast between the depicted loyalty of the Jewish leaders to Moses and the supposed disloyalty of the blind man to Moses.[52] Third, the additional use of ἡμεῖς at the beginning of v. 29 (ἡμεῖς οἴδαμεν) further reinforces the contrast between associating with Jesus and associating oneself with Jesus over against associating oneself with Moses.[53] Finally, the use of the pronoun ἐκείνου in v. 28 by the Pharisees (σὺ μαθητὴς εἶ ἐκείνου), instead of the personal name Jesus, also exhibits the tension between the Pharisees and Jesus. In this way, John depicts the Jewish leaders as viewing Jesus and Moses as competing figures. But even though "the Jews" are depicted as viewing themselves as the disciples of Moses and label the blind man as a disciple of "that man," there is no indication in their polemical discourse that they view Jesus as the replacement of Moses (9:24–31). Thus, instead of presenting Jesus as one who supplants Moses, John depicts Jesus to be in concert with Moses not only in John 9 but also in the rest of the Gospel.

John's previous reference to Moses in 5:45–47 indicates that Jesus and Moses are concomitant figures. John writes:

> Do not think that I will accuse you before the Father, the one accusing you is Moses, in whom you have set your hope. If you believed (ἐπιστεύετε, imperfect) Moses, you would believe (ἐπιστεύετε, imperfect) me, because he wrote concerning me. But if his writings you do not believe (πιστεύετε, present), how will you believe (πιστεύσετε, future) my words.

The four instances of πιστεύω in this passage stress that believing in Moses should mature into believing in Jesus (note the tense changes in πιστεύω from imperfect to present to future). In effect, the two figures are not presented as being in conflict with each other; rather, Jesus is depicted as continuing the message of Moses.[54] The declaration that Moses will accuse those who reject Jesus is the strongest indication that Jesus and Moses had a similar mission. According to John, the Jewish leaders erroneously set the authority of Moses against the authority of Jesus (9:28–29), and in so doing they misunderstood the role of Moses, who is depicted by John as a witness to Jesus rather than as an antagonist to Jesus (1:45; 5:45–47).[55] Thus, it seems preferable to argue that John does not place Jesus *against* Moses as much as John presents Jesus as the figure who continues Moses' role (1:41, 45; 5:46).[56]

John Ashton also uses the two-level reading with respect to John 9 to defend the assertion that Jesus ousts Moses.[57] It is presumed that there is only one messianic confession during the time of Jesus, that is, Peter's declaration in Matthew 16:16; consequently there is no compelling evidence for a Christological conflict between Jesus/disciples and the Pharisees/"the Jews" until the time of the Johannine community (i.e., the events reflected in John 9).[58] Since a few dozen followers of Jesus would not pose a challenge to the established Jewish religion, the accusation against the blind man in 9:28 is presumably inconceivable during Jesus' lifetime.[59] Consequently, it is assumed that the conflict between Jesus and "the Jews" is a later interpolation into the story of Jesus.[60] However, in the Synoptic Gospels, although there is no additional instance of a Christological confession per se by a specific individual (see Matthew 16:16=Mark 8:29), the animosity of the high priest, chief priests, scribes, and elders toward Jesus that led to his crucifixion is still traced to Jesus' claims of his messianic status (Matthew 26:57–68=Mark 14:53–64=Luke 22:66–23:5).

In sum, it is not necessary to affirm the two-level reading of John 9 or to accept the relationship between the *Birkat ha-Minim* and the expulsion passages, or to subscribe to the theory that Jesus supplants Moses, in order to affirm the setting of hostility as the historical background to the Gospel of John. Irrespective of the timing of the conflict between "the Jews" and Jewish Christians, reading John's Gospel in light of this hostility, which may have formed part of the outlook of the Johannine believers, further reinforces the value of the rewards for continuous discipleship.

## HOSTILITY IN THE GOSPEL OF JOHN

In this section I will argue that John's Gospel is filled with evidence of hostility toward Jesus' followers from "the Jews" and "the world." It is this internal evidence that prompts this author to conclude that John deploys the rewards of following Jesus (explained in the previous chapters) as incentives toward continuous discipleship.

From the outset, John sets his narrative in a framework of conflict.[61] In 1:11 John writes, "he came to his own and his own did not receive him." The empathic placement of "his own" (τὰ ἴδια) and its repetition as οἱ ἴδιοι adds further emphasis.[62] Although there is no explicit mention of opposition to Jesus in this verse, the audiences are made aware that Jesus will experience rejection, and this proves true as the Johannine narrative develops, ultimately climaxing in Jesus' crucifixion. This opposition, however, does not cease with Jesus' crucifixion, but is subsequently directed at his disciples (e.g., 16:1–2; 20:19). John presents two groups of antagonists who exhibit hostility toward the Father, Jesus, the Spirit, and the disciples: "the world" and "the Jews."

## "The World" in the Gospel of John

John projects a complex portrayal of "the world" (ὁ κόσμος) through the seventy-eight appearances of the term. On the one hand, John presents "the world" from a positive vantage point. God loves "the world" (3:16–17) that was created by the Word (1:10), and Jesus desires that "the world" may be saved (17:21). God sent his Son to save "the world" (3:16–17; 4:42; 6:33, 51; 12:47), and Jesus came into "the world" (1:9; 3:19; 6:14; 10:36; 11:27; 18:37) to remove its sin (1:29). Thus, John presents "the world" as a mission field for Jesus that is in need of salvation (8:26; 14:31; 16:28; 17:18, 21, 23; 18:20, 37; 21:25). On the other hand, despite the various passages that depict "the world" with a positive or neutral connotation (7:4; 11:9; 12:19, 25; 16:21; 17:5, 13, 24; 18:20; 21:25), John also characterizes "the world" to be at enmity with God, Jesus, the Paraclete/Spirit, and believers.

First, John describes "the world" as a place that is hostile to God (15:21–24; 17:25) and has rejected the Son (3:19). "The world" is characterized by sin (1:29; 16:8), darkness (8:12; 9:5; 12:46), false peace (14:27), hatred toward Jesus (7:7; 15:18–19), and "the world" is under the power of the ruler of "the world" (12:31; 14:30; 16:11). "The world" does not know Jesus (1:10) or God (17:25), rejects the Spirit (14:17), and rejoices at Jesus' death (16:20). Jesus, however, does not belong to "the world," and Jesus' kingdom is not of this "world" (18:36). Jesus came to judge "the world" (9:39; 12:31), and to overcome it (16:33) and its ruler (12:31; 14:30; 16:11). Thus, John presents "the world" at odds with the person and message of Jesus.

Second, John indicates that "the world" rejects the disciples of Jesus. "The world" refers to those who do not belong to the community of Jesus' followers, while, in contrast, the disciples of Jesus are those who are saved out of "the world" (15:19; 17:6).[63] Though Jesus and the disciples are *in* "the world," they are not *of* "the world" (17:14, 16). According to John's dualistic perspective within the narrative, one either *is* from the present "world" or *is not* from the present "world" (8:23). After Jesus' departure from this "world," the disciples remain in "the world" (13:1; 17), and their function is to continue Jesus' mission (17:18; 20:21). However, John demonstrates that as "the world" hated Jesus, so "the world" continues to hate the followers of Jesus (15:18–19; 17:14). In fact, the degree of "the world's" hostility toward the disciples is such that the disciples demonstrate a need for protection from "the world" (17:9–15). Inasmuch as "the world" is hostile toward the disciples, Jesus calls the disciples to seek comfort in Jesus, specifically in Jesus' victory over "the world" (16:33).

Third, John demonstrates that the Paraclete/Spirit endured the same hostile reception from "the world" that Jesus and his disciples suffered. John makes clear that Jesus' mission in "the world" continues after his departure not only through the disciples (15:27), but also through the Paraclete/Spirit as the Paraclete/Spirit convicts "the world" of sin, righteousness, and judgment (16:8–11).[64] But, again, as "the world" did not receive or know Jesus or God (1:10–11; 17:25) or his disciples (15:18–19; 17:14), so "the world" does not know or receive the Paraclete/Spirit (14:17).

In the end, John depicts "the world" expressing hostility toward God, Jesus, the Paraclete/Spirit, and the disciples.

## The Identity of "the Jews"

John presents "the Jews" as being part of and representative of "the world," specifically in their shared hostile response to God, Jesus, the disciples, and the Paraclete. First, in 15:24–25 John considers "the Jews" to be part of "the world," inasmuch as he speaks about "the world's" hatred for him and for the disciples and at the same time associates "their law," in v. 25 (i.e., the law of "the Jews") with "the world's" hatred.[65] Second, in 7:1–24 John depicts "the Jews" seeking to kill Jesus (vv. 1, 19), and in the very same context Jesus speaks specifically of "the world" hating him (v. 7). Third, John attributes a similar relationship of "the Jews" to Jesus, the Father, and the Spirit as he does of "the world" to Jesus, the Father, and the Spirit. That is, ultimately "the Jews," just as "the world," do not know Jesus, the Father, or the Spirit (1:10; 5:37, 43; 7:28; 8:19, 55; 14:17; 17:25). In this way, then, John presents "the Jews" as representatives of "the world" in their antagonism toward Jesus and his followers.[66]

Regarding the identity of "the Jews," John demonstrates that while "the Jews" is a referent to a single group that generally expresses hostility toward Jesus and his disciples, this group, nonetheless, consists of smaller groups that exhibit fractured loyalties with regard to Jesus and his followers.[67] There are fifty-one references to "the Jews" in John and in thirty-eight of the fifty-one occurrences the term has a negative connotation.[68] Studies on the identity of "the Jews" in John abound, proposing to see them as Judeans, Diaspora Jews, high officials, or simply as "representatives of unbelief."[69] None of these proposals, however, captures the full essence of the Johannine use of "the Jews" as a character, since John's usage includes qualities in the designation that transcend any single category proposed above.[70] A more nuanced understanding of the identity of "the Jews" is that the designation "the Jews" is a "distinct religious group in Jesus' time."[71] That is, the group is generally depicted as being hostile toward Jesus, and yet, the group is also depicted as being internally fractured with regard to its view of Jesus.[72] For example, that, on the one hand, the resurrection of Lazarus prompted many "Jews" to believe in Jesus (11:45; 12:11), and, on the other, it roused other "Jews" to plan to put Jesus to death (11:46–53).⁷³ This proposal not only explains John's general use of "the Jews" as a group that is hostile toward Jesus but it also explains the internal discord between certain members of "the Jews" with respect to their reception or rejection of Jesus. Furthermore, this definition of "the Jews" aids audiences in understanding the secret believers in Jesus who were members of this group that was hostile to Jesus (3:1–11; 12:42; 19:38), and why these secret believers in Jesus feared to make this confession publicly on account of the repercussions they might suffer from "the Jews." Thus, this view encapsulates the usage of "the Jews" in different passages and identifies the complexity of "the Jews" as a character in John to refer to individuals who are hostile to Jesus and to those who are sympathetic to Jesus.

## The Hostility between "the Jews," Jesus, and His Disciples

John depicts the antagonism from "the Jews" toward Jesus' followers through references to the fear of "the Jews" (7:13; 9:22; 12:4—fear of the Pharisees; 19:38; 20:19) and expulsion from the synagogue (9:22; 12:42; 16:2). John features "the Jews" as employing fear and expulsion to restrain members of the Jewish community from becoming disciples of Jesus.

The first mention of the fear of "the Jews" is in reference to Jesus' sympathizers fearing repercussions from "the Jews" for open dialogue about Jesus (7:13). The context of 7:13 is the festival of the Tabernacles and the sentiment in the crowd concerning Jesus was schismatic—some complained, others affirmed him as a good man, still others viewed him as a deceiver, but no one spoke of him openly for fear of "the Jews" (7:12–13). The nature of this fear seems to be related to the apprehension of suffering consequences for being associated with Jesus, that is, of being subjected to the persecution of "the Jews" that was directed at Jesus; for "the Jews" were seeking to kill Jesus (7:1, 13, 25–26). This is not the only mention in John of "the Jews" seeking to kill Jesus, the earlier reference appearing in 5:1–18, in which John employs the imperfect "persecuted" (διώκω, 5:16, see also 15:20) to express their aggression and relentless pursuit of Jesus.⁷⁴ According to 5:1–18, after Jesus healed the lame man, "the Jews" sought to kill Jesus for breaking the Sabbath and for claiming that God was his father, which in their understanding placed Jesus on a par with God (5:18).⁷⁵ The narrative in John 7, then, alludes to 5:1–18 in that in 7:23 Jesus attributes the Jewish aggression toward him expressed in John 7 to his prior healing of the lame man in John 5. Moreover, in the flow of the narrative, John 7 records Jesus' first reappearance in Jerusalem since the story in John 5; thus John 5 and 7 should be linked in that the events in John 5 prompted the persecution in John 7. Inasmuch as Jesus was a target of persecution at the hands of "the Jews," the idea of associating with Jesus aroused fear among the members of the Jewish community and among the sympathizers of Jesus that the persecution directed at Jesus would be applied to those who might be associated with him (15:18, 20).

The second reference to the fear of "the Jews" is in 9:22, where expulsion from the synagogue (ἀποσυνάγωγος) is presented as the basis for the fear. In 9:22, although the primary questions concerning Jesus are directed toward the blind man and while he is the chief target of the ridicule by "the Jews" until he is cast out of the synagogue (9:28, 34), the characters who express fear of "the Jews" in this pericope are the blind man's parents.[76] In their attempt to ascertain the full account of Jesus granting sight to the blind man, "the Jews" summoned the blind man's parents to answer questions about their son's condition from birth and to explain the process by which he was healed (9:18–21). However, John indicates that the parents deflected from answering the questions because of their fear of "the Jews" (9:22–23), that is, evidently because they feared being put out of the synagogue (9:22).[77] This pericope suggests that there was a general understanding among the Judeans that any affirmation of Jesus as the Messiah could result in hostility from "the Jews."[78]

The third mention of fear is in 12:42–43 where John refers to fearing the Pharisees, and this occurrence is also linked with expulsion from the synagogue. This pericope is unique in two respects. First, in contrast to 9:22, where the potential victims of the expulsion were common Judeans, in 12:42, the target is Jewish rulers. Second, the nature of the fear is further nuanced by being linked to the glory that comes with being associated with a synagogue. As 12:43 reads: "For they loved human praise more than praise that comes from God." Ultimately, this passage explains the phenomenon of refusing to associate with Jesus publicly for two interconnected reasons—the fear of expulsion from the synagogue and the love of the praise that comes from association with the synagogue.

Expulsion from the synagogue is also mentioned in 16:2, where the victims are the disciples. In this verse, the reference to "offering service to God" (λατρείαν προσφέρειν τῷ θεῷ) suggests that the antagonists were primarily Jewish, as opposed to Roman. In the New Testament, the noun "service" (λατρεία) appears four times in addition to John 16:2, and on three of those occasions, it is in reference to sacrificial ministry to God (Romans 9:4; Hebrews 9:1, 6), while in one instance it is a metaphoric allusion to the same (12:1).[79] Since in John 16:2, λατρεία is appended to προσφέρειν, it carries the same connotation of cultic service to God.[80] Paul serves as an illustration of this type of service in Galatians 1:13–14 (see also Acts 22:3–4) where he refers to zeal for God producing hostility toward Christians.

The fourth mention of the fear of "the Jews" is in 19:38 where Joseph of Arimathea feared consequences from his colleagues for associating with Jesus. While not much is stated regarding the identity of Joseph of Arimathea in 19:38–42 (see Mark 15:43; Luke 23:50 where he is designated as a ruler), the text makes clear that he was a disciple of Jesus, but that he believed in Jesus secretly for fear of "the Jews." Despite the brevity of this narrative, this pericope corroborates the statement in 12:42 that some Jewish leaders believed in Jesus but were afraid to confess this belief.[81] Joseph's request to take the body of Jesus in order to bury it suggests that he ultimately mustered sufficient courage to overcome the fear of "the Jews" and to act in accordance with his belief in Jesus irrespective of the consequences he might suffer for public association with Jesus (see Mark 15:43).[82]

Another such sympathizer of Jesus with whom John's audiences would be familiar is Nicodemus. Scholarly opinion regarding Nicodemus varies, as he is considered to be an unbeliever, a partial believer, an ambiguous disciple, a true disciple, a secret disciple, a member of the establishment confronting a fringe sect, or as "the prime example of one whose expression of faith is dictated by his fear of 'the Jews.'"[83] While it is beyond the scope of this book to delve into matters of the characterization of Nicodemus, it is important to take note of Nicodemus' initial secretive interest in Jesus (3:1–15), of his subsequent attempted defense of Jesus before the Jewish leaders (7:50–52), and of his ultimate expression of honor at Jesus' burial (19:38–42).[84] Nicodemus' first appearance in John—in which he meets with Jesus at night seemingly in order to keep the meeting secret—suggests that he feared to be exposed as Jesus' sympathizer (2:23–3:2).[85] As in the case of Joseph of Arimathea, Nicodemus' secrecy corresponds to the narrator's commentary in 12:42 that the fear of reprisals from the Jewish leaders arguably prevented other Jews from associating with Jesus publicly.

In his second appearance in the Gospel (7:50–52), however, Nicodemus seems to advocate on Jesus' behalf in that he challenges the Pharisees concerning their apparent neglect of the law in their investigation of Jesus (7:51). As a result, Nicodemus is served an insult by the Pharisees of being insignificant in that they accuse him of sharing a common geographic origin with Jesus, that is, Galilee (7:52).[86] This narrative illustrates how even a Jewish leader may be intimidated by "the Jews" for expressing sympathy toward or association with Jesus. In his final appearance (19:39), Nicodemus is portrayed honoring Jesus publicly at his burial.[87] Nicodemus appears in this scene together with Joseph of Arimathea, who, as already noted above, was explicitly introduced as a secret disciple of Jesus (19:38). Potentially, then, Nicodemus, along with Joseph of Arimathea, serves as an illustration of a Jewish leader who initially was a secret believer in Jesus for fear of "the Jews" (19:38), but who ultimately overcame this fear and exhibited his association with and belief in Jesus publicly.[88]

The final mention of the fear of "the Jews" is in 20:19 where the disciples are gathered behind locked doors. This reminds John's audiences of Jesus' warning to his disciples of future hostility directed at them (16:2). John 20:19 illustrates that the pressure and persecution implemented by "the Jews" against Jesus and those who were sympathetic to his mission was effective to such a degree that his most loyal followers feared for their safety because of public display of their faith in Jesus. John 20:19 differs from the previous references to the fear of "the Jews" in that the followers of Jesus no longer fear the act of professing their belief in Jesus, but, instead, they fear the actual and apparently imminent repercussions for publicly associating with Jesus. In 18:19, the high priest focuses on Jesus' disciples as part of the interrogation and since Jesus was executed, the disciples would have reason to hide from "the Jews" in 20:19. Certainly Peter's threefold denial in 18:17–27 is in response to the fear of being identified as Jesus' disciple (and incur negative consequences) as observable in the sixfold use of "disciple" (μαθητής) and the use of "follow" (ἀκολουθέω) in 18:15–27.

In the end, John's references to the expulsion from the synagogue and to the fear of "the Jews" reveal hostility from "the Jews" toward Jesus and his disciples.

## CONCLUSION: CONFLICT AND THE PURPOSE OF THE GOSPEL OF JOHN

The hostility from "the Jews" and "the world" toward Jesus and his disciples provides the general historical background against which the benefits of discipleship can be understood as compensatory rewards for following Jesus. In John, every chapter contains elements of opposition toward Jesus or his followers.[89] John's references to the fear of "the Jews," expulsion from the synagogue, and the animosity from "the world" is congruent with the evidence from the other New Testament writings.[90] This atmosphere of opposition created a need for John to write a Gospel that narrated an account of analogous hostility and that provided a paradigm for an appropriate response to this hostility, ultimately to encourage his readers to maintain their commitment to Jesus. To counter potential defection in response to opposition (16:2), John deploys images that accent relational intimacy between Jesus and his followers.

The Jewish hostility might have been a factor in the then-current experience of Johannine believers, or it might have been an experience of prior time, which continued to form part of the outlook of Johannine believers.[91] Expulsion from the synagogue resulted in being ostracized from the social life in the Jewish community and in losing the identity determined by association with the synagogue. John counters the fear of hostility with the encouragement that following Jesus would provide a new and a more desirable identity, one that was incomparable with the Jewish life defined by the local synagogue.[92] For example, though the blind man was put out of the local synagogue (9:34), he obtained and embraced a new identity in the Messiah (9:35–38). Also, although the disciples confined themselves in the upper room for fear of "the Jews" (20:19), in a post-resurrection visit from Jesus they were reinvigorated with courage to remain faithful until the end on account of their association with Jesus (21:19, 23–25).

John's message to his readers who perhaps lived in conflict with their neighbors (9:8–13) and authorities (9:14–34) is that continuous commitment to Jesus results in rewards that outweigh the privileges obtained within the Jewish community. Discipleship with Jesus places Jesus' followers into the divine family, keeps them in an abiding relationship with the Father and the Son through the Spirit that is experienced in the present time and culminates in the future, and designates them as royal friends of Jesus. Reading the Gospel of John against the canvas of hostility toward Jesus' followers and recognizing the benefits of continuous commitment to Jesus, Johannine discipleship becomes appealing as a worthwhile pursuit even in the face of opposition.

## NOTES

1. In 12:42, John mentions fear of the Pharisees instead of fear of "the Jews."
2. Köstenberger has recently attempted to revive this approach. He writes:

"[T]he Fourth Gospel's emphasis on Jesus as the fulfillment of the symbolism surrounding various Jewish festivals and institutions—including the temple—can very plausibly be read against the backdrop of the then-recent destruction of the second temple as one possible element occasioning its composition. If this sketch is essentially correct, at least in its general contours, John would have formulated his Christology at least in part in the context of the crisis of belief engendered by the destruction of the temple. The gospel could then be understood, at least in part, as an effort to respond to the religious vacuum which resulted from the temple's destruction by pointing, not to a temporary, but a permanent solution: Jesus' replacement of the temple in the religious experience of his people by himself." Andreas J. Köstenberger, "The Destruction of the Second Temple and the Composition of the Fourth Gospel," in *Challenging Perspectives on the Gospel of John*, ed. John Lierman (Tübingen: Mohr Siebeck, 2006), 215.

Motyer suggests that the author of John placed the trauma of the temple destruction in a culture where various Jewish sects defined their identity in reference to the temple. The elimination of the temple prompted these sects to seek individualism to make themselves known and John's Gospel was one such group "seeking to bring order into the social chaos." Motyer, *Father*, 103. For similar proposals, see W. D. Davies, "Reflections on Aspects of the Jewish Background of the Gospel of John," in *Exploring the Gospel of John: In Honor of D. Moody Smith* ed. R. Alan Culpepper and C. Clifton

Black (Louisville: Westminster John Knox, 1996), 43–64, citing 56; J. A. Draper, "Temple, Tabernacle and Mystical Experience in John," *Neot* 31 no. 2 (1997): 263, 285; Alan R. Kerr, *The Temple of Jesus' Body: The Temple Theme in the Gospel of John*, JSNTSup 220 (London: Sheffield Academic Press, 2002), 31–33, 371–76; Peter W. L. Walker, *Jesus and the Holy City: New Testament Perspectives on Jerusalem* (Grand Rapids, MI: Eerdmans, 1996), 195, 198; Westcott, *John*, xxxviii.

3. Köstenberger, "Destruction," 215. The generally accepted date of John is 80–100 CE. See, Behm et al., *Introduction*, 175; Brown, *John*, lxxxvi; Keener, *John*, 142; Moloney, *John*, 2–6; Tellbe, *Christ-Believers*, 35; Trebilco, *Early Christians*, 272.

4. Köstenberger, "Destruction," 216.

5. Köstenberger, "Destruction," 216–21.

6. Köstenberger, "Destruction," 228.

7. Köstenberger sees the Christological purpose, Köstenberger, "Destruction," 228–42. Stegemann links Jesus' death and resurrection with the temple destruction. Ekkehard W. Stegemann, "Zur Tempelreinigung im Johannesevangelium," in *Die Hebräische Bibel und ihre zweifache Nachgeschichte. Festschrift für Rolf Rendtorff zum 65. Geburtstag*, ed. Christian Macholz Erhard Blum, Rolf Rendtorff, Ekkehard Stegemann (Neukirchen-Vluyn: Neukirchener, 1990), 511–12.

8. Köstenberger lists the following passages in support of his argument: 1:14, 51; 2:14–22; 4:19–24; 7:1–8:59; 9:38; 10:22–39; 11:48–52; 20:28. Köstenberger, "Destruction," 230. The dominant view is still the Johannine community hypothesis as discussed in any major commentary.

9. Martyn, *History*. Kysar has a synthesis of the rise, influence, and the erosion of this hypothesis. Kysar, *Voyages*, 237–45.

10. Martyn was not the first to promote the dual reading of the text. Bultmann engaged in a similar approach when he posited one character against another to represent wider communities at odds with each other. Bultmann suggested that the struggle between the Beloved Disciple and Peter within John reflects competition between the Hellenistic church and the Palestinian church. Bultmann, *John*, 484–85.

11. For the actual language of the curse, see Solomon Schecter and Israel Abrahams, "Genizah Specimens," *JQR* 10 (1898): 654–61.

12. Martyn, *History*.

13. Defenders of the two level reading are: Paul N. Anderson, *The Fourth Gospel and the Quest for Jesus: Modern Foundations Reconsidered* 321 (London: T & T Clark, 2006), 34, 65, 197; Ashton, *Origins*; Barrett, *John*, 361–62; Brown, *Community*, lxx–lxxv, lxxxv, 380; Bultmann, *John*, 239; Collins, *These Things*, 49–55; Davies, "Reflections on Aspects of the Jewish Background of the Gospel of John," 51; Hays, *Gospels*, 303; Marius Heemstra, *The Fiscus Judaicus and the Parting of the Ways*, WUNT 2.277 (Tübingen: Mohr Siebeck, 2010), 159–89; Howard-Brook, *Children*, 20; John S. Kloppenborg, "Disaffiliation in Associations and the 'Ἀποσυνάγωγος' of John," *TS* 61 no. 1 (2011): 1–16; Joel Marcus, "*Birkat ha-Minim* Revisited," *NTS* 55 (2009): 523–51; Richey, *Roman*, 51–64; Trozzo, *Ethics*, 109–17. Bernier divides this movement into two traditions—(1) classic Martynian which holds to two-level reading of John and affirms the link between the *Birkat ha-Minim* and the Johannine

expulsion passages and (2) Neo-Martynian which holds to a two-level reading but rejects the link between the expulsion passages and the *Birkat ha-Minim*. Jonathan Bernier, *Aposynagōgos and the Historical Jesus in John: Rethinking the Historicity of the Johannine Expulsion Passages*, BIS 122 (Boston: Brill, 2013), 11–13.

14. Meeks called the *Birkat ha-Minim* a "red herring in Johannine research." Meeks, "Breaking Away," 102. Robinson calls the thesis a "highly imaginative reconstruction of the history of the fourth gospel" and sees no "compelling reason to assign it a [decree to expel Christians from synagogues] to a situation that obtained only at the end of the first century." Robinson, *Redating*, 273–74. Kysar changed from declaring that the *Birkat ha-Minim* theory "convincingly exhibits the fact that the Fourth Gospel was written in response to the expulsion of Jewish Christians from their synagogues and the condemnation of Christians as heretics." Robert Kysar, "Community and Gospel: Vectors in Fourth Gospel Criticism," *Int* 21 (1977): 363. Kysar now maintains that "there was no formal and widespread ban against Christians participating in synagogue worship, and the division between the church and synagogue more likely occurred little by little on a local basis." Kysar, *Voyages*, 240. For a critique of the sectarian and two-level reading of John, see Hamid-Khani, *Revelation*, 174–208. For additional critiques of the *Birkat ha-Minim*, see Bauckham, ed. *Gospels*; Bernier, *Aposynagōgos*; Frey, "Diaspora," 186; Douglas R. A. Hare, *The Theme of Jewish Persecution of Christians in the Gospel according to St. Matthew*, SNTSMS 6 (Cambridge: Cambridge University Press, 1967), 48–56; Edward W. Klink, *The Sheep of the Fold: The Audience and Origin of the Gospel of John*, SNTSMS 141 (Cambridge: Cambridge University Press, 2007); Adele Reinhartz, *Befriending the Beloved Disciple: A Jewish Reading of the Gospel of John* (New York: Continuum, 2001), 37–53; Adele Reinhartz, "Incarnation and Covenant: The Fourth Gospel through the Lens of Trauma Theory," *Int* 69 no. 1 (2015): 36–37. The dating of the *Birkat ha-Minim* is evaluated by Gedalyahu Alon, "Jewish Christians: The Parting of the Ways," in *The Jews in Their Land in the Talmudic Age (70–640 CE)*, ed. Gershon Levi (Jerusalem: Magnes Press, 1980), 288–307; Ashton, *Origins*; Bernier, *Aposynagōgos*; Brown, "Other Sheep," 5–22; Brown et al., *Introduction*, 151–88; Carroll, "Fourth Gospel," 19–32; Maurice Casey, *Is John's Gospel True?* (London: Routledge, 1996), 98–110; Shaye J. D. Cohen, "The Significance of Yavneh: Pharisees, Rabbis and the End of Jewish Sectarianism," 55 (1984): 27–53; Raimo Hakola, *Identity Matters: John, the Jews, and Jewishness*, NovTSup 118 (Leiden: Brill, 2005), 45–55; Hengel, *Johannine Question*, 114–19; William Horbury, "Extirpation and Excommunication," *VT* 35 (1985): 13–38; S. T. Katz, "Issues in the Separation of Judaism and Christianity after 70 C.E.: A Reconsideration," *JBL* 103 (1984): 43–76; Keener, *John*, 207–14; Reuven Kimelman, "*Birkat Ha-Minim* and the Lack of Evidence for an Anti-Christian Jewish Prayer in Late Antiquity," in *Jewish and Christian Self-Definition*, ed. E. P. Sanders, A. I. Baumgarten, and Alan Mendelson (Philadelphia: Fortress, 1981), 226–44; Edward W. Klink, "Expulsion from the Synagogue? Rethinking a Johannine Anachronism," *TynBul* 59 no. 1 (2008): 99–118; Kloppenborg, "Disaffiliation," 1–16; Celestino G. Lingad, *The Problems of Jewish Christians in the Johannine Community*, Tesi gregoriana Serie teologia 73 (Roma: Editrice Pontificia Università Gregoriana, 2001), 66–109; Martyn, *History*,

37–62, 156–57; Motyer, *Father*, 92–94; John Painter, "John 9 and the Interpretation of the Fourth Gospel," *JSNT* 28 (1986): 31–61; *TDNT*, s.v. "ἀποσυνάγωγος," 7:848–52; Hermann Leberecht Strack and Paul Billerbeck, *Kommentar zum Neuen Testament aus Talmud und Midrasch*, 6 vols. (München: Beck, 1922), IV:293–333; G. M. Styler, "The Persecution of Christians in John 15:18–16:4a," in *Essays on John*, ed. Barnabas Lindars and C. M. Tuckett (Leuven: Leuven University Press, 1992), 48–69; Pieter Willem van der Horst, "The *Birkhat ha-Minim* in Recent Research," *ExpTim* 105 (1993/1994): 363–68; Urban C. Von Wahlde, "The Terms for Religious Authorities in the Fourth Gospel: A Key to Literary-Strata," *JBL* 98 no. 2 (1979): 231–53.

15. Heemstra, *Fiscus Judaicus*, 63.
16. Heemstra, *Fiscus Judaicus*, 1–66.
17. Heemstra, *Fiscus Judaicus*, 179.
18. Heemstra, *Fiscus Judaicus*, 179.
19. Heemstra, *Fiscus Judaicus*, 187.
20. Heemstra, *Fiscus Judaicus*, 186–89.
21. Heemstra, *Fiscus Judaicus*, 187, 201–207.
22. Heemstra, *Fiscus Judaicus*, 179. Heemstra cites m. Sanh. 10.1, which reads: "The following are those who do not have a portion in the world to come: the one who says there is no resurrection of the dead, [the one who says] the Torah is not from Heaven, and the *'apiqoros*." Heemstra, *Fiscus Judaicus*, 169.

23. Kloppenborg, "Disaffiliation," 3 fn. 14.

24. Lawrence H. Schiffman, "At the Crossroads: Tannaitic Perspectives on the Jewish-Christian Schism," in *Jewish and Christian Self-Definition*, ed. E. P. Sanders, A. I. Baumgarten, and Alan Mendelson (London: SCM, 1981), 152. Schiffman argues that the *Birkat ha-Minim* sought to exclude heretics from serving as precentors in the synagogue. He affirms the *Birkat ha-Minim* as targeting Jewish Christians (*minim*) and Gentile Christians (*notzrim*) but because of the evidence from Justin Martyr, Origen, and Epiphanius, he dates the final version of the benediction to second century CE. He allows for the possibility that the Johannine expulsion passages were a result of the institution of this benediction. Schiffman, "At the Crossroads," 149–56.

25. Heemstra, *Fiscus Judaicus*, 159–89, citing 186.

26. Hengel, *Johannine Question*, 114–15. Hengel writes that the *Birkat ha-Minim* should be viewed as "simply the ultimate consequence of a development full of combat and suffering." Hengel, *Johannine Question*, 115.

27. Heemstra, *Fiscus Judaicus*, 176. Heemstra cites Pliny's letter to Trajan, *Ep.* 10.96 but the letter does not assert that their hostility toward believers in Jesus is rooted in the worship of Roman gods.

28. If we look back to 15:18–25 as the context for 16:2b, it seems best to identify the antagonism of "the Jews" as representative of "the world," since in 15:25 Jesus cites the Jewish Scriptures to explain their antagonism toward him and the disciples. Similarly, Chennattu, *Discipleship*, 123 fn. 132; Thompson, *John*, 335–36; Tolmie, *Farewell*, 215.

29. Bernier, *Aposynagōgos*, 41, 45–46.

30. Bernier argues that the decision to pay Judas to betray Jesus (Luke 22:45) and the decision by "the Jews" to deceive the Roman centurion to bring out Paul so they might kill him (Acts 23:20) must not have come through formal legislation, rather by an ad hoc decision of the leaders. Thus, he reasons because ἀποσυνάγωγος is paired with συντίθημι in 9:22, it speaks to the informal nature of the decision. Bernier, *Aposynagōgos*, 68–74. The informal meaning of συντίθημι is also supported by Josephus who uses the term about eighty times, half of which refer to official decrees and half to non-official decrees. Bernier, *Aposynagōgos*, 70.

31. Bernier, *Aposynagōgos*, 70.

32. Bernier, *Aposynagōgos*, 68–74.

33. Bernier, *Aposynagōgos*, 73–74.

34. Cf. Hare and Kloppenborg who argue that social misbehavior was the impetus for ἀποσυνάγωγος. Chennattu rightly points to the confession of Jesus as Messiah as the cause for the conflict between "the Jews" and the disciples. However, I think she reads too much into John when she concludes that John's response to the expulsion passages is to take the Old Testament covenant metaphor and redefine it, broaden it, and apply it to the relationship between God and the Johannine community. Rather, I argue that John picks up on certain Old Testament themes in his explanation of Jesus' identity but in reference to the disciples, John deploys a variety of images to stimulate continuous discipleship. Chennattu, *Discipleship*, 194–211; Hare, *Persecution*, 48–56; Kloppenborg, "Disaffiliation," 1–16.

35. Bernier, *Aposynagōgos*, 95–176.

36. Adele Reinhartz, "Reading History in the Fourth Gospel," in *What We Have Heard from the Beginning: The Past, Present, and Future of Johannine Studies*, ed. Tom Thatcher (Waco, TX: Baylor University Press, 2007), 193.

37. Reinhartz, *Befriending*, 41.

38. Reinhartz, *Befriending*, 37–53.

39. Reinhartz, *Befriending*, 39–48.

40. So, Reinhartz, "Women," 17.

41. Reinhartz, *Befriending*, 49–50. For defense of οὗτός...οἴδαμεν...αὐτὸν οἶμαι referring to a single eyewitness in 21:24–25 (see also 19:35), which would suggest a high probability of historical accuracy of the Johannine narrative, see Richard Bauckham, *Jesus and the Eyewitnesses: The Gospels as Eyewitness Testimony* (Grand Rapids, MI: Eerdmans, 2006), 358–411; Howard M. Jackson, "Ancient Self-Referential Conventions and Their Implications of the Authorship and Integrity of the Gospel of John," *JTS* 50 (1999): 1–34. For defense of multiple authors in 21:24–25 and thus reduced historicity in John, see R. Alan Culpepper, "John 21:24–25: The Johannine Sphragis," in *John, Jesus, and History: Aspects of Historicity in the Fourth Gospel*, ed. Paul N. Anderson, Felix Just, and Tom Thatcher (Atlanta, GA: SBL Press, 2007), 349–64; Andrew T. Lincoln, "The Beloved Disciple as Eyewitness and the Fourth Gospel as Witness," *JSNT* 85 (2002): 11. For broader discussions concerning the historicity of John, see Paul N. Anderson, Felix Just, and Tom Thatcher, *John, Jesus, and History*, 3 vols. (Atlanta, GA: SBL Press, 2007–2016).

42. Reinhartz, *Befriending*, 50.

43. Arguments adopted from Bernier, *Aposynagōgos*, 24. Bernier derives his methodology from Ben F. Meyer, "Locating Lonerganian Hermeneutics," in *Critical Realism and the New Testament*, ed. Ben F. Meyer (Eugene, OR: Pickwick, 1989), 1–16; Ben F. Meyer, "Lonergan's Breakthrough and the Aims of Jesus," in *Critical Realism and the New Testament*, ed. Ben F. Meyer (Eugene, OR: Pickwick, 1989), 147–56.

44. Bernier, *Aposynagōgos*, 114–34; Hengel, *Johannine Question*, 119; Klink, "Expulsion," 117–18; Reinhartz, *Befriending*, 50–53; Trebilco, *Early Christians*, 240.

45. Ashton, *Origins*, 9. For a discussion on when the final break between Judaism and Christianity occurred, see the following works: for the break before 70 CE, Giorgio Jossa, *Jews or Christians?: The Followers of Jesus in Search of Their Own Identity*, WUNT 202 (Tübingen: Mohr Siebeck, 2006), 102–21. For the break ca. 96 CE, Heemstra, *Fiscus Judaicus*, 165, 201–203. For the break ca. 135 CE, James D. G. Dunn, *The Partings of the Ways: Between Christianity and Judaism and Their Significance for the Character of Christianity*, 2nd ed. (London: SCM, 2006), 312–18.

46. Ashton, *Origins*, 3.

47. Ashton, *Origins*, 9.

48. Ashton, *Origins*, 142–44.

49. With reference to John 1:17, Ashton writes, "with this sentence, Moses has been ousted from his position at the heart of the Jewish religion; his privileged role as God's intermediary has been taken away from him and conferred instead on Christ." Ashton, *Origins*, 167.

50. Ashton, *Origins*, 9, 22, 142–43.

51. Ashton, *Origins*, 17–18, 93–94, 141.

52. This emphatic use of the pronoun σύ is also seen in 9:17 (τί σὺ λέγεις περὶ αὐτοῦ), where the blind man is set against the Pharisees (λέγουσιν οὖν τῷ τυφλῷ πάλιν) with the dual use of the verb λέγω. Barrett, *John*, 360.

53. Keener, *John*, 791.

54. In his critique of Ashton, Bennema says, "While agreeing with Ashton's main point that the fourth evangelist presents Jesus as superseding Moses, I see this more in terms of Jesus going *beyond* Moses rather than *against* Moses." Cornelis Bennema, "Review of *The Gospel of John and Christian Origins*," *JETS* 58 no. 2 (June 2015): 398.

55. Beasley-Murray, *John*, 158. John 5:45–47 supports the notion that true belief in Moses will lead to belief in Jesus. The perfect tense of ἠλπίκατε in 5:45 may accent the long-standing commitment of "the Jews" to Moses even when faced with a type of "new Moses" (see 6:14; 7:40). See also Meeks who writes, "Moses only wrote of Jesus and true belief in Moses led to belief in Jesus." Meeks, *Prophet-King*, 319.

56. Shin argues for moral progress as John's understanding of discipleship and in the response of the blind man to the Jewish leaders. He observes that "Moses is nothing more than an instrument of God whose role is to witness to Jesus (5:46)." Moreover, he read John 3:14 through the rhetorical device *synkrisis* and concluded that John does not present Jesus as negating Moses and the serpent, but Jesus is superior for he offers something far greater to the people. Shin, *Ethics*, 68, 116.

57. Ashton, *Origins*, 76–78.

58. As cited by Ashton, *Origins*, 77. "This statement [John 9:28] is scarcely conceivable in Jesus' lifetime, since it recognizes discipleship to Jesus not only as antithetical, but also as somehow comparable, to discipleship to Moses. It is, on the other hand, easily understood under circumstances in which the synagogue has begun to view the Christian movement as an essential and more or less clearly distinguishable rival." Original from Martyn, *History*, 47.

59. Ashton writes: "There is not the slightest indication that there was any controversy over this title [Christ] between Jesus and the Pharisees, or between Jesus and any other Jewish group. Indeed, it is safe to say that such a controversy is highly unlikely to have occurred in Jesus' lifetime." Ashton, *Origins*, 77–78.

60. Ashton maintains that when John "implicates the Pharisees, along with the chief priests, in the two attempts on Jesus' life—first in the earlier episode in the temple (7:32, 45) and then in the final, successful, effort (11:47, 57; 18:3)—he is probably retrojecting his current enmity with the Pharisees back into the story." Ashton, *Origins*, 51.

61. John's references to hostility toward Jesus and Jesus' followers is congruent with the religious milieu of early Christianity presented by the other New Testament writings (e.g., Acts 4, 5, 7, 8, 9; 2 Corinthians 11:24–25; Galatians 1:13; 1 Thessalonians 2:14–16; Revelation 3:9). Gorman insightfully shows how the mission of God is being extended and fulfilled by Jesus and subsequently by the disciples to their adversaries in John (e.g., "the world," "the Jews," Nicodemus, Samaritan woman). See Gorman, *Abide and Go*, 160–78.

62. John repeats the phrase "his own" in 10:3–4, 12; 13:1; 15:19 to distinguish between Jesus' followers and those who reject him.

63. Culpepper, "Realized," 275.

64. Tolmie explains the work of the Paraclete in 16:8, ἐλέγξει τὸν κόσμον περὶ ἁμαρτίας καὶ περὶ δικαιοσύνης καὶ περὶ κρίσεως, is proof of "the world's" wrongdoing. The lack of the articles before each noun suggests that general ideas are meant rather than individual issues. Tolmie, *Farewell*, 86 fn. 44.

65. See also John 7:19, 23 where Jesus associates the law with "the Jews."

66. Rainbow, *Theology*, 136.

67. The definition of "the Jews" discussed here is based on Bennema's study from Cornelis Bennema, "The Identity and Composition of ΟΙ ΙΟΥΔΑΙΟΙ in the Gospel of John," *TynBul* 60 no. 2 (2009): 239–63. Myers argues for John's presentation of the ambiguous response of "the Jews" toward Jesus which allows for the readers of John to identify with "the Jews'" tension between belief and unbelief in John. Alicia D. Myers, "Just Opponents?: Ambiguity, Empathy, and the Jews in the Gospel of John," in *Johannine Ethics: The Moral World of the Gospel and Epistles of John*, ed. Sherri Brown and Christopher W. Skinner (Minneapolis, MN: Fortress Press, 2017), 159–76.

68. John 2:18, 20; 5:10, 15, 16, 18; 6:41, 52; 7:1, 13, 35; 8:22, 48, 52, 57; 9:18, 22 (2x); 10:19, 24, 31, 33; 11:8, 45, 54; 13:33; 18:12, 14, 20, 31, 36; 19:7, 12, 14, 21, 31, 38; 20:19. Other passages refer to Jewish customs, the title "king of the Jews," and ethnicity.

69. For a survey of "the Jews" as a literary character in John, see Urban C. Von Wahlde, "The Johannine 'Jews': A Critical Survey," *NTS* 28 (1982): 33–60. For

specific proposals on "the Jews" in John, see John Ashton, "The Identity and Function of the Ioudaioi in the Fourth Gospel," *NovT* 27 no. 1 (1985): 40–75; Bennema, "Identity," 239–63; Brown et al., *Introduction*, 160–72; Chris Keith, Hurtado, Larry W., *Jesus among Friends and Enemies: A Historical and Literary Introduction to Jesus in the Gospels* (Grand Rapids, MI: Baker, 2011), 199–217; Marinus de Jonge, "The Conflict between Jesus and the Jews and the Radical Christology of the Fourth Gospel," *PRSt* 20 no. 4 (1993): 341–55; T. Dozemann, "Sperma Abraham in Jn 8 and Related Literature," *CBQ* 42 (1980): 342–58; Hakola, *Identity*; Janis E. Leibig, "John and 'the Jews': Theological Antisemitism in the Fourth Gospel," *JES* 20 no. 2 (1983): 209–34; Judith Lieu, "Anti-Judaism, the Jews, and the Worlds of the Fourth Gospel," in *The Gospel of John and Christian Theology*, ed. Richard Bauckham and Carl Mosser (Grand Rapids, MI: Eerdmans, 2008), 168–82; Malcolm F. Lowe, "Who Were the 'Ioudaioi,'" *NovT* 18 no. 2 (1976): 101–30; Wayne A. Meeks, "'Am I a Jew?'—Johannine Christianity and Judaism," in *Christianity, Judaism, and Other Greco-Roman Cults: Studies for Morton Smith at Sixty*, ed. Jacob Neusner (Leiden: Brill, 1975), 164–85; Stephen Motyer, "Bridging the Gap: How Might the Fourth Gospel Help Us Cope with the Legacy of Christianity's Exclusive Claim over against Judaism?," in *The Gospel of John and Christian Theology*, ed. Richard Bauckham and Carl Mosser (Grand Rapids, MI: Eerdmans, 2008), 183–92; Schnackenburg, *John*, 1:286–87; Fernando F. Segovia, "The Love and Hatred of Jesus and Johannine Sectarianism," *CBQ* 43 no. 2 (1981): 258–72; Smith, *John*, 34–38; Von Wahlde, "Terms for Religious Authorities," 231–53; Urban C. Von Wahlde, "Literary Structure and Theological Argument in Three Discourses with the Jews in the Fourth Gospel," *JBL* 103 no. 4 (1984): 575–84. Judeans: Lowe, "Who Were the 'Ioudaioi,'" 119–24. Diaspora Jews: North, *Journey*, 148–67. High officials: Von Wahlde, "Johannine 'Jews,'" 33–60. Representatives of unbelief: Bultmann, *John*, 86.

70. John Ashton, *Studying John: Approaches to the Fourth Gospel* (Oxford: Clarendon Press, 1994), 63, 70.

71. Bennema, "Identity," 263; Motyer, *Father*, 46–57.

72. Bennema explains "the Jews" as follows:

> Οἱ Ἰουδαῖοι in the Gospel of John are a particular religious group within Judaism—the (strict) Torah- and temple-loyalists who are mainly located in Jerusalem and Judaea but could also have been present in Galilee. Their leaders consist of the chief priests who had the power of control and policymaking, and the Pharisees who had the 'power' of influence. We argued that John had a single referent in mind—albeit the referent is a composite group which does not present a uniform response. Οἱ Ἰουδαῖοι as a group is and remains hostile towards Jesus, but it is also divided about him and some individual Ἰουδαῖοι were able to express sympathy and even belief in Jesus—though not always in the full Johannine sense." Bennema, "Identity," 262.

73. Bennema, "Identity," 260–62.

74. The imperfect tense in 5:16 can be customary, Beasley-Murray translates it as "used to persecute," see Beasley-Murray, *John*, 68. Ingressive seems to be more appropriate since this is the first mention of Jewish leaders' persecution of Jesus. For the ingressive view, see Brown, *John*, 212–13; Harris, *John*, 109. John also uses ζητέω to convey the idea of pursuing Jesus with the intent of persecution. There are

twenty-nine combined references to Jesus being sought (ζητέω, twenty-three of thirty-four total uses in John)/found (εὑρίσκω, six of total nineteen in John) and in only five of these twenty-nine combined references to Jesus is he sought/found with positive intent (1:38, 41, 45; 13:33; 20:15). In thirteen occurrences his seekers have ill intent, with the majority of the references being to arrest/kill him (5:18; 7:1, 19, 20, 25, 30; 8:37, 40; 10:39; 11:8; 18:4, 7, 8). In the remaining eleven uses of ζητέω/εὑρίσκω, the meaning of seeking/finding appears to be neutral (6:24, 25, 26; 7:11, 34 (2x), 35, 36 (2x); 8:21; 11:56), but even in some of these eleven passages a negative meaning can also be deduced. Thus, in *pace* Pazdan, who attributes a positive meaning to ζητέω-εὑρίσκω as part of her paradigm of Johannine discipleship, most of the uses of ζητέω-εὑρίσκω have a negative connotation. Pazdan, "Discipleship," 267–300. The other passages denoting the Jewish opposition to Jesus are: 5:16–18; 7:1, 13, 19–20, 25, 30, 32, 44; 8:20, 37, 40, 59; 10:39; 11:8, 46–53, 57.

75. The lame man in John 5:15 illustrates the extent of influence the religious leaders had on him, such that the lame man's allegiance to the Jewish leaders prompted him to return to "the Jews" and turn on Jesus even after being healed by him. The majority of commentators view the lame man negatively. However, Staley suggests that the lame man is a faithful witness because he testified of Jesus' power. Resseguie also views the lame man as a faithful witness to Jesus' miracle based on the consistently positive use of ἀναγγέλλω in John (e.g., 4:25; 16:13–15). However, it is imbalanced to elevate a single verb above the rest of the contextual evidence to the contrary. Second, in the other passages, ἀναγγέλλω is attributed to persons who had previously expressed a favorable view of Jesus. Thus, Resseguie's argument is not convincing. Beck points to the lame man picking up his mat and witnessing to "the Jews" concerning his own healing as evidence of receiving Jesus' words, obeying Jesus, and believing in Jesus. Yet all these attempts to interpret the lame man positively fall short for the following reasons: (1) it is not the most natural reading of the text, especially since (2) there is no comment on the lame man's faith, (3) the lame man does not respond with affirmation to Jesus' question nor express joy for his healing, (4) the result of the lame man's testimony to "the Jews" is the persecution of Jesus, (5) the lame man does not follow Jesus after he is healed, and (6) Jesus points out his sin for which the man does not repent (5:14). Beck, *Discipleship*, 86–91; James M. Howard, "The Significance of Minor Characters in the Gospel of John," *BSac* 163 (2006): 71–73; Resseguie, *Strange*, 134–38; Jeffrey L. Staley, "Stumbling in the Dark, Reaching for the Light: Reading Character in John 5 and 9," *Semeia* 53 (1991): 58–64.

76. Note the use of ἐκβάλλω in John 9:34 that is similar to its use in Luke 6:22.

77. Beasley-Murray suggests that their fear would have been baseless unless they were ready to confess Jesus as a prophet sent by God because of their son's miraculous healing, but refrained from openly supporting Jesus because of their fear of the consequences. Beasley-Murray, *John*, 157.

78. Okure perceptively points out that "the primary causes which led to departures from the Johannine community were internal and doctrinal rather than external and social, for instance, ejection from the synagogue. . . . If the Johannine evidence be taken at its face value, the fear of ejection from the synagogue is seen as the reason

for remaining a crypto-Christian, a hidden confessor of Jesus (9:22; 12:42–43; 19:38), not for refusing to believe in him." Okure, *Approach*, 259–60.

79. The verb λατρεύω is scattered throughout the New Testament with the same meaning of service to God, with the only exception being Romans 1:25 where Paul refers to serving the creation in contrast with serving God.

80. Strathmann notes, "The concrete idea of sacrifice seems always to cling to the noun no less than to the verb." *TDNT*, s.v. "λατρεύω, λατρεία," 4:65.

81. Farelly also links 12:42–43 with 19:38–42 and observes that Joseph's involvement at Jesus' burial is his attempt to "confess his allegiance," which is in stark contrast to the absence of the disciples at the burial, an act that "can hardly go unnoticed." The disciples' absence further reinforces the notion of the fear of "the Jews." Farelly, *Disciples*, 80.

82. It is beyond the scope of this book to discuss whether Joseph of Arimathea displays traits of true belief. Bennema judges his interaction with Jesus as reflecting inadequate faith from John's point of view. Bennema, *Encountering*, 190–95. In contrast to Bennema, Joseph of Arimathea is presented positively through a comparison of John's account with Mark 15:43. Hunt et al., eds., *Character*, 646–57.

83. True disciple: Beirne calls Nicodemus an example of full discipleship (103). J. M. Auwers, "La nuit de Nicodème (Jn 3.2; 19.39) ou l'ombre du langage," *RB* 97 (1990): 501; Beirne, *Women and Men*, 67–104; Brown, *Community*, 72, fn. 128; Brown, *Death*, 1266; Bultmann, *John*, 133, fn. 2; Sandra Marie Schneiders, *Written That You May Believe: Encountering Jesus in the Fourth Gospel* (New York: Crossroad, 1999), 119. Unbeliever: Collins, *These Things*, 15, 58; de Jonge writes, "[Nicodemus] does not belong to the children of God," de Jonge, *Stranger*, 29–47, citing 42. Partial believer: Culpepper, *Anatomy*, 135–36, 233; Sean Freyne, "Vilifying the Other and Defining the Self," in *To See Ourselves as Others See Us: Christians, Jews, "Others" in Late Antiquity*, ed. Jacob Neusner (Chico, CA: Scholars Press, 1985), 127; Francis J. Moloney, *Belief in the Word: Reading the Fourth Gospel, John 1–4* (Minneapolis, MN: Fortress, 1993), 121. Ambiguous disciple: J. M. Bassler, "Mixed Signals: Nicodemus in the Fourth Gospel," *JBL* 108 no. 4 (1989); Beck, *Discipleship*, 63–70; Hylen, *Imperfect*, 23–40; Gabi Renz, "Nicodemus: An Ambiguous Disciple? A Narrative Sensitive Investigation," in *Challenging Perspectives on the Gospel of John*, ed. John Lierman (Tübingen: Mohr Siebeck, 2006), 254–83. Beck writes, "Nicodemus' final allegiance is an unresolved indeterminacy in the Fourth Gospel. . . . He stands in the text as a potential disciple who has progressed toward, but has not yet arrived at an appropriate response to Jesus . . . in the end his indecision is a decision not to commit." Beck, *Discipleship*, 69. Secret disciple: Bennema, *Encountering*, 83; Conway, *Men and Women*, 86, 101; Martyn, *History*, 87; Smith, *John*, 366. Member of the establishment: David K. Rensberger, *Johannine Faith and Liberating Community* (Philadelphia: Westminster Press, 1988), 115. Prime example of faith: Steven A. Hunt, "Nicodemus, Lazarus, and the Fear of 'the Jews' in the Fourth Gospel," in *Repetitions and Variations in the Fourth Gospel: Style, Text, Interpretation*, ed. Gilbert van Belle, Michael Labahn, and P. Maritz (Leuven; Walpole, MA: Peeters, 2009), 201.

84. See Bennema, *Encountering*, 77–85; Hunt et al., eds., *Character*, 249–59; Craig R. Koester, "Theological Complexity and the Characterization of Nicodemus in John's Gospel," in *Characters and Characterization in the Gospel of John*, ed. Christopher W. Skinner (London: T & T Clark, 2013), 165–81. For a more positive presentation of Nicodemus from the spatial/temporal point of view, see Resseguie, *Strange*, 120–27.

85. In reference to the darkness–light symbolism, most commentators agree that it is more than just a temporal marker. Barrett, *John*, 204–205; Brown, *John*, 130; Carson, *John*, 186; Conway, *Men and Women*, 92–93; Koester, *Symbolism*, 47; Morris, *John*, 187, fn. 8; Renz, "Nicodemus," 261, fn. 26. Cotterrell and Turner dissent and interpret the reference to the night as merely a chronological marker because John did not mark it by moving it to the front of the clause which would have been typical to accent this feature in the narrate (see Matthew 28:13; Luke 21:37). Peter Cotterell and Max Turner, *Linguistics & Biblical Interpretation* (Downers Grove, IL: InterVarsity, 1989), 282. The lexical overlap between 2:23–25 and 3:1–2 suggests that Nicodemus had some level of belief in Jesus. For John 2:23–3:15 as a single pericope, see Bennema, *Encountering*, 79, fn. 15.

86. Hylen supposes that Nicodemus' response to the question from the Jewish leaders suggests that he is in the category of the Pharisees who believed in Jesus. Hylen, *Imperfect*, 33.

87. Bauckham concludes that Nicodemus' honor of Jesus at his burial is fitting for a king. Bauckham, *Testimony*, 165. See also Beirne, *Women and Men*, 86; Keener, *John*, 1157, 1162.

88. Contra Beck who does not view Nicodemus as a model disciple because there is no evidence of a faith response and Nicodemus does not witness to others. While John does not narrate a confession from Nicodemus, the spices he brought for Jesus' burial suggest Nicodemus' recognition of Jesus' kingship. Beck, *Discipleship*, 63–70. Shin evaluates Nicodemus through an ethical reading and concludes that the placement of Nicodemus' narrative early on in the Gospel demonstrates the importance of new birth to the process of discipleship. Moreover, the darkness reference in the story of Nicodemus suggests that he has not come fully into the light and thus at best he is an ambiguous disciple. The ethical reading sends the message to the readers that "any attachment to darkness must be abandoned entirely in order for the *Light* to take over" which is necessary of true discipleship. Shin, *Ethics*, 77–79.

89. 1:11; 2:18–21; 3:11, 36; 4:1–3, 44; 5:16–18; 6:60–66; 7:1, 13, 19–20, 25, 30, 32, 44; 8:20, 37, 40, 59; 9:22, 28, 34; 10:39; 11:8, 46–53, 57; 12:10, 19, 42; 13:2, 21; 14:27, 30; 15:18–27; 16:2, 33; 17:14; chs. 18–19; 19:38; 20:19; 21:18.

90. Bennema writes, "The conflict between Jesus and the Jewish religious authorities of his time is probably paradigmatic of the conflicts his followers will face in later times—whether Jewish Christians versus synagogue Judaism (16.2) or believers/church versus the world at large (15.18–16.4; 17.14–16). Hence . . . John 9.22 and 12.42 may simply reflect the general situation towards the end of the first century." Bennema, *Power*, 251–52.

91. Okure similarly observes: "The Evangelist seeks to understand his own situation and problems in the light of Jesus' own situation." Okure, *Approach*, 259; cf. Bernier, *Aposynagōgos*, 133–34.

92. Brown and Moloney make a similar connection: "The Gospel was written in good part to deepen the faith of believers so that they could understand that what they had gained by way of God's life more than made up for what had been lost in their former religious adhesion. The evangelist speaks to those who accepted Jesus, thereby becoming God's children, begotten not by human intervention but by God (1:12–13), in order to make them appreciate the life they had been given." Brown et al., *Introduction*, 182.

# Conclusion

This study presents the benefits of discipleship in John's Gospel as motivations for continuous commitment to Jesus. John encourages devotion to Jesus by featuring certain themes that can be grouped under three primary categories and designated as compensatory benefits of commitment to Jesus in light of the potential cost of discipleship. These three benefits are as follows: membership in the divine family, the abiding presence of the Father and the Son through the Spirit with the believer, and royal friendship with Jesus. John deployed corollary benefits as additional themes that fill out John's bouquet of benefits that are conferred upon the disciple who continuously believes in Jesus.

The proposal that John deploys the above themes as compensatory benefits of discipleship rests on three points. First, the inclusion of the promise of life in the purpose statement forges a link between discipleship and the reward for believing in Jesus as the Messiah (20:31). Notwithstanding the debate regarding the tense of "that you may believe" (πιστεύ[σ]ητε) in 20:31, the present participle in the clause, "that by believing you may have life in his name" (ἵνα πιστεύοντες ζωὴν ἔχητε ἐν τῷ ὀνόματι αὐτοῦ) functions modally and thus suggests that life is obtained through continuous belief in his name.[1] John's juxtaposition of belief with the resultant benefit of life indicates to his audiences that there are benefits for believing. Second, a chiastic reading of John's prologue suggests that 1:12b is the central point of the prologue, that is, the *Logos* became human to give believers the right to become children of God. This benefit of becoming a child of God is conferred specifically on the individual who continuously believes in his name (τοῖς πιστεύουσιν, v. 12).[2] The third reason to view benefits as motivators for discipleship is John's frequent presentation of the theme of discipleship in the context of opposition that might prompt defection.

After introducing the argument of the present study and situating it in the scholarly literature on Johannine discipleship, the first two chapters focused on the benefit of membership in the divine family as the first primary reward of continuous discipleship. The prominence of familial terminology in John and the placement of the family theme in the prologue suggests a chiasm in 1:1–18 with the focal point being in 1:12b—"who believed in his name, he gave the right to become children of God." This chiasm essentially forms two *inclusios*: the first *inclusio* in the public ministry of Jesus (1:12–13 with 12:36) and the second *inclusio* of the entire Gospel (1:12–13 with 20:17 and 21:5). The focus of chapter 2 was the theme of life (ζωή) in juxtaposition to kinship terminology, which suggests that the promise of life should be understood as the ability and the quality of the believer to exist and relate *within* the divine family. Membership in the divine family yields the corollary benefits of love, knowledge of God and of the truth, freedom from sin, walking in the light, salvation, avoidance of judgment/destruction, resurrection, protection, performance of great works, affirmation of genuine discipleship, honor, glory, and unity/oneness of the Father and the Son with the other disciples. These benefits enhance the believer's experience in the divine family.

Chapter 3 featured abiding as the second primary benefit in John. Abiding was presented as a promise that is experienced by the disciple in the present time (14:23) and in the future (14:2–3). Abiding should be understood as a major motif because of the frequent occurrence and the peculiar meaning of "abide/abiding place" (μένω/μονή) in the Gospel. John situates his presentation of the theme of abiding in the Old Testament imagery of God dwelling with his people. John subsequently develops the abiding of the Father and the Son through the Spirit with(in) the believer (14:1–3, 15–24), and the believer fulfilling his obligation to abide in Jesus (15:1–11), which results in additional corollary benefits—fruit, the Paraclete, peace, joy, answered requests, love, confirmation of genuine discipleship, avoidance of judgment, and the ability to perform great works. The promise of God's abiding presence reaches its zenith in eschatology when Jesus will provide a dwelling place (μονή) for his disciples (14:2–3).

In chapters 4 and 5 royal friendship was discussed as the third primary benefit in John. Friendship is a key theme in John because 15:12–17 is set apart as a separate unit within the Farewell Discourse through (1) the use of ταῦτα λελάληκα (v. 11) and the parallel clause ταῦτα ἐντέλλομαι (v. 17), and (2) through the repeated command "to love one another" (vv. 12, 17). Moreover, the extended narrative on friendship and the exegesis of 15:12–17 establish friendship as a significant and distinct benefit in the Gospel. Based on the uniqueness of the friendship motif in the Gospel, I argued that John depicts Jesus as a royal figure who invites his followers into a friendship in which the followers experience the honor and privileges of being members of his royal circle. There are three reasons why 15:12–17 is best understood through the lens of royal friendship. First, classical Greek, Roman, and Hellenistic writings provide a literary context in which the term "friends" (φίλοι) bears political overtones in 15:12–17. Second, John presents Jesus as a king (1:49; 3:3–5; 6:14–15; 12:13–15; 18:33–19:21), which suggests that Jesus is a royal friend to his followers. Third, the context of 15:12–17 contains the imagery and language of a shepherd-king, subordination, election, obligations, and benefits that would have characterized ancient royal friendship.

In chapter 6 I argued that John's Gospel is filled with references to hostility against Jesus and his followers that form the backdrop for John's call to continuous discipleship. On account of the fear of expulsion from the synagogues (9:22; 12:42; 16:2), opposition from the Jewish leadership (7:13; 9:22; 12:42; 19:38; 20:19), and hatred from "the world" (15:18–27; 17:14), there is a possibility of apostasy by Jesus' followers (16:1–2). John's presentation of membership in the divine family, the abiding presence of the Father and the Son through the Spirit with the believer, and royal friendship with Jesus are to be understood as incentives for John's audiences to remain faithful to Jesus in light of the potential opposition for belief in Jesus.

In 6:66–67, John depicts a scene in which many of Jesus' disciples cease to follow him. In response, John portrays Jesus as asking his disciples, "Do you also wish to go away?" Peter functions as the representative of "the twelve" when he replies: "Lord, to whom will we go? You have the words of eternal life. We have believed and we have come to know that you are the Holy One of God" (6:68). Peter's verbal allegiance was appended to his belief that Jesus' teaching would result in eternal life.[3] The question Jesus posed to his disciples, "Do you also wish to go away?" serves as a resounding echo to the audiences of the Gospel whom John encourages to emulate Peter's response and to recognize that certain benefits await the believer in Jesus (1:12; 14:1–3; 15:13–16; 20:31). John extends membership in the divine family, the abiding presence of the Father and the Son through the Spirit with the believer, and royal friendship with Jesus, along with numerous corollary benefits to encourage continuous discipleship and curtail potential defection by the followers of Jesus (8:31; 6:60–71; 15:8). This is the call to John's audiences in all times and places, to believe and follow Jesus no matter the cost.

## NOTES

1. Harris, *John*, 336.
2. John deploys the verb πιστεύω in the present tense fifty of ninety-eight times.
3. Harris, *John*, 147.

# Bibliography

Accame, Silvio. *Il dominio romano in Grecia dalla guerra acaica ad Augusto*. Studi pubblicati dal R. Istituto italiano per la storia antica fasc 4. Roma: Roma. A. Signorelli, 1946.

Achtemeier, Elizabeth. "Jesus Christ, the Light of the Word: The Biblical Understanding of Light and Darkness." *Interpretation* 17 (1963): 439–49.

Aeschylus. *Persians. Seven against Thebes. The Suppliants. Prometheus Bound*. Translated by Alan H. Sommerstein. LCL. Cambridge, MA: Harvard University Press, 2008.

Akala, Adesola Joan. *The Son-Father Relationship and Christological Symbolism in the Gospel of John*. LNTS 505. London: Bloomsbury.

Aland, Kurt, and Barbara Aland. *The Text of the New Testament: An Introduction to the Critical Editions and to the Theory and Practice of Modern Textual Criticism*. Grand Rapids, MI: Eerdmans, 1987.

Allison, Dale C. "The Living Water (John 4:10–14; 6:35c; 7:37–39)." *St. Vladimir's Theological Quarterly* 30 (1986): 143–57.

Alon, Gedalyahu. "Jewish Christians: The Parting of the Ways." In *The Jews in Their Land in the Talmudic Age (70–640 CE)*, edited by Gershon Levi, 1, 288–307. Jerusalem: Magnes Press, 1980.

Andersen, Francis I. "Enoch, Second Book of." In *The Anchor Bible Dictionary*, edited by David Noel Freedman, 2, 516–22. New York: Doubleday, 1992.

Anderson, Paul N. *The Christology of the Fourth Gospel: Its Unity and Disunity in the Light of John 6*. WUNT 2.78. Tübingen: Mohr, 1996.

———. *The Fourth Gospel and the Quest for Jesus: Modern Foundations Reconsidered*. London: T & T Clark, 2006.

Anderson, Paul N, Felix Just, and Tom Thatcher. *John, Jesus, and History*. 3 vols. Atlanta, GA: SBL Press, 2007–2016.

Appasamy, A. J. *The Johannine Doctrine of Life: A Study of Christian and Indian Thought*. London: Society for Promoting Christian Knowledge, 1934.

Aristotle. *The Art of Rhetoric*. Translated by John Henry Freese. LCL. London: Heinemann, 1926.

———. *Nicomachean Ethics*. Translated by H. Rackham. 23 vols. Cambridge, MA: Harvard University Press, 1975.
Arndt, William, Frederick W. Danker, and Walter Bauer. "ἁρπάζω." In *A Greek-English Lexicon of the New Testament and Other Early Christian Literature*. Chicago: University of Chicago, 2000.
———. "ἕλκω." In *A Greek-English Lexicon of the New Testament and Other Early Christian Literature*. Chicago: University of Chicago, 2000.
———. "Καῖσαρ." In *A Greek-English Lexicon of the New Testament and Other Early Christian Literature*. Chicago: University of Chicago, 2000.
———. "μονή." In *A Greek-English Lexicon of the New Testament and Other Early Christian Literature*. Chicago: University of Chicago, 2000.
Ashton, John. *Studying John: Approaches to the Fourth Gospel*. Oxford: Clarendon Press, 1994.
———. *The Gospel of John and Christian Origins*. Minneapolis: Fortress, 2014.
———. "The Identity and Function of the Ioudaioi in the Fourth Gospel." *Novum Testamentum* 27, no. 1 (1985): 40–75.
———. *Understanding the Fourth Gospel*. 2nd ed. Oxford: Oxford University Press, 2007.
Attridge, Harold W. "Johannine Christianity." In *Essays on John and Hebrews*, edited by Harold W. Attridge, 3–19. Tübingen: Mohr Siebeck, 2010.
———. "Plato, Plutarch, and John: Three Symposia about Love." In *Beyond the Gnostic Gospels: Studies Building on the Work of Elaine Pagels*, edited by Elaine H. Pagels, Eduard Iricinschi, Lance Jenott, Nicola Denzey Lewis, and Philippa Townsend, 367–78. Tübingen: Mohr Siebeck, 2013.
Aune, David Edward. *The New Testament in Its Literary Environment*. LEC 8. Philadelphia: Westminster Press, 1987.
Auwers, J. M. "La nuit de Nicodème (Jn 3.2; 19.39) ou l'ombre du langage." *Revue Biblique* 97 (1990): 481–503.
Badian, Ernst. "Amicitia." In *Brill's New Pauly*, edited by Hubert Cancik, Helmuth Schneider, Manfred Landfester, Christine F. Salazar, and August Friedrich von Pauly. Leiden: Brill, 2005.
Baffes, Melanie. "Christology and Discipleship in John 7:37–38." *Biblical Theology Bulletin* 41, no. 3 (2011): 144–50.
Balsdon, John Percy V. D., and Barbara M. Levick. "Aelius Seianus, Lucius (Sejanus)." In *The Oxford Classical Dictionary*, edited by Simon Hornblower and Antony Spawforth, lv, 1640 p. Oxford; New York: Oxford University Press, 2003.
Bammel, C. P. "Farewell Discourse in Patristic Exegesis." *Neotestamentica* 25, no. 2 (1991): 193–207.
Bammel, Von Ernst. "φίλος τοῦ Καίσαρος." *Theologische Literaturzeitung* 77, no. 4 (1952): 205–10.
Barrett, C. K. *The Gospel According to St. John*. 2nd ed. London: SPCK, 1978.
Bassler, J. M. "Mixed Signals: Nicodemus in the Fourth Gospel." *Journal of Biblical Literature* 108, no. 4 (1989): 635–46.
Bauckham, Richard. *Jesus and the Eyewitnesses: The Gospels as Eyewitness Testimony*. Grand Rapids, MI: Eerdmans, 2006.

―――. *Gospel of Glory: Major Themes in Johannine Theology*. Grand Rapids, MI: Baker, 2015.

―――. "Messianism According to the Gospel of John." In *Challenging Perspectives on the Gospel of John*, edited by John Lierman, 34–68. Tübingen: Mohr Siebeck, 2006.

―――. *The Testimony of the Beloved Disciple: Narrative, History, and Theology in the Gospel of John*. Grand Rapids, MI: Baker, 2007.

―――. ed. *The Gospels for All Christians: Rethinking the Gospel Audiences*. Grand Rapids, MI: Eerdmans, 1998.

Bautch, Kelly Coblentz. "Enoch, First Book of." In *The New Interpreter's Dictionary of the Bible*, edited by Katharine Doob Sakenfeld, Samuel E. Balentine, and Brian K. Blount, 2, 258. Nashville, TN: Abingdon Press, 2009.

Beasley-Murray, G. R. *Gospel of Life: Theology in the Fourth Gospel*. Peabody, MA: Hendrickson, 1991.

―――. *John*. Word Biblical Themes. Dallas, TX: Word, 1989.

Beck, David R. *The Discipleship Paradigm: Readers and Anonymous Characters in the Fourth Gospel*. BIS 27. Leiden: Brill, 1997.

Becker, J. *Das Evangelium des Johannes*. 2 vols. ÖTK 4/1–2. Gütersloh: Gerd Mohn; Würzburg: Echter, 1979–81.

Behm, Johannes. "παράκλητος." In *The Theological Dictionary of the New Testament*, edited by Gerhard Kittel, Gerhard Friedrich, and Geoffrey William Bromiley, 5, 800–814. Grand Rapids, MI: Eerdmans, 1964.

Behm, Johannes, Werner Georg Kümmel, and Paul Feine. *Introduction to the New Testament*. Translated by Jr. A. J. Mattill. Revised ed. Nashville, TN: Abingdon Press, 1966.

Beirne, Margaret M. *Women and Men in the Fourth Gospel: A Genuine Discipleship of Equals*. JSNTSup 242. London: Sheffield Academic Press, 2003.

Bennema, Cornelis. *A Theory of Character in New Testament Narrative*. Minneapolis, MN: Fortress, 2014.

―――. "Christ, the Spirit and the Knowledge of God: A Study in Johannine Epistemology." In *The Bible and Epistemology: Biblical Soundings on the Knowledge of God*, edited by M. Healy and R. Parry, 107–33. Milton Keynes, U.K.: Paternoster, 2007.

―――. *Encountering Jesus: Character Studies in the Gospel of John*. Colorado Springs, CO: Paternoster, 2009.

―――. "Review of *The Gospel of John and Christian Origins*." *Journal of Evangelical Theological Society* 58, no. 2 (June 2015): 397–401.

―――. "The Identity and Composition of ΟΙ ΙΟΥΔΑΙΟΙ in the Gospel of John." *Tyndale Bulletin* 60, no. 2 (2009): 239–63.

―――. *The Power of Saving Wisdom: An Investigation of Spirit and Wisdom in Relation to the Soteriology of the Fourth Gospel*. WUNT 2.148. Tübingen: J.C.B. Mohr, 2002.

Bernard, J. H., and A. H. McNeile. *A Critical and Exegetical Commentary on the Gospel According to St. John*. 2 vols. ICC. New York: Charles Scribner & Sons, 1929.

Bernier, Jonathan. *Aposynagōgos and the Historical Jesus in John: Rethinking the Historicity of the Johannine Expulsion Passages*. BIS 122. Boston: Brill, 2013.
Betz, Hans Dieter. "Nachfolge und Nachahmung Jesu Christi im Neuen Testament." Habilitationsschrift, Mainz, 1967.
Beutler, Johannes S. J. "Faith and Confession: The Purpose of John." In *Texts about Faith and Confession*, edited by Rudolf Hoppe und Ulrich Berges, 101–13. Bonn: V & R Unipress; Bonn University Press, 2012.
Bickerman, E. J. *Institutions des Séleucides*. Haut-commissariat de la république française en Syrie et au Liban service des antiquités bibliothèque archéologique et historique XXVI. Paris: P. Geuthner, 1938.
Bieringer, Reimund. "My Kingship is Not of This World." In *The Myriad Christ: Plurality and the Quest for Unity in Contemporary Christology*, edited by Terrence Merrigan and Jacques Haers, 159–75. Leuven: University Press; Uitgeverij Peeters, 2000.
Bieringer, Reimund, Didier Pollefeyt, and F. Vandecasteele-Vanneuville, eds. *Anti-Judaism and the Fourth Gospel: Papers of the Leuven Colloquium 2000* no. 1. Assen, Netherlands: Royal Van Gorcum, 2001.
Blank, Josef. *Krisis: Untersuchungen zur johanneischen Christologie und Eschatologie*. Lambertus-Verlag: Freiburg im Breisgau, 1964.
Blass, Friedrich, Albert Debrunner, and Robert Walter Funk. *A Greek Grammar of the New Testament and Other Early Christian Literature*. Chicago: University of Chicago, 1961.
Bode, Edward Lynn. *The First Easter Morning: The Gospel Accounts of the Women's Visit to the Tomb of Jesus*. Analecta Biblica 45. Rome: Biblical Institute Press, 1970.
Boismard, M. E. "L'évolution du thème eschatologique dans les traditions johanniques." *Revue biblique* 68 (1961): 507–24.
———. *Le prologue de saint Jean*. Paris, 1953.
Bond, Helen K. "Herod, Family." In *The New Interpreter's Dictionary of the Bible*, edited by Samuel E. Balentine, Katharine Doob Sakenfeld, Brian K. Blount, et al., 2, 790. Nashville, TN: Abingdon Press, 2006.
———. *Pontius Pilate in History and Interpretation*. SNTSMS 100. Cambridge: Cambridge University Press, 1998.
Borgen, Peder. *Bread from Heaven: An Exegetical Study of the Concept of Manna in the Gospel of John and the Writings of Philo*. NovTSup 10. Leiden: E. J. Brill, 1965.
Borig, Rainer. *Der wahre Weinstock: Untersuchungen zu Jo 15, 1–10*. SANT 16. München: Kösel, 1967.
Bowman, John. "The Fourth Gospel and the Samaritans." *BJRL* 40 (1958): 298–308.
Braund, David. *Rome and the Friendly King: The Character of the Client Kingship*. London; New York: Croom Helm; St. Martin's Press, 1984.
Brock, Ann Graham. "The Significance of Φιλέω and Φίλος in the Tradition of Jesus Sayings and in the Early Christian Communities." *The Harvard Theological Review* 90, no. 4 (October 1997): 393–409.
Brodie, Thomas L. *The Gospel According to John: A Literary and Theological Commentary*. New York: Oxford University Press, 1993.

Brooks, Roger. "Mishnah." In *The Anchor Bible Dictionary*, edited by David Noel Freedman, 4, 871–73. New York: Doubleday, 1992.

Brown, Raymond E. *The Gospel According to John*. 2 vols. AB 29–29A. New York: Doubleday, 1966.

———. "'Other Sheep Not of This Fold': The Johannine Perspective on Christian Diversity in the Late First Century." *Journal of Biblical Literature* 97 (1978): 5–22.

———. *The Community of the Beloved Disciple*. New York: Paulist Press, 1979.

———. *The Death of the Messiah: From Gethsemane to the Grave A Commentary on the Passion Narratives in the Four Gospels*. 2 vols. ABRL. New York: Doubleday, 1994.

———. "The Paraclete in the Fourth Gospel." *New Testament Studies* 13 (1967): 113–32.

———. "The Prologue of the Gospel of John: John 1:1–18." *Review and Expositor* 62, no. 4 (1965): 429–39.

Brown, Raymond E., and Francis J. Moloney. *An Introduction to the Gospel of John*. ABRL. New York: Doubleday, 2003.

Brown, Sherri. "Believing in the Gospel of John: The Ethical Imperative to Becoming Children of God." In *Johannine Ethics: The Moral World of the Gospel and Epistles of John*, edited by Sherri Brown, and Christopher W. Skinner, 3–24. Minneapolis, MN: Fortress Press, 2017.

———. "Water Imagery and the Power and Presence of God in the Gospel of John." *Theology Today* 72, no. 3 (2015): 289–98.

———. "What Is Truth? Jesus, Pilate, and the Staging of the Dialogue of the Cross in John 18:28–19:16a." *The Catholic Biblical Quarterly* 77, no. 1 (2015): 69–86.

———. "What's in an Ending? John 21 and the Performative Force of an Epilogue." *Perspectives in Religious Studies* 42 no. 1 (2015): 29–42.

Brownlee, William H. "Whence the Gospel According to John?" In *John and Qumran*, edited by Raymond E. Brown and James H. Charlesworth, 166–94. London: Geoffrey Chapman, 1972.

Brunson, Andrew C. *Psalm 118 in the Gospel of John: An Intertextual Study on the New Exodus Pattern in the Theology of John*. WUNT 2.158. Tübingen: Mohr Siebeck, 2003.

Brunt, P. A. *The Fall of the Roman Republic and Related Essays*. Oxford: Clarendon Press, 1988.

Bultmann, Rudolf. "γινώσκω." In *The Theological Dictionary of the New Testament*, edited by Gerhard Kittel, Gerhard Friedrich, and Geoffrey William Bromiley, 1, 689–719. Grand Rapids, MI: Eerdmans, 1985.

———. "ζάω." In *The Theological Dictionary of the New Testament*, edited by Gerhard Kittel, Gerhard Friedrich, and Geoffrey William Bromiley, 2, 832–75. Grand Rapids, MI: Eerdmans, 1985.

———. *The Gospel of John: A Commentary*. Oxford: B. Blackwell, 1971.

———. *Theology of the New Testament*. 2 vols. New York: Charles Scribner & Sons, 1951.

Burnett, F. W. "Characterization and Reader Construction of Characters in the Gospels." *Semeia* 63 (1993): 3–28.

Burridge, Richard A. *What Are the Gospels? A Comparison with Graeco-Roman Biography*. SNTSMS 70, edited by G. N. Stanton. Cambridge: Cambridge University Press, 1992.

Campbell, Constantine R. *Advances in the Study of Greek: New Insights for Reading the New Testament*. Grand Rapids, MI: Zondervan, 2015.

———. *Basics of Verbal Aspect in Biblical Greek*. Grand Rapids, MI: Zondervan, 2008.

Carroll, Kenneth L. "The Fourth Gospel and the Exclusion of Christians from the Synagogues." *BJRL* 40, no. 1 (1957): 19–32.

Carson, D. A. *The Gospel According to John*. Grand Rapids, MI: Eerdmans, 1991.

———. "The Purpose of the Fourth Gospel: John 20:31 Reconsidered." *Journal of Biblical Literature* 6 (1987): 639–51.

———. "Understanding Misunderstandings in the Fourth Gospel." *Tyndale Bulletin* 33 (1982): 59–91.

Carter, Warren. *John and Empire: Initial Explorations*. New York: T & T Clark, 2008.

Casey, Maurice. *Is John's Gospel True?* London: Routledge, 1996.

Charles, R. H., and August Dillmann. *The Book of Enoch*. Oxford: Clarendon Press, 1893.

Charlesworth, James H., ed. *The Old Testament Pseudepigrapha*. New York: Doubleday, 1983.

Chennattu, Rekha M. *Johannine Discipleship as a Covenant Relationship*. Peabody, MA: Hendrickson, 2006.

———. "Les femmes dans la mission de l'église: interprétation de Jean 4." *Bulletin de littérature ecclésiastique* 108, no. 3 (2007): 381–96.

Cicero. *Letters to Atticus*. Translated by D. R. Shackleton Bailey. 4 vols. LCL. Cambridge, MA: Harvard University Press, 1999.

———. *On Old Age. On Friendship. On Divination*. Translated by W. A. Falconer. LCL. Cambridge, MA: Harvard University Press, 1923.

Clark-Soles, Jaime. "'I Will Raise [Whom?] Up on the Last Day': Anthropology as a Feature of Johannine Eschatology." In *New Currents through John: A Global Perspective*, edited by Francisco Lozada and Tom Thatcher, 29–53. Atlanta: SBL Press, 2006.

Cohen, Shaye J. D. "The Significance of Yavneh: Pharisees, Rabbis and the End of Jewish Sectarianism." *Hebrew Union College Annual* 55 (1984): 27–53.

Collins, Raymond F. *These Things Have Been Written: Studies on the Fourth Gospel*. Grand Rapids, MI: Eerdmans, 1990.

Coloe, Mary L. *Dwelling in the Household of God: Johannine Ecclesiology and Spirituality*. Collegeville, MN: Liturgical Press, 2007.

———. *God Dwells with Us: Temple Symbolism in the Fourth Gospel*. Collegeville, MN: Liturgical Press, 2001.

———. "The Woman of Samaria: Her Characterization, Narrative, and Theological Significance." In *Characters and Characterization in the Gospel of John*, edited by Christopher W. Skinner, 182–96. London: Bloomsbury T & T Clark, 2013.

Conway, Colleen M. *Men and Women in the Fourth Gospel: Gender and Johannine Characterization*. SBLDS 167. Atlanta, GA: SBL Press, 1999.

———. "Speaking through Ambiguity: Minor Characters in the Fourth Gospel." *Biblical Interpretation* 10, no. 3 (2002): 324–41.
Cotterell, Peter, and Max Turner. *Linguistics & Biblical Interpretation*. Downers Grove, IL: InterVarsity, 1989.
Crook, Zeba A. "Fictive-Friendship and the Fourth Gospel." *HTS Teologiese Studies/ Theological Studies* 67, no. 3 (2011): 1–7.
Culpepper, R. Alan. *Anatomy of the Fourth Gospel: A Study in Literary Design*. Philadelphia: Fortress, 1983.
———. "John 21:24–25: The Johannine Sphragis." In *John, Jesus, and History: Aspects of Historicity in the Fourth Gospel*, edited by Paul N. Anderson, Felix Just and Tom Thatcher, 2, 349–64. Atlanta, GA: SBL Press, 2007.
———. "The Pivot of John's Prologue." *New Testament Studies* 27, no. 1 (1980): 1–31.
———. "Realized Eschatology in the Experience of the Johannine Community." In *The Resurrection of Jesus in the Gospel of John*, edited by Craig R. Koester and R. Bieringer, 253–76. Tübingen: Mohr Siebeck, 2008.
Culy, Martin M. *Echoes of Friendship in the Gospel of John*. NTM 30. Sheffield, England: Sheffield Press, 2010.
Cuss, Dominique. *Imperial Cult and Honorary Terms in the New Testament*. Paradosis, Contributions to the History of Early Christian Literature and Theology 23. Fribourg: University Press, 1974.
Davies, W. D. "Reflections on Aspects of the Jewish Background of the Gospel of John." In *Exploring the Gospel of John: In Honor of D. Moody Smith*, edited by R. Alan Culpepper and C. Clifton Black, 43–64. Louisville: Westminster John Knox, 1996.
Davis, J. C. "The Johannine Concept of Eternal Life as a Present Possession." *Restoration Quarterly* 27 (1984): 161–69.
De Boer, M. C. "Narrative Criticism, Historical Criticism, and the Gospel of John." *Journal for the Study of the New Testament* 47 (1992): 35–58.
De Jonge, Marinus. "The Conflict between Jesus and the Jews and the Radical Christology of the Fourth Gospel." *Perspectives in Religious Studies* 20, no. 4 (1993): 341–55.
———. *Jesus: Stranger from Heaven and Son of God*. Sources for Biblical Study 11. Missoula, MT: Scholars Press, 1977.
De la Potterie, Ignace. "Οἶδα et γινώσκω: Les deux modes de la connaissance dans le quatrième évangile." *Biblica* 40, no. 3 (1959): 709–25.
———. "The Truth in Saint John." In *The Interpretation of John*, edited by John Ashton, 67–81. Philadelphia: Fortress, 1986.
De Smidt, J. C. "A Perspective on John 15:1–8." *Neotestamentica* 25, no. 2 (1991): 251–72.
Deissmann, Adolf. *Bible Studies: Contributions Chiefly from Papyri and Inscriptions to the History of the Language, the Literature, and the Religion of Hellenistic Judaism and Primitive Christianity*. Edinburgh: T & T Clark, 1901.
———. *Light from the Ancient East: The New Testament Illustrated by Recently Discovered Texts of the Graeco-Roman World*. 4th ed. London: Hodder and Stoughton, 1927.

Dio, Cassius. *Roman History*. Translated by Earnest Cary. 9 vols. LCL. London: Harvard University Press, 1924.
Dodd, C. H. *Historical Tradition in the Fourth Gospel*. Cambridge: University Press, 1963.
———. *The Interpretation of the Fourth Gospel*. Cambridge: University Press, 1953.
Domeris, William R. "Christology and Community: A Study of the Social Matrix of the Fourth Gospel." *Journal of Theology for Southern Africa* 64 (1988): 49–56.
———. "The Farewell Discourse: An Anthropological Perspective." *Neotestamentica* 25, no. 2 (1991): 233–50.
Dozemann, T. "Sperma Abraham in Jn 8 and Related Literature." *Catholic Biblical Quarterly* 42 (1980): 342–58.
Draper, J. A. "Temple, Tabernacle and Mystical Experience in John." *Neotestamentica* 31, no. 2 (1997): 263–88.
Du Rand, J. A. "Perspectives on Johannine Discipleship According to the Farewell Discourses." *Neotestamentica* 25, no. 2 (1991): 311–25.
Dunn, James D. G. *Jesus Remembered*. Grand Rapids, MI: Eerdmans, 2003.
———. "John VI—A Eucharistic Discourse?" *New Testament Studies* 17 (1971): 328–38.
———. "Let John Be John: A Gospel for Its Time." In *Das Evangelium und die Evangelien: Vorträge vom Tübinger Symposium 1982*, edited by Peter Stuhlmacher, 309–39. Tübingen: Mohr, 1983.
———. *The Partings of the Ways: Between Christianity and Judaism and Their Significance for the Character of Christianity*. 2nd ed. London: SCM, 2006.
Eisenstadt, S. N., and L. Roniger. *Patrons, Clients and Friends: Interpersonal Relations and the Structure of Trust in Society*. Themes in the Social Sciences. Cambridge: Cambridge University Press, 1984.
Elliott, Susan M. "John 15:15—Not Slaves but Friends: Slavery and Friendship Imagery and the Clarification of the Disciples' Relationship to Jesus in the Johannine Farewell Discourse." In *Proceedings of the Eastern Great Lakes and Midwest Society of Biblical Literature*, 31–46. Toronto, 1993.
Epictetus, and William Abbott Oldfather. *Discourses, Books 1–2*. Translated by W. A. Oldfather. 2 vols. LCL. Cambridge, MA: Harvard University Press, 1925.
———. *Epictetus; the Discourses as Reported by Arrian, the Manual and Fragments, with an English Translation*. Translated by William Abbott Oldfather. 2 vols. LCL. London, New York: W. Heinemann; G. P. Putnam's sons, 1956.
Esler, Philip F. "Community and Gospel in Early Christianity: A Response to Richard Bauckham's Gospels for all Christians." *Scottish Journal of Theology* 51, no. 2 (1998): 235–48.
Evans, Craig A. *Ancient Texts for New Testament Studies: A Guide to the Background Literature*. Peabody, MA: Hendrickson, 2005.
Farelly, Nicolas. *The Disciples in the Fourth Gospel: A Narrative Analysis of Their Faith and Understanding*. WUNT 2.290. Tübingen: Mohr Siebeck, 2010.
Feuillet, André. *Études johanniques*. Museum Lessianum Section biblique 4. Paris: Desclée de Brouwer, 1962.
———. *Johannine Studies*. Staten Island, NY: Alba House, 1964.

———. *Le prologue du quatrième évangile*. Paris: Desclée de Brouwer, 1968.
———. "Le triomphe du fils de l'homme." In *La venue du messie: messianisme et eschatologie*, 149–71. Desclée de Brouwer, 1962.
Filson, Floyd F. "The Gospel of Life: A Study of the Gospel of John." In *Current Issues in New Testament Interpretation in honor of O. A. Piper*, edited by W. Klassen and G. F. Snyder, 111–23. New York: Harper, 1962.
Findlay, J. Alexander. *The Way, the Truth and the Life*. London: Hodder and Stoughton, 1940.
Fitzgerald, John T. "Christian Friendship: John, Paul, and the Philippians." *Interpretation* (July 2007): 284–96.
———. *Friendship, Flattery, and Frankness of Speech: Studies on Friendship in the New Testament World*. NovTSup 82. Leiden: Brill, 1996.
———. *Greco-Roman Perspectives on Friendship*. RBS 34. Atlanta: Scholars Press, 1997.
Foerster. "ἁρπάζω." In *The Theological Dictionary of the New Testament*, edited by Gerhard Kittel, Gerhard Friedrich, and Geoffrey William Bromiley, 1, 472–74. Grand Rapids, MI: Eerdmans, 1964.
Ford, J. Massyngberde. *Redeemer-Friend and Mother: Salvation in Antiquity and in the Gospel of John*. Minneapolis, MN: Fortress, 1997.
Freed, Edwin E. "Samaritan Influence in the Gospel of John." *Catholic Biblical Quarterly* 30 (1968): 580–87.
Frey, Jörg. "The Diaspora-Jewish Background of the Fourth Gospel." *Svensk exegetisk årsbok* 77 (2012): 169–96.
———. "From the 'Kingdom of God' to 'Eternal Life': The Transformation of Theological Language in the Fourth Gospel." In *John, Jesus, and History, Volume 3: Glimpses of Jesus through the Johannine Jesus*, edited by Paul N. Anderson, Felix Just, and Tom Thatcher, 439–58. Atlanta, GA: SBL Press, 2016.
Freyne, Sean. "Vilifying the Other and Defining the Self." In *To See Ourselves as Others See Us: Christians, Jews, "Others" in Late Antiquity*, edited by Jacob Neusner, 117–43. Chico, CA: Scholars Press, 1985.
Gaius. *Gai Institutiones or Institutes of Roman Law*. Translated by Edward Poste. Oxford: The Clarendon Press, 1904.
Garland, David E. *Luke*. ZECNT. Grand Rapids, MI: Zondervan, 2011.
Garnsey, Peter, and Richard P. Saller. *The Roman Empire: Economy, Society, and Culture*. Berkeley, CA: University of California Press, 1987.
Glasson, T. F. *Moses in the Fourth Gospel*. SBT 40. Naperville, IL: A.R. Allenson, 1963.
Gold, Barbara K. *Literary Patronage in Greece and Rome*. Chapel Hill, NC: University of North Carolina, 1987.
Goldstein, Jonathan A. *I Maccabees*. AB 41. New York: Doubleday, 1976.
Gorman, Michael J. *Abide and Go: Missional Theosis in the Gospel of John*. Eugene, OR: Cascade Books, 2018.
Gornish, Yisroel. *The Mishnah Volume 3: Rosh Hashanah, Yoma, Succah*. 4 vols. Edited by Nosson Scherman and Meir Zlotowitz. Brooklyn, NY: Mesorah Publications, Ltd, 1980.

Greimas, A. J. "Elements of a Narrative Grammar." *Diacritics* 7 (1977): 23–40.
Grenfell, Bernard P., and Arthur S. Hunt, eds. *The Oxyrhynchus Papyri Part IV*. London: Egypt Exploration Fund, 1904.
Grindheim, Sigurd. "Faith in Jesus: The Historical Jesus and the Object of Faith." *Biblica* 97, no. 1 (2016): 79–100.
Gundry, Robert. "In My Father's House Are Many *Monai* (John 14:2)." *Zeitschrift für die neutestamentliche Wissenschaft* 58 (1967): 68–72.
Haenchen, Ernst, Robert Walter Funk, and Ulrich Busse. *John: A Commentary on the Gospel of John*. 2 vols. Hermeneia. Philadelphia: Fortress, 1984.
Hahn, Ferdinand, August Strobel, and Eduard Schweizer. *Die Anfänge der Kirche im Neuen Testament*. Göttingen; Minneapolis: Vandenhoeck u. Ruprecht; Augsburg Pub. House, 1967.
Hakola, Raimo. *Identity Matters: John, the Jews, and Jewishness*. NovTSup 118. Leiden: Brill, 2005.
Hamid-Khani, Saeed. *Revelation and Concealment of Christ: A Theological Inquiry into the Elusive Language of the Fourth Gospel*. WUNT 2.120. Tübingen: Mohr Siebeck, 2000.
Hanson, K. C. "All in the Family: Kinship in Agrarian Roman Palestine." In *The Social World of the New Testament: Insights and Models*, edited by Jerome H. Neyrey and Eric Clark Stewart, 27–46. Peabody, MA: Hendrickson, 2008.
Hare, Douglas R. A. *The Theme of Jewish Persecution of Christians in the Gospel According to St. Matthew*. SNTSMS 6. Cambridge: Cambridge University Press, 1967.
Harris, Elizabeth. *Prologue and Gospel: The Theology of the Fourth Evangelist*. JSNTSup 107. Sheffield, England: Sheffield Academic Press, 1994.
Harris, Murray J. *John*. EGGNT, edited by Robert W. Yarbrough and Andreas J. Köstenberger. Nashville, TN: B&H Academic, 2015.
———. *Prepositions and Theology in the Greek New Testament*. Grand Rapids, MI: Zondervan, 2011.
Harstine, Stan. *Moses as a Character in the Fourth Gospel: A Study of Ancient Reading Techniques*. JSNTSup 229. London: Sheffield Academic Press, 2002.
Hartin, P. J. "Remain in Me (John 15:5): The Foundation of the Ethical and Its Consequences in the Farewell Discourses." *Neotestamentica* 25, no. 2 (1991): 341–56.
Hays, Richard B. *Echoes of Scripture in the Gospels*. Waco: Baylor University Press, 2016.
Heemstra, Marius. *The Fiscus Judaicus and the Parting of the Ways*. WUNT 2.277. Tübingen: Mohr Siebeck, 2010.
Heise, Jürgen. *Bleiben: Menein in den johanneischen Schriften*. Tübingen: J. C. B. Mohr (Paul Siebeck), 1967.
Hellerman, Joseph H. *The Ancient Church as Family*. Minneapolis, MN: Fortress, 2001.
Hengel, Martin. *The Johannine Question*. London: SCM, 1989.
———. *Studies in Early Christology*. Edinburgh: T & T Clark, 1995.

Hera, Marianus Pale. *Christology and Discipleship in John 17*. WUNT 2.342. Tübingen: Mohr Siebeck, 2013.

Herman, G. "The 'Friends' of the Early Hellenistic Rulers: Servants or Officials?" *Talanta* 12–13 (1980–1981): 103–49.

Heuss, Alfred. *Die völkerrechtlichen Grundlagen der römischen Aussenpolitik in republikanischer Zeit*. Klio Beiheft XXXI. Leipzig: Dieterich, 1933.

Horbury, William. "Extirpation and Excommunication." *Vetus Testamentum* 35 (1985): 13–38.

Howard-Brook, Wes. *Becoming Children of God: John's Gospel and Radical Discipleship*. Maryknoll, NY: Orbis Books, 1994.

Howard, James M. "The Significance of Minor Characters in the Gospel of John." *Bibliotheca Sacra* 163 (2006): 63–78.

Hunt, Steven A. "Nicodemus, Lazarus, and the Fear of 'the Jews' in the Fourth Gospel." In *Repetitions and Variations in the Fourth Gospel: Style, Text, Interpretation*, edited by Gilbert van Belle, Michael Labahn, and P. Maritz, 199–212. Leuven; Walpole, MA: Peeters, 2009.

Hunt, Steven A., D. F. Tolmie, and Ruben Zimmermann, eds. *Character Studies in the Fourth Gospel*, WUNT 314. Tübingen: Mohr Siebeck, 2013.

Hunter, Archibald M. *According to John: The New Look at the Fourth Gospel*. Philadelphia, PA: Westminster Press, 1968.

———. *The Work and Words of Jesus*. Rev. ed. London: SCM, 1950.

Hurtado, Larry W. *Lord Jesus Christ: Devotion to Jesus in Earliest Christianity*. Grand Rapids, MI: Eerdmans, 2003.

———. "Participationism and Messiah Christology in Paul: YHWH's Return to Zion. A New Catalyst for Earliest High Christology?" In *God and the Faithfulness of Paul: A Critical Examination of the Pauline Theology of N.T. Wright*, edited by Christoph Heilig, J. Thomas Hewitt, and Michael F. Bird, 417–38. Tübingen: Mohr Siebeck, 2016.

Hurtado, Larry W., and Paul Owen. *'Who Is This Son of Man?': The Latest Scholarship on a Puzzling Expression of the Historical Jesus*. LNTS 390. London; New York: T & T Clark, 2011.

Hutter, Horst. *Politics as Friendship: The Origins of Classical Notions of Politics in the Theory and Practice of Friendship*. Waterloo, ON: Wilfrid Laurier University Press, 1978.

Hwang, Won-Ha, and J. G. van der Watt. "The Identity of the Recipients of the Fourth Gospel in the Light of the Purpose of the Gospel." *HTS Teologiese Studies/ Theological Studies* 63, no. 2 (2007): 683–98.

Hylen, Susan. *Imperfect Believers: Ambiguous Characters in the Gospel of John*. Louisville, KY: Westminster John Knox Press, 2009.

Iamblichus. *Life of Pythagoras*. Translated by Thomas Taylor. London: J. M. Watkins, 1818.

Ihenacho, David Asonye. *The Community of Eternal Life: The Study of the Meaning of Life for the Johannine Community*. Lanham, MD: University Press of America, 2001.

Jackson, Howard M. "Ancient Self-Referential Conventions and Their Implications of the Authorship and Integrity of the Gospel of John." *Journal of Theological Studies* 50 (1999): 1–34.

Jaubert, Anne. "L'image de la vigne (Jean 15)." In *Oikonomia: Heilsgeschichte als Thema der Theologie*, edited by Felix Christ, 93–99. Hamburg–Bergstedt: Herbert Reich Evang. Verlag GmbH, 1967.

Jerumanis, Pascal-Marie. *Réaliser la communion avec Dieu: croire, vivre et demeurer dans l'évangile selon S. Jean*. Études bibliques 32. Paris: J. Gabalda, 1996.

Jiménez, Ramón Moreno. "El Discipulo de Jesucristo segun el evangelio de S. Juan." *Estudios Bíblicos* 30 (1971): 269–311.

Johnston, George. "The Allegory of the Vine: An Exposition of John 15:1–17." *Canadian Journal of Theology* 3/4 (1957/58): 150–58.

Josephus, Flavius. *Jewish Antiquities*. Translated by H. St. J. Thackeray and Ralph Marcus. 8 vols. LCL. Cambridge, MA: Harvard University Press, 1950.

Jossa, Giorgio. *Jews or Christians?: The Followers of Jesus in Search of Their Own Identity*. WUNT 202. Tübingen: Mohr Siebeck, 2006.

Kaczmarek, David. *An Introduction to Language in the Johannine Community: Love, Friendship, and Discipleship in the Gospel According to John*. Minneapolis, MN: Xlibris, 2008.

Kanagaraj, Jey J. *'Mysticism' in the Gospel of John: An Inquiry into Its Background*. JSNTSup 158. Sheffield: Sheffield Academic Press, 1998.

Katz, S. T. "Issues in the Separation of Judaism and Christianity after 70 C.E.: A Reconsideration." *Journal of Biblical Literature* 103 (1984): 43–76.

Kee, H. C. "Knowing the Truth: Epistemology and Community in the Fourth Gospel." In *Neotestamentica et Philonica: Studies in Honor of Peder Borgen*, edited by D. E. Aune, T. Seland and J. H. Ulrichsen, 254–80. Leiden: Brill, 2002.

Keener, Craig S. *Christobiography: Memory, History, and the Reliability of the Gospels*. Grand Rapids, MI: Eerdmans, 2019.

———. *The Gospel of John*. 2 vols. Peabody, MA: Hendrickson, 2003.

———. "'We Beheld His Glory!' (John 1:14)." In *John, Jesus, and History, Volume 2: Aspects of Historicity in the Fourth Gospel*, edited by Paul N. Anderson, Felix Just and Tom Thatcher, 15–25. Atlanta: SBL Press, 2009.

———. "'What Is Truth?': Pilate's Perspective on Jesus in John 18:33–38." In *John, Jesus, and History, Volume 3: Glimpses of Jesus through the Johannine Jesus*, edited by Paul N. Anderson, Felix Just, and Tom Thatcher, 77–94. Atlanta, GA: SBL Press, 2016.

Keith, Chris, and Larry W. Hurtado. *Jesus among Friends and Enemies: A Historical and Literary Introduction to Jesus in the Gospels*. Grand Rapids, MI: Baker, 2011.

Kerr, Alan R. *The Temple of Jesus' Body: The Temple Theme in the Gospel of John*. JSNTSup 220. London: Sheffield Academic Press, 2002.

Kimelman, Reuven. "*Birkat Ha-Minim* and the Lack of Evidence for an Anti-Christian Jewish Prayer in Late Antiquity." In *Jewish and Christian Self-Definition*, edited by E. P. Sanders, A. I. Baumgarten, and Alan Mendelson, 2, 226–44. Philadelphia: Fortress, 1981.

Klink, Edward W. "Expulsion from the Synagogue? Rethinking a Johannine Anachronism." *Tyndale Bulletin* 59, no. 1 (2008): 99–118.
———. *John*. ZECNT, edited by Clinton E. Arnold. Grand Rapids, MI: Zondervan, 2016.
———. *The Audience of the Gospels: The Origin and Function of the Gospels in Early Christianity*. LNTS 353. London: T & T Clark, 2010.
———. *The Sheep of the Fold: The Audience and Origin of the Gospel of John*. SNTSMS 141. Cambridge: Cambridge University Press, 2007.
Kloppenborg, John S. "Disaffiliation in Associations and the 'Ἀποσυνάγωγος' of John." *HTS Teologiese Studies/Theological Studies* 61, no. 1 (2011): 1–16.
Knight, William E. "Defining Discipleship in the Fourth Gospel: A Narrative Analysis of the Motif for the Implied Reader." Ph.D. Dissertation, New Orleans Baptist Theological Seminary, 2001.
Koester, Craig R. *Symbolism in the Fourth Gospel: Meaning, Mystery, Community*. 2nd ed. Minneapolis, MN: Fortress, 2003.
———. "Theological Complexity and the Characterization of Nicodemus in John's Gospel." In *Characters and Characterization in the Gospel of John*, edited by Christopher W. Skinner, 165–81. London: T & T Clark, 2013.
Koester, Helmut. *Introduction to the New Testament*. New York: Walter De Gruyter, 1982.
Konstan, David. *Friendship in the Classical World*. Cambridge: Cambridge University Press, 1997.
Köstenberger, Andreas J. "The Destruction of the Second Temple and the Composition of the Fourth Gospel." In *Challenging Perspectives on the Gospel of John*, edited by John Lierman, 69–108. Tübingen: Mohr Siebeck, 2006.
———. "Early Doubts of the Apostolic Authorship of the Fourth Gospel in the History of Modern Biblical Criticism." In *Studies on John and Gender: A Decade of Scholarship*, 17–47. New York: P. Lang, 2001.
———. *John*. BECNT. Grand Rapids, MI: Baker, 2004.
———. *The Missions of Jesus and the Disciples According to the Fourth Gospel: With Implications for the Fourth Gospel's Purpose and the Mission of the Contemporary Church*. Grand Rapids, MI: Eerdmans, 1998.
———. *A Theology of John's Gospel and Letters*. Biblical Theology of the New Testament. Grand Rapids, MI: Zondervan, 2009.
Kunst, Christiane. "Römische Adoption: zur Strategie einer Familienorganisation." Universität Potsdam, 2005.
Kysar, Robert. "Community and Gospel: Vectors in Fourth Gospel Criticism." *Interpretation* 21 (1977): 355–66.
———. *Voyages with John: Charting the Fourth Gospel*. Waco, TX: Baylor University Press, 2005.
Laertius, Diogenes. *Lives of Eminent Philosophers*. Translated by R. D. Hicks. 2 vols. LCL. Cambridge, MA: Harvard University Press, 1925.
Lamb, David. "Review of *Echoes of Friendship in the Gospel of John* by Martin Culy." *Biblical Theology Bulletin* 42, no. 1 (2012): 51–52.

———. *Text, Context and the Johannine Community: A Sociolinguistic Analysis of the Johannine Writings*. LNTS 477. London: Bloomsbury, 2015.
Lee, Dorothy A. "Abiding in the Fourth Gospel: A Case-study in Feminist Biblical Theology." *Pacifica* 10 (1997): 123–36.
———. *Hallowed in Truth and Love: Spirituality in the Johannine Literature*. Eugene, OR: Wipf & Stock, 2012.
———. *The Symbolic Narratives of the Fourth Gospel: The Interplay of Form and Meaning*. JSNTSup 95. Sheffield: JSOT Press, 1994.
Leibig, Janis E. "John and 'the Jews': Theological Antisemitism in the Fourth Gospel." *Journal of Ecumenical Studies* 20, no. 2 (1983): 209–34.
Lémanon, Jean-Pierre. *Pilate et la gouvernement de la Judée: textes et monuments*. Paris: Gabalda, 1981.
Lieu, Judith. "Anti-Judaism, the Jews, and the Worlds of the Fourth Gospel." In *The Gospel of John and Christian Theology*, edited by Richard Bauckham and Carl Mosser, 168–82. Grand Rapids, MI: Eerdmans, 2008.
Lincoln, Andrew T. "The Beloved Disciple as Eyewitness and the Fourth Gospel as Witness." *Journal for the Study of the New Testament* 85 (2002): 3–26.
———. *The Gospel According to Saint John*. BNTC. Peabody, MA: Hendrickson, 2005.
———. *Truth on Trial: The Lawsuit Motif in the Fourth Gospel*. Peabody, MA: Hendrickson, 2000.
Lindars, Barnabas. *The Gospel of John*. NCB. London: Oliphants, 1972.
Lingad, Celestino G. *The Problems of Jewish Christians in the Johannine Community*. Tesi gregoriana Serie teologia 73. Roma: Editrice Pontificia Università Gregoriana, 2001.
Lowe, Malcolm F. "Who Were the 'Ioudaioi,'" *Novum Testamentum* 18, no. 2 (1976): 101–30.
Lucian. *Lucian*. Translated by A. M. Harmon. 8 vols. LCL. Cambridge, MA: Harvard University Press, 1936.
Macaskill, Grant. "Enoch, Second Book of." In *The New Interpreter's Dictionary of the Bible* edited by Katharine Doob Sakenfeld, Samuel E. Balentine, and Brian K. Blount, 2, 261. Nashville, TN: Abingdon Press, 2009.
*Maccabees, 1–4*. The Holy Bible: New Revised Standard Version. Nashville, TN: Thomas Nelson Publishers, 1989.
Maccini, Robert Gordon. *Her Testimony Is True: Women as Witnesses According to John*. JSNTSup 125. Sheffield: Sheffield Academic Press, 1996.
Malina, Bruce J. *The New Testament World: Insights from Cultural Anthropology*. 3rd ed. Louisville, KY: Westminster John Knox Press, 2001.
Malina, Bruce J., and Richard L. Rohrbaugh. *Social-Science Commentary on the Gospel of John*. Minneapolis, MN: Fortress, 1998.
Marcus, Joel. "*Birkat ha-Minim* Revisited." *New Testamenet Studies* 55 (2009): 523–51.
———. "Rivers of Living Water from Jesus' Belly, John 7:38." *Journal of Biblical Literature* 117 (1998): 328–30.
Marsh, John. *The Gospel of St. John*. The Pelican Gospel commentaries. Harmondsworth: Penguin, 1968.

Marshall, I. Howard. *New Testament Theology: Many Witnesses, One Gospel.* Downers Grove, IL: InterVarsity, 2004.

———. *The Gospel of Luke.* NIGTC. Grand Rapids, MI: Eerdmans, 1978.

Martial, and D. R. Shackleton Bailey. *Epigrams.* 3 vols. LCL. Cambridge, MA: Harvard University Press, 1993.

Martyn, J. Louis. *History and Theology in the Fourth Gospel.* 1st ed. New York: Harper & Row, 1968. Reprint, Westminster John Knox Press, 2003.

———. *The Gospel of John in Christian History: Essays for Interpreters.* New York, NY: Paulist Press, 1978.

Mbamalu, Abiola. "'Life' in the Fourth Gospel and its Resonances with Genesis 1–3." *In die Skriflig* 38, no. 1 (2014): 1–5.

McCaffrey, James. *The House with Many Rooms: The Temple Theme of Jn. 14, 2–3.* Analecta biblica 114. Roma: Editrice Pontificio Istituto Biblico, 1988.

McCool, F. J. "Living Water in John." In *The Bible in Current Catholic Thought: In Honor of M. Gruenthaner*, edited by J. L. McKenzie, 226–33. New York: Herder & Herder, 1962.

McGrath, James F. *John's Apologetic Christology: Legitimation and Development in Johannine Christology.* SNTSMS 111. Cambridge: Cambridge University Press, 2001.

McHugh, John. *John 1–4.* ICC. London; New York: T & T Clark, 2009.

McKeever, Michael C. "Born of God: The 'Virgin Birth' of Believers in the Fourth Gospel." In *But These Are Written: Essays on Johannine Literature in Honor of Professor Benny C. Aker*, edited by Craig S. Keener, Jeremy S. Crenshaw, and Jordan D. May, 121–38. Eugene, OR: Pickwick Publications, 2014.

Meeks, Wayne. "'Am I a Jew?'—Johannine Christianity and Judaism." In *Christianity, Judaism, and Other Greco-Roman Cults: Studies for Morton Smith at Sixty*, edited by Jacob Neusner, 1, 164–85. Leiden: Brill, 1975.

———. "Breaking Away: Three New Testament Pictures of Christianity's Separation from the Jewish Communities." In *'To See Ourselves as Others See Us': Christians, Jews, 'Others' in Late Antiquity*, edited by Jacob Neusner, Ernest S. Frerichs, and Caroline McCracken-Flesher, 93–115. Chico, CA: Scholars Press Studies in the Humanities, 1985.

———. "The Man from Heaven in Johannine Sectarianism." *Journal of Biblical Literature* 91, no. 1 (1972): 44–72.

———. *The Prophet-King: Moses Traditions and the Johannine Christology.* Leiden: Brill, 1967.

Menken, Maarten J. J. "'Born of God' or 'Begotten by God'? A Translation Problem in the Johannine Writings." In *Studies in John's Gospel and Epistles: Collected Essays*, 13–28. Leuven: Peeters, 2015.

———. "John 6:51c–58: Eucharist or Christology." In *Critical Readings of John 6*, edited by R. Alan Culpepper, 183–204. Leiden: Brill, 1997.

Metzger, Bruce Manning. *A Textual Commentary on the Greek New Testament.* 2nd ed. Stuttgart: Deutsche Bibelgesellschaft/German Bible Society, 1994.

Meyer, Ben F. "Locating Lonerganian Hermeneutics." In *Critical Realism and the New Testament*, edited by Ben F. Meyer, 1–16. Eugene, OR: Pickwick, 1989.

———. "Lonergan's Breakthrough and the Aims of Jesus." In *Critical Realism and the New Testament*, edited by Ben F. Meyer, 147–56. Eugene, OR: Pickwick, 1989.

Middleton, J. Richard. *A New Heaven and a New Earth: Reclaiming Biblical Eschatology*. Grand Rapids, MI: Baker, 2014.

Millar, Fergus. *The Emperor in the Roman World: 31 BC–AD 337*. London: Duckworth, 1977.

Moloney, Francis J. *Belief in the Word: Reading the Fourth Gospel, John 1–4*. Minneapolis, MN: Fortress, 1993.

———. *Glory Not Dishonor: Reading John 13–21*. Minneapolis, MN: Augsburg Fortress, 1998.

———. "John 20: A Journey Completed." *Australasian Catholic Record* 59 (1982): 417–32.

———. *Love in the Gospel of John: An Exegetical, Theological, and Literary Study*. Grand Rapids, MI: Baker, 2013.

———. *Signs and Shadows: Reading John 5–12*. Minneapolis, MN: Fortress, 1996.

———. *The Gospel of John*. SP 4. Collegeville, MN: Liturgical Press, 1998.

———. *The Gospel of John: Text and Context*. Leiden: Brill, 2005.

Moltmann, Jürgen. "Open Friendship: Aristotelian and Christian Concepts of Friendship." In *The Changing Face of Friendship*, edited by Leroy S. Rouner, 29–42. Notre Dame, IN: University of Notre Dame, 1994.

Morris, Leon. *The Gospel According to John*. Rev. ed. NICNT. Grand Rapids, MI: Eerdmans, 1995.

Motyer, Stephen. "Bridging the Gap: How Might the Fourth Gospel Help Us Cope with the Legacy of Christianity's Exclusive Claim over against Judaism?" In *The Gospel of John and Christian Theology*, edited by Richard Bauckham and Carl Mosser, 143–67. Grand Rapids, MI: Eerdmans, 2008.

———. "Method in Fourth Gospel Studies: A Way Out of an Impasse?" *JSNT* 66 (1997): 27–44.

———. *Your Father the Devil?: A New Approach to John and "the Jews"*. PBTM. Carlisle: Paternoster, 1997.

Moule, C. F. D. "A Neglected Factor in the Interpretation of Johannine Eschatology." In *Studies in John: Presented to Professor Dr. J. N. Sevenster on the Occasion of his Seventieth Birthday*, 155–60. Leiden: Brill, 1970.

———. "The Meaning of 'Life' in the Gospels and Epistles of St. John: A Study in the Story of Lazarus, John 11:1–44." *Theology* 78 (March 1975): 114–25.

Mussner, Franz. *Zōē; Die Anschauung vom "Leben" im vierten Evangelium*. Münchener theologische Studien, 1. Historische Abteilung, 5. München: Karl Zink Verlag, 1952.

Myers, Alicia D. "Just Opponents?: Ambiguity, Empathy, and the Jews in the Gospel of John." In *Johannine Ethics: The Moral World of the Gospel and Epistles of John*, edited by Sherri Brown and Christopher W. Skinner, 159–76. Minneapolis, MN: Fortress Press, 2017.

Neyrey, Jerome H. *The Gospel of John in Cultural and Rhetorical Perspective*. Grand Rapids, MI: Eerdmans, 2009.

Ng, Wai-Yee. *Water Symbolism in John: An Eschatological Interpretation.* New York: Peter Lang, 2001.
Nickelsburg, George W. E. "Enoch, First Book of." In *The Anchor Bible Dictionary*, edited by David Noel Freedman, 2, 508–16. New York: Double Day, 1992.
———. *Resurrection, Immortality, and Eternal Life in Intertestamental Judaism and Early Christianity.* Expanded ed. HTS 56. Cambridge, MA: Harvard University Press, 2006.
North, Wendy E. S. *A Journey Round John: Tradition, Interpretation, and Context in the Fourth Gospel.* LNTS 534. Edited by Chris Keith. London: Bloomsbury, 2015.
O'Day, Gail R. "Jesus as Friend in the Gospel of John." *Interpretation* (April 2004): 144–57.
———. "Toward a Narrative-Critical Study of John." *Interpretation* 49, no. 4 (1995): 341–46.
O'Grady, John F. *According to John: The Witness of the Beloved Disciple.* New York: Paulist Press, 1999.
Okure, Teresa. *The Johannine Approach to Mission: A Contextual Study of John 4:1–42.* WUNT 2.31. Tübingen: J.C.B. Mohr, 1988.
Oliver, W. H., and A. G. van Aarde. "The Community of Faith as a Dwelling-Place of the Father: βασιλεία τοῦ θεοῦ As Household of God in the Johannine Farewell Discourse(s)." *Neotestamentica* 25, no. 2 (1991): 379–400.
P. W. von Martitz, E. Schweizer, E. Lohse, and W. Schneemelcher. "υἱός, υἱοθεσία." In *The Theological Dictionary of the New Testament*, edited by Gerhard Kittel, Gerhard Friedrich and Geoffrey William Bromiley, 8, 334–97. Grand Rapids, MI: Eerdmans, 1964.
Painter, John. "John 9 and the Interpretation of the Fourth Gospel." *Journal for the Study of the New Testament* 28 (1986): 31–61.
———. "Jesus and the Quest for Eternal Life." In *Critical Readings of John 6*, edited by R. Alan Culpepper, 61–94. Leiden: Brill, 1997.
———. *The Quest for the Messiah.* 2nd ed. Nashvile, TN: Abingdon, 1993.
Pazdan, Mary M. "Discipleship as the Appropriation of Eschatological Salvation in the Fourth Gospel." Ph.D. Diss., University of St. Michael's College, 1982.
Pearson, Lionel Ignacius Cusack. *Popular Ethics in Ancient Greece.* Stanford, CA: Stanford University Press, 1962.
Peppard, Michael. *The Son of God in the Roman World: Divine Sonship in Its Social and Political Context.* Oxford: Oxford University Press, 2011.
Philo. *On Flight and Finding. On the Change of Names. On Dreams.* Translated by F. H. Colson and G. H. Whitaker. LCL. Cambridge, MA: Harvard University Press, 1934.
———. *On the Unchangeableness of God—On Husbandry—Concerning Noah's Work as a Planter—On Drunkenness—On Sobriety.* LCL. Cambridge, MA: Harvard University Press, 1930.
Pisarek, Stanislaw. "Christ the Son and the Father-Farmer in the Image of the Vine (Jn 15.1–11, 12–17)." In *Testimony and Interpretation: Early Christology in its Judeo-Hellenistic Milieu: Studies in Honor of Petr Pokorný*, edited by Jiri Mrazek and Jan Roskovec, 240–46. London; New York: T & T Clark, 2004.

Plato. *Lysis, Symposium, Gorgias*. Translated by W. R. M. Lamb. LCL. Cambridge, MA: Harvard University Press, 1925.

———. *Plato, with an English Translation. I, Euthyphro; Apology; Crito; Phaedo; Phaedrus*. Translated by Harold North Fowler. LCL. Cambridge: Harvard University Press, 1947.

Pliny. *Letters, and Panegyricus*. Translated by Betty Radice. 2 vols. LCL. Cambridge, MA: Harvard University Press, 1969.

Plutarch. *Moralia*. Translated by Babbitt, Frank Cole. 15 vols. LCL. Cambridge, MA: Harvard University Press, 1936.

Poirier, John C. "Hanukkah in the Narrative Chronology of the Fourth Gospel." *New Testament Studies* 54 (2008): 465–78.

Porter, Stanley E. *John and His Gospel, and Jesus: In Pursuit of the Johannine Voice*. Grand Rapids, MI: Eerdmans, 2015.

Porton, Gary G. "Talmud." In *The Anchor Bible Dictionary*, edited by David Noel Freedman, 6, 310–15. New York: Doubleday, 1992.

Puthenkandathil, Eldho. *Philos: A Designation for the Jesus-Disciple Relationship— An Exegetico-Theological Investigation of the Term in the Fourth Gospel*. European University Studies 23.475. Frankfurt am Main: P. Lang, 1993.

Quast, Kevin. *Reading the Gospel of John: An Introduction*. New York: Paulist Press, 1991.

Rainbow, Paul A. *Johannine Theology: The Gospel, the Epistles and the Apocalypse*. Downers Grove, IL: IVP Academic, 2014.

Ramelli, Ilaria. "'Simon Son of Jonah, Do You Love Me?' Some Reflections on John 21:15." *Novum Testamentum* 50 (2008): 332–50.

Rebell, Walter. *Gemeinde als Gegenwelt: zur soziologischen und didaktischen Funktion des Johannesevangeliums*. BBET 20. Frankfurt: Peter Lang, 1987.

Reinhartz, Adele. *Befriending the Beloved Disciple: A Jewish Reading of the Gospel of John*. New York: Continuum, 2001.

———. "Incarnation and Covenant: The Fourth Gospel through the Lens of Trauma Theory." *Interpretation* 69, no. 1 (2015): 35–48.

———. "The Lyin' King? Deception and Christology in the Gospel of John." In *Johannine Ethics: The Moral World of the Gospel and Epistles of John*, edited by Sherri Brown and Christopher W. Skinner, 117–33. Minneapolis, MN: Fortress Press, 2017.

———. "Reading History in the Fourth Gospel." In *What We Have Heard from the Beginning: The Past, Present, and Future of Johannine Studies*, edited by Tom Thatcher, 190–94. Waco, TX: Baylor University Press, 2007.

———. "Women in the Johannine Community: An Exercise in Historical Imagination." In *A Feminist Companion to John*, edited by Amy-Jill Levine and Marianne Blickenstaff, 2, 14–33. London: Sheffield Academic Press, 2003.

Rengstorf. "μαθητής." In *The Theological Dictionary of the New Testament*, edited by Gerhard Kittel, Gerhard Friedrich, and Geoffrey W. Bromiley, 4, 415–61. Grand Rapids, MI: Eerdmans, 1964.

Rensberger, David K. *Johannine Faith and Liberating Community*. Philadelphia: Westminster Press, 1988.

———. "The Politics of John: The Trial of Jesus in the Fourth Gospel." *Journal of Biblical Literature* 103, no. 3 (1984): 395–411.
Renz, Gabi. "Nicodemus: An Ambiguous Disciple? A Narrative Sensitive Investigation." In *Challenging Perspectives on the Gospel of John*, edited by John Lierman, 255–83. Tübingen: Mohr Siebeck, 2006.
Resseguie, James L. *Narrative Criticism of the New Testament: An Introduction*. Grand Rapids, MI: Baker, 2005.
———. *The Strange Gospel: Narrative Design and Point of View in John*. BIS 56. Leiden: Brill, 2001.
Reynolds, Benjamin E. *The Apocalyptic Son of Man in the Gospel of John*. WUNT 249. Tübingen: Mohr Siebeck, 2008.
Richey, Lance Byron. *Roman Imperial Ideology and the Gospel of John*. The CBQMS 43. Washington, DC: Catholic Biblical Association of America, 2007.
Ridderbos, Herman N. *The Gospel According to John: A Theological Commentary*. Grand Rapids, MI: Eerdmans, 1997.
———. "The Structure and Scope of the Prologue to the Gospel of John." In *The Composition of John's Gospel: Selected Studies from 'Novum Testamentum,'* edited by David E. Orton, 41–62. Leiden: Brill, 1999.
Ringe, Sharon H. *Wisdom's Friends: Community and Christology in the Fourth Gospel*. Louisville, KY: Westminster John Knox Press, 1999.
Robinson, John A. T. "The Destination and Purpose of St. John's Gospel." *New Testament Studies* 6 (1959/60).
———. *Jesus and His Coming: The Emergence of a Doctrine*. London: SCM, 1957.
———. *Redating the New Testament*. London: S.C.M. Press, 1976.
———. "The Relation of the Prologue to the Gospel of John." *New Testamenet Studies* 9, no. 2 (January 1963): 120–29.
Rubenstein, Jeffrey L. *The History of Sukkot in the Second Temple and Rabbinic Periods*. BJS 302. Atlanta: Scholars Press, 1995.
Saller, Richard P. "Patronage and Friendship in Early Imperial Rome: Drawing the Distinction." In *Patronage in Ancient Society*, edited by Andrew Wallace-Hadrill, 49–87. London; New York: Routledge, 1989.
Schecter, Solomon, and Israel Abrahams. "Genizah Specimens." *Jewish Quarterly Review* 10 (1898): 654–61.
Schiffman, Lawrence H. "At the Crossroads: Tannaitic Perspectives on the Jewish-Christian Schism." In *Jewish and Christian Self-Definition*, edited by E. P. Sanders, A. I. Baumgarten, and Alan Mendelson, 2, 115–56, 338–52. London: SCM, 1981.
Schnackenburg, Rudolf. *The Gospel According to St. John*. Translated by David Smith and G. A. Kon. 3 vols. New York: Crossroad, 1982.
Schneemelcher, Wilhelm, and R. McL. Wilson. *New Testament Apocrypha*. 2 vols. Revised ed. Cambridge; Louisville, KY: J. Clarke & Co.; Westminster/John Knox Press, 1991.
Schneiders, Sandra. "The Foot Washing (John 13:1–20): An Experiment in Hermeneutics." *Catholic Biblical Quarterly* 43 (1981): 76–92.
———. "Review of *Johannine Discipleship as a Covenant Relationship*." *Catholic Biblical Quarterly* 69, no. 3 (July 2007): 575–76.

———. *Written That You May Believe: Encountering Jesus in the Fourth Gospel*. New York: Crossroad, 1999.
Schnelle, Udo. *Das Evangelium nach Johannes*. Leipzig: Evangelische Verlagsanstalt, 1998.
———. *Theology of the New Testament*. Grand Rapids, MI: Baker, 2009.
Scholer, David M., ed. *Social Distinctives of the Christians in the First Century: Pivotal Essays by E. A. Judge*. Peabody, MA: Hendrickson, 2008.
Scholtissek, Klaus. *In ihm sein und bleiben: die Sprache der Immanenz in den johanneischen Schriften*. Herders biblische Studien Bd 21. Freiburg; New York: Herder, 2000.
Schottroff, L. "ζῶ, ζωή, ἧς, ἡ." In *Exegetical Dictionary of the New Testament*, edited by Horst Robert Balz and Gerhard Schneider, 2, 105–109. Edinburgh: T & T Clark, 1990.
Schrage. "ἀποσυνάγωγος." In *The Theological Dictionary of the New Testament*, edited by Gerhard Kittel, Gerhard Friedrich, and Geoffrey W. Bromiley, 7, 848–52. Grand Rapids, MI: Eerdmans, 1964.
Schulz, Anselm. *Nachfolgen und Nachahmen; Studien über das Verhältnis der neutestamentlichen Jüngerschaft zur urchristlichen Vorbildethik*. SANT 6. München: Kösel-Verlag, 1962.
Schütz, Eduard. "Knowledge." In *The New International Dictionary of New Testament Theology*, edited by Colin Brown, 2, 390–409. Grand Rapids, MI: Zondervan, 1986.
Schweizer, Eduard. *Lordship and Discipleship*. London, England: SCM, 1960.
Scott, Martin. *Sophia and the Johannine Jesus*. JSNTSup 71. Sheffield: JSOT, 1992.
*Scriptores Historiae Augustae*. Translated by David Magie. 3 vols. LCL. London: William Heinemann, 1932.
Segovia, Fernando F. "The Love and Hatred of Jesus and Johannine Sectarianism." *Catholic Biblical Quarterly* 43, no. 2 (1981): 258–72.
———. *Love Relationships in the Johannine Tradition*. SBLDS 58. Chico, CA: Scholars Press, 1982.
———. *The Farewell of the Word: The Johannine Call to Abide*. Minneapolis, MN: Fortress, 1991.
———. "John 15:18–16:4a: A First Addition to the Original Farewell Discourse?" *The Catholic Biblical Quarterly* 45 (1983): 210–30.
———. "The Theology and Provenance of John 15:1–17." *Journal of Biblical Literature* 101, no. 1 (1982): 115–28.
Seneca, Lucius Annaeus. *Declamations, Controversiae*. Translated by Thomas H. Corcoran. 2 vols. LCL. London: Heinemann, 1974.
———. *Epistulae Morales*. Translated by Richard M. Gummere. 3 vols. LCL. Cambridge, MA: Harvard University Press, 1953.
Shepherd, David. "'Do You Love Me?' A Narrative-Critical Reappraisal of ἀγαπάω and φιλέω in John 21:15–17." *Journal of Biblical Literature* 129, no. 4 (2010): 777–92.
Shin, Sookgoo. *Ethics in the Gospel of John: Discipleship as Moral Progress*. BIS 168. Leiden; Boston: Brill, 2019.

Simon, U. E. "Eternal Life in the Fourth Gospel." In *Studies in the Fourth Gospel*, edited by F. L. Cross, 97–109. London: A. R. Mowbray & Co., 1957.

Skinner, Christopher W. "John the Baptist: Witness and Embodiment of the Prologue in the Gospel of John." In *Characters and Characterization in the Gospel of John*, 147–64. London: Bloomsbury T & T Clark, 2013.

Smith, D. Moody Jr. *John*. ANTC. Nashville, TN: Abingdon Press, 1999.

Smyth, Herbert Weir. *Greek Grammar*. Cambridge, MA: Harvard University Press, 1956.

Spaulding, Mary B. *Commemorative Identities: Jewish Social Memory and the Johannine Feast of Booths*. LNTS 396. London: T & T Clark, 2009.

Spicq, Ceslas. *Notes de lexicographie néo-testamentaire*. I, II, + Supplément vols. Orbis biblicus et orientalis 22/1–3. Fribourg, Suisse; Göttingen: Éditions universitaires; Vandenhoeck & Ruprecht, 1978–1982.

Stählin. "φιλέω." In *The Theological Dictionary of the New Testament*, edited by Gerhard Kittel, Gerhard Friedrich, and Geoffrey W. Bromiley, 9, 112–71. Grand Rapids, MI: Eerdmans, 1985.

Staley, Jeffrey L. "Stumbling in the Dark, Reaching for the Light: Reading Character in John 5 and 9." *Semeia* 53 (1991): 55–80.

Stambaugh, John E., and David L. Balch. *The New Testament in Its Social Environment*. LEC 2. Philadelphia: Westminster Press, 1986.

Stegemann, Ekkehard W. "Zur Tempelreinigung im Johannesevangelium." In *Die Hebräische Bibel und ihre zweifache Nachgeschichte. Festschrift für Rolf Rendtorff zum 65. Geburtstag*, edited by Christian Macholz Erhard Blum, Rolf Rendtorff, Ekkehard Stegemann, 503–16. Neukirchen-Vluyn: Neukirchener, 1990.

Stevens, George Barker. *The Johannine Theology: A Study of the Doctrinal Contents of the Gospels and Epistles of the Apostle John*. New York: C. Scribner's Sons, 1894.

Stibbe, Mark. *John*. Readings: A New Biblical Commentary. Sheffield: JSOT Press, 1993.

———. "Telling the Father's Story." In *Challenging Perspectives on the Gospel of John*, edited by John Lierman, 170–93. Tübingen: Mohr Siebeck, 2006.

Strack, Hermann Leberecht, and Paul Billerbeck. *Kommentar zum Neuen Testament aus Talmud und Midrasch*. 6 vols. München: Beck, 1922.

Strathmann. "λατρεύω, λατρεία." In *The Theological Dictionary of the New Testament*, edited by Gerhard Kittel, Gerhard Friedrich, and Geoffrey William Bromiley, 4, 58–65. Grand Rapids, MI: Eerdmans, 1985.

Streett, Andrew. *The Vine and the Son of Man*. Minneapolis, MN: Fortress, 2014.

Styler, G. M. "The Persecution of Christians in John 15:18–16:4a." In *Essays on John*, edited by Barnabas Lindars and C. M. Tuckett, 48–69. Leuven: Leuven University Press, 1992.

Suetonius. *The Lives of the Caesars*. Translated by John Carew Rolfe. 2 vols. LCL. Cambridge, MA: Harvard University Press, 1997.

Summers, Steve. *Friendship: Exploring Its Implications for the Church in Postmodernity*. T & T Clark Theology 7. London; New York: T & T Clark, 2009.

Täubler, Eugen. *Imperium romanum*. Leipzig and Berlin: Teubner, 1913.
Tellbe, Mikael. *Christ-Believers in Ephesus: A Textual Analysis of Early Christian Identity Formation in a Local Perspective*. WUNT 242. Tübingen: Mohr Siebeck, 2009.
Temple, P. J. "The Eucharist in St. John 6." *Catholic Biblical Quarterly* 9 (1947): 442–52.
Theophilos, Michael P. "John 15.14 and the ΦΙΛ-Lexeme in Light of Numismatic Evidence: Friendship or Obedience?" *New Testament Studies* 64 (2018): 33–43.
Thompson, Marianne Meye. *John: A Commentary*. NTL. Louisville, KY: Westminster John Knox Press, 2015.
———. *The God of the Gospel of John*. Grand Rapids, MI: Eerdmans, 2001.
Tolmie, D. F. *Jesus' Farewell to the Disciples: John 13:1–17:26 in Narratological Perspective*. BIS 12. Leiden: Brill, 1995.
———. "The Characterization of God in the Fourth Gospel." *Journal for the Study of the New Testament* 69 (1998): 57–75.
Tovey, Derek. *Narrative Art and Act in the Fourth Gospel*. JSNTSup 151. Sheffield: Sheffield Academic Press, 1997.
Trebilco, Paul. *The Early Christians in Ephesus from Paul to Ignatius*. WUNT 166. Tübingen: Mohr Siebeck, 2004.
Trozzo, Lindsey M. *Exploring Johannine Ethics: A Rhetorical Approach to Moral Efficacy in the Fourth Gospel Narrative*. WUNT2 449. Tübingen: Mohr Siebeck, 2017.
Trumbower, Jeffrey A. *Born from Above: The Anthropology of the Gospel of John*. HUT 29. Tübingen: J.C.B. Mohr, 1992.
Unnik, W. C. Van. "The Purpose of St. John's Gospel." *Studia Evangelica* (1959): 382–411.
Van der Horst, Pieter Willem. "The *Birkhat ha-Minim* in Recent Research." *Expository Times* 105 (1993/1994): 363–68.
Van der Merwe, Dirk G. "Towards a Theological Understanding of Johannine Discipleship." *Neotestamentica* 31, no. 2 (1997): 339–59.
Van der Watt, J. G. "A New Look at John 5:25–9 in the Light of the Use of the Term 'Eternal Life' in the Gospel According to John." *Neotestamentica* 19 (1985): 71–86.
———. *An Introduction to the Johannine Gospel and Letters*. T & T Clark Approaches to Biblical Studies. London; New York: T & T Clark, 2007.
———. "Everlasting Life in John and the Permanence of Salvation: The Life Metaphor in John's Gospel." *Testamentum Imperium* 1 (2005–2007): 1–12.
———. *Family of the King: Dynamics of Metaphor in the Gospel According to John*. BIS 47. Leiden: Brill, 2000.
———. "Some Reflections on the Historicity of the Words 'Laying Down Your Life for Your Friends' in John 15:13." In *John, Jesus, and History, Volume 3: Glimpses of Jesus through the Johannine Jesus*, edited by Paul N. Anderson, Felix Just and Tom Thatcher, 481–91. Atlanta, GA: SBL Press, 2016.

———. "The Use of αἰώνιος in the Concept ζωὴ αἰώνιος in John's Gospel." *Novum Testamentum* 31, no. 3 (1989): 217–28.
Van Tilborg, Sjef. *Imaginative Love in John*. BIS 2. Leiden: Brill, 1993.
———. *Reading John in Ephesus*. NovTSup 83. Leiden: Brill, 1996.
Varghese, Johns. *The Imagery of Love in the Gospel of John*. Rome, Italy: Gregorian & Biblical Press, 2009.
Vellanickal, Matthew. "Discipleship According to the Gospel of John." *Jeevadhara* 10 (1980): 131–47.
———. *The Divine Sonship of Christians in the Johannine Writings*. Anelecta Biblica 72. Rome: Biblical Institute Press, 1977.
Vhumani Magezi, and Peter Manzanga. "A Study to Establish the Most Plausible Background to the Fourth Gospel (John)." *HTS Teologiese Studies/Theological Studies* 66, no. 1 (2010): 1–7.
Visotzky, Burton A. "Midrash." In *The New Interpreter's Dictionary of the Bible*, edited by Samuel E. Balentine, Katharine Doob Sakenfeld, Brian K. Blount, et al., 2, 790. Nashville, TN: Abingdon Press, 2006.
Volf, Miroslav. "Johannine Dualism and Contemporary Pluralism." In *The Gospel of John and Christian Theology*, edited by Richard Bauckham and Carl Mosser, 19–50. Grand Rapids, MI: Eerdmans, 2008.
Von Wahlde, Urban C. "Literary Structure and Theological Argument in Three Discourses with the Jews in the Fourth Gospel." *Journal of Biblical Literature* 103, no. 4 (1984): 575–84.
———. "The Johannine 'Jews': A Critical Survey." *New Testament Studies* 28 (1982): 33–60.
———. "The Terms for Religious Authorities in the Fourth Gospel: A Key to Literary-Strata." *Journal of Biblical Literature* 98, no. 2 (1979): 231–53.
Waetjen, Herman C. *The Gospel of the Beloved Disciple*. London: T & T Clark, 2005.
Walker, Peter W. L. *Jesus and the Holy City: New Testament Perspectives on Jerusalem*. Grand Rapids, MI: Eerdmans, 1996.
Wallace, Daniel B. *Greek Grammar Beyond the Basics: An Exegetical Syntax of the New Testament*. Grand Rapids, MI: Zondervan, 1996.
———. "John 5,2 and the Date of the Fourth Gospel." *Biblica* 71, no. 2 (1990): 177–205.
Weiser, A. "Καῖσαρ." In *Exegetical Dictionary of the New Testament*, edited by Horst Robert Balz and Gerhard Schneider, 2, 235–36. Edinburgh: T & T Clark, 1990.
Weissenrieder, Annette. "Spirit and Rebirth in the Gospel of John." *Religion & Theology* 21 (2014): 58–85.
Westcott, Brooke Foss. *The Gospel According to St. John*. Grand Rapids, MI: Eerdmans, 1978.
Westermann, Claus. *The Gospel of John in the Light of the Old Testament*. Peabody, MA: Hendrickson, 1998.
Willett, Michael E. *Wisdom Christology in the Fourth Gospel*. San Francisco, CA: Mellen Research University Press, 1992.

Witherington, Ben. *John's Wisdom: A Commentary on the Fourth Gospel*. Louisville, KY: Westminster John Knox Press, 1995.

Wolf, E. "Kinship, Friendship, and Patron-Client Relations." In *The Social Anthropology of Complex Societies*, edited by Michael Banton, 1–22. London: Tavistock Publications, 1966.

Zahn, Theodor. *Das Evangelium des Johannes*. Kommentar zum Neuen Testament. Leipzig: Diechert, 1921.

# Index

Note: Page numbers in *italics* denotes tables.

abandonment, 7, 67, 84n131, 100, 179n88
abiding, 6, 12, 85–109; abide/abiding place, symbolic meaning, *2*, 87–95, 109n89, 182; challenge to, 97, 109n86; as a condition for the believer, 85, 87, 96; corollary benefits of, 69, 85, 87, 97–102, 182; with the Father and the Son through the Spirit, 85, 88, 89, 92–95, 101–2, 169, 182; in love, 94; New Testament references, 87–95, 104n31; believer as the temple, 90; heaven as the locale of the Father's house, 88–92; Jesus' body as the temple, 89–90; Old Testament references, 85–87, 182; Enoch's depiction, 91–92; Exodus narrative, 86; Ezekiel's depiction, 87; Maccabees' prayer, 90–91; in the tabernacle, 86; in the temple, 86–87; in the pillar of cloud, 86; in the pillar of fire, 86; as a present and eschatological promise, 85, 88–95, 101, 106n58, 182
Abraham, 32, 38, 42n3, 46n40, 47n54, 113, 122nn11–12, 160

adoption, 33, 41
agency, 10, 24n51, 77n63, 94, 118, 119
Agrippa I, 119
Akala, Adesola Joan, 13, 47n54, 102n9
Alexander, 120, 121
*amicitia*, 112, 119
answered requests, 1, 8, 85, 98–99, 101, 121, 129, 142, 144, 150n57, 182
Antiochus IV (Epiphanes), 120
Antipater, 125n58
anxiety, 98, 100, 114
apostasy, 109n86, 183
Appasamy, A. J., 73n13
Aristotle, 113–15
ark of the covenant, 86, 87
ascension, 41, 88, 93
Ashton, John, 22n35, 102n2, 160, 162, 174n49, 174n54, 175nn59–60
Augustus, 125n60, 136
Aune, David Edward, 20n28, 22n35

Baffes, Melanie, 13, 26n81
baptism, 45nn29–31
Barabbas, 148n31
Bauckham, Richard, 21n34, 22n35, 48n67, 49n73, 50n84, 147n26, 179n87

Beasley-Murray, G. R., 108n74, 174n55, 176n74, 177n77
Beck, David, 14, 26–27n97, 77n63, 177n75, 179n88
belief/believe/believing, discipleship and, 1–2, 4–7, 10, 16nn3–5, 17n12, 17n15, 17n17, 30, 31, 35, 39, 42, 43n9, 55–56, 60–67, 69, 72n9, 78n82, 84n131, 98, 99, 100–101, 142, 144, 150n53, 153n96, 160, 164, 167, 168, 169, 174n55, 175n67, 176n72, 178n82, 179n85, 181, 183
Beloved Disciple, 4–5, 14, 18n18, 26n97, 36, 84n133, 103, 131, 146n5, 170n10
Bennema, Cornelis, 11–12, 16n4, 17n17, 45nn31–32, 49n69, 73n13, 74n21, 80n100, 81n107, 82n115, 83n120, 103n18, 124n46, 174n54, 175n67, 178n82, 179n90
Bernier, Jonathan, 158–59, 170–71, 173n30, 174n43
betrayal, 100, 130, 148, 173n30
*bios*, 22n35
*Birkat ha-Minim*, 156–59, 162, 170–71nn13–14, 172n24
blind man, 6, 26n97, 33, 65, 66, 79n93, 156, 159, 161, 162, 166, 169, 174n52, 174n56
body and blood, Jesus', 7, 36, 69
Borgen, Peder, 82n118
"born of God," 30–36, 44n24
"born of water and spirit," 34, 45n29, 45n32
Brock, Ann Graham, 145n5
Brodie, Thomas L., 151n67, 152n85
Brown, Raymond, 81n107, 135, 148n29
Brown, Sherri, 44n19, 75–76n41, 77n55, 80n102, 105n49, 122n12, 148n27, 148n31, 180n92
Brunson, Andrew C., 132, 146n8
Bultmann, Rudolf, 20n29, 48n55, 73n13, 77n54, 81n110, 105n51, 107n59, 170n10
Burridge, Richard A., 22n35

Caesar, 20n26, 118–20, 125n58, 127n72, 132, 135–37, 148n31, 148nn34–35, 149n44
change of heart, 34
Chennattu, Rekha, 12, 49–50n81, 49n71, 81n107, 105n49, 105n51, 107n59, 122n7, 173n34
children of God, 6, 12, 30, 31–36, 119; becoming/right to become, 32–34, 180n92, 181, 182; born of God/begotten by God, 31–32, 34, 44n24, 46n39; drawn by the Father, 35; given to Jesus, 34, 35; Old Testament references, 42n4; as righteous, 42n4; as sheep, 34
Christology, 10, 13, 16n10, 26n81, 27n97, 39, 44n19, 46n44, 68, 84n129, 112, 133, 134, 141, 146n8, 156, 162, 169n2
church fathers, 93
cleansing, 96
*clientela*, 119
cloud, symbolism, 102n5
Coloe, Mary, 88–89
comfort, 100, 108n85
commandments, 94, 96–97
constancy, 99
courage, 108n85
covenant, 10, 12, 25n71
the cross, 17n12, 82n115
Culpepper, R. Alan, 14
Culy, Martin, 12–13, 124n44, 124n46

darkness, 6, 47, 48n55, 60–66, 70, 77n60, 77n66, 78n78, 79nn91–92, 103n10, 109n86, 163, 178n88, 179n85
David, 3, 135, 139, 146n8
death, 4, 22n35, 37, 41, 46n43, 52, 53, 57–62, 68, 69, 76n41, 78n81, 91, 112–14, 126n61, 130, 139, 141, 144, 146n8, 149n48, 151n62, 152n77, 157–58, 163, 165, 170n7
Deissmann, Adolf, 127n72
de Jonge, Marinus, 10, 13, 46n39

de la Potterie, Ignace, 46n44
descent-ascent motif, 10, 23n39, 24n51
desertion, 3, 6–7, 69, 70, 83n121, 84n131, 100, 137, 144, 168, 181, 183
devil, 35, 37, 38, 42n3, 46n40, 52, 61
disciple(s): *vs.* apostle, 3; as branches, 96, 97, 108n71, 138; desertion of Jesus, 3, 6–7, 69, 70, 83n121, 84n131, 100, 137, 144, 168, 181, 183; future, 5; genuine/true/authentic, 1, 5, 8, 10–13, 20n25, 35–38, 46n43, 47n46, 48n65, 64, 85, 97, 99–102, 131, 142, 167, 179n88, 182; inner circle of, 3, 7, 10, 138, 144; terminology, 3–5, 9
discipleship: challenges, 95–97, 155–80; cost of, 1, 145, 152n78, 155, 181, 183; covenant, 12, 25n71; defined, 1–3; expressions/manifestations of, 2, 10–14, 16n5, 85, 95–97; as moral progress, 14, 16n4; moral progression of, 14; nature of, 10–11; Old Testament references, 3, 12; prominence of, 3–5; scholarship on, 10–14; and spirituality, 13, 72n9
discipleship, rewards and benefits of, 1, 5–9; abiding, 6, 12, 85–109; friendship with Jesus, 7, 8, 12–13, 20n27, 111–27, 129–53, 182–83; membership in the divine family, 7–8, 12, 29–50; Son-Father relationship, 7, 8, 12, 13, 30, 39–40, 48n66. *See also under individual entries*
divine family, 7–8, 12, 29–50; abiding presence within, 85–109; corollary benefits of membership, 36–42, 182; freedom from sin, 37–38, 182; honor and glory, 40–42, 182; knowledge of God and the truth, 36–37, 182; love, 182; unity, 38–40, 182; disciples as children (of God), 29–30, 31–36, 182; disciples as Jesus' brothers, 29, 30, 31, 41; Father-Son relationship, 30, 31, 36, 38–40, 47n54, 48n66, 51–58, 63
Dodd, C. H., 21n34, 60–61, 72n3, 73n13, 77n60
Domitian, 125n61, 157
dualism, 11, 20n29, 63, 77n66, 163, 169

early church/church, 83n118, 90, 103n18, 130, 170n10, 171n14, 179n90. *See also* Johannine community
Easter, 24n40, 105n51
ecclesiology, 10, 112, 159
Egypt, 47, 121, 127n72, 139, 145
election, 12, 138, 141–44, 152n83, 183
Epiphanius, 172n24
equality, 12–13, 117–18, 124n47, 131, 139, 145n5, 151n64
Eucharist, 83n118
Exodus narrative, 65, 82n114, 86, 94, 102n3, 112, 122n8

faith, 4, 14, 17n15, 18n18, 22, 30, 33, 38, 43n9, 84n131, 91, 107n62, 108n81, 167, 168, 177n75, 178n82
faithfulness, 11, 102n9, 113, 114
fallen angels, 92
Farelly, Nicolas, 14, 17n15, 27n98, 80n105, 84n131, 178n81
Farewell Discourse, 10–11, 53, 99, 101, 103n18, 106n59, 111–12, 115, 137, 143, 149n48, 151n69, 152n76, 182
fear: Jesus' admonition not to, 98, 100, 130; of "the Jews," 64, 68, 98, 134, 155–80
Feast of Dedication, 79n88
Feast of the Tabernacles, 147n22
feeding of the 5,000, 68, 83n119
festivals/feasts, 9, 65, 147n22, 160, 165, 169n2
*fiscus Judaicus*, 156–58
foot washing, 2, 25n71, 124n41, 138, 140–41
Ford, 83n118, 149n46, 150n61
forefathers, 42n3

forgiveness, 49n71, 98
freedom from sin, 1, 8, 36, 37–38, 60, 182
friendship, 12–13, 20n27, 111–27; *amicitia/clientele* (Roman model), 119–20, 126n71, 135–36; Aristotelian notion, 113–15; benefits of, 121, 122n2, 131, 137, 182–83; familial/kinship relationships, 116–17, 124n38; Father-Son, 117–18, 124n47; fictive-kinship (Greek model), 113–16; with God, 112–13, 122nn11–12, 130; ideal, 117–18, 124n47; and Jesus' commissioning, 118–19; and love, 130–31, 137, 140–41, 151n69; Maccabean narrative, 120–21; New Testament meanings, 129–31; political, 120–21, 136; royal/imperial. *See* royal friendship
fruit/fruit-bearing, 1, 2, 8, 11, 85, 95–101, 103n10, 106n59, 107n60, 107n62, 114, 118–19, 121, 129, 131, 137, 142, 144, 150n57, 153n90, 182

Galilee, 167, 176
Garden of Gethsemane, 78n81
Garland, David E., 145n1
glorification, 13, 40, 41, 48n55, 97, 98, 133–34, 145
glory, 1, 8, 34, 36, 39, 40–42, 47n54, 58, 86–87, 94, 99, 102n4, 102n9, 122n8, 166, 182
Gnosticism, 73n13
God: abiding presence of/glory of, 85–109; election of Israel, 142; as the Father-king, 117, 124n42; feminine aspects of, 83n118; immanence of, 47n54, 101; knowledge of, 1, 8, 12, 36–37, 46, 49, 51, 54–57, 58, 63, 64, 74n22, 129, 142, 160, 182; love of, 49n71, 94, 95–97, 99, 107n61, 108n81, 123n27, 129, 142, 152n76, 153n90; service to/zeal for, 22n34, 41, 131, 140, 158, 166, 178n79; as the vinedresser, 97, 108n71; will of,
38; word of, 37, 71, 76n43, 103n10; wrath of, 60, 77n55, 89–90, 91, 103n10
Goldstein, Jonathan A., 126nn70–71
Good Shepherd, 56–57, 138–39, 145, 151n62
Gorman, Michael, 13, 26n86, 42n2, 48n66, 72n9, 152n76, 153n90, 175n61
Gospel of John: audiences, 9–10, 21–22n34; authorship of, 9–10; benefits of discipleship, 181–83; *Birkat ha-Minim* and, 156–59; Farewell Discourse, 10–11; historical setting, 155–62; identity of "the Jews," 164–65, 176n72; Jewish hostility toward Jesus and disciples, 162–63, 165–68, 175n61, 176–77nn74–75; portrayal of the world, 163–64; prologue, 5–8, 13, 19n21, 29–30, 39, 51, 63, 102n9, 181–82; purpose statement, 3–5, 7, 13, 17n17, 51, 77n63, 181; themes and imagery, 9–10, 11, 23n37; two-level reading, 14, 156, 159–60, 162, 170–71n13
great(er) works, performance of, 1, 8, 36, 40, 48nn65–66, 57, 85, 95, 97, 102, 182

Hahn, Ferdinand, 16n9, 24n40, 140
Hanson, K. C., 49n77
Hare, Douglas R. A., 173n34
hating one's life, 2, 16n5, 41, 49n75
hearing: and believing, 62, 76n44; God's word, 2, 35, 37, 38, 43n7, 46n42, 58; Jesus' voice, 2, 6, 56–57; the truth, 37
heaven, 13, 35, 45n29, 69, 82n118, 83n120, 86, 88–92, 157
Heemstra, Marius, 156–57, 172n27
Hengel, Martin, 146n13, 158, 172n26
Hera, Marianus, 13, 16n10, 17n12, 24n40
heresy/heretics, 156–58, 171n14, 172n24

Herod, 20n27, 119, 130, 147n20
high priest, 118, 120, 125n58, 162, 168
Holy Spirit: body as the temple of, 89–90; friendship with, 122n5; indwelling/abiding/abiding presence of, 1, 10, 45, 85, 90, 92–95, 106n55, 108n74; and new birth, 34, 45n29; of peace, 98; the Promised One, 93, 97; the revealer of truth, 40, 97–98; role in a disciple's life, 34, 45n29, 97–98; unity/oneness of, 40; the world does not know/receive, 164
honor, 1, 8, 36, 38, 40–42, 58, 119, 120, 130, 167, 179n87, 182–83
Hosanna, 134, 147n22
Hurtado, Larry W., 146n8
Hylen, Susan, 47n48, 179n86
Hyrcanus, 125n58

imitation of Jesus, 13–14, 16n4, 26n87, 152, 153n90
immanence, 47n54, 101
incarnation, 6, 30, 32, 61, 65, 77n60, 83n120, 86, 112
*inclusio*, 7, 17n12, 29–30, 60, 62, 99, 111, 138, 151n69, 182
inclusivity, 3, 12, 17n12, 108n81, 131
individualism, 31, 58, 75n41, 169n2
intimacy, 20n25, 49n73, 50, 57, 63, 102n5, 114, 116, 118, 122n15, 124n46, 140, 144, 151n68, 168
Isaac, 47n54, 105n38
Israel/Israelite, 34, 42n4, 50n81, 77n55, 82n114, 86–87, 107n59, 112, 122n7, 135, 142, 147n16, 147–48n26, 157

Jacob, 42n3, 160
Jerusalem, 65, 82n114, 87, 88, 89, 90, 104n35, 132, 134, 137, 146n8, 147n22, 149n46, 159, 160, 165, 176n72
Jesus: ascension of, 41, 88, 93; attempted murder of, 27n97, 35, 38, 65, 164, 165, 177; body as the temple, 90, 92; as the bread of life, 83n120; burial of, 149n46, 167, 178n81, 179nn87–88; command to love, 2, 10, 12, 99–100, 119, 124n41, 138–41, 143, 150n57, 151n69, 152nn79–80, 182; compassion of, 83n119; crucifixion of, 13, 22, 48n66, 64, 82n115, 135, 162; divinity of, 5, 35, 83n119; Father's love for, 94, 99, 107n61, 131; feeding of the 5,000, 68, 83n118; as good shepherd, 56–57, 138–39, 145, 151n62; as High Priest, 7; hostility/opposition toward, 6–7, 38, 135–36, 155–80, 183; kingship of, 5, 52, 119–20, 129–53, 182–83; as Lamb of God, 132; as the life, 48, 51–52; as light of the world, 6, 8, 30, 47n54, 53, 60–66, 70, 71, 77n66, 77n68, 78n88, 91; as living water, 26n81, 66–69, 80nn100–101, 80–81n107, 82n114; as Lord, 5, 52, 117, 118–19, 134; love for the church, 130; as mediator, 86–87, 112, 116, 160; as Messiah, 2, 4, 22, 62, 64, 67, 81n107, 91, 130, 132–33, 135, 139, 156, 157, 159, 166, 169, 173n34, 181; mission of, 13, 22n35, 24n51, 36, 40, 42n2, 49n71, 74n22, 80n102, 108n81, 152n85, 153, 175n61; and Moses, parallels between, 3, 6, 12, 33, 46, 86, 94, 102n2, 112–13, 122n8, 122n12, 132–33, 146n8, 160–62, 174n49, 174nn54–56, 175n58; obedience to the Father, 37, 94–95, 97; Passion of, 22n35, 132, 134–37, 139; personification of God's presence, 59, 63, 83n120, 86–87; prayer of consecration, 51; public ministry of, 7, 17n12, 29, 63, 64, 182; as Rabbi, 132–33, 151n74; refusal to attempted coronation, 133–34; resurrection of, 1, 8, 13, 14, 18n18, 24n40, 27n98, 36, 48n66, 49–50n81, 53, 57–59, 62, 69, 70, 71, 76n41, 76n46, 92, 93, 98, 146n8,

156, 165, 169, 170n7, 172n22, 182; as the revealer, 20n29, 39, 48n55; as the savior, 36, 52, 67–68; suffering of, 13; trial of, 7, 135, 141, 147n20, 149n44; triumphal entry into Jerusalem, 134–35, 137, 147n22, 149n46; as the truth, 36–37; unity/oneness/abiding with/in the Father, 39–40, 92–95, 102n9, 107n61; as the vine, 36, 40, 50n84, 96, 97, 107n59, 108n71, 138, 142, 150n53, 153; walking with, 69, 71, 78n78, 83n121; withdrawal of, 87, 147n20
the Jews, 3, 38; as Abraham's descendants, 38, 42n3, 46n40, 61; attempted murder of Jesus, 27n97, 35, 38, 65, 164, 165, 177; Diaspora, 9; fear of, 155, 165–68, 177–78n78, 178n81; hostility/opposition toward Jesus, 6–7, 38, 135–36, 155–80, 183; identity of, 19n23, 164–65, 166; Jesus' accusation of, 38, 55; as Moses' disciples, 3, 33; persecution/expulsion of Jewish Christians, 22n34, 27n97, 37, 155–80; as (secret) believers, 35, 38, 165–68; service to God, 166, 178n79; slavery of, 47n48
Jiménez, Ramón, 10
Johannine community, 10, 155–80; believers as Jesus' body, 88, 89–90; and destruction of the Jewish temple, 155–56; first-century persecution of, 156–59; membership, 12
John the Baptist, 3, 6, 20n26, 26–27n97, 36, 130, 143
Jonathan, 104n35, 120, 126n70
Joseph (father of Jesus), 42n3
Joseph of Arimathea, 166–67, 178nn81–82
Josephus, 102n6, 104n35, 125n58, 173n30
Joshua, 139
joy, 1, 6, 8, 49n81, 85, 97, 98–99, 101, 113, 114, 129, 142, 177n75, 182

Judaism, 12, 158, 160, 176n72, 179n90
Judas, 14, 70, 83n121, 100, 109n86, 130, 135, 173n30
Judea/Judeans, 6, 136, 164, 166
judgment, avoidance of, 1, 8, 36, 48n55, 52, 53, 57, 58, 59, 60–64, 66, 71, 75n36, 77n54, 77n60, 78n81, 78n85, 85, 91, 97, 101–2, 149n46, 164, 182
*Jupiter Capitolinus*, 156–57
Justin Martyr, 172n24

Kaczmarek, David, 12, 145n5
Kanagaraj, Jay J., 94
Kee, H. C. Kee, 73–74n18
Keener, Craig S., 122n8, 146n8, 149n45
kingdom of God, 34, 45n32, 52, 124n43, 132, 133
"king of Israel," 132–35, 137, 145, 147n26
"King of 'the Jews'", 132, 134, 135, 147n26
Klink, Edward, 22n35
Kloppenborg, John S., 173n34
knowledge of God, 1, 8, 10, 12, 14, 20, 36–37, 39, 40, 46n43, 49n69, 51, 53, 54–57, 58, 63, 64, 66, 67, 73–74n18, 74nn21–22, 84n131, 93, 118, 121, 129, 142, 144, 160, 182
Koester, Craig, 141
Köstenberger, Andreas, 11, 17n13, 45n32, 169n2
*kyrios*, 116
Kysar, Robert, 76n41, 170n9, 171n14

Lamb, David A., 25n72, 124n48
lame man, 26n97, 27n97, 32, 165–66, 177n75
Last Discourse, 101
law, 82n118, 132, 160, 164, 167, 175n65
Lazarus, 20n26, 112, 130–31, 165
Lee, Dorothy, 13, 103n10, 108n71, 109n89, 122n5, 152n76
Levi, 113

# Index

life (physical/eternal): abundant, 6, 57,
71; benefit of, 1, 6, 7, 10, 51–84;
and bread, 68–71, 78n75, 83n120,
103n10; and darkness, 60–66,
77n60, 77n66, 78n78; entering/
seeing the kingdom of God, 52; and
eschatology, 57–62; Father-Son
relationship, 53, 71; and food, 76n53;
and the Holy Spirit, 71; in Indian
thought, 73n13; and judgment, 71;
and knowledge, 54–57, 73–74n18;
and light, 62–66, 77n66; loss of,
76n53; notion of, 53–54, 71, 72n3;
promise of, 7, 31, 34, 41–42, 48n55,
62, 66–68, 153n90, 181, 182;
salvation and, 72n9; *vs.* spiritual,
51–52, 73n15, 73n17, 76n53; and
water, 66–68, 78n75; words of, 71,
76n44, 183
light: and darkness, 47n54, 62–66, 70,
77n60, 77nn66–67, 78n78, 79n92,
179n85, 179n88; walking in the,
1, 6, 8, 36, 60–66, 70, 71, 72n9,
77n60, 77n66, 78n85, 79n90, 79n92,
105n43, 182
living water, 26n81, 66–69, 80nn100–
101, 80nn107–8, 82n114, 97
*Logos*, 6, 8, 29–30, 32, 33–34, 36, 39,
44n23, 47n55, 65, 69, 86, 181
love, and discipleship, 1, 2, 6, 10–14,
16n4, 18, 36–38, 47, 49, 72n9, 85,
87, 94–101, 105, 106n59, 107nn60–
62, 108nn80–81, 111–15, 118–19,
123n27, 124n41, 129–43, 138,
150n53, 150n57, 151n69, 152–53,
166, 182
loyalty, 2, 4, 7, 33, 83n121, 100,
119–20, 136, 138, 143, 144, 161,
164, 168

Marshall, Howard, 145n1
Martha, 27n97, 59, 62, 70, 77n63, 159
Martyn, J. Louis, 14, 25n72, 75n34,
156, 170n10
martyrdom, 22n34, 158

Mary (Martha's sister), 159
Mary Magdalene, 14, 27n98, 41, 49n81
Mary the mother of Jesus, 26n97,
50n81, 103n18, 134
Mattathias, 120
McGrath, James F., 83n118
Meeks, Wayne A., 146n8, 148n29,
149n44, 151n62, 171n14, 174n55
miracles, 68, 133, 177
mission, 10–14, 16n4, 22n35, 24n40,
24n51, 26n87, 36, 39, 40, 42n2,
47n54, 48n66, 49n71, 67, 74n22,
80n102, 81n108, 95–98, 102n9,
108n81, 114, 118, 130, 140, 142,
144, 152n76, 153n90, 161, 163–64,
168, 175n61
Moltmann, Jürgen, 113
moral progression, 14, 16n4, 79n93,
174n56
Moses, 3, 6, 12, 33, 46, 86, 94, 102n2,
112–13, 122n8, 122n12, 132, 133,
146n8, 160–62, 174n49, 174n56,
174nn54–56, 175n58
Motyer, Stephen, 169n2
Mussner, Franz, 72n9, 73n13
mutuality, 10, 12, 13, 55, 57, 85, 94,
95, 108n81, 113, 116, 117–18, 120,
122, 124n47, 141, 151n67, 152n85,
157
mysticism, 73n13, 82n118

name change, 12
narratology, 11, 15
Nathaniel, 27n97, 50n84, 132–35
Nerva, 157
Neyrey, Jerome H., 47n46
Nicodemus, 26n97, 34, 45n30, 50n84,
81n108, 133, 167, 175n61, 178n83,
179n84, 179nn87–88

obedience, 10, 35, 37, 38, 94, 95–96,
97, 99, 101, 116, 119, 137, 139–40,
142, 144
official of Capernaum, 26n97, 42n3
*oikos*, 116

Okure, Teresa, 108n81, 177–78n78, 179n91
Origen, 172n24

Painter, John, 49n69, 82n118, 83n121
Palestine, 108n81, 156
Paraclete, 11, 49n69, 56, 85, 88, 90, 93–98, 101, 105n49, 105n51, 106n55, 122n5, 160, 163–64, 175n64, 182
*parousia*, 77n54, 93, 103n20, 104n22, 105n51, 146n8
Paul, 158, 166, 173n30, 178n79
Pazdan, Mary, 13, 16n5, 26n81, 106n58, 177n74
peace, 1, 6, 8, 85, 97, 98, 101, 108n75, 121, 136, 163, 182
Pentateuch, 86
Peppard, Michael, 47n54
persecution, 1, 20n27, 22n34, 27n97, 73n14, 121, 140, 144, 155–60, 168
perseverance, 17n15, 111
Peter, 4–5, 7, 14, 18n18, 26–27n97, 50n84, 51, 70, 83n121, 84n133, 100, 131, 141, 145, 162, 168, 170n10, 183
Pharisees, 6–7, 64, 66, 134, 158, 161, 162, 165, 166, 167, 169n1, 174n52, 175nn59–60, 176n72, 179n86
Philo, 90, 104n33, 114, 119, 122nn11–12
Pilate, 20nn26–27, 36, 119, 130, 135–37, 145, 147n26, 148n27, 148n31, 148n35, 149n45
pillar of cloud, 86
pillar of fire, 65, 86
Pliny, 119
Plutarch, 14, 26n87, 108n80, 114
prayer, 51, 91, 95, 112. *See also* answered requests
priestly office, 119
protection, 1, 8, 36, 46, 49n71, 57, 60, 64, 99, 101, 102n5, 119, 143, 163, 182
pruning, 97, 107n68, 108n71
Ptolemy, 120, 126n70, 127n72, 149n39

quality of life, 51

Rainbow, Paul A., 20n29, 54
Reinhartz, Adele, 46n44, 81n107, 159
Rengstorf, Karl, 2, 16n7
Resseguie, James, 11, 81n107, 84n133, 109n86, 177
the righteous, 91–92, 113
righteousness, 1, 8, 13, 14, 18n18, 24n40, 27n98, 36, 48n66, 49–50n81, 53, 57–59, 62, 69, 70, 71, 76n41, 76n46, 92, 93, 98, 146n8, 156, 164–65, 169, 170n7, 172n22, 182
Risen Lord, 22n35
royal friendship (Jesus' kingship/kingdom), 119–20, 129–53, 182–83; benefits of, 142–43, 144, 153n90, 153n94, 182–83; disciples' transition from slaves to friends, 137–41; and election/commissioning, 141–42, 144, 152n83, 183; Jesus' rejection of public coronation, 133–34; Jewish rejection of Jesus, 132, 135–36, 148n29, 148n31, 159, 183; John the Baptist, 130, 143; kingdom terminology, 132–33; and Lazarus, 130–31; and love, 131, 138, 140–41, 143, 151n69, 152n79; and Moses, 133; and Nathaniel, 132–33, 134; and Shepherd-King, 138–39, 150n58, 151nn62–63, 183; and social disparity, 139–41, 144, 183

sacrament, 83n118
sacrifice, 25n71, 47n54, 86, 102n6, 113–14, 124n41, 130, 141, 142, 166, 178n80
salvation, 1, 3, 8, 11, 35, 36, 37, 45n32, 57, 59, 72n9, 79n83, 80n101, 163, 182
Samaritan woman, 26n97, 66–69, 80n102, 81nn108–10, 175n61
Schiffman, Lawrence H., 157, 172n24
schism, 165
Schnackenburg, Rudolf, 10, 44n24, 54, 65, 73n17, 107n62, 107n66, 108n74, 147n16
Schweizer, Eduard, 23–24n40

Second Temple period, 88, 90, 169n2
Segovia, Fernando F., 10, 24n46, 48n56, 107n61, 108n85, 115, 150n53, 151n70, 153n96
Sejanus, Lucius Aelius, 136, 148n35
Seleucid, 120, 149n39
self-sacrifice, 25, 130, 141
Seneca, 113–14
sheep, 6, 34, 40, 51, 56–57, 75n34, 84n133, 112, 139
Shema, 49n73
Shin, Sookgoo, 14, 16n4, 20n25, 26n87, 48n64, 78n78, 79n93, 81n108, 103n18, 122n15, 152n76, 174n56, 179n88
sin, freedom from, 1, 8, 36, 37–38, 46, 48n55, 52, 59–63, 79n91, 103n10, 163, 164, 177n75, 182
Sinai, 82n118
slavery, 37, 38, 46n43, 47n48, 115, 118, 124n46, 130
Son of God, 2, 4, 22n35, 30, 39, 48n57, 48n59, 48n61, 62, 94, 132, 133, 147n25
Son of Man, 59, 61, 91–92, 132, 133
soteriology, 11, 16, 26n81, 43n7, 62, 77n62, 122n5
Stegemann, Ekkehard W., 170n7
Stephen, 158
Strobel, August, 24n40
Sukkot, 47n48, 65, 68, 78nn87–88, 81n111, 160
synagogue, 9, 12, 22n34, 64, 79n93, 118, 144, 156–60, 165, 166, 168–69, 171n14, 172n24, 175n58, 177n78, 179n90, 183
Synoptic Gospels, 8, 16–17n11, 20n27, 30, 43n9, 134, 159, 162

tabernacle, 86–87, 102n9
temple, 9, 65, 68, 86–90, 102n6, 102n9, 118, 147n22, 160, 169n2, 175n60, 176n72; destruction of, 155–57, 169n2
temple tax, 156–57
tent of meeting, 86, 87

Theophilos, Michael P., 148n35
theosis, 13, 26n86, 42n2, 90, 153n90
Thomas, 4, 5, 14, 26–27n97, 52, 55, 66, 70, 88, 89, 108n75
Tiberius, 136, 139, 148n35
Tolmie, D. Francois, 10, 48n65, 109n86, 151n68, 152n77, 175n64
Torah, 80n101, 87, 122n8, 157, 172n22, 176n72
Trajan, 125n61, 172n27
treason, 136, 149
tribulation, 98
trinitarian theology, 10, 48n67
Trozzo, Lindsey, 22n35, 26n87, 83n119, 103n18, 108n81
trust, 20n25, 122, 130
truth, 1, 8, 36–37, 38, 40, 46nn43–44, 48n56, 55, 56, 61, 74n21, 97–98, 115, 149n45, 182
the twelve, 3, 7, 9, 70, 83n121

unity, 1, 6, 8, 9, 10, 12–14, 16n4, 26n87, 36, 38–40, 48n67, 49n71, 49n73, 50n84, 83n119, 117–18, 124n47, 131, 145n5, 152n76, 182

van der Merwe, Dirk G., 24n51
van der Watt, Jan, 11, 45n32, 71nn1–2, 72n5, 73n14, 76n41, 76n46, 78n77, 147n16, 148n35
van Tilborg, Sjef, 116, 124nn41–42, 135
Vellanickal, Matthew, 43n18, 47n46, 47n49
Vespasian, 156–57
vineyard, 107n59

walking with Jesus, 1, 6, 8, 36, 63–64, 69, 71, 78n85, 83n121, 182
water: living, 53, 62, 66–68, 69, 70, 71, 78n75, 79n98, 80–81n107, 80nn100–102, 82n114, 91, 97; and spirit, birth from, 26n81, 34, 45n29, 45nn31–32
wedding, 130
the wicked, 91–92
wilderness, 82n114, 86

Wisdom, 11, 80n101, 83n118, 83n120, 112, 122n3, 122n45

witnessing, and discipleship, 1, 2, 5, 12, 14, 17n15, 27n97, 44n19, 67, 80n105, 81nn107–8, 92, 93, 95, 96, 107n62, 133, 137, 143, 145, 160, 161, 174n56, 177n75, 179n88

the world: darkness in, 63; friendship of, 111–27; vs. God's kingdom, 132–53; God's love for, 61, 65, 108n81, 118, 153n90, 163–64; Jesus as light of, 63, 65, 78n88; Jesus/disciples hated by, 93, 98, 155–80; Johannine portrayal of, 49n71, 163–64; judgment of, 61, 64, 77n54, 78n81; peace in, 98; tribulation in, 98

worldview, 14, 16n4

worship/worshippers, 36, 66, 67, 79n95, 87, 160, 171, 172n27

Wright, N.T., 146n8

YHWH, 3, 50n81, 102n3, 107n59, 122n7, 146n8

# About the Author

**Mark Zhakevich** is the chair of the New Testament Department at The Master's Seminary in Los Angeles, CA. He holds a BA from the University of California, Los Angeles, an MDiv and a ThM from The Master's Seminary, and a PhD in the New Testament and Christian Origins from the University of Edinburgh.

www.ingramcontent.com/pod-product-compliance
Lightning Source LLC
Chambersburg PA
CBHW050904300426
44111CB00010B/1371